In the Face of Adversity

Literature and Translation

Literature and Translation is a series for books that address literary translation and for books of literary translation. Its emphasis is on diversity of genre, culture, period and approach. The series uses an open access publishing model to disseminate widely developments in the theory and practice of translation, as well as translations into English of literature from around the world.

Series editor: Timothy Mathews is Emeritus Professor of French and Comparative Criticism, UCL.

In the Face of Adversity

Translating difference and dissent

Thomas Nolden (ed.)

In honour of Lawrence A. Rosenwald

First published in 2023 by
UCL Press
University College London
Gower Street
London WC1E 6BT

Available to download free: www.uclpress.co.uk

Collection © Editors, 2023
Text © Contributors, 2023
Images © Contributors and copyright holders named in captions, 2023

The authors have asserted their rights under the Copyright, Designs and Patents Act 1988 to be identified as the authors of this work.

A CIP catalogue record for this book is available from The British Library.

Any third-party material in this book is not covered by the book's Creative Commons licence. Details of the copyright ownership and permitted use of third-party material is given in the image (or extract) credit lines. If you would like to reuse any third-party material not covered by the book's Creative Commons licence, you will need to obtain permission directly from the copyright owner.

This book is published under a Creative Commons Attribution-Non-Commercial 4.0 International licence (CC BY-NC 4.0), https://creativecommons.org/licenses/by-nc/4.0/. This licence allows you to share and adapt the work for non-commercial use providing attribution is made to the author and publisher (but not in any way that suggests that they endorse you or your use of the work) and any changes are indicated. Attribution should include the following information:

Nolden, T. (ed), 2023. *In the Face of Adversity: Translating difference and dissent*. London: UCL Press. https://doi.org/10.14324/111.9781800083691

Further details about Creative Commons licences are available at https://creativecommons.org/licenses/

ISBN: 978-1-80008-371-4 (Hbk.)
ISBN: 978-1-80008-370-7 (Pbk.)
ISBN: 978-1-80008-369-1 (PDF)
ISBN: 978-1-80008-372-1 (epub)
DOI: https://doi.org/10.14324/111.9781800083691

Financial support for the publication of this volume was provided by Wellesley College, Mass.

Contents

Notes on Contributors	vii
List of Figures	xi
List of Tables	xii
Acknowledgements	xiii

Introduction — 1
Thomas Nolden

Part I: Modes of Perseverance: Translating the Jewish Tradition — 17

1. Lamentations 3: A Four-Voiced Rendering — 19
   Edward L. Greenstein

2. Isaiah 1 in Translation and Contexts — 33
   Everett Fox

3. Emma Lazarus, Heinrich Heine and the Splendid Galaxy of Jewish Poetry — 41
   Abigail Gillman

4. City of the Dead or The Dead City? Yitskhok-Leybush Peretz as Self-Translator — 65
   Efrat Gal-Ed

Part II: Modes of Intervention: Translating Dissent and Diversity — 93

5. How George Eliot Came to Write — 95
   Gail Twersky Reimer

6. Venture, Courage, Ruin: Karin Michaëlis in Translation
   Across Genre and Time   112
   Katherine Hollander

7. Lu Xun's Unfaithful Translation of Science Fiction:
   Rewriting Chinese Literary History   129
   Mingwei Song

8. Translating Chinese Science Fiction into English:
   Decolonization and Reconciliation on a Cultural Battlefield   145
   Emily Xueni Jin

9. Whose Voice(s)?: Authorship, Translation, and Diversity
   in Contemporary Children's Literature   160
   Isabelle Chen

**Part III: Modes of Remedialization: Translating
           Beyond the Text**   **177**

10. Seeing Images, Thinking of Words: Visual Art
    as Translation   179
    Werner Sollors

11. Theatre without Theatres: Performance
    Transmission as Translation   193
    Sarah Bay-Cheng

12. From Miami to Hong Kong: Sounding Transnational
    Queerness and Translation in *Moonlight*   207
    K. E. Goldschmitt

13. Crowd Noise: Collective Turbulence in Modern Opera   221
    Martin Brody

14. Creative Translation in Emerson's Idealism   237
    Kenneth P. Winkler

Index   254

Notes on Contributors

Sarah Bay-Cheng currently serves as the Dean of the School of the Arts, Media, Performance and Design at York University. She previously served as Chair and Professor of Theatre and Dance at Bowdoin College and as the founding Director of Graduate Studies in Theatre & Performance at the University at Buffalo (UB), SUNY. In 2012, she founded the Technē Institute for Arts and Emerging Technology at UB, a collaboration that connected faculty researchers and students working at the intersection of art, computer science, design, engineering, media and performance. Her research focuses on the intersections among performance and media including histories of cinema, experimental theatre, social media and computer technology in contemporary performance.

Martin Brody is the Catherine Mills Davis Professor Emeritus of Music at Wellesley College, a composer of concert music and historian of modern music – especially music of the Cold War in relation to other arts. He teaches composition, theory and history of music, with a special emphasis on twentieth-century and recent music. He is especially interested in pedagogy that connects music to the study of other arts, philosophy and cultural history. He also enjoys teaching all aspects of music theory, especially in relation to questions of musical cognition and aesthetics.

Isabelle Chen is a PhD candidate in the Department of French and Italian at Princeton University, where she primarily studies twentieth-century narratives of migration and exile. She has a great interest in multilingual literature and language politics, inspired both by her professional experience in the publishing industry and by her undergraduate work with Larry Rosenwald, including a particularly rich and formative experience in his seminar 'Translation and the multilingual world'.

Everett Fox is the Allen M. Glick Professor of Judaic and Biblical Studies at Clark University. His main scholarly focus is the rhetoric and internal coherence of the Hebrew Bible, and how they may be emphasized in translation. Among his many publications are *Scripture and Translation* (a translation of Buber and Rosenzweig, *Die Schrift und ihre Verdeutschung*), which he edited and translated together with Lawrence Rosenwald. His *The Five Books of Moses: (The Schocken Bible, Volume 1)*

A New English Translation with Commentary and Notes was published in 1995, *Give Us a King!: A New English Translation of the Book of Samuel* in 1999 and *The Early Prophets: Joshua, Judges, Samuel, Kings* in 2014.

Efrat Gal-Ed is Professor of Yiddish Literature and Culture at the Institute for History at Heinrich Heine University in Düsseldorf, where she heads the section of Yiddish Research and Editions. Her recent publications include *Niemandssprache: Itzik Manger – ein europäischer Dichter* (2016); *Das Buch der Jüdischen Jahresfeste* (revised edition, 2019); and *Crossing the Border: an anthology of modern Yiddish short stories* (in Yiddish), edited with Simon Neuberg and Daria Vakhrushova (2021).

Abigail Gillman is Professor of Hebrew, German and Comparative Literature in the Department of World Languages and Literatures at Boston University, where she is also affiliated faculty in the Elie Wiesel Center for Jewish Studies and the Graduate Program on Religion. She is the author of *Viennese Jewish Modernism: Freud, Hofmannsthal, Beer-Hofmann and Schnitzler* (2009) and *A History of German Jewish Bible Translation* (2018). Her essay 'Martin Buber's Message to Postwar Germany' (2014) won the 2015 Egon Schwarz Prize for an Outstanding Essay in the Area of German Jewish Studies.

K. E. Goldschmitt is Associate Professor of Music at Wellesley College. They publish on the transnational mediation of music, musicians and music technology, especially involving the Lusophone world. Their first book is *Bossa Mundo: Brazilian music in transnational media industries* (2020) and they co-edited a special issue of *American Music* 'Platforms, Labor, and Community in Online Listening'. Prior to Wellesley, Goldschmitt held research and teaching positions at University of Cambridge, New College of Florida and Colby College.

Edward L. Greenstein is Professor Emeritus of Bible at Bar-Ilan University. Greenstein began teaching there in 2006, where he also headed the Institute for Jewish Biblical Interpretation and held the Meiser Chair in Biblical Studies. He also served as Chair of the Interdisciplinary Graduate Program in Hermeneutics and Cultural Studies. Prior to that, he served as Professor at Tel Aviv University from 1996 to 2006. From 1976 through 1996, he taught at the Jewish Theological Seminary in New York, where he became Professor of Bible in 1989. He has also taught at the Columbia University Graduate School, Yale University, Princeton University, Union Theological Seminary, the Hebrew University of Jerusalem and other institutions of higher learning.

Katherine Hollander is a poet, historian, and Brecht scholar. She holds an MA in creative writing and a PhD in modern European history, both from Boston University. She is the editor of a student edition of *Mother Courage and her*

Children (Bloomsbury/Methuen, 2022) and the author of a collection of poems, *My German Dictionary* (Waywiser Press, 2019), which won the Anthony Hecht Poetry Prize. She serves as poetry and reviews editor for Consequence, a literary journal and organization dedicated to illuminating the culture and consequences of war and geopolitical violence, and is a lecturer in poetry at Tufts University. Her poetry and scholarship have been published in *New German Critique, The Brecht Yearbook, Salmagundi, Literary Imagination*, and elsewhere.

Emily Xueni Jin is currently pursuing a PhD in East Asian Languages and Literature at Yale University while also working as a science fiction and fantasy translator. As one of the core members of the Clarkesworld-Storycom collaborative project on publishing English translations of Chinese science fiction, she has worked with various prominent Chinese SF writers. Her most recent Chinese to English translations can be found in *AI2041: ten visions for our future* (2021), a collection of science fiction and essays co-written by Dr Kaifu Lee and Chen Qiufan and *The Way Spring Arrives and Other Stories* (2022), a Chinese science fiction and fantasy anthology written, edited and translated by women and non-binary creators. Her most recent English-to-Chinese translation, 'The Search for Philip K. Dick', the first biography of PKD in Chinese, was published in July 2020 by Eight Light Minutes.

Thomas Nolden received his PhD from Yale University and is currently Professor of German Studies and Comparative Literary Studies at Wellesley College. He has taught at the University of California at Berkeley, the Freie Universität Berlin and as visiting professor at Brandeis University, the Massachusetts Institute of Technology and the summer school of the University of Graz (Austria). He has been a member of the Coordinating Committee for the Comparative History of Literatures in European Languages Series (part of the International Comparative Literature Association). Among his book publications are *'An einen jungen Dichter': Studien zur epistolaren Poetik* ['Letters to a Young Poet': studies in epistolary poetics]; *Junge jüdische Literatur. Konzentrisches Schreiben in der Gegenwart* [Young Jewish Writing in Contemporary Austria and Germany]; *Voices from the Diaspora. Jewish Women Writing in Contemporary Europe*, co-edited with Frances Malino; *Contemporary Jewish Writing in Europe. A Guide*, co-edited with Vivian Liska; *In Lieu of Memory: contemporary Jewish writing in France*; *Beyond the Textual: practices of translation and adaptation*.

Gail Twersky Reimer is the founder and former Executive Director of the Jewish Women's Archive. A graduate of Sarah Lawrence College, Reimer began her professional career as a faculty member at Wellesley College shortly after receiving her PhD in English and American Literature from Rutgers University. She is the co-editor of two pathbreaking anthologies of Jewish women's writings – *Reading Ruth: women reclaim a sacred story* and *Beginning Anew: a woman's companion to the high holy days*.

Werner Sollors received his PhD from the Freie Universität Berlin and taught there, at Columbia University, at the Universitá degli Studi di Venezia, and at Harvard University, where he is now Henry B. and Anne M. Cabot Professor of English, *Emeritus*. Co-editor, with Greil Marcus, of *A New Literary History of America*, he is the author of *Beyond Ethnicity, Neither Black nor White yet Both, Ethnic Modernism, The Temptation of Despair, African American Writing, Challenges of Diversity, Schrift in bildender Kunst*, and *Ein Kind in Bergen-Belsen / Un Bambino a Bergen-Belsen*. His edited books include *The Return of Thematic Criticism and Multilingual America*.

Mingwei Song is Professor of Chinese at Wellesley College, where he specializes in modern Chinese literature and intellectual history, science fiction, youth culture, posthuman theories and the Neo-Baroque aesthetics. He is the author of *Young China: national rejuvenation and the bildungsroman, 1900–1959* (2015) and *Fear of Seeing: the politics and poetics of Chinese science fiction* (forthcoming). He is the co-editor of *The Reincarnated Giant: an anthology of twenty-first-century Chinese science fiction* (2018). He has translated works by David Damrosch, Delmore Schwartz, and A.S. Byatt into Chinese, and his own academic works as well as his short stories and poems have been translated into German, French, Italian, Japanese, Russian, Spanish, Korean, and Hindi.

Kenneth P. Winkler is Kingman Brewster, Jr Professor of Philosophy at Yale University and the author of *Berkeley: an interpretation*. He has published numerous articles and essays and edited *The Cambridge Companion to Berkeley*, Berkeley's *A Treatise Concerning the Principles of Human Knowledge* and an abridgment of Locke's *Essay concerning Human Understanding*. From 2000 to 2005 he served as editor of the journal *Hume Studies*.

List of Figures

10.1 Mawande Ka Zenzile, 'Calling a Spade a Spade' (2016. Cow dung and oil on canvas, 154 × 172cm). © Stevenson, Amsterdam, Cape Town, Johannesburg. 180

10.2 Heinrich Meyring, 'Moses Receiving the Law on Mount Sinai' (1684. Carrara marble, High Altar front. San Moisè, Venice. Werner Sollors). 182

List of Tables

4.1	Interlinear comparison of עיר המתים (City of the dead) and די טויטע שטאָט (The dead city)	76
4.2	Interlinear comparison of עיר המתים (City of the dead) and די טויטע שטאָט (The dead city)	77
4.3	Interlinear comparison of עיר המתים (City of the dead) and די טויטע שטאָט (The dead city)	80
4.4	Interlinear comparison of עיר המתים (City of the dead) and די טויטע שטאָט (The dead city)	82
4.5	Interlinear comparison of עיר המתים (City of the dead) and די טויטע שטאָט (The dead city)	84

Acknowledgements

This volume is the result of the remarkable willingness of friends, colleagues and students of Lawrence A. Rosenwald to join together to celebrate the work of an outstanding scholar, academic and mentor, with their commitment and ideas. They need to be recognized for their innovative takes on questions about translation that are central to Larry Rosenwald's intellectual inquiries. I would also like to acknowledge Andrew Shennan, Provost of Wellesley College, who saluted and supported the project of this volume early on, as a way to publicly express gratitude and admiration for Larry Rosenwald's innumerable contributions to the academic community. Chris Penfold, the editor at UCL Press, judiciously shepherded the volume from its inception to its final form. Last, but not least, I acknowledge with gratitude Katharina Christoph who was involved in each phase of the formation of this book, generously offering her precious time, sound judgment, and close attention to the *minutiae* of en dashes just as much as to the conceptualization of the volume as a whole. Without her, this would have been a lesser book.

Introduction
Thomas Nolden

The central concern of this volume can be best delineated with an observation about pacifism by critic, translator and activist Lawrence A. Rosenwald, to whom this collection is dedicated. Rosenwald writes that 'serious pacifism has to be realistic, tragic, and responsible'.[1] Indeed, serious translation, too, must be realistic, tragic and responsible – attributes that are taken into account by the authors of the chapters assembled in this collection. The contributors to this volume demonstrate that the politics of translation will often present the translator with the indisputable economic, cultural, societal and racial circumstances of and surrounding their work, and they must be realistic in rendering them appropriately. One of the tragedies of translation that is relevant to this collection pertains to the inability of the translator to control the reception of their work, to assure that their choices and decisions will be appreciated by the reader the way that the translator intended. And yet, in the face of many such adverse realities and linguistic conundrums, the translator remains resolute in their responsibility to expose difficult and precarious texts to readers and, in turn, expose those same readers to at times fraught expressions of difference and dissent.

I.

The very fact that we can find a theory both of translation and of pacifism right at the traverse of the many vectors of the rich *œuvre* of a scholar and critic like Rosenwald alerts us to the moral relevance of translation as a practice of perseverance and of intervention, and as a practice that can give voice to diverse experiences and opposing points of view.

The chapters of this collection address various aspects of the relationship between text, translator and reader in historical, political or cultural situations that, for one reason or another, are anything but neutral. Indeed, these chapters illustrate how literary records of extreme and often painful experiences are at risk of being stripped of their authenticity when not carefully handled by the translator; how cultural moments in which the translation of a text that would have otherwise fallen into oblivion instead gave rise to a translator who enabled its preservation while ultimately coming into their own as an author as a result; how the difficulties the translator faces in intercultural or transnational constellations in which prejudice plays a role endangers projects meant to facilitate mutual understanding; how musical scores can effectively capture and render queerness into transcultural phenomena, thereby invoking spaces that are as much (and perhaps more) about healing as they are about suffering. In sum, this volume demonstrates that translation has never existed as a purely subjective and individual practice; rather, it has always been inevitably and inextricably linked to sweeping discourses of geopolitics and power.

The title of this collection, then, is meant to be understood in several ways at once: it refers to the dynamics of rendering texts that articulate particular notions of adverse circumstances as well as situations in which translators have themselves encountered adversity in undertaking their work. 'Translating in the face of adversity' also explores some of the venues that artists have pursued by transferring artistic expressions from one medium into another in order to preserve and disseminate important experiences in a culture that has turned from being primarily text-based to one that is more and more 'visual' (W.J.T. Mitchell).

II.

A look back at the beginning of the history and theory of translation shows that the type of inquiry that this volume pursues is anything but part of the historical core of established understandings of translation. The criteria and practices that have inspired the way we have typically thought about translation since the times of John Dryden – often credited as one of the first true theorists of translation in modern times – were developed in the context of translating texts that were revered by their authors because they represented some of the 'crowning achievements' and cultural norms of Western civilization. And it stands to reason that these criteria, and the practices that developed alongside them, indeed reflect the elevated status of the materials on which translators like John Dryden or Ben Johnson before him were honing their ideas and refining their skills.

But even long before Neoclassical scholars and writers set out to promote the paradigms that have since been governing modern understandings of the work of the translator, their early theological predecessors had already forged impactful standards and expectations to guide the act of rendering a source into the vernaculars of the day. The Church Fathers, followed eventually by the translators of the Renaissance all the way through the Enlightenment, positioned the translator as akin to the disciple. Translation theory and practices were a by-product of an evangelizing apparatus, a surplus effect of an attempt to strengthen and reinforce religious institutions.

A glance at an even earlier moment in Western translation theory confirms the imbalance of power inscribed into the relationship between translator and the translated texts. In their discussions about the principles that the translator should follow, St Augustine stated in a letter to St Jerome written in AD 403:

> I have since heard that you have translated Job out of the original Hebrew, although in your own translation of the same prophet from the Greek tongue we had already a version of that book. In that earlier version you marked with asterisks the words found in the Hebrew but wanting in the Greek, and with obelisks the words found in the Greek but wanting in the Hebrew; and this was done with such astonishing exactness, that in some places we have every word distinguished by a separate asterisk, as a sign that these words are in the Hebrew, but not in the Greek. Now, however, in this more recent version from the Hebrew, there is not the same scrupulous fidelity as to the words; and it perplexes any thoughtful reader to understand either what was the reason for marking the asterisks in the former version with so much care that they indicate the absence from the Greek version of even the smallest grammatical particles which have not been rendered from the Hebrew, or what is the reason for so much less care having been taken in this recent version from the Hebrew to secure that these same particles be found in their own places.[2]

At this point, it suffices to call attention to the fact that the project of translation has been, from its inception in early Christianity onwards, understood as a transaction devoted to solidifying the reputation and dissemination of an authoritative source. The excruciating attention to the original's every detail then functions simultaneously as a confession of the translators' own faith in the sanctity of the source. This is essential as nothing less than the unity of the Christian church appears to be at stake in the mind of Church Father Augustine:

> For my part, I would much rather that you would furnish us with a translation of the Greek version ... For if your translation begins to be more generally read in many churches, it will be a grievous thing that, in the reading of Scripture, differences must arise between the Latin Churches and the Greek Churches, especially seeing that the discrepancy is easily condemned in a Latin version by the production of the original in Greek, which is a language very widely known.[3]

Following St Augustine's lead further back into the contexts of Latin and Greek letters, it becomes clear that the Roman authors conceived theoretical insights into the practice of translation that closely resemble the ones we have been using ever since. Comparing the advantages and disadvantages associated with literal as well as with freer forms of translation (*imitatio* and *aemulatio*), author-translators like Horace and Cicero in the first century BCE had forged their discourses, too, while working on the commanding texts that they considered part of a venerable tradition. It was these traditions that translators believed they had an obligation to uphold. The claim that translation is a Roman intervention (dating back to the translation of the *Odyssey* by a Greek captive adopted and eventually freed by an illustrious Roman family) may indeed be hard to prove. And yet the very absence of a veritable Greek theory of translation that equals the astonishing efforts made by Roman authors and translators is telling in itself. It appears to confirm the assumption that theorizing about the task of the translator was, to a large degree, the by-product of debates that focused on how to best secure the reputation of preeminent texts whose elevated status needed to be preserved for the future. After all, ancient Greek culture is not known to have been informed by translating or adapting literary artefacts of non-Greek origins. Philosophers like Plato or historians and geographers like Herodotus were undoubtedly cognizant of and often fascinated by non-Greek cultures, but they never quoted them – so we must assume that the Greeks never engaged in translating these sources.

In any case, from this vantage point, the debates among Renaissance and Enlightenment translators can be understood as a second take on a set of problems outlined centuries earlier. Their ideas and techniques were impacted by their unquestioned understanding that Ovid's *Epistles* or Horace's *Ars Poetica* represented authoritative texts. And they were informed by the conviction that the status and the authoritative claims of these texts needed to be rendered and disseminated just as carefully as the words found within them. Articulating their views in prominent places such as the forewords to their translations was indicative of the translators' reverence for the cultural monuments whose reputation they set out to secure.

III.

It is itself a sign of our own ongoing difficulty to critically examine the underpinnings of our cultural history that we have yet to understand in more general terms how the types of texts that instigated translation theory (such as scripture and the ancient classics) impacted its core sets of paradigms. Thus, it comes as no surprise that a thorough critique of the way we have understood translation has since been offered by critics like Homi K. Bhabha, Tejaswini Niranjana and Gayatri Chakravorty Spivak who were able to discern our Western 'sanctioned ignorance' by pointing to the experiences articulated in voices that are often muted, ignored or distorted. They took issue with the long-established notion that translators are the 'silent' or the 'hidden masters of culture' (Maurice Blanchot) and called out their complicity in ongoing projects of cultural imperialism. After all, the Western translator had promoted the cause of geopolitically-significant distribution of established Western political ideologies and cultural canons at the same time as their religious counterparts were using their craft to proselytize the non-Christian Other. Alerting Western translation theory to the fundamental question 'Can the subaltern speak?', Spivak drew attention to the colonial vestiges inscribed in the theory and praxis of translation and pivoted the discourse towards the native informer, the non-Western woman whose utterances need to be translated and appreciated rather than silenced. Yet even Spivak found herself drawn into the dynamics of translation that had historically predicated the fame of the translator on the reputation of the text they were translating. Spivak at one point recalled that her English translation of Derrida's *Of Grammatology*, the founding document of Deconstruction, was responsible for launching her own career as a critic – a career whose origins can be traced back to her now famous 'Translator's Preface' (1976).

While critics like Spivak must be given due credit for radically probing the 'Who' in the question 'Who is being translated?', they postulate in the same vein that the 'Who' in the query 'Who is translating?' ought to be categorically related to the subject of the utterances that are being rendered into a different language. The emergence of the postcolonial feminist translator in the late 1980s culminated in the debate that made global headlines following Amanda Gorman's recitation of her poem 'The Hill We Climb' at the inauguration of United States President Joseph Biden in January 2020. The claim arose that the 'positionality' (Stuart Hall) of the author can only be fully comprehended and legitimately rendered by a translator who shares with the author commensurable experiences, if not an identical history, of oppression. Anything less would taint the poem with the politics of cultural appropriation.

This more recent moment in Western translation history marks just how far we have come in considering this basic intercultural tool. To be sure, the monumental efforts of translating first the literary monuments of Greek antiquity, then scripture and eventually the texts of classical antiquity, triggered a theoretical reflex that produced the conservative, Augustinian maxim of literal adherence to the original text. And yet, this is clearly only one part of the dynamics that ensued. It also generated the Jeromian impetus to instead adapt the word of the original to the language and culture of the contemporary audiences. It is not an exaggeration to say that the figure of the cultural iconoclast most powerfully entered the stage of the modern world in the learned debates about the translation of gospel. The gesture of justifying one's liberty of ignoring, moving away from or knowingly interfering with parts of established tradition by pointing to the need of the here and now was methodically rehearsed in the battles fought among the translators and interpreters of texts that were central to a culture's identity. Literalist translations are what have held our 'imagined communities' (Benedict Anderson) in place while more free forms of rendering have moved them on. Martin Luther's epochal translation of the Bible serves as a monument to the latter; judiciary practices of justices claiming to read the Constitution as 'originalists' powerfully stand in for the former. To bring the argument back into the realm of literature: the *bon mot* attributed to Robert Frost that 'poetry is what gets lost in translation' proves as many times correct as the observation that mis-translations of poetry also succeed in engendering new poetry and forms of literary expression – and thus pushing literature ahead in time and space.

It is of course a matter of speculation which path the theory of translation may have taken if translation had not emerged in the proselytizing service of disseminating the claims of 'supreme' texts. It may certainly be worthwhile to identify more thoroughly those strands in the history of translation that developed in areas less preoccupied with the solidification of cultural norms and societal codes. And it would be intriguing to compare their translative preferences to the core tradition of translation outlined above.

IV.

The aims pursued by this collection are related, yet follow a slightly different ambition: rather than asking what may have gotten lost in the dynamics of translation history at large, the authors of this collection are concerned with the question of how texts have been imperilled by getting lost without translation or how specific translations have obscured the proper place of a text in world literature. They discuss how specific translation practices can rescue texts from being lost and thus address translation as a project of making available and preserving a corpus of texts that would otherwise be in danger of becoming censored, misperceived or ignored. In this regard, they, too, are part of a heritage discipline which explores ways of securing legacies of texts for future generations of readers. The authors of this collection look at translation and adaptation as a project of curating textual models of personal, communal or collective perseverance. And they offer insights into the dynamics of cultural inclusion and exclusion through a series of theoretical frameworks as well as through a set of concrete case studies drawn from different cultural and historical contexts. While the expansive historical scope of the collection samples translation studies from Jewish scripture all the way to modern Chinese science fiction, its thematic scope encompasses various modes of translation (including adaptations into different hybrid and new media) and a large range of topics that speak to important issues of present-day concern.

The title of Part I of this collection references contemporary efforts of translating as a mode of perseverance. 'Modes of Perseverance: Translating the Jewish Tradition' sets the stage for the collection as a whole, both in regards to its historical and thematic scope and in the array of the methodologies employed. The case studies presented here offer reconceptualizations of the Jewish experience by commenting on and adding to iterative acts of translation that try to relate historical experiences to present-day audiences. The chapters examine the translator's role in capturing and wresting from history important modes of perseverance and resistance in the face of political and social adversity. The translator is aware of the need to expose texts to contrasting and complementary post-biblical traditions and to the concerns raised by such exposure. Scripture has always been at risk of losing some notions of its particularity once translation relates it to the contemporary world. And yet this section demonstrates that it may lose its relevance if the translator is incapable or uninterested in embedding it in the language of today's discourses.

This part of the volume thus seeks to discuss how rendering the imperilled voices of Jewish writing into different lingual and historical traditions is a necessary yet precarious undertaking that reflects the understanding of Jewish cultures as both enriched and jeopardized by the politics of translation. And it succeeds in outlining the ways in which the perseverance found in biblical and post-biblical Jewish writing requires the translator to pay heed to the interplay between religious and non-religious language and languages.

By setting out with an annotated 'four-voiced rendering' of Lamentations 3, Edward L. Greenstein's chapter calls attention to a text that articulates the traumatic experience surrounding the destruction of Jerusalem by the Babylonian army. Opening the inquiry of the volume with a chapter that examines the difficulties encountered in the rendering of an experience of great hardship and adversity, Greenstein points to the tall order of translation as a part of the command to remember the pain inflicted throughout history. The Jewish imperative of *zakhor* signals a first and powerful paradigm in the long history of translating the experience of endurance *vis-a-vis* the tribulations of the past.

Following Greenstein's expository chapter, Everett Fox addresses in his contribution yet another set of complexities encountered when translating the Hebrew Bible in the twenty-first century. 'Isaiah 1 in Translation and Contexts' captures the challenges of rendering the book's complicated rhetoric and possibly performative nature over time. Fox engages in a conversation on the principles of translating scripture with Greenstein and, of course, with Martin Buber and Franz Rosenzweig. After all, it was their monumental Bible translation that famously strove 'to create distance for the reader, not to bridge it'.[4] Fox, too, operates on a minute philological level when considering the precarious subject matter as well as the prophetic tropes that surface in Isaiah. Fox sets these prophetic tropes against a background of the present to ask how a translation can make visible a text's emphasis on the sickness of the body politic, the oppression of the powerless and the corruption of public institutions.

In 'Heinrich Heine and the Splendid Galaxy of Jewish Poetry', Abigail Gillman illustrates the dynamics translators reckon with when rendering Jewish prose and poetry into diasporic languages and literatures. In doing so, Gillman pays close attention to the cultural context surrounding the kinship between the exiled German Romantic poet Heinrich Heine and American Jewish poet Emma Lazarus. According to Gillman, Lazarus eschewed the 'anxiety of influence' (Harold Bloom) and succeeded in 'translating herself into an American Jewish writer' largely through her own translations of Heine. In addition to reconstructing Lazarus' work as a translator of Heine's writings, Gillman reads some of the key texts in which Lazarus articulates a notion of Jewish identity against the backdrop of Heine's poetry. Underlying both of these modern renderings, the palimpsest of Hebrew scripture thus becomes visible. Lazarus pursues Heine's 'mediaeval Jewish heritage' to orient her own poetic agenda towards an understanding of Jewish literature in which the act of translation is not merely a utilitarian tool, but also an essential part.

In her chapter 'City of the Dead or The Dead City? Yitskhok-Leybush Peretz as Self-Translator', Efrat Gal-Ed directs attention to a story Peretz first published in 1892 in Hebrew with the title *'ir-hametim* ('City of the Dead') when he was preoccupied with the dire situation of Polish-Jewish *shtetl* life. Gal-Ed provides a close, interlinear reading of the differences between the Hebrew and Peretz's subsequent Yiddish publication of the story in 1901 under the title *di toyte shtot* ('The Dead City'). The synoptic comparison of the two versions yields crucial insights into the dynamic at play: whereas the Yiddish story succeeds in making oral discourse literary, the Hebrew version appears to render literary language colloquial. Both become visible as a means to capture the fragile state of Jewish existence in the Polish province. Gal-Ed contextualizes these observations in the historical development of Yiddish as a language with a strong oral tradition, compared to Hebrew, which, at this point, comprised a more robust literary tradition.

Part II, entitled 'Modes of Intervention: Translating Dissent and Diversity', concentrates on a set of key questions posed by translation while exploring innovative renderings of literary texts, both early and contemporary, that emanate from various Western and non-Western cultural traditions. Whether tracing iterative translations of a single story across decades and political divides or identifying the problematic cultural and racial preconceptions present in the translations of particular texts, the contributors to this part show the susceptibility of translation to implicit collective bias about the Other. Drawing on close readings of individual texts alongside examinations of their historical contexts, they study how intercultural dynamics can impact the politics of translation at several levels, from stylistic minutiae to large-scale processes such as the economics of distribution and politics of censorship. By introducing case studies from Asian literary contexts alongside European ones, this part raises compelling questions about ethnic, political and cultural intersectionality in the translation of texts ranging from nineteenth-century philosophical discourse to contemporary children's literature. A renewed focus on these dynamics in literary translation in light of global reckonings on racial and social justice provides a necessary and long overdue reassessment of the conventions and preconceptions inherent in crosscultural linguistic intervention and interpretation.

The examples of dissent that are discussed in this part entail nineteenth-century critiques of religious orthodoxy (Feuerbach) and of the divine origin of the gospels (Strauss) which – translated by George Eliot – gave rise to her own literary career. They also make reference to intertextual connections between twentieth-century antiwar writers in pre-World War II Europe and in the civil war-torn Democratic Republic of the Congo. Last, but not least, they pertain to the formation of the genre of science fiction in China, informed by translations from French and Japanese authors, where it advanced as a medium of conveying dissent from the official ideology of technological progress.

Gail Twersky Reimer opens this part of the volume by returning to the moment in George Eliot's life when she published her first book, an anonymous translation of Strauss' *The Life of Jesus, Critically Examined* (*Das Leben Jesu*), followed by a translation of Feuerbach's *Essence of Christianity* (*Wesen des Christentums*) under her real name, Marian Evans. As in the previous chapters, questions surface that concern the apt rendering of sacred language, though Strauss and Feuerbach themselves had pushed theology to the brink, falling victim to their new brand of historically-informed scholarship of the Bible. In her chapter 'How George Eliot Came to Write', Reimer dissects young Eliot's approach to the works of Strauss and Feuerbach that eventually destroyed the established paradigms of Christian theology. Reimer contextualizes Eliot's formative work and years as a translator within the contemporary discussion about the status and the task of the translator before turning to the factors that led the young translator to become interested in Strauss' theological treatise. Reimer demonstrates how Eliot crafted her own approach to her translations of the Young Hegelians and, with it, also crafted a venue that would allow for her own inception as an independent writer.

Katherine Hollander's 'Venture, Courage, Ruin: Karin Michaëlis in Translation Across Genre and Time' shifts the discussion from the translation of radical theological texts to pieces of pacifist fiction. She sets her discussion of the novel *Mette Trap og Hendes Unger* (1922) by Danish feminist author Karin Michaëlis against a set of cognate texts, including Bertolt Brecht's *Mother Courage* (1939) and Lynn Nottage's acclaimed play *Ruined* (2008). Hollander reads the latter two as iterative 'translations' of Michaëlis' story over time; Brecht's *Courage*, written in the shadow of the Third Reich, is set during the Thirty Years War and Nottage's *Ruined* set in a modern, civil-war torn Democratic Republic of the Congo. As critic and author Ngũgĩ Wa Thiong'o has pointed to the impact of Brechtian dramaturgy on African literature, Hollander understands the connections between the Marxist messaging of Brecht's antiwar theatre and Nottage's play as existing on a translational continuum going back to Michaëlis. The corpus of texts Hollander brings into conversation with one another illuminate strategies over time of representing the dire situation of women in exploitative historical settings and the economic factors that force them to make complicated decisions to ensure the survival of themselves and their communities.

Mingwei Song's chapter moves the focus from the discussion of the translative forces that have shaped the Western segment of world literature to the dynamics at play within East Asian writing and to the complex relationship between the works of Chinese authors and their Western readership. 'Lu Xun's Unfaithful Translation of Science Fiction: Rewriting Chinese Literary History' turns to the moment in literary history at the turn of the twentieth century when science fiction and utopian fiction became popular genres among Chinese readers. Song focuses on translations by writer Lu Xun who, as a student in Japan, introduced science fiction novels and stories (among them a rather obscure short story by American woman author Louise J. Strong) to Chinese audiences. Song shows how the translation of non-Chinese texts engendered a genre of writing that allowed Chinese authors to depict what they perceived as the menacing future of modernity. In their 'unfaithful' attitude towards the original texts, Lu Xun's translations reveal the tension between the attitudes of twentieth-century intellectuals toward science, Enlightenment and progress, as well as the Chinese government's attempt at engineering the 'Chinese dream'. His translations remain a palimpsest that records the reservations the new wave of Chinese science fiction harbours for the politics of China and this nation's ideological investment into relentless, ever-accelerating technologization.

Emily Xueni Jin addresses the role of translation of Chinese science fiction in her chapter as well, though from the point of view of rendering texts into English. In 'Translating Chinese Science Fiction into English: Decolonization and Reconciliation on a Cultural Battlefield', Jin sets out to discuss the perceived 'Chineseness' of contemporary Chinese science fiction writing and the challenges such an essentialization poses to translation. Jin asks how Chinese science fiction translators, fully aware of the context in which they work, navigate the treacherous international political landscape and struggle with cultural decolonization. Using Liu Cixin's novel *The Three-Body Problem* as a case study to discuss manifestations of orientalism in the translation of Chinese science fiction, Jin shows how translation of Chinese science fiction into the Anglophone world has become a political and cultural 'battlefield'. Jin's analysis reflects the emphasis the Chinese state places on translation as inadvertently revealing orientalist proclivities when it uses translated Chinese science fiction's prestige in a Western-centric global market as a metric for success.

Isabelle Chen's chapter 'Whose Voice(s)?: Authorship, Translation, and Diversity in Contemporary Children's Literature' concludes this part of the volume by expanding the query beyond the scope of individual national literatures. Chen discusses the claim that characters from traditionally underrepresented backgrounds should be written by authors of this same background because specific experiences of marginalization are in a sense 'untranslatable' across the borders of identity and group affiliation. In a field increasingly concerned with this metaphorical untranslatability of lived experience, Chen inquires how translators can strike a balance between a linguistic understanding of a text and the singular cultural context in which the author creates it. Drawing upon sources from canonical translation theory to tweets about kid-lit, Chen focuses on the intersection of voice, authorship and translation, and considers to what extent their relationship has evolved in parallel with the industry's heightened sensitivity to ethnic and linguistic difference. Elizabeth Acevedo's young adult novel-in-verse, *The Poet X*, and its translations into Spanish (by Silvina Poch) and French (by Clémentine Beauvais) serve as a case study to analyse this complex relationship.

Part III and the volume's final part, 'Modes of Remedialization: Translating Beyond the Text', pitches the notion of translation beyond the domain of the text *per se* and points to the various ways in which theories and practices of translation intersect with the fine arts, film and new media. Understanding translation as encompassing the remedialization of texts into the sister arts not only poses challenges but raises poignant questions about the task of capturing imperilled voices. Thus, this part offers insights into diverse media and their affordances in an effort to continue long-standing dialogues on the creative transformation of the spoken or written word into the visual and performing arts.

The opening chapter returns to the beginnings of Western theories of translation and reminds us that non-textual media have been used as early as the fifteenth century to comment on the relationship between translation and original text. Looking at Albrecht Dürer's depiction of the translator St Jerome, we come to understand that adaptation and translation are, as a matter of fact, coeval. The following chapters push the line of this argument into an examination of contemporary modes of remedialization. Like their counterparts in the earlier parts of the volume, these chapters simultaneously address how translation and adaptation projects of the past are rife with implications for the present, precisely because they speak to collective experiences and moments in history that, at times, uncannily resemble the political constellations in which we find ourselves today.

This part of the volume concludes the arc of the thematic and historical span of the volume by examining how acts of translation inform contemporary queer film and even pandemic-era digital theatre. It closes with the intriguing observation that present-day virtual performances are being (mis-)perceived in exactly the same manner in which translation theory, from its beginnings on, had disavowed translation as a deficient derivative of the original.

Werner Sollors' 'Seeing Images, Thinking of Words: Visual Art as Translation' redirects focus to the translation dispute between Jerome and Augustine mentioned at the beginning of this introduction. While concentrating on a specific object, a pumpkin, in Albrecht Dürer's engraving *Der Heilige Hieronymus im Gehäus* (*Saint Jerome in his Study*, 1514), Sollors unveils the presence of a theoretical discourse on translation in the hagiographic depiction of St Jerome. Focusing on the power of visual representation, this chapter addresses the ability of the image to translate questions of scripture by placing them into the realm of a non-linguistic medium. Sollors sets the stage for his scholarly inquiry by analysing an explicitly political painting by contemporary artist Mawande Ka Zenzile, whose visual language is predicated on an English-language expression whose racist implications the painting powerfully exposes.

Sarah Bay-Cheng's 'Theatre without Theatres: Performance Transmission as Translation' transitions the discussion about adaptation and translation to the present by likening the debate about digital theatre to ongoing debates about translation. Bay-Cheng expounds on those debates that decry both digital theatre and translated texts as inferior, deviative and deficient compared to the original, and uses these paradigms to appreciate digital theatre as translated theatre. Bay-Cheng turns to Walter Benjamin's notion of the 'dialectical image' to understand how the medial translation provided by digital theatre can accentuate features that an audience may otherwise miss in the theatre. The 'meaning' of the original can thus be more effectively rendered through the technological features of the 'inaccurate' medium of the digital representation of the original performance. Expanding the reading of digital performance as a form of translated theatre, the chapter ultimately borrows from translation theory to apprehend the current phenomenon of theatre across media and to suggest future directions of live art post-pandemic.

K. E. Goldschmitt's chapter addresses the potential inherent in established musical vernaculars to translate the experience of otherness. Focusing on a specific motion picture soundtrack, 'From Miami to Hong Kong: Sounding Transnational Queerness and Translation in *Moonlight* (2016)' traces how directors use musical scores to translate queerness into a transnational and transcultural phenomenon able to be captured and celebrated in music. Analysing the example of Barry Jenkins' musical choices for *Moonlight*, Goldschmitt illustrates how pop music cues can connect a film's thematic elements to other minority filmmaking traditions and translate them across various cultural contexts. The chapter follows the various acts of transnational and transcultural translations of a Mexican song that originated in Wong Kar-Wai's film about two gay men from Hong Kong vacationing in Argentina before it was heard in Almodóvar's *Hable Con Ella*, and eventually in Jenkins' *Moonlight*, which is set in Miami's historically-Black Liberty City neighborhood, allowing it to partake in a 'sonic afro-modernity' (Weheliye).

Martin Brody analyses the disruption of conventional musical aesthetics when rendering turbulence in the performance of modern operas. Accepting the difficult task of translating a collective voice of dissent and dissonance into a musical language, the composer has to find ways of conveying a people's expression of distress in the language of music. His chapter 'Crowd Noise: Collective Turbulence in Modern Opera' discusses how the musical articulation of communal experiences and emotions appear to question the very genre of opera itself. Scanning examples from Puccini's *Turandot* and Mussorgsky's *Boris Godunov*, Brody focuses on Arnold Schoenberg's translation of the Mosaic legend into his twelve-tone opera *Moses und Aron*. Schoenberg captures the dynamics of a people delving into a mob with the realities of rising authoritarianism in mind and pushes the sonic articulation of the mob's sentiment to a point well beyond the musical order of the opera.

This part of the volume, and with it the volume itself, concludes with Kenneth P. Winkler's chapter 'Creative Translation in Emerson's Idealism', which expands on L. Rosenwald's reading of the diaristic traditions that impacted the form of Ralph Waldo Emerson's journals. Rather than merely looking at the formal continuities between the Puritan diary and Emerson's, Winkler details how Emerson responded to the idea of continuous creation endorsed by the Puritan diarist Jonathan Edwards. The chapter examines how Emerson advanced his own understanding of the doctrine of continuous creation as a form of translation, a creative appropriation that would become a formative element in Emerson's idealism. Here, divine creation is understood as the continuous act of retranslating the original act of creating the world at every moment anew while at the same moment preserving the original act of inception.

V.

> Making an argument that translation matters means taking a risk. Once we win, once we persuade the skeptical world to care more about translation than it has previously, we have called the djinn out of the bottle and cannot put it back; we cannot keep the now-attentive world from directing to particular translations and translators the fierce scrutiny it previously directed elsewhere. That is for the better; but such scrutiny will both raise reputations and lower them, enforce truths but also explode dogmas, assay gold as gold and pyrite as pyrite.[5]

While the contributors to this volume have responded to this claim by L. Rosenwald in various ways, they all endorse the central charge underlying his hope that 'translation matters'. They apply scrutiny to the history of translational practices and they apply ingenuity and creativity to the exploration of new ways of rendering marginal and precarious texts – as well as texts that are central to various traditions – relevant for and pertinent to today's contexts and concerns. Their chapters demonstrate how translation can indeed 'enforce truths' by understanding it as a mode of perseverance predicated on continuous acts of improving access to historical records of pain and trauma. But they also illustrate that translation is capable of 'exploding dogmas' when articulating dissent and difference: *by rendering oppositional voices, it becomes an articulation of difference and dissent itself.*

The volume as a whole, then, is meant to lay the groundwork for an expansion of current theorizing about translation: analogous to the way we appreciate texts as elements in a complex network of past, present and future texts that we refer to as 'literature', we must also consider texts and non-textual media as elements of a larger network of translations. While we have suitable terms for the former ('literature' as the intertextual dynamics that connects each part – text – to a larger whole of all the texts), we still lack adequate terms for the latter. Still missing is a concept that – analogous to the notion of 'intertextuality' – could aptly capture the interrelatedness of translations among each other *and* of the interrelatedness of each text to the whole of literature as a network of translated texts. Still missing is also a concept that – analogous to the notion of 'literature' – would aptly acknowledge the fuller understanding of literature not just as an ensemble of *original* acts of literary articulations, but also as an ensemble of translations.

Rosenwald reminds us that 'making an argument that translation matters means taking a risk'. But naming *how* it matters means taking a risk, too – one for which this volume aspires to offer insights and encouragement.

Notes

1. Rosenwald, 'Notes on pacifism', 94.
2. 'Letter 71'.
3. 'Letter 71'.
4. Batnitzky, 'Translation as transcendence', 87.
5. Rosenwald, 'Imagining a world where translation matters', 126.

Bibliography

Batnitzky, Leora. 'Translation as transcendence: a glimpse into the workshop of the Buber-Rosenzweig Bible translation'. *New German Critique*, no. 70, 1997, pp. 87–116.

'Letter 71'. *The Works of Aurelius Augustine, Bishop of Hippo. A New Translation*, edited by Rev. Marcus Dods, translated by Rev. J.G. Cunningham. T. & T. Clark. 1875.

Rosenwald, Lawrence A. 'Notes on pacifism'. *The Antioch Review*, vol. 65 no. 1, Winter 2007, pp. 93–106.

Rosenwald, Lawrence A. 'Imagining a world where translation matters. Review of Edith Grossman's *Why Translation Matters*'. *Raritan*, vol. 31, no. 4, 2012, pp. 119–30.

Part I
**Modes of Perseverance:
Translating the Jewish Tradition**

1
Lamentations 3: A Four-Voiced Rendering

Edward L. Greenstein

Introduction I: the poetics

The biblical book of Lamentations comprises a sequence of five poems. The first four are a mixture of lament and complaint, and the fifth is a petition for relief from the deity.[1] The poems all revolve around the siege and destruction of Jerusalem by the Babylonian army in the years 587–586 BCE. Although they relate to the events surrounding that national catastrophe,[2] leaving the city and its temple devastated and leading to the exile of thousands of its people, the poems do not narrate the history – they evoke it in order to express the trauma that is felt, grieve the losses and shake an angry finger at YHWH, Israel's God, who several of the poets blame for punishing the people for their sins in a highly disproportionate manner.[3]

The poems provide a many-sided perspective on the depredations that accompanied the siege and destruction: starvation, disease and death within the walls of the besieged city; death from warfare; deportation of a substantial portion of the population; desolation among the burnt city's ruins. But they are not arranged in chronological order. The first poem dwells on the aftermath of the destruction. The second delineates the destruction itself and the deity's role in carrying it out. (The theological orientation of the poems, characterizing extreme divine wrath, eschews any mention of the historical perpetrators of the catastrophe – the Babylonians.) The third poem, on which I shall elaborate below, combines complaint and meditation. The fourth, in many ways comparable in tone and style to the second, delves into the human losses and the grievances they provoke. The fifth, as said, is a petitionary prayer to repair the broken relationship between the people and their God.

Each of the first four poems is constructed, verse by verse, as an alphabetic acrostic.[4] Each verse begins with a succeeding letter of the Hebrew alphabet. Such a rigid programme of prosodic structure might have produced a choppy cascade of verses. However, the poets, for the most part, ran themes, motifs and language from one verse to the next, creating units that override the verse-divisions produced by the acrostic. This flow from verse to verse is most apparent in Lamentations 3. That poem, which is the focus of this chapter, organizes the acrostic in three verses at a time, each of them beginning with the same letter. Nevertheless, several themes and motifs begin in the midst of one letter-unit and end in the midst of the next. For example, verses 12–13 straddle letters *dalet* and *he*, in which the latter clearly resumes the theme of the speaker feeling himself the target of the deity's arrows; and verses 19–20, which both begin with the letter *zayin* – and the same word – belong to two different speakers (see below). Similarly, verse 48 begins with the letter *peh*, just as verse 47 does; but verse 48 belongs to a voice that speaks in the singular, while verse 47 belongs to the preceding speaker, whose language is formulated in the plural.

This strategy of maintaining the flow dovetails with another peculiarity of Lamentations, in contrast to more typical biblical poetry. It is generally the case that the basic unit of biblical verse is a couplet of two parallel lines. This parallelism takes the form of a prosodic balance between the lines, or a repetition of syntactic structure from one line to the next, or the distribution of a conventional pair of words (for example, heaven–earth, earth–dust, father–mother, eat–drink) between the two lines – or, in many if not most instances, a combination of two or three of these features.[5] Moreover, there is generally a syntactic break or caesura at the end of each line. Most of the couplets (or triplets) in Lamentations work this way as well. For example, Lamentations 1:8: 'A sin has Jerusalem sinned; / Therefore has she become pitiful. / All those who had respected her scorn her, / For they have seen her nakedness'. But a relatively large number of verses in Lamentations feature enjambment, as one line runs into the next without any syntactic break.[6] For example, Lamentations 1:3: 'Judah has gone into exile / after affliction and great travail ... All those who pursued her overtook her / in the narrow straits'. Such enjambment can be found in Lamentations 3 as well; it is always reflected in my translation.

One of the widespread tropes in biblical poetry, which abounds in Lamentations as well, is wordplay and sound-play.[7] This surface phenomenon, which functions more deeply in linking terms, motifs and ideas, is notoriously hard to convey in translation. I have endeavoured to replicate something of this in my rendering, but the reader will imagine, quite correctly, that such phenomena are often missed. Most obviously, I have made very little effort to reproduce the alphabetic acrostic.[8] But I have tried to reproduce some of the more salient instances of sound-play (see, for example, verse 47); and, in adhering as much as possible to a relatively literal style, I have rendered recurrent terms largely by the same English gloss. Intelligibility has trumped consistency; but in cases in which I need to render the same word or stem differently, I provide a note to alert the reader (see, for example, on verses 9–13, where 'walkways' and 'stepped down' share the same stem).

Introduction II: the voices

Scholars have remarked on the diversity of genres and speakers in Lamentations 3.[9] However, no translation of which I am aware presents the diverse sections of the poem as the discourse of distinctly different speakers. I find in this poem a drama of argument, reaction and echo. The reader of a translation, often lacking access to rhetorical and linguistic cues in the source, is apt to miss the clash of voices. In fact, these voices can, at least in part, be identified – not with respect to a particular individual or group but to a set of types. Before delineating these types, I should explain as simply as I can the bases for distinguishing the voices.[10]

From verse 1 through verse 39 the speaker employs the first person singular. From verse 40 through verse 47 the discourse is formulated in the first person plural. At verse 48 an individual voice takes over and there is no reason to think that it does not continue till the poem's end in verse 66. Within the first section expressed in the first person singular, there are two clearly opposed voices. The first complains in a manner that is strongly reminiscent of Job – a voice that claims to have been wronged and battered (verses 1 through 19).[11] The second is the response of a pious interlocutor, like Job's companions, who exhorts the first speaker to disregard the injustices, stop complaining and wait patiently for restoration by the deity.[12] Following that conventional counsel, an apparent audience to this squaring-off ponders its own best course of (re)action – synthesizing the attitude of the Job-like character while seeming to adopt the interlocutor-like character's advice. When the collective voice concludes by evoking the profound devastation they endured, another singular voice emerges, the voice of personified Jerusalem, who spoke throughout the second half of Lamentations 1 (see below).

The reader may wonder why the poet does not introduce the speakers, as in the book of Job. Such introductions are conventionally dispensed with within ancient Near Eastern literature. For example, the Babylonian 'Theodicy' comprises a stanza-by-stanza dialogue between a complaining sufferer and his pious friend,[13] and the biblical Song of Songs comprises, for the most part, alternating discourse between a female and male lover. In neither case are the speakers identified.

Before elaborating a bit on the identification of these voices, there are two philological matters I need to address. First, yes, Lamentations 3 begins, literally, 'I am the man who has seen oppression'. It is therefore universally assumed that the speaker is male.[14] However, the term 'man' (*geber*) is a technical term indicating a pious 'man' whose suffering may be unjust. Compare, for example, this use of the term in Psalm 88:5, a highly Job-like prayer: 'I am reckoned with those who descend into the pit [that is, the grave]; / I am like a man (*geber*) without any strength'. Mesopotamian complaints of pious sufferers employ a semantically equivalent term, 'man' or 'young man'.[15] But the most prominent example of a righteous sufferer who refers to himself and is referred to by others as the 'man' (*geber*) is Job (for example, 3:3, 23; 22:2). Accordingly, the term 'man' indicates a type, not a gender – even though all our examples, like almost all speakers in ancient Near Eastern texts, are men. One should not assume that the speaker in the first section of Lamentations 3, nor that the speakers in the succeeding sections, are male. There is nothing in the speaker's language (such as a gendered verb form) to indicate maleness.[16]

A second philological point is crucial to establishing that the speaker in the fourth section of Lamentations 3 is female. Verse 51 is routinely rendered: 'My eyes cause me grief / at the fate of all the young women in my city' (New Revised Standard Version). It is presumed by most commentators and translators that the individual voice in this verse and the surrounding section is male and, for many, the same speaker who opens the discourse in verse 1. However, from a linguistic perspective, this interpretation of the verse is unlikely. To make (their) sense of it, other translators interpret the preposition *min*, most often 'from', as 'on account of'. Thus, a more literal translation, in the spirit of the translation cited above, is: 'My eyes cause me grief / on account of all the young women of my city'.

The problem is that when used in the full syntactic construction we find here, the preposition does not ordinarily mean 'on account of' but rather 'more than'. When it is said of or by someone that so-and-so A is such-and-such 'more than' B, A is an individual member of the group B. Let me clarify with a couple of examples, each employing the preposition *min* in its comparative ('more than') function. From 1 Samuel 18:30: 'David [A] had more success than all the servants of Saul [B]' (New Revised Standard Version). From Esther 2:17: 'the king loved Esther [A] more than all the other women [B]' (New Revised Standard Version). David belongs to the servants of Saul, and Esther belongs to the women. It is therefore most likely that Lamentations 3:51 features one of the young women of the city lamenting, saying that she is pained by what she has seen even more than her cohort. One of the city's maidens is speaking. That insight suggests that, in the entire fourth section of the poem, the voice is female.

We are now prepared to identify the types of the speakers in Lamentations 3.

The first is a Joban type. The speaker in verses 1–19 makes use of motifs and even some language that echoes those of Job, another person tormented by the deity, whose appeals on high seem to be barred. I am not maintaining that Lamentations is drawing on the book of Job as we know it, which, with many others, I hold to be a Persian period work composed a century or more later.[17] To my mind, the parallels result from two ancient Hebrew poets developing the same type – the pious sufferer.[18] I have indicated many of the parallels in the notes to the translation. But for the sake of making the point here, compare the following:

> Lam 3:12: He's stepped down on his bow and set me up / As a target for his arrow.
>
> Job 7:20: Why have you made me your target? / How could I be a burden to you?[19]
>
> Lam 3:14: I am a laughingstock among my people, / The taunt they sing every damn day.
>
> Job 17:6: He has set me up as a popular taunt; / I have become like spit in the face.

The second speaker (verses 20–39) is hardly a more reflective version of the sufferer, who suddenly chooses to repent and hope in the deity's compassion. The second speaker recalls the interlocutors of Job, who urge him to abandon what they see as a slippery slope toward blasphemy and rely on God's charitable nature. Compare, for example, what the speaker in the second part of our poem tells the first speaker with what Eliphaz advises Job:

> Lam 3:32: For whenever he afflicts, he (then) shows mercy / In accord with his many kindnesses.
>
> Job 5:17–18: Happy is the mortal whom Eloah reproves – / Do not reject Shaddai's discipline. / For once he inflicts pain, he binds up; / Once he strikes, his own hands heal.

The fact that the second speaker is addressing the complaints of a pious sufferer type, like Job, and not a victim of the devastation of Jerusalem in particular is apparent from Lamentations 3:35–36, in which the speaker insists that the deity would never pervert justice, using terms reminiscent of Job's companion Zophar in Job 8:3: 'Would El corrupt what is just? / Would Shaddai corrupt what is right?' The first speaker in Lamentations 3 said nothing about divine injustice. The issue of the deity's (in)justice, in forensic terms, is a central topic in the dialogues of Job, but not in our first speaker's discourse.[20] The poet would seem to have in mind a response to a contention by a Job-like figure, going beyond what the first speaker is said to have said. This factor makes the identification of the first and second speakers as types of the pious sufferer and his companion as certain as can be.

As noted above, the switch to first person plural discourse in Lamentations 3:40 signals the change of speaker from an individual to a group. Scholars posit that the collective is the community of which the preceding speaker is a member. The tenor of the community's discourse conforms neither to the complaining voice in the first part of the poem nor to the penitent voice of the second part. It is a tense combination of both. Immediately after confessing their sinfulness (verses 40–42), they protest that the deity refuses to hear their prayers (verses 43–44), in a manner resembling the Joban complaint that the deity is remote and aloof. The following lines continue the Job-like complaints of being mocked (verses 45–46). If, as many commentators maintain, the community takes up its prayer at the pious prompting of the preceding speaker, the community can hardly be understood to follow directions. The Joban voice of the first speaker in the poem seems to hold sway.

The biting rhetoric of the communal voice provides an appropriate background to the final section of the poem, in which a female voice (see above), a daughter of Zion, laments her situation in a manner that unmistakably echoes the emotional evocations of the personified city of

Jerusalem in Lamentations 1.[21] The opening reference to weeping (Lam 3:48–51) reprises one of the most salient images of the first chapter in Lamentations (verses 2, 16), in which the personified city wells up in tears. Our speaker's cry for vengeance on her tormentors (Lam 3:64–66) echoes a similar appeal by the Daughter of Zion in Lamentations 1:22. But she also seeks justice from the deity (Lam 3:58–59), an appeal, as said above, that is inappropriate to the desolated city but characteristic of the type of a righteous sufferer like Job.

Many of the annotations to the translation indicate parallels to the sorts of texts each speaker represents, supporting their typological identification.

Translation

A sufferer's complaint

[1–3]   I am the one[22] who has seen oppression
By the rod of his wrath.[23]
Me he drove to walk
In darkness without light.[24]
Against me he turns his hand
Every damn day.[25]

[4–6]   He has worn away my flesh and my skin,
He has shattered my bones.[26]
Constructed (siege-works) and encircled me
In abject-condition and hardship.[27]
In a dark place he has settled me
Like the forever dead.

[7–8]   He's erected before me a fence
So I cannot get out;
He's made my chains so heavy!
Though I cry out in supplication,
He shuts out my prayer.[28]

[9–11] He's fenced in my walkways with hewn-stone,[29]
My paths he's made crooked.
A bear in ambush is he to me,
A lion in a covert![30]
He's set brambles in my walkways and mangled me;[31]
He's left me desolate.

[12–13] He's stepped down[32] on his bow and set me up
As a target for his arrow.[33]
He's thrust into my innards
The sons of his quiver.[34]

[14–15]   I'm a laughingstock among my people,
          The taunt they sing every damn day.[35]
          He's sated me with poisonous herbs,[36]
          Saturated me with wormwood.
[16]   He's ground my teeth into the gravel,
          Stamped me into the dust.
[17–18]   I'm deprived of any peace of mind,
          I've forgotten any good.
          I thought, 'Lost is any future,
          Any hope, from YHWH'.[37]
[19]   Pay mind to my affliction and wretched state – [38]
          Wormwood and abject-condition!

A companion's response
[20–24]   Pay mind, pay mind,
          As my spirit speaks[39] to me.
          This I declare[40] to my heart,
          Which is why I have hope.
          YHWH's kindnesses have not reached an end,
          His mercies are not spent.
          They're renewed every morning.
          Great (O LORD) is your faithfulness!
          'YHWH is my lot', say I to myself –
          That is why I have hope in him.
[25–26]   Good is YHWH to those who rely on him,
          To a person[41] who seeks him.
          Good it is that one wait in quiet-patience
          For YHWH's salvation.
[27–30]   Good it is for one[42] to bear
          The yoke in one's youth;
          That he sit alone and be silent
          When he carries his yoke;[43]
          That he put his mouth into the dirt – [44]
          There yet may be a future!
          That he turn his cheek to one who strikes him;[45]
          That he accept the scorn.
[31–33]   For he will not abandon forever,
          Not the LORD!
          For whenever he afflicts, he (then) shows mercy
          In accord with his many kindnesses.[46]
          For it is not in his heart to torment
          And afflict someone's children.[47]
[33–36]   By crushing under his feet
          All the earth's prisoners;[48]

IN THE FACE OF ADVERSITY

	By skewing a man's case
	In the court of the Most High;
	By corrupting a human's lawsuit –
	(As though) the LORD does not see.[49]
[37–39]	Who after all gave the order – and it was?
	(What) is there that the LORD did not command?
	Do not from the Most High's mouth come
	The bad things and the good?[50]
	So why should a living human complain[51] –
	Why should one[52] – about one's penalties?[53]

The community takes stock

[40–42]	We must examine our ways, probe them,
	And turn back to YHWH!
	We must lift our hearts on our palms
	To the Deity in the heavens!
	We have rebelled and revolted –
	You have not forgiven.[54]
[43–44]	You have screened us out in anger and persecuted;
	You have slain, shown no mercy!
	You have screened yourself in a cloud
	So no prayer could pass through![55]
[45–46]	Foul[56] and abhorred you have made us
	To all other peoples.
	They open their mouths wide against us –
	All our enemies do.[57]
[47]	Terror and entrapment[58] are what we have,
	Wreckage and breakdown.[59]

The personified Daughter of Zion laments

[48–51]	Streams of water my eye runs down[60]
	O'er the breakdown of the Daughter of My People.[61]
	My eye flows, will not stand still,
	For lack of respite,
	Till he looks down and sees –
	YHWH from the heavens does.[62]
	My eye has made me suffer
	More than all my city's daughters.[63]
[52–53]	They have hunted me down like a bird –
	My enemies, without cause.[64]
	They have confined me in the pit,
	And thrown stones at me.
[54–57]	Water rushes over my head;
	I think, 'I'm cut off!'[65]
	I call your name, O YHWH,

                From the pit down below.
                Pray hear my voice!
                Let your ear not ignore
                My cry for relief, my appeal!
                Pray draw close when I call you,
                Pray tell me, 'Do not fear!'

[58–59] You (once) took, O LORD, the side of my defence;[66]
                You (once) gave me redemption.
                You (once) saw, O YHWH, the corruption of my case.
                Pray judge me a fair judgement!

[60–63] You have seen all their vengeance,
                All their plotting against me.
                You have heard their scorn, O YHWH,
                All their plotting against me –
                The mouthings[67] of my attackers and their mutterings[68]
                Go against me every damn day.
                Pray look at them when they sit and when they rise –
                I am the butt of their jingles.[69]

[64–66] Turn on them, O YHWH, the retribution
                That befits what their hands have done![70]
                Bestow upon them an aching heart,[71]
                The execration they are due!
                Chase them in anger and wipe them out
                From under YHWH's heavens![72]

Conclusion

Separating out the diverse voices in Lamentations 3 transforms what has mostly been taken as a reflection and invocation by a single individual into a drama of argument, recalling those of Job and his companions, followed by an audience reaction, in which the perspective of Job appears to prevail, and a reprise of a stricken Jerusalem, lamenting her fate in a manner that echoes the Job-like figure who initiated the poem's discourse. I understand it to be among the tasks of the translator to convey that drama.

Notes

1. For analysis of Lamentations according to genres, see Westermann, *Lamentations*, and Gerstenberger, *Lamentations*. I am pleased to offer this translation in tribute to Larry Rosenwald, a great translator and scholar of literature, who some decades ago gave me the encouragement I needed to engage in translation.
2. For a summary of the historical context, see Berlin, 'Exile and diaspora in the Bible'.
3. On the anger expressed toward the deity in Lamentations, see Greenstein, 'The Wrath at God in the book of Lamentations'.

4. The poetic function of the acrostic is much discussed. I concur with those who find in it a curb on emotional flailing, a dynamic tension between order and chaos, or, as Assis suggests, between passion and reflection; see, for example, Assis, 'The alphabetic acrostic in the book of Lamentations'. The fifth poem, Lamentations 5, does not exhibit an acrostic but contains twenty-two verses, one for each letter of the Hebrew alphabet.
5. On the structure of biblical poetry, see, for example, Greenstein, 'Hebrew poetry: Biblical poetry'.
6. See especially Dobbs-Allsopp, 'The enjambing line in Lamentations', 'The effects of enjambment in Lamentations'.
7. See, for example, Greenstein, 'Wordplay (Hebrew)'; Rendsburg, *How the Bible is Written*, 335–91. On the poetics of Lamentations, see further Thomas, *Poetry and Theology in the Book of Lamentations*, 83–95.
8. Only one translation I know makes a consistent attempt to begin each verse with a succeeding letter of the English alphabet: Slavitt, *The Book of Lamentations*. The results are sometimes ludicrous.
9. See the survey of opinions in House, *Lamentations*, 404–5. See also Grossberg, *Centripetal and Centrifugal Structures*, 92–3; Lee, *The Singers of Lamentations*, 164, 168, 180–1. House himself (405) maintains that there is only one speaker throughout, finding 'a similarity of message in all sections of the text'. Hillers (*Lamentations*, 64), among others, regards the speaker as an individual 'everyman'. Berlin (*Lamentations*, 84–5), among others, identifies the speaker as 'the personified voice of the exile'. However, the individual speaking in Lamentations 3:14 makes reference to 'my people', which would make little sense if the individual were a personification of a community; see Hillers, *Lamentations*, 62. Mintz (*Ḥurban*, 39–40) sees a fluid relationship between an individual and a community; compare Salters, *Lamentations*, 185–7; Thomas, *Poetry and Theology in the Book of Lamentations*, 172–3, 196. As the reader will soon see, I concur with those who discern four distinct voices, one after the other, in this poem.
10. In what immediately follows, I draw on an academic study and a semi-academic study of mine: Greenstein, 'A woman's voice in Lamentations' (in Hebrew), and Greenstein, 'Voices in Lamentations' (in English). One will find several additional bibliographic references there.
11. Cf., for example, Gordis, *The Song of Songs and Lamentations*, 174; Berlin, *Lamentations*, 85. Classical rabbinic exegesis has already made the comparison; see, for example, *Lamentations Rabbah*, ed. S. Buber (Vilna, 1898), 123–4 (Hebrew); *Pesiqta de-Rav Kahana*, ed. B. Mandelbaum (New York, 1962), 272–3 (Hebrew).
12. Cf., for example, Gordis, *The Song of Songs and Lamentations*, 175; Berlin, *Lamentations*, 85. In spite of the clash of perspectives, few commentators maintain that the second speaker is different from the first. Cf., for example, this formulation of Landy, 'Lamentations', 332: 'The poet talks like Job one minute, and like one of Job's friends the next. He seems unaware of the contradiction'.
13. For a new edition, translation and commentary, see Oshima, *Babylonian Poems of Pious Sufferers*.
14. For a relatively recent characterization of this 'strong man', see Hens-Piazza, *Lamentations*, 39–44 and passim.
15. See Klein, *Lamentations*, 213–14; cf. Renkema, *Lamentations*, 351–2.
16. The verb 'who has seen' (*ra'ah*) in the first line is masculine, but it is governed by the term 'man', which, I am claiming, describes a type, not a gender.
17. See, for example, Greenstein, *Job*, xxvii–xxviii.
18. Cf., for example, Gerstenberger, *Psalms, Part 2, and Lamentations*, 493, who adduces several parallels to psalms of individual complaint.
19. This and all translations from Job are from Greenstein, *Job*.
20. On Job's lawsuit against the deity, see, for example, Greenstein, 'A forensic understanding of the speech from the whirlwind'; Magdalene, *On the Scales of Righteousness*.
21. Cf., for example, Provan, *Lamentations*, 81.
22. Literally, 'the man', as it is almost always translated; an exception is the New Revised Standard Version. For the sense of 'pious sufferer', see the discussion above.
23. Cf., for example, Isaiah 10:5. The image represents the foreign power that carried out the deity's punishment of Judah: the Babylonian army. 'His' refers to the deity, who, it has been plausibly suggested, was mentioned explicitly in the final verses of the preceding poem, Lamentations 2:20–22; for example, Provan, *Lamentations*, 80–1.

24. 'Darkness' is imprisonment; 'to see the light' is to go free (see Isaiah 9:1: 'The people walking in darkness have seen a great light; / Dwellers in a deathly-dark land – a light shines on them'). Cf. Job 30:26. This symbolic motif recurs in verse 6, where being settled in darkness is commensurate with being imprisoned. For discussion and biblical parallels, see for example Hillers, *Lamentations*, 67.
25. The addition of 'damn', which is not represented lexically in the source, is meant to reflect the tone of the discourse and to call attention to the recurrence of the phrase 'every damn day' in the poem.
26. Cf. Job 7:5; 16:7–8; 19:26–27; 30:16–18.
27. Cf. Job 10:20–22; 19:6, 12.
28. Cf. Job 30:20–21.
29. Cf. Job 19:8. 'Hewn stone' suggests a deliberate plan of obstruction; cf., for example, Salters, *Lamentations*, 203.
30. Cf. Job 10:16.
31. Cf. Job 16:12. For a discussion of the unique verb rendered here 'mangled', see, for example, Salters, *Lamentations*, 206–8.
32. 'Stepped down' (*darak*) is cognate to 'walkway' (*derek*) in verses 9–11. Holding the bow down with one's foot is a well-documented ancient practice.
33. Cf. Job 6:4 and even more precisely 7:20.
34. Cf. Job 16:13.
35. Cf. Job 17:6; 30:1, 9.
36. Cf. Job 9:18; also 20:25.
37. Cf. Job 17:15.
38. An echo of the description of abject Zion in Lamentations 1:7.
39. Reading with the written form (*Ketib*) instead of the read form (*Qeri*) of the traditional Hebrew text.
40. Cf. the usage of *heshib ruaḥ*, 'return breath' in the sense of declaring, in Job 13:13; 15:13; et al.
41. The same term as 'spirit' and 'self' (*nepesh*).
42. Literally, 'a man'; but see verse 1 and my discussion surrounding it above.
43. Reading 'his yoke' (*'ullo*) for 'upon him' (*'alaw*). Carrying the yoke is an ancient Near Eastern metaphor for being subject to another's control; for example, 1 Kings 12:11, 14; Jeremiah 27:11–12. If one reads *'ullo* 'his yoke' for *'alu* 'they ascended' in Lamentations 1:14 (so several moderns), there is an echo of that verse here. Note that the term *'ol* 'yoke' occurs earlier in that same verse.
44. That he silence himself.
45. A widespread gesture of insult in the ancient Near East. Cf. Job's complaint in 16:10.
46. Cf. Eliphaz to Job in Job 5:17–18: 'Happy is the mortal whom Eloah reproves – / Do not reject Shaddai's discipline. / For once he inflicts pain, he binds up; / Once he strikes, his own hands heal'.
47. Literally, 'the sons of a man'. The suffering of children is particularly poignant in Lamentations; see, for example, 2:11–12, 19–20; 4:4–5.
48. Job describes the tranquil existence of 'prisoners' in the netherworld (3:18).
49. Job complains that the deity would corrupt any trial at which he could make his complaint; see, for example, Job 9:15–35. Eliphaz insists that the deity does see what goes on and enacts justice; see Job 22:12–20.
50. Cf. Isaiah 45:7 and Amos 3:6.
51. The verb for 'complain' evokes the so-called murmurings of the Israelites in the wilderness (Numbers 11:1); cf., for example, Thomas, *Poetry and Theology in the Book of Lamentations*, 207–8.
52. Literally 'a man', reverting to verse 1 above.
53. More literally, '(the consequences of) one's sins'.
54. Cf. Job 7:20–21.
55. Cf. Job 21:22 as explicated in 22:13–14; 23:12. For Job, the deity cannot see from behind the clouds (see also 3:23). For his pious interlocutor Eliphaz, his perch high in heaven affords the deity an ideal vantage point.
56. For a discussion of this unique word, see, for example, Salters, *Lamentations*, 255.
57. Cf. Job in 16:10.
58. The punning dyad is also found in Jeremiah 48:43.
59. A punning dyad.

60. Cf. Jerusalem in Lamentations 1:16: 'Over all these (depredations) I weep! / My eye, my eye runs down with water!'
61. The city, Zion or Jerusalem.
62. The appeal to the deity to 'see' and 'look' recurs in Jerusalem's complaint in Lamentations 1 (verses 9, 11, 20).
63. From a linguistic point of view, this is the most likely sense. It is ordinarily rendered something like: 'My eye afflicts me on account of (what has happened to) all the daughters of my city'. Translators have been misled by their presumption that a male, not a female, is speaking.
64. Cf. Job in 10:16: 'If (my head) were to loom, you would hunt me down like a lion'.
65. Cf. the petition of Jonah in 2:4–7. The complaint is a stock motif, hardly appropriate if taken literally.
66. For this widespread phrase, asking the deity to take up one's cause, see, for example, Micah 7:9; Psalm 43:1; 74:22; 119:154.
67. Literally, 'lips' – which might also, as in Akkadian, suggest hostile spells.
68. The term for 'pronouncements' belongs to a stem that always refers to utterance, to making a sound; see recently Greenstein, 'The heart as an organ of speech in Biblical Hebrew'. It is usually misunderstood in the sense of 'thought' or 'meditation'. I owe the gloss 'mutterings' to Jessica Sacks in Sacks (ed.), *Koren Tanakh Maalot*.
69. Cf. the first, Joban, speaker in this poem (verse 14 above) and the parallel in Job 17:6.
70. Cf. Lamentations 1:21–22.
71. 'Aching' in the unique Hebrew phrase (*meginnat*) echoes both 'their mutterings' (*hegyonam*, verse 62) and 'their jingles' (*manginatam*, verse 63). For a rich survey of possible derivations, see, for example, Salters, *Lamentations*, 277–8. There may be a slight corruption in the writing, for the meaning seems to call for a form of the stem *ygy* 'suffer distress'; see the compelling considerations of Renkema, *Lamentations*, 467–8.
72. There is a sound play between 'wipe out' and 'heavens'.

Bibliography

Assis, Elie. 'The alphabetic acrostic in the Book of Lamentations'. *Catholic Biblical Quarterly*, vol. 69, 2007, pp. 710–24.
Berlin, Adele. *Lamentations: a commentary*. John Knox Press, 2002.
Berlin, Adele. 'Exile and diaspora in the Bible'. *The Oxford Handbook of the Jewish Diaspora*, edited by Hasia R. Diner. Oxford University Press, 2018, pp. 23–40.
Buber, S. (ed.) *Lamentations Rabbah*. Vilna, 1898.
Dobbs-Allsopp, F.W. 'The enjambing line in Lamentations: a taxonomy (part 1)'. *Zeitschrift für die alttestamentliche Wissenschaft*, vol. 113, 2001, pp. 219–39.
Dobbs-Allsopp, F.W. 'The effects of enjambment in Lamentations (part 2)'. *Zeitschrift für die alttestamentliche Wissenschaft*, vol. 113, 2001, pp. 370–85.
Gerstenberger, Erhard S. *Psalms, Part 2, and Lamentations*. Eerdmans, 2001.
Gordis, Robert. *The Song of Songs and Lamentations: a study, modern translation and commentary*, revised edition. Ktav, 1974.
Greenstein, Edward L. 'Wordplay (Hebrew)'. *Anchor Bible Dictionary*, 6 vols., edited by David Noel Freedman. Doubleday, 1992, vol. 6, pp. 68–71.
Greenstein, Edward L. 'A forensic understanding of the speech from the whirlwind'. *Texts, Temples and Traditions: a tribute to Menahem Haran*, edited by Michael V. Fox et al. Eisenbrauns, 1996, pp. 241–58.
Greenstein, Edward L. 'The Wrath at God in the Book of Lamentations'. *The Problem of Evil and its Symbols in Jewish and Christian Tradition*, edited by Henning G. Reventlow and Yair Hoffman. T & T Clark International/Continuum, 2004, pp. 29–42.
Greenstein, Edward L. 'Hebrew poetry: Biblical poetry'. *Princeton Encyclopedia of Poetry and Poetics*, 4th rev. ed., edited by Roland Greene. Princeton University Press, 2012, pp. 601–9.
Greenstein, Edward L. 'Voices in Lamentations: dialogues in trauma'. *TheTorah.com* (July 2015). https://www.thetorah.com/article/voices-in-lamentations-dialogues-in-trauma. Accessed 26 December 2021.

Greenstein, Edward L. 'A woman's voice in Lamentations 3'. *Shenaton: An Annual for Biblical and Ancient Near Eastern Studies*, vol. 24, 2016, pp. 167–76.

Greenstein, Edward L. *Job: a new translation*. Yale University Press, 2019.

Greenstein, Edward L. 'The heart as an organ of speech in Biblical Hebrew'. *Semitic, Biblical and Jewish Studies in Honor of Richard C. Steiner*, edited by Mordechai Z. Cohen, Aaron Koller, Adina Moshavi. Yeshiva University Press / Mossad Bialik, 2020, pp. 206–18 (English section).

Grossberg, Daniel. *Centripetal and Centrifugal Structures in Biblical Poetry*. Scholars Press, 1989.

Hens-Piazza, Gina. *Lamentations*. Collegeville, MN, 2017.

Hillers, Delbert R. *Lamentations: a new translation with introduction and commentary*. Doubleday, 1972.

House, Paul R. *Lamentations*. Thomas Nelson, 2004.

Klein, Jacob. *Lamentations: introduction and commentary*. Am Oved / Hebrew University Magnes Press, 2017 (Hebrew).

Landy, Francis. 'Lamentations'. *The Literary Guide to the Bible*, edited by Robert Alter and Frank Kermode. Harvard University Press, 1987, pp. 329–34.

Lee, Nancy C. *The Singers of Lamentations: cities under siege, from Ur to Jerusalem to Sarajevo ...* . Brill, 2002.

Magdalene, F. Rachel. *On the Scales of Righteousness: Neo-Babylonian trial law and the book of Job*. Brown Judaic Studies, 2007.

Mandelbaum, B. (ed.) *Pesiqta de-Rav Kahana*, New York, 1962.

Mintz, Alan. *Ḥurban: responses to catastrophe in Hebrew literature*. Columbia University Press, 1984.

Oshima, Takayoshi. *Babylonian Poems of Pious Sufferers*. Mohr Siebeck, 2014.

Provan, Iain W. *Lamentations*. Marshall Pickering / Eerdmans, 1991.

Rendsburg, Gary A. *How the Bible is Written*. Hendrickson, 2019.

Renkema, Johan. *Lamentations*, translated by Brian Doyle. Peeters, 1998.

Sacks, Jonathan, editor. *The Koren Tanakh Maalot, Magerman Edition (Hebrew and English edition)*. Koren Publishers, 2021.

Salters, R.B. *A Critical and Exegetical Commentary on Lamentations*. T & T Clark International, 2010.

Slavitt, David R. *The Book of Lamentations: a meditation and translation*. Johns Hopkins University Press, 2001.

Thomas, Heath A. *Poetry and Theology in the Book of Lamentations: the aesthetics of the open text*. Sheffield Phoenix Press, 2013.

Westermann, Claus. *Lamentations: issues and interpretation*, translated by Charles Muenchow. Fortress Press, 1994.

2
Isaiah 1 in Translation and Contexts
Everett Fox

Over a quarter of a century ago, Larry Rosenwald helped me realize a long-desired goal of rendering Martin Buber's and Franz Rosenzweig's collected essays on Bible translation, *Die Schrift und ihre Verdeutschung*, into English (published as *Scripture and Translation*). To this project he contributed not only the great bulk of the translation work but also an introductory essay on 'Buber and Rosenzweig's challenge to Bible translation' and he has subsequently written and spoken widely on the topic. So it feels to me doubly appropriate on this occasion to present below a fresh translation of the opening chapter of the book of Isaiah, whose concerns for language and social justice are echoed by Buber's concerns, and indeed by Rosenwald's own.

The texts of the prophetic books of the Bible offer a unique and challenging display of exalted but also difficult poetry. They reflect what must have been overwhelming life experiences amid the clash of ancient empires, with the relatively small kingdoms of Israel and Judah caught in the middle. This was the backdrop for the prophets' total involvement in their contemporary world, even to the point of risking their lives to deliver uncompromising messages of social and political criticism. They must be understood in this light rather than being characterized as soothsayers, as is often done.

At the same time, we cannot precisely reconstruct the circumstances under which these texts came into being. Do they represent the prophets' own authentic words? Are they later reconstructed by their disciples? Have portions been added by a later hand? Were prophetic texts originally performed, and how? Scholars make a living attempting to answer these questions, but here I shall focus not on the reconstruction of an *Urtext* but rather on the rhetorical features and impact of what has come down to us. This demands the joining of translation and performance – not an imagined ancient performance, but rather one that takes its cues from the language of the text as we have it. Analogously, what we are dealing with is not like a period performance of a Beethoven symphony, with smaller forces, valveless French horns and the like, but one in which carefully thought-out tempo and dynamics, not to mention the inspiration of the moment, convey something indelible of the structure and power of the work.

In that context, the principles laid out in the Buber-Rosenzweig Bible translation (1925–62) may illuminate the text of Isaiah 1. Without seeking to translate a translation, I have tried to follow three of these principles in my rendering of the Hebrew text. First, there is the question of line division. The layout is meant to echo the breathing cadences of the Hebrew, drawing the audience into an immediate sensory reaction to what is being said. Second, one must pay attention to significant repetitions or key images in the text. That means preserving the Hebrew's links between verses when appropriate (for example, God's castigating of the Israelites' 'many sacrifices' and 'many prayers' in verses 11 and 15, and other doublings such as Sodom and Amora and mention of the orphan and the widow). Finally, one must attempt to intuit what might be called the 'stage tone' of the chapter, that is, the amount of textual energy needed to convey the import of the prophet's words. As is well known, the pre-medieval texts of the Hebrew Bible contain no punctuation, which forces the translator to either minimally supply it in the conventional form of periods, commas and semicolons, or else take the plunge into giving the reader some idea of performance possibilities. In this case, what is required is the strategic insertion of exclamation points, imperative in speeches such as the ones we encounter in Isaiah 1. A fine example of this approach has recently been demonstrated in Ed Greenstein's *Job: a new translation*, where the English rendition of Job's impassioned opening harangue in the third chapter is daringly but, in my view, appropriately accompanied by thirteen uses of the exclamation point in just seven verses. Neither the revered King James Version nor more recent translations such as those of Stephen Mitchell and Robert Alter use any at all. Martin Buber pointed the way by including seven in his German rendition. In my translation of the excerpt from Isaiah 1, I have not shied away from doing something similar to reflect how I hear the text and how I feel it must be presented.

As regards content, Isaiah 1 consciously serves as the beginning of the entire prophetic corpus, which covers some fifteen books of the Hebrew Bible. After a brief introduction (v. 1) which enumerates the eighth-century BCE Judean kings during whose reign Isaiah delivered his messages, it proceeds to powerfully lay out a series of themes that will recur in his book and those of other prophets as well. These include rebellion against Israel's traditional covenant values, the graphic illness of the body politic, the inevitable invasion and destruction of Jerusalem by foreigners, the emptiness of conventional piety when it is not combined with social justice, the corruption of leadership and the never-lost possibilities of redemption. In a sense, this text is a potpourri of prophetic tropes.

In the interests of getting immediately to Isaiah's address itself, I have omitted verse 1, with its king list, below. I have also omitted the chapter's last four verses, which may be from a later hand, in order to end on a more positive note than the description of 'crushing of rebels and sinners together' (v. 28) permits. With these few textual caveats, here is Isaiah's memorable opening speech, cast in an English translation that is meant to be read aloud.

2   Hearken, O heavens, give ear, O earth,
    for YHWH has spoken:
    Children have I reared and raised,
    and they have been disloyal to me!
3   An ox knows its owner,
    a donkey its master's crib—
    Israel does not know,
    My people does not comprehend!
4   *Hoy,*
    sinful nation,
    a people heavy with iniquity,
    wicked seed,
    ruin-bringing children!
    They have forsaken YHWH,
    they have spurned the Holy One of Israel,
    become estranged, [gone] backward!
5   For what will you be struck down again,
    [that] you continue to turn away?
    Every head has become sick,
    every heart is faint;
6   from the sole of the foot up to the head,
    there is no soundness in it –
    bruise and sore and open wound,
    not drained, not bandaged,
    not pressed out with oil!
7   Your land is desolation,
    your towns burned with fire;

>   your soil—before your [eyes], strangers eat from it.
>   Yes, desolation,
>   as [one] overthrown by strangers!
> 8 Daughter Zion is left
>   like a hut in a vineyard,
>   like a shack in a cucumber-patch,
>   like a town under siege.
> 9 Had not YHWH of the Forces-on-High
>   left us a small remnant,
>   like Sedom we'd have become,
>   like 'Amora we would have been!
> 10 Hearken to the word of YHWH,
>   O chieftains of Sedom,
>   give ear to our God's Instruction,
>   O people of 'Amora:
> 11 What need have I of your many sacrifices?
>   – the Utterance of YHWH.
>   I am sated with the offerings-up of rams
>   and the suet of well-nourished beasts;
>   in the blood of bulls and lambs and goats
>   I take no pleasure!
> 12 When you come to appear in my presence,
>   who requests this at your hand,
>   [this] trampling of my courtyards?
> 13 Bring no more false offerings;
>   incense is an abomination to me!
>   New Moon, Sabbath,
>   proclaiming of holy proclamation –
>   I cannot [stand them]:
>   idolatry along with [Day of] Restraint!
> 14 Your New Moons and your fixed-times, my very being hates,
>   they have become a burden to me –
>   I am weary of bearing them!
> 15 And when you spread out your palms,
>   I will hide my eyes from you;
>   when you offer many prayers,
>   I will not hearken—
>   your hands are filled with blood!
> 16 Wash, cleanse yourselves,
>   remove the evil of your doings from before my eyes!
>   Cease evil!
> 17 Learn [to do] good,
>   seek justice,

strengthen the oppressed;
defend the orphan's rights,
plead the widow's cause!

18 Come now, let us reach an understanding
– YHWH has declared:
If your sins be like scarlet,
like snow shall they be made white;
if they be reddened like crimson,
like [pure] wool shall they be!

19 If you are willing and hearken,
the good-things of the land shall you eat;

20 but if you refuse and rebel,
by the sword shall you be eaten!
Indeed, the mouth of YHWH has spoken.

21 O how she has become a whore,
the trustworthy city!
Filled with justice,
righteousness [once] dwelled in her –
but now, murderers!

22 Your silver has turned into dross,
your liquor is mixed with water.

23 Your rulers are rogues,
companions of thieves;
each one loves a bribe,
pursues [illicit] gifts.
The orphan they do not defend,
the cause of the widow does not reach them!

24 Therefore,
the Utterance of the Lord of the Forces-on-High,
the Mighty One of Israel:
Hoy,
I will get satisfaction on my enemies,
I will take vengeance on my foes!

25 Then I will turn my hand toward you
and smelt out your dross as with lye,
and I will remove all your slag!

26 And I will restore your judges as at the first,
your counsellors as at the beginning.
After that you will [once more] be called:
'Town of righteousness,
trustworthy city'.

27 Zion will be redeemed through justice,
and those who return to her, through righteousness.

Notes

2. *Hearken ... heavens:* Heb. *shim'u shamayim*. The alliteration demands the audience's attention from the start.
3. *YHWH:* the unpronounceable name of God in the Bible, euphemistically translated as 'Lord' since antiquity. *Israel does not know:* many translations insert 'but' at the beginning of the sentence. I see its omission as purposeful, encouraging the performer to use body language to provide the necessary contrast.
4. *Hoy:* an exclamation, traditionally translated as 'Ah'.
5. *estranged:* Hebrew uncertain, but the sound of *nazoru* is picked up in v. 7 by *zarim*, 'strangers'.
6. *pressed out with oil:* olive oil, applied as a balm for wounds.
7. *overthrown:* describing the destruction of a city, as in the famous case of Sodom and Gomorrah in Gen. 19 (see v. 10).
8. *Daughter Zion:* others, 'Fair Zion' or 'the Daughter of Zion', a common personification of Jerusalem in biblical poetry.
9. *YHWH of the Forces-on-High:* God as the leader of the 'heavenly host', the angels or other divine beings.
10. *Sedom ...'Amora:* trad. 'Sodom ... Gomorrah'.
11. *the Utterance of YHWH:* a divine oracle.
12. *in my presence:* at the Temple in Jerusalem.
13. *New Moon:* a holy day at the head of each month. *[Day of] Restraint:* Heb. unclear, although it occurs as designation for the last day of certain festivals.
14. *fixed-times:* holy days. *Burden ... bearing:* echoing the Hebrew *nil'eiti neso* at the end of the sentence.
15. *spread out your palms:* the typical physical motion of praying in the Bible.
16. *Wash:* unlike Lady Macbeth's, the blood-filled hands here can be washed clean. The verb introduces a set of nine imperatives which are directives for a teetering society to reverse course. Theoretically, one could punctuate each with an exclamation point.
17. *strengthen:* following Akkadian; others, 'defend, aid', 'relieve' or 'make happy'
18. *like [pure] wool:* presumably white.
21. *O how she has become a whore, the trustworthy city:* the *ah*-sounding endings of the first five Hebrew words here mimic sounds of mourning, similar to the opening lines of the later book of Lamentations.
23. *Rulers ... rogues:* Heb. *sarayikh sorerim* (following Blenkinsopp 2000). *orphan ... widow:* the classic examples of those who are deemed defenceless in the ancient Near East.
26. *And I will restore your judges as at the first, / your counsellors as at the beginning:* these two lines, with their heartfelt hopes for the future, were adopted by the ancient rabbis, in plea form, into the Amidah, the core prayer recited by religious Jews thrice daily.

Contexts old and new

As I have hinted at above, the task of the Bible translator is in one sense artistic and based, once the niceties of philology are duly observed, on the exigencies of performance. But as is the case with all performances, audiences and their needs change over time. This is particularly true for Isaiah 1, and indeed for most of the prophetic texts in the Hebrew Bible. Over the millennia it has been read, or rather read into, by a variety of interpreters, themselves typically affected by the ideological and religious worlds they inhabit as well as by the text itself. The Talmudic

Rabbis, for example, established the chapter as a yearly reading on the Sabbath before the Ninth of Av, the traditional date of the destruction of both the First and Second Temples. The Church Fathers frequently applied Isaiah's condemnation of his contemporaries to the Jews of Jesus' and their own time, an unfortunate interpretation which endured into the Middle Ages and beyond. A comprehensive accounting of reception history can be found in Sawyer (2018).

In truth, Isaiah's rants seem eerily familiar. It does not take much to find, in his words, strong connections to our present predicaments with the text's emphasis on the sickness of the body politic, the oppression of the powerless, the transgressions of religious leaders amid professions of piety and the corruption of public institutions. Historically speaking, these issues are not confined to one time or one place, but what sets Isaiah 1 apart is the eloquence and vehemence with which the prophet speaks. I have always wondered what would happen if Isaiah or one of his fellow prophets were to be invited to speak at a contemporary church or synagogue service. If he were to choose the very words of chapter 1, as passionately delivered as they warrant, I predict that he would be forcibly removed from the premises, or worse. The juxtaposition of Israel with dumb animals in verse 3, the description of a seriously ill or wounded body in verses 5–6, the likening of Israel to the wicked cities of Abraham's time (9–10) and the characterization of Jerusalem as a whore in verse 21 – all of these images remain as shocking to today's audiences as they must have been to ancient ones.

We should not, however, ignore the positive side of Isaiah's words. The biting criticisms brought by the prophet are interwoven in this chapter with pleas to turn toward justice (v. 17), the recognition that blood can be washed away from violent hands (vv. 16–18) and the prayer that princes who are bribe-loving rogues (v. 23) might be replaced by those resembling the righteous judges of old (v. 26).

Ironically, the very inclusion of a book such as Isaiah in the sacred canon of the Bible has, to a certain extent, blunted his words or even tamed them. Divorced from their original context, they may have lost some of their steam with time, relegating their author to the state of a revered rather than an irksome figure. But as Buber would maintain, careful translation and the restoring of the text to its spoken character may awaken in its hearers a renewed sense of appreciation, or even a willingness to become more attentive to the urgency of the prophet's words. In that urgency, thanks to the artistry of the poet, the ancient words still have life, aimed as they are at a world on the brink.

Bibliography

Alter, Robert. *The Wisdom Books: Job, proverbs and ecclesiastes: a translation*. W.W. Norton & Company, 2010.

Blenkinsopp, Joseph. *Isaiah 1–39: a new translation with introduction and commentary*. The Anchor Yale Bible vol. 19. Doubleday, 2000.

Buber, Martin and Franz Rosenzweig. *Die Schrift und ihre Verdeutschung*. Schocken Verlag, 1936.

Greenstein, Edward L. *Job: a new translation*. Yale University Press, 2020.

Mitchell, Stephen. *The Book of Job*. North Point Press, 1987.

Rosenwald, Lawrence and Everett Fox. *Scripture and Translation*. Indiana University Press, 1994.

Sawyer, John F.A. *Isaiah Through the Centuries*. Wiley Blackwell Bible Commentaries. John Wiley & Sons, 2018.

3
Emma Lazarus, Heinrich Heine and the Splendid Galaxy of Jewish Poetry

Abigail Gillman

> Let but an Ezra rise anew,
> To lift the BANNER OF THE JEW!
>
> Emma Lazarus[1]

I.

When seen from the outside, the lives of Heinrich Heine (1797–1856) and Emma Lazarus (1849–87) look about as different as the two female figures with which their most famous poems are associated: the Loreley and the Statue of Liberty.[2] The mythic Loreley, who sits above a mass of rock overlooking the Rhine river, is a siren whose seductive song, captured by Heine's ballad, caused many shipwrecks. Across the ocean, Lady Liberty, given voice by Emma Lazarus' 'The New Colossus', stands majestic in New York Harbour, her torch lighting the way for countless immigrants to the new world. The popular fame of both Lazarus and Heine is in each case linked to a single now monumental poem which overshadows their lives and legacies.

Many important affinities connect the German Harry Heine, as he was originally called, to the American Emma Lazarus. They were both proud poets of Jewish exile, in its many ancient and modern forms, who responded boldly, as artists and thinkers, to the Jewish and universal questions of the nineteenth century. Their childhoods were shaped by wars – the French Revolution and the American Civil War – as well as by persecution and anti-Semitism. Writing in German and English respectively, their voices were heard internationally in their lifetimes, even as their words spoke (and have never stopped speaking) to Jews. They used the pen as a sword. They understood the essential role of history, of a usable Jewish past, in forging Jewish culture in a new world. They had clear visions of how to write new songs by the rivers of Babylon.

Emma Lazarus' legacy as an American Jewish poet continues to grow. Already in 1906, she was called 'the most eminent Jewish poet since Heine and Judah Löb Gordon'.[3] And in the early twenty-first century, she was credited with an even more impressive achievement: 'Emma Lazarus (1849–1887)', wrote Lichtenstein and Schor, 'an internationally known poet and essayist, created the role of the American Jewish writer'. They continue:

> In her own day Lazarus was, by any standard, a famous writer; indeed, her eminent father's obituary identified him as the father of the poet Emma Lazarus. Whether she was writing blistering essays about anti-Semitism, soaring transcendentalist sonnets, or erudite poems about mythology, art and literature, Lazarus was read by more American readers than any other Jewish writer of her century. At the same time, she was more deeply invested in her own identity as an American writer, and in the future of American letters, than any of her Jewish contemporaries. Lazarus succeeded, decades before the twentieth century, in the double task of becoming an eminent woman writer, and in creating, for an international audience, the persona of an American Jewish writer.[4]

These authors credit Lazarus with three remarkable achievements. She established herself as a popular American writer. She carved out her place as a female author of international acclaim. And she established as well the identity of the Jewish-American writer. How did she do it? John Hollander provides a lead, noting that 'she felt [Heine] to be her major precursor both as a Jew and a romantic ironist'.[5] I would add that it was largely through her efforts as a translator of Heine that Lazarus translated herself into an American Jewish writer. Most who research Lazarus' writings focus on her contributions to women's literature, American literature and Jewish literature.[6] A notable exception is the article by another New York poet-translator, Aaron Kramer, of 1956.[7] Hollander notes, 'In her lifelong devotion to verse in other languages and the importance of translation for her own poetry, Lazarus belongs to the line of American poets running from Longfellow to Pound, Robert Lowell and W.S. Merwin'.[8] Lazarus also belongs to the genealogy of important Jewish poet-translators, and she broke new ground in this regard.

Considering her lifelong involvement with Heine also addresses a discrepancy in accounts of Lazarus' Jewish identity. In their co-authored article about Lazarus for the *Jewish Encyclopaedia* of 1906, Cyrus Adler and Henrietta Szold emphasized, as many others would thereafter, that the immigration of Russian Jews to America provided her a 'Jewish theme':

> Hitherto her life had held no Jewish inspiration. Though of Sephardic stock, and ostensibly Orthodox in belief, her family had hitherto not participated in the activities of the Synagogue or of the Jewish community. Contact with the unfortunates from Russia led her to study the Bible, the Hebrew language, Judaism and Jewish history.[9]

While this account makes sense, it short-changes the intellectual whose engagement with Jewish authors and questions predates her activities of the 1880s. Heine gave Lazarus a Jewish theme, but also a patrimony, a muse.

Lazarus and Heine had many common sources of inspiration, first and foremost, their ancestry: both descended of Ashkenazi fathers and Sephardic mothers. Sephardic parentage was a mark of nobility and *yichus* (privilege) in the nineteenth century, especially if one valued secular culture and poetry. They both drew inspiration from the Hebrew Bible; from Jewish history (especially exile and persecution); and from the Diwan, the Hebrew poetry of medieval Spain. This was the 'three-fold cord' (Ecclesiastes 4:12) securing their Jewishness; it was the cultural capital of the modern Jewish poet. They were further nourished by the tensions of Hellenism vs. Hebraism, and Christianity vs. Judaism; by mythology, French culture and classical art; by music (Lazarus wrote poems inspired by classical music); by what Asher D. Biemann calls 'statue love'.[10] As prolific prose writers and journalists with socialist principles, they fought the social struggles of their day, expressing convictions with vehemence and prophetic ardour. As poets, their strongest affinity was to romantic irony, experimentation with poetic form and modernism *avant la lettre*. They were deeply engaged in the poetic circles and movements of their day; Lazarus, who lived in New York (with travels to Boston and Europe), corresponded with Emerson, Longfellow and Henry James. Both were cosmopolitan Jewish writers, in some ways too Jewish and in other ways, not Jewish enough. Inevitably, they met complicated receptions as Jewish writers, in their own time and after their deaths, and it was a challenge to 'place' them and their oeuvres with respect to the usual movements and options – nationalism, Judaism, Zionism, socialism, romanticism and modernism. It is hard to do because both were pioneers as well as prophets; children of the nineteenth century, who 'overcame their time in themselves' (Nietzsche). Both died young of illness: Heine at fifty-nine, Lazarus at thirty-eight.

In Mark Gelber's 1992 volume *The Jewish Reception of Heinrich Heine,* one of the first volumes in English on the topic, Lazarus is mentioned only by Jeffrey L. Sammons.[11] But what Sammons writes is crucial: he calls Emma Lazarus 'the pioneer of Jewish Heine reception in America'.[12] By this Sammons means that Lazarus was one of the first Jews to write about Heine in America; keep in mind that Heine's collected works in German were first published in twenty-one volumes between 1861 and 1866, during Lazarus' teenage years. But the influence of Heine goes further. She looked to Heine as an example of a modern Jewish poet. For that is what Heine himself was, within German literature, and within modern Jewish literature. Jeffrey Grossman explains: 'Heine appropriates elements from the Jewish sphere to generate within German literature a repertoire of Jewish cultural allusions and *a new Jewish cultural space*, a space occurring beyond the sphere of traditional Jewish culture, but at the interior of the sphere of German culture.'[13] Following Heine, but very much on her own terms, Emma Lazarus undertook two mutually dependent challenges: 'finding a new place for Jews and new roles for writers within [the majority] culture'.[14]

II.

Heine's impact on Lazarus was not only through his poetry and biography. For Lazarus, as for other Anglo-Jewish women poets of her generation,[15] Heine provided a bridge to a golden age of Jewish poetry: to the Hebrew poets of mediaeval Spain, to Judah Halevi, Ibn Gabirol, Ibn Ezra and many others. This body of poetry was anthologized and translated into German in the early nineteenth century by scholars Michael Sachs (1845) and Abraham Geiger (1851). Heine himself encountered Halevi in Michael Sachs' volume *Die religiöse Poesie der Juden in Spanien,* which combined an historical account with an anthology.[16]

Lazarus' own involvement with Hebrew poetry began in 1877, when Rabbi Gustav Gottheil, an eminent German-born Reform Rabbi, who had just been appointed senior Rabbi of Temple Emanu-El, asked her to translate some hymns by the mediaeval poets from German into English for a new prayer book; Gottheil went on to publish a book of

Jewish hymns in 1886 (with the music in a separate volume). Lazarus agreed, despite her lack of religiosity. Five years later, she started studying Hebrew in order to read the poetry in the original, and published a translation of one poem from Hebrew in 1883. She inserted other new translations from Halevi in her second major essay on Heine in 1884. In the same essay, she radically reconceptualizes Heine's oeuvre – not only the *Hebrew Melodies*, but also the early poems of the Lyrical Intermezzo – as 'a seed sprung from the golden branch that flourished in Hebrew Spain between the years 1000 and 1200'.[17]

The historical role of Heine as a bridge to Hebrew poetry took on an entirely new significance when I moved to Tel Aviv in the course of writing this chapter. In Tel Aviv University's Sourasky Library, I found only one English volume of Lazarus' poetry alongside three English biographies and a volume of correspondence; I could not locate any translations of Lazarus' poetry into Hebrew. In stark contrast, hundreds of volumes of Heine's works fill several shelves, among them multiple sets in German alongside secondary sources in all languages, and numerous volumes of Heine in Hebrew translation.

In those volumes of Heine in Hebrew, I discovered another group of pioneers: the Hebrew poets who made room for Heine within the new modern Hebrew literature, Zionist literature and Israeli culture.

To give Heine – not only a tortured poet of exile, but an apostate – a home in a Jewish language was a challenge on many counts. My initial research into this chapter in Heine reception showed me that Heine posed a series of problems. The first problem was about membership. Heine converted, and for many decades there would be no streets named after him. Is Heine one of ours? Translation into Hebrew offered a way to reclaim him. A second problem pertained to imitation. Everyone knew Heine's poems. They had been reared on those poems. Yitzchak Katzenelson wrote that not only did he sing Heine's poems, but once having translated them, and 'redeemed' them, he recognized them to be his own 'children': it is an uncanny allusion to Heine's poem about encountering his own doppelgänger in the window of his beloved's house. The dilemma was how to write love poetry without imitating or plagiarizing Heine. Another problem for any translator is Heine's irony. How does one capture romantic irony in translation? How to translate, without reromanticizing?

Fundamentally, the Hebrew and Israeli poets saw themselves as continuing Heine's own project of carving out a new space for Jewish poetry – which always already entailed returning to Jehuda Halevi. As poets, translators and editors, Hebrew writers appreciated that the Book of Songs uses Halevi and many other points of reference to constellate one location (for example, the North of the lonely pine tree or the North Sea) with a significant other (in this example, the East of the palm tree or of Halevi's pilgrimage) to create complex semiotic spaces.[18]

Na'ama Rokem argues that Hebrew translations of Heine in the twentieth century are 'an efficient barometer of the transformation of Hebrew literature and its relation to questions of prose, media, pragmatics and space'.[19]

Emma Lazarus was not afraid of Heine, nor did she see him as a problem to be overcome. Yet, the reception of Heine in Hebrew, in her lifetime and beyond, must contribute to an understanding of just how Heine 'called on Emma Lazarus to write as a Jew', and why she listened.[20]

III.

Emma Lazarus began translating Heine, along with Goethe, Schiller, French and Italian poetry, as a teenager, during the Civil War. Her first book, *Poems and Translations* (1866) 'written between the ages of fourteen and sixteen' as the title page notes, was published privately by her father and also dedicated to him. An expanded version of the book, published one year later by Hurd and Houghton, has three sections: original pieces; translations from the German of songs from Heinrich Heine; and translations from the French of songs from Alexandre Dumas and songs from Victor Hugo.

Lazarus' early poems are about love, nature, the seasons. The ode 'A Spring Morning' has eight stanzas, starting with

> O wondrous Earth! Thou blossomest with joys,
> With starry flowers, and with downy sod;
> In thy grand forest-temple what can man,
>   Save fall and worship God![21]

Many poems speak of death and war. 'The Prussian's Story' begins with a newspaper item from July 1866 from the Franco-Prussian War. A number take up classical mythology, giving voice to Greek heroines such as Aphrodite, Daphne, Clytie speaking her love to Apollo, and 'Penelope's Choice' about her decision to marry Ulysses and leave her father. Two bear epigrams from the Bible, from Proverbs and Ecclesiastes: 'Remember' has an epigram from Ecclesiastes xii:1: 'Remember now thy Creator from the days of thy youth'. This volume also includes 'Song from Alexander Dumas', one short poem 'From Schiller', and several translations of Heine, beginning with 'Fischer Mädchen' and ending with 'Ich glaub' nicht an den Himmel'.

Lazarus' second book, *Admetus and Other Poems* (1871),[22] dedicated to 'my friend Ralph Waldo Emerson', contained extensive translations from Goethe's *Faust* and from the Italian poet Leopardi, and on the very last page, 'Song from Heine', where she oddly rendered only three of the six stanzas of Heine's provocative poem, 'Mein Herz mein Herz ist traurig' with its unexpected, pointed ending: 'Ich wollt, er schösse mich tot!' ('I wish he would shoot me dead!'). Lazarus' choice to omit the lighthearted stanzas two through four sharpens the poem and reveals her confidence as a poet-translator.

Only fifteen years after her first book, Lazarus' *Poems and Ballads of Heinrich Heine,* with almost 150 translations of Heine's poems, appeared in 1881 with R. Worthington Press in New York. Her selections include twelve early poems; the cycle of 100 poems *Heimkehr,* which she titled *Homeward Bound,* 1823–4, including the famous 'Loreley' poem, the (now) complete version of the song from the prior volume, 'Mein Herz mein Herz ist traurig' and 'I, a most wretched Atlas'. She includes selections from 'Songs to Seraphine' and two complete 'North Sea cycles'. Here I can only begin to demonstrate how well her technique matched that of the original poet. In the words of a reviewer for *The Boston Transcript,* 'Miss Lazarus' version is a copy of an artist's work made by an artist's hand'.[23] The reviewer from the *New York Herald* praised her: 'She is terse, sparing of words, direct, has a keen musical ear, and a good command of language'.[24] Another noted, 'The renderings from the original are remarkably close, and enjoy the same freedom from involution or straining after effect that makes most of Heine's works limpid and places some of it at the very front of German literature'.[25]

Let us look at a poem from the *Lyrisches Intermezzo,* 'Ein Fichtenbaum steht einsam', and compare Emma Lazarus' version to those of Hal Draper and Louis Untermeyer.

Heine:
Ein Fichtenbaum steht einsam
Im Norden auf kahler Höh'.
Ihn schläfert; mit weißer Decke
Umhüllen ihn Eis und Schnee.

Er träumt von einer Palme,
Die, fern im Morgenland,
Einsam und schweigend trauert
Auf brennender Felsenwand.

Lazarus:
There stands a lonely pine-tree
In the north, on a barren height;
He sleeps while the ice and snow flakes
Swathe him in folds of white.

He dreameth of a palm-tree
Far in the sunrise-land,
Lonely and silent longing
On her burning bank of sand.[26]

Draper:
A pine is standing lonely
In the North on a bare plateau.
He sleeps; a bright white blanket
Enshrouds him in ice and snow.

He's dreaming of a palm tree
Far away in the Eastern land
Lonely and silently mourning
On a sunburnt rocky strand.[27]

Untermeyer:
A pine tree stands so lonely
In the North where the high winds blow,
He sleeps; and the whitest blanket
Wraps him in ice and snow.[28]

He dreams – dreams of a palm-tree
That far in an Orient land,
Languishes, lonely and drooping,
Upon the burning sand.[29]

In this comparison, Lazarus' artful simplicity comes into focus. Both Draper and Untermeyer try to be faithful to the original by ending stanza one with 'ice and snow', but doing so forces them to falsify Heine's simple *Höh'*, or height; Draper renders Heine's impure rhyme *Höh' / Schnee* with a perfect rhyme *plateau / snow*, but the Latinate word adds artifice; Untermeyer's 'where the high winds blow' comes from nowhere, and the same goes for 'sunburnt rocky strand'. Draper's 'is standing' and 'is dreaming' are likely only used to lengthen the metre. Perhaps Untermeyer added 'drooping' to help us visualize a real palm tree, but nothing could be further from Heine's intention. Incidentally, Draper and many of the Hebrew translators render 'trauern' as mourning; Lazarus is one of the few who understands the imagined tree is 'longing', not mourning.

Consider Lazarus' rendering of the simple, yet malicious, 'Du bist wie eine Blume', where 'seemest' is cleverly added, ostensibly to preserve the German metre:

> Thou seemest like a flower
> So pure, and fair, and bright;
> A melancholy yearning
> Steals o'er me at thy sight.
>
> I fain would lay in blessing
> My hands upon thy hair,
> Imploring God to keep thee,
> So bright and pure, and fair.[30]

Lazarus' metrically precise translation of 'Zu fragmentarisch sind Welt und Leben' shows that she is equally attuned to Heine's wit.

> Heine:
> Zu fragmentarisch ist Welt und Leben!
> Ich will mich zum deutschen Professor begeben.
> Der weiß das Leben zusammenzusetzen,
> Und er macht ein verständlich System daraus;
> mit seinen Nachtmützen und Schlafrockfetzen
> Stopft er die Lücken des Weltenbaus.
>
> Lazarus:
> Our life and the world have too fragment-like grown;
> To the German Professor I'll hie me anon
> Who sets in straight order all things overhurled.
> He will draw up a sensible system, I think,
> With his nightgown and nightcap he'll stop every chink
> In this tumble-down edifice known as the world.[31]

In the case of Heine's famous Saint Simonist poem, which begins 'Auf diesem Felsen bauen wir', translation can make or break the theological point. Here is Lazarus' translation in full:

> Come, let us build upon this rock,
> > The Church of God's last lover,
> The third New Testament's revealed,
> > The agony is over.
>
> Refuted is the second book
> > That fooled us through long ages.
> The stupid torture of the flesh
> > Is not for modern sages.
>
> Hear'st thou the Lord in the dark sea,
> > With thousand voices speaking?
> See'st thou o'erhead the thousand lights
> > Of God's own glory breaking?
>
> The holy God dwells in the light,
> > As in the dark abysses.
> For God is everything that is:
> > His breath is in our kisses.[32]

See how admirably Lazarus does justice to the final lines stanza in German:

> Der heilge Gott der ist im Licht
> Wie in den Finsternissen;
> Und Gott ist alles was da ist;
> Er ist in unsern Küssen.

In comparison, Untermeyer's free rendering of the stanza sounds almost Christian:

> God's beauty moves through light and dark,
> Through bright and secret places;
> His spirit lives in all that is –
> Even in our embraces.[33]

Lastly, I share the irresistible, final stanza of 'Question' ('Fragen'), with its brutal, assonant last line:

> Heine:
> Es murmeln die Wogen ihr ew'ges Gemurmel,
> Es wehet der Wind, es fliehen die Wolken,
> Es blinken die Sterne, gleichgültig und kalt,
> Und ein Narr wartet auf Antwort.

Lazarus:
The waves murmur their eternal murmur,
The winds blow, the clouds flow past.
Cold and indifferent twinkle the stars,
And a fool awaits an answer.[34]

What makes Lazarus a great translator of Heine is quite simply her precision. She avoids sentimentality and artifice in order to preserve his sparse style, nuance and tone.

IV.

Lazarus prefaced her volume *Poems and Ballads of Heinrich Heine* of 1881 with a modestly titled 'Biographical Sketch', written a few years earlier in 1876–7. Lazarus opens the essay with telling details and a bold, unapologetic treatment of the poet's conversion to Christianity. She notes the impact of the French occupation of Düsseldorf on 'the formation of his character'; his 'Gallic liveliness and mobility which pre-eminently distinguish him among German authors'; and the fact that he was raised 'with a rigid adherence to the Hebrew faith', leading to 'ineradicable sympathy with things Jewish, and his inveterate antagonism to the principles and results of Christianity'.[35] The second paragraph deals directly with the controversial subject of Heine's 'proselytism'. Lazarus notes: 'It was well-known that this [i.e., entering the university, practising law] would necessitate Harry's adoption of Christianity; but his proselytism did not strike those whom it most nearly concerned in the same way as it has impressed the world'.[36] She allows Heine to speak for himself, quoting his 1823 letter to Moser:

> 'Here the question of baptism enters; none of my family is opposed to it except myself; but this *myself* is of a peculiar nature. With my mode of thinking, you can imagine that the mere act of baptism is indifferent to me; that even symbolically I do not consider it of any importance, and that I shall only dedicate myself more entirely to upholding the rights of my unhappy brethren. But, nevertheless, I find it beneath my dignity and a taint upon my honour, to allow myself to be baptised in order to hold office in Prussia. I understand very well the Psalmist's[37] words: "Good God, give me my daily bread, that I may not blaspheme thy name!"'[38] (Poems xi)

Lazarus' account is remarkably different from Lady Katie Magnus' discussion of this sensitive topic in *Jewish Portraits,* where she laments that Heine 'sold his soul',[39] and from many discussions in Hebrew prefaces to Heine's works in the next decades, which dwell on the pathos of Heine's torn soul, guilt, collective shame, betrayal and a sin for which his many years of suffering was a kind of penance. Lazarus chose to quote Heine because any summary threatens to falsify his position. Heine refused to justify his own position, and so does the artist who follows him. Implicit here is that Heine does not need Lazarus or anyone else to 'redeem' him. His reference to 'upholding the rights of my unhappy brethren' mirrors her own mission, and the poignant reference to the Bible subtly restores to Heine his prophetic and even reverent stance, as do the words 'dignity' and 'honour'.

The essay follows him to the bitter end of his life, reduced (in his words) to a 'poor, fatally-ill Jew'. Again, Lazarus makes room for Heine's own voice, allowing the poet to express who he was, and who he was not, by the end of his life:

> I must expressly contradict the rumor that I have retreated to the threshold of any sort of church, or that I have reposed upon its bosom. No! My religious views and convictions have remained free from all churchdom; no belfry chime has allured me, no altar taper has dazzled me. I have trifled with no symbol, and have not utterly renounced my reason. I have forsworn nothing – not even my old pagan-gods, from whom it is true I have parted, but parted in love and friendship.

> 'I am no longer a divine biped', he wrote. 'I am no longer the freest German after Goethe, as Ruge named me in healthier days. I am no longer the great hero No. 2, who was compared with the grape-crowned Dionysius, whilst my colleague No. 1 enjoyed the title of a Grand Ducal Weimarian Jupiter. I am no longer a joyous, somewhat corpulent Hellenist, laughing cheerfully down upon the melancholy Nazarenes. I am now a poor fatally-ill Jew, an emaciated picture of woe, an unhappy man.'[40]

The essay was criticized for not focusing enough on Heine's Jewishness. Apparently, the criticism inspired her to compose a second essay in response.[41] As Young notes, the second essay 'defends his right to be judged as a poet'[42] and, in so doing, it entails something wholly absent from the first: a celebration of Heine's relationship to the mediaeval

Hebrew poets. It was not a portrait of Heine the Jew, but of Heine, the Jewish poet, that emerges there.

Many believe that Lazarus engaged with Jewish themes only after 1882, as that was when she began a strident campaign against anti-Semitism. Her sister promoted this myth after her death. In the 1880s, she threw herself into the cause of helping immigrants. The same Rabbi Gottheil who had first introduced her to mediaeval Jewish poetry took Lazarus to visit Ward Island where the Russian Jewish refugees were arriving.[43] She saw the miserable conditions with her own eyes. Her outrage led her to publish numerous essays in the *American Hebrew*, purposefully not under her own name, to publicize the conditions in the Schiff building and the HIAS (Hebrew Immigrant Aid Society) shelter. She even started an organization to resettle immigrants in Palestine; she became a Zionist over a decade before Theodor Herzl published *Der Judenstaat*. But Young argues that the campaign had begun already in the 1870s. Lazarus was also learning Hebrew in these years, in the interest of reading mediaeval Spanish poetry without relying on German translation.

Just one year after the Heine volume, Lazarus' collection *Songs of a Semite* was published by *The American Hebrew*, founded in New York City in 1879. In this unabashed title, a response perhaps to the newly coined word 'anti-Semitism', the naïve, almost biblical word 'songs' provokes as much as the word 'Semite'. The volume as a whole conveys Lazarus' idea of what it meant to be a Jewish writer at the end of the nineteenth century: it entailed biblically inspired poetry; formal experimentation; historical tragedy; an imitation of Heine; and translations from Hebrew poetry. It confirms Hollander's interpretation that Heine had become her 'major precursor both as a Jew and a romantic ironist'.

The volume opens with *The Dance to Death*, a five-act historical tragedy dedicated to the memory of George Eliot, 'the illustrious writer, who did most among the artists of our day towards elevating and ennobling *the spirit of Jewish nationality*'.[44] Another implied inspiration was Heine's *Der Rabbi von Bacherach*, which she deeply admired. The dance, most simply, refers to the embrace of martyrdom by a Jewish community in fourteenth-century Germany as they go to their fiery death. In her brief endnote, she emphasizes her concern with the history of Jewish persecution and martyrdom: 'The Plot and incidents of the Tragedy are taken from a little narrative entitled 'Der Tanz zum Tode: ein Nachtstück aus dem vierzehnten Jahrhundert (the Dance to Death – a Night-piece of the fourteenth century) by Richard Reinhard. Compiled from authentic documents communicated by Professor Franz Delitzsch.'[45] The Dance is followed by seven 'songs' on Jewish themes. I will look at one example of how Lazarus 'achieved a tone of ironic prophetic vehemence'.[46]

Many of the poems on Jewish themes are downright nationalistic ('The Banner of a Jew'; 'Bar Kochba'; 'the New Ezekiel'). But what is her method in the odd poem 'The Valley of Baca', subtitled 'Psalm 84'?[47] Lazarus had translated Heine's poem 'Vale of Tears', but other than the title, it does not obviously relate to that text. Her title refers to the cryptic Hebrew phrase 'Emek Habacha' (Psalm 84:7), which the Vulgate mistranslated as 'valley of tears', but which probably refers to a location on the way to Jerusalem. Lazarus' approach to the Psalm, if one can speculate, was to lift out a single, enigmatic verse, which was extremely difficult to interpret, and to imagine her own scenario.

Unlike her poem, Psalm 84 as a whole describes a joyful pilgrimage to Jerusalem, with the singer exulting in the stages of the journey and anticipating entering God's 'Dwelling – Place', the House of the Lord, namely the Temple. Many phrases from the Psalm have found their way into liturgy and even everyday parlance. 'How lovely is your dwelling-place / O Lord of Hosts'. 'Happy are those who dwell in Your house; they forever praise You. Selah'.

Lazarus drew from verses 6–8:

Happy is the man who finds refuge in you,
whose mind is on the pilgrim highways.
They pass through the Valley of Baca,
regarding it as a place of springs,
as if the early rain had covered it with blessing.
They go from rampart to rampart (or: strength to strength / hayil el hayil).

The enigmatic verse that inspired her poem depicts, at least in many translations, the low point of the pilgrim's journey. Her poem narrates the scenario of a Christ-like wanderer who passes through the valley, having 'beheld the sword / Of terror of the angel of the Lord' and is nearly broken. She uses the phrase 'The valley of the shadow and of death' (line 30), which conflates the Valley of Baca with the (also mistranslated) 'Valley of the Shadow of Death' (tzalmavet) in Psalm 23. She also borrows from Psalm 84 the phrase 'dwelling-place' (line 6). In the first line, 'a brackish lake' perhaps echoes the Hebrew word for blessing (brachot in verse 7) or pools of water (brechot); and the image of the warrior as a 'steadfast soul' echoes verse 12, 'those who go with integrity'; but above all, Lazarus takes the words 'from strength to strength he goes' (line 29).

In sum, the poem does not so much allude to the Bible as use it as a tangent. The use of quoted material, in the manner of documentary poetics, enables her to create a psalm of her own.

The book's third section, 'Translations from Heine and two imitations', includes her renderings of Heine's 'Donna Clara', followed by two imitations, her original poems in the same verse form, 'Don Pedrillo' and 'Fra Pedrillo'. With these poems, Lazarus fulfilled the poet's intention to complete Heine's intended trilogy. Young speculates about this text: 'why did the acculturated Emma Lazarus, at that time just twenty-seven years of age, choose to finish Heine's task? This was her first work published in a Jewish journal [*The Messenger*]'.[48] Without directly answering the questions, Young emphasizes 'the real bond between them – the sympathy in the blood, the deep, tragic, Judaic passion of eighteen hundred years that was smouldering in her own heart', which she feels many biographers ignore.

The last and largest section of *Songs of a Semite*, 'Translations from the Hebrew Poets of Medieval Spain', includes nineteen poems by Solomon ben Judah Gabirol, Judah Ben Halevi and Moses Ben Esra. These are mostly religious poems, in various forms and genres; many of them rhyme in her English renderings. Most likely these are retranslations from German, as a few sources mention that Lazarus published her first translation directly from Hebrew in *The American Hebrew* on 11 May 1883.

In this final collection, Hebrew poems outnumber the translations from Heine and poems from Lazarus' own pen. Lazarus desired to promote and make better known this newly discovered corpus of poetry, and, following the example of George Eliot, do her part 'towards elevating and ennobling the spirit of Jewish nationality'. In her fifth of the fifteen *Epistles to the Hebrews,* essays on Jewish literature, history and religion published between 3 November 1882 and 23 February 1883, Lazarus decried the 'ignorance which prevails' in Christian society regarding Jewish customs and culture. The names of Halevi, Ibn Gabirol, Moses ben Ezra, Alcharisi, as well as Mendelssohn and Maimonides, are dropped throughout that essay, along with references to the Bible and Psalms, to refute Christian critics who believe 'We all know that Jews have no literature!'[49]

V.

Two years after *Songs of a Semite*, Lazarus published her second essay on Heine in *The Century* in 1884. It was occasioned (she writes) by the recent publication in Germany of Heine's lost memoir. The essay's 'epigram' is the sonnet 'Venus of the Louvre', which I discuss below. Many new and different translations of Heine's poems are integrated into the article, as

Kramer observes; not only did she take on new types of poetry (including 'Jehuda ben Halevi' from *Hebräische Melodien* in the *Romanzero*, 1851, and the ballad 'The Silesian Weavers' of 1844) but her style of translating had developed and matured. Movingly, Kramer writes that Lazarus was on the path to becoming a 'complete translator of Heine'.[50]

Ostensibly in response to the criticism of the first essay, Lazarus asserts at the outset that Heine is many things, but ultimately a 'Poet', and 'it is only as a poet that we shall consider him in these pages'.[51] Lazarus' characterization is so Heine-esque, it bears quoting directly:

> He loves to defy, to shock, even to revolt, his warmest admirers; no prejudices are sacred, no associations are reverend to him. Romanticism; Hellenism; Hebraism; Teutonism, – he swears allegiance to each and all in turn, and invariably concludes with a mock and parody to all in turn ... A mocking voice calls out from his pages, 'I am a Jew, I am a Christian, I am tragedy, I am comedy – Heraclitus and Democritus in one – a Greek, a Hebrew, an adorer of despotism incarnate in Napoleon, an admirer of Communism embodied in Proudhon – a Latin, a Teuton, a beast, a devil, a god!' Thus he bewitches us amid roguish laughter, streaming tears, and fiery eloquence. In reality Heine is all and none of these; he is a Poet, and in each phase of human development that passes before his contemplation his plastic mind seizes and reproduces an image of beauty and inspiration. It is only as a poet that we shall consider him in these pages ...[52]

Without simplifying Heine's 'bewitching' persona, Lazarus proceeds to offer a definitive and original interpretation of his poetic genius. Even his early folksongs broke new ground in expressing something quite modern: 'the *Weltschmerz* of the nineteenth century'.[53] In the most famous collection 'Lyrical Intermezzo', 'Heine attains his fullest and richest lyrical expression'.[54] But she also drops a clue as to her ultimate thesis: 'we must go back to the Hebrew poets of Palestine and Spain to find a parallel in literature for the magnificent imagery and voluptuous orientalism of the "Intermezzo"'.[55]

Another noteworthy development is her turn to prose translation for rendering Heine's consummately ironic 'They sat and drank at the tea-table' and five other poems. Kramer sees the birth of the new technique she would adopt fully in 'By the Waters of Babylon', published posthumously:

It is strange that none of the recent writers on Emma Lazarus should have republished, or at least mentioned, these remarkable versions of key Heine poems which are in a completely different vein from those she had hitherto tackled. The unrhymed, paragraph form used for some of these poems appears closely related to the form of her last work 'By the Waters of Babylon', and may indeed be a clue to her change in technique.[56]

Joshua Logan Wall writes that Lazarus was the first since Baudelaire to adopt the genre 'Little poems in prose', and that her formal experiment presaged the documentary poetics of modernism.[57] I further propose that the turn to prose translation indicated a new interest in the prosaic, pragmatic, political legacy of Heine – an approach that Na'ama Rokem develops in her analysis of Heine's reception in Zionist literature.

Lazarus' celebration of the North Sea Poems, whose theme 'was one never before enlarged upon in German literature: the glory and beauty of the sea', contains yet another reference to Hebraism. 'His muse here blends in a symmetrical whole the sunny mythology of Hellas, the rude spirit of the Goths, and the Hebraic diction and imagery'.[58] Heine is indeed reputed to have borrowed imagery from Halevi's sea voyage poems. Lazarus continues to emphasize that Heine's popularity in German was undeniable proof of his 'Teutonic spirit and genius', and that Germany, as depicted in *Atta Troll* and *Germany, a Winter's Tale* was his ultimate homeland. Earlier in the essay, she notes the influence of *Minnesang*, mediaeval German love poetry, including as evidence her version of the penultimate poem of the 100 poem cycle. Heine, with his blend of humour, irony and anguish, was the exemplary German poet.

This theme conveys, as Esther Schor argues, that in this essay Lazarus reframes 'the fatal and irreconcilable dualism which formed the basis of his nature' as that between German and Jew, rather than Hellene and the Hebrew; moreover, as a German Jew, Heine's dualism was 'a dark, nightmare vision of the double life she was trying to live as an American and as a Jew'.[59] But far more startling is the extraordinary turn from the Jewish to the Hebraic. As she does with the striking proliferation of Hebrew poems on the pages of her *Songs of a Semite,* Lazarus explicitly states that the Hebraic tradition 'grafted' onto the Germanic to shape Heine's poetics, and she inserts new translations of Halevi as her evidence. Thus, midway through a paragraph devoted to Heine's love of Germany, we find a pregnant 'but':

> But it was the graft of a foreign tree that gave him his rich and spicy aroma, his glowing color, his flavor of the Orient. His was a seed sprung from the golden branch that flourished in Hebrew Spain between the years 1000 and 1200. Whoever looks into the poetry of the medieval Spanish Jews will see that Heine, the modern, cynical German-Parisian, owns a place among these devout and ardent mystics who preceded him by fully eight centuries. The 'Intermezzo', so new and individual in German literature, is but a well-sustained continuation of the 'Divan' and 'Gazelles' of Judah Halevi, or the thinly veiled sensuousness of Alcharisi and Ibu [sic] Ezra.[60]

The American female artist seeking a fuller lineage emphasizes Heine's mediaeval Jewish heritage. In the process of constructing Heine's artistic past, including Christian and Teutonic influences, she finds direct textual evidence of borrowings from the poetry of mediaeval Jewish Spain. He is 'graft of a foreign tree' and a 'seed sprung from the golden branch' who 'owns a place' among his mystic forebears; the Intermezzo is a 'well-sustained continuation' of Halevi's 'Divan' and the Arabic genre of *ghazal*. In the following lines, she almost accuses Heine of plagiarism, but she pulls back, instead writing that he 'unwittingly repeated the notes which rang so sweetly in his ears'. And then comes the clincher: 'What the world thought distinctively characteristic of the man was often simply a mode of expression *peculiar to his people at their best*'.[61] 'Peculiar' means 'particular'. This is a radical claim. Is it hyperbole, or does she believe that what made Heine Heine was a poetic genius that only the best of the Jewish poets possessed? She goes on to include two quotations from her own Hebrew translations of Halevi that could easily have been 'inserted into the heart of the "Intermezzo"', and then several stanzas of Heine's ballad 'Jehuda ben Halevi', describing the 'lamentation for Jerusalem', for a city reduced to 'grey heaps of rubbish', 'mighty ruins' and 'broken temple-columns'. The section concludes:

> If Heine had never written any other Judaic poems than this ballad of 'Halevi', and the verses we are about to quote [the dedication to the 'Rabbi of Bacherach'] he would deserve a high place in that splendid galaxy which includes not only Halevi and Gabirol, but David, Isaiah, and the author of Job.[62]

Now Heine assumes his proper place: in the 'splendid galaxy', the Jewish pantheon, with the biblical prophets, the mediaeval poets, Deborah, woman of torches, Rachel, 'Mother of Exiles'; Ezra the scribe, who 'raised the banner of the Jew', and bequeathed the Torah to Jews of his generation in a new Hebrew script; and Moses Mendelssohn, who also used German translation to make the Bible accessible to his compatriots. Yet after this highest praise, Lazarus pulls back rather than risk idealizing Heine's Jewishness.

> But it would convey a false impression to insist unduly upon the Hebrew element in Heine's genius, or to deduce therefrom the notion that he was religiously at one with his people. His sympathy with them was sympathy of race, not of creed, and, as we have said it, it alternated with an equally strong revulsion in favor of Greek forms and ideas of beauty. Nor did it ever restrain him from showering his pitiless arrows of ridicule upon the chosen race.[63]

Lazarus concludes her essay by describing her visit to Heine's grave in Montmartre. She worried at first to see him an 'exile and outcast' even in death: 'He lies in the stony heart of Paris amidst the hideous monuments decked with artificial wreaths of bead and wire that form the usual adornments of a French cemetery'.[64] But upon closer reflection, she saw that the cemetery itself resembles a ruin – a 'rubbish and wreck' like the destroyed Jerusalem of Lamentations – and she understands he is in his proper place after all.

> Yet no! Even now, more than a quarter of a century after his death, perhaps he is better thus. The day before I visited his tomb, the barrier wall between the Jewish and Christian portions of the cemetery of Montmartre had been demolished by order of the French government. As I saw the rubbish and wreck left by the work of humane destruction, I could not but reflect with bitterness that the day had not yet dawned beyond the Rhine, when Germany, free from race-hatred and bigotry, is worthy and ready to receive her illustrious Semitic son.[65]

These sad lines, written a few decades before the Shoah, have a prophetic character. By way of postscript, I include the following episode from Lazarus' life, based on the account of her sister Josephine Lazarus:

> Two years after these words appeared in print, Emma Lazarus was again in Paris – this time herself, at the age of thirty-seven, 'a pale, death-stricken Jew'. Once again came the lifelong analogy, which

she herself pointed out now, to the German master. Her thoughts were of Heine, on his 'mattress-grave' in Paris thirty years earlier. She, too, the last time she went out, dragged herself to the Louvre, to the feet of Venus, 'the goddess without arms, who could not help'.[66]

Why did she return to the Louvre with her last strength to visit the statue? Lazarus' kinship with Heine, her 'lifelong analogy ... to the German master', is immortalized in the sonnet 'Venus of the Louvre' which opened the second Heine essay. I quote the final ten lines:

> When first the enthralled enchantress from afar
> Dazzled mine eyes, I saw not her alone,
> Serenely poised on her world-worshipped throne,
> As when she guided once her dove-drawn car,-
> But at her feet a pale, death-stricken Jew,
> Her life adorer, sobbed farewell to love.
> Here *Heine* wept! Here still he weeps anew,
> Nor ever shall his shadow lift or move
> While mourns one ardent heart, one poet-brain,
> For vanished Hellas and Hebraic pain.[67]

Lazarus' eyes meet the bright gaze of the goddess, but it is the shadow, the dying Jew, who arouses her pathos. The one who wept in the Louvre now weeps 'here', in a Jewish poem. Whose is the ardent heart? Whose the poet brain? Emma and Harry merge into one – united by love, art, death and deep ambivalence towards Hellas. Hebraic pain lives on into the present.[68]

We see the profound, lifelong kinship Emma Lazarus felt for Heinrich Heine realized in a range of writings, but especially in the act and significance of translation. By placing her affinity with Heine in the foreground, we illuminate and appreciate Lazarus' career as an English translator of German, Jewish and Hebrew poetry. Heine enabled Lazarus to consolidate a lineage of great poets reaching back to the Bible, a starry constellation that she made visible through translation.

And what of Lazarus' heirs, the Hebrew writers in Europe and Palestine? For them, Heine was a problem. I quote two excerpts from the most famous Hebrew utterance on the subject of translating Heine by Hayyim Nachman Bialik. First: 'Remember Heine. In no case would I have ransomed the famous statue of Heine, but would rather permit it to be transported from place to place, now and forever.'[69] The second part of Bialik's *cri de coeur* is an imperative to redeem him through translation. 'There is no greater way to fulfil the commandment of "redeeming captives" than to translate Heine's poetry into Hebrew – this Jew, whose suffering was penance for his sin, and whose death made peace between himself and the God of Israel'.[70] The two parts of Bialik's statement are not contradictory. They express that Heine is what Leslie Morris calls the ultimate 'translated Jew'.[71] His diasporic spirit; the wound that cannot close; the 'Hebraic pain'; it all beckoned to Jewish poets from Lazarus onwards, who imitated, translated and built their own oeuvres around him. The fascinating story of his reception continues to guide scholars into the space of the translated Jewish text – a haunted house; a palimpsest; a transit point; a place of 'no-homeland'[72] – and into the 'splendid galaxy' of Jewish poetry.

Notes

1. Emma Lazarus' poem 'The Banner of the Jew' was first published in *Critic* 2 (18 June 1882), 164.
2. Author's note: Larry Rosenwald was the first person I heard speak about translation as a literary enterprise worthy of study. Through his scholarship, translations and vivid personal example, Larry helped create the field of Jewish translation history. I also acknowledge my teacher Jeffrey Sammons who died in 2021. Sammons first introduced me to Heine in a course on 'Germans and Jews: The Literary Encounter'. Sammons' claim that composers 're-romanticized' Heine's songs shapes my thinking about the temptation to reromanticize them in translation. I also wish to thank Susan David Bernstein, Lilach Lachman, Lilach Naishtat, Michal Peles-Almagor, Jeffrey Grossman, Willi Goetschel and Jan Kühne, for helpful conversations during the writing of this chapter.
3. 'Emma Lazarus'. *The Jewish Encyclopedia*. www.jewishencyclopedia.org.
4. Lichtenstein and Schor, 'Emma Lazarus'. Emphasis my own.
5. Hollander, 'Introduction', xviii.
6. Ranen Omer-Sherman's chapter 'Emma Lazarus, Zion and Jewish Modernity', mentions Heine twice. Though Omer-Sherman offers important insights into the ideological tensions in Lazarus' writings, Heine does not figure in those discussions. Those tensions manifested in her poems are addressed productively in Shira Wolosky, 'Emma Lazarus Transnational', in the *Oxford Handbook of the Bible in America*. 'Instead of privileging a dissolution of borders that suspends identity, Lazarus's texts open the possibility of multiple memberships as an ongoing unfolding of the self and its commitments' (390).
7. Aaron Kramer, 'The Link Between Heinrich Heine and Emma Lazarus'. Kramer's own volume of Heine translations was published in 1948.
8. Hollander, 'Introduction', xiv.
9. Adler and Szold, 'Emma Lazarus'. Bialik, *The Hebrew Book*, 198–9.
10. Biemann, *Dreaming of Michelangelo. Jewish Variations on a Modern Theme*.
11. Sammons also questions whether she matched his irony and malicious sardonic temper, agreeing somewhat with the assessment of H.B. Sachs in his 1916 book *Heine in America*: 'Very curious is the link between that bitter, mocking, cynical spirit and the refined, gentle spirit of Emma Lazarus'.
12. Gelber, *The Jewish Reception of Heinrich Heine*, 206.
13. Grossman, 'Heine and Jewish culture', 275. Emphasis my own.
14. Grossman, 'Heine and Jewish culture', 276.
15. Amy Levy (1861–89), British poet and novelist, the second Jewish woman to study at Cambridge, translated poems by Heine and by Spanish Jewish poets for another ground breaking Anglo-Jewish volume, *Jewish Portraits* (1897), by Lady Katie Magnus (1844–1924). Luke Devine writes, 'Heine was Levy's "favourite poet"', and he interprets her poem 'Borderland' as a

'reading of Heine', and, partly by way of Heine, a 'refiguring of the Song of Songs'. See Devine, 'I sleep, but my heart waketh', 219–40.
16. See Jeffrey Grossman in Cook, ed., 269–76.
17. Hollander, 'Introduction', xvii–xviii.
18. Rokem, *Prosaic Conditions*, 25.
19. Rokem, *Prosaic Conditions*, xxi. In entering into the conversation on Heine in Hebrew translation, I have learned much from Rokem, *Prosaic Conditions;* Jacobs, *Strange Cocktail,* and Jan Kühne's forthcoming essay, 'Nathan Alterman's bilingual adaptation of Heinrich Heine's 'Loreley' (2022).
20. Schor, *Emma Lazarus,* 76.
21. Lazarus, *Poems and Translations,* 174. Dated 20 May 1866.
22. Published by Cambridge: Riverside. NY Hurd and Houghton.
23. The citation from Henry T. Tuckerman's review, together with promotional material and excerpts from other reviews, are found in the back matter to *Songs of a Semite* (1882).
24. Lazarus, *Songs of a Semite*, 81.
25. Lazarus, *Songs of a Semite*, 81.
26. Heine and Lazarus, *Poems,* 161.
27. Trans. Hal Draper published by Oxford University Press and Suhrkamp/Insel Verlag (1984).
28. Heine and Untermeyer, *Poems of Heinrich Heine,* 35.
29. Untermeyer, *Poems of Heinrich Heine: Three Hundred and Twenty-five Poems.*
30. Heine and Lazarus, *Poems,* 101.
31. Heine and Lazarus, *Poems,* 108.
32. Lazarus, *Poems and Translations,* 141.
33. Heine and Untermeyer, *Poems,* 218.
34. Heine and Lazarus, *Poems,* 215–16.
35. Heine and Lazarus, *Poems,* viii.
36. Heine and Lazarus, *Poems*, xi.
37. These words are not from Psalms but from Proverbs 30.
38. Heine and Lazarus, *Poems,* xi. 'Keep falsehood and lies far from me; give me neither poverty nor riches, but give me only my daily bread. Otherwise, I may have too much and disown you and say, 'Who is the LORD?' Or I may become poor and steal, and so dishonor the name of my God'. (Proverbs 30: 8–9, New International Version.)
39. Magnus, *Jewish Portraits,* 72.
40. Heine and Lazarus, *Poems,* xxi–xxii.
41. Her second essay, 'The poet Heine', appeared in *The Century Illustrated Monthly Magazine*, 29, N.S. 7 (November 1884–April 1885), 210–11. Available on Hathi Trust.
42. Young, *Emma Lazarus in Her World*, 42.
43. On 11 July 1885, *The New York Times* reported, 'At a meeting of the Finance Committee of the Commissioners of Emigration yesterday it was decided to call a meeting of the board for next Monday in order to discuss a communication received from the District Attorney in regard to the sanitary condition of Castle Garden' (8). This was the main immigration station until Ellis Island opened in 1892.
44. Lazarus. *Songs of a Semite*
45. According to Mary Cronk Farrel, 'Richard Reinhard's 1877 *Der Tanz zum Tode* celebrated the courage and faith of 600 Jews who were killed, many burned to death, in Nordhausen, Germany, in 1349. The massacre was one of hundreds throughout Europe during the plague, where Jews were accused of causing the Black Death. 'The Story behind Lady Liberty'.
46. Hollander, 'Introduction', xviii.
47. Lazarus, *Songs of a Semite,* 55–6.
48. Young, *Emma Lazarus in Her World,* 37.
49. Lazarus, *An Epistle to the Hebrews*, 26–9.
50. Kramer, 'The link between Heinrich Heine and Emma Lazarus', 256.
51. Lazarus, 'The poet Heine', 211.
52. Lazarus, 'The poet Heine', 211.
53. Lazarus, 'The poet Heine', 212.
54. Lazarus, 'The poet Heine', 212.
55. Lazarus, 'The poet Heine', 212.
56. Kramer, 'The Link Between Heinrich Heine and Emma Lazarus', 255–6.

57. 'Though Lazarus' formal experiments remain overlooked, after her turn to Jewish history and subjectivity she increasingly develops a document-based poetics that, less than forty years after her death, would become a central practice of modernist poetics. Considering the experience of religious and ethnic otherness pushes her to seek out forms beyond the limits of poetic convention'. See Wall, 'Talking Hebrew in every language under the sun', 30.
58. Lazarus, 'The poet Heine', 213.
59. Schor, *Emma Lazarus,* 210.
60. Lazarus, 'The poet Heine', 215.
61. Lazarus, 'The poet Heine', 215–16. Emphasis my own.
62. Lazarus, 'The poet Heine', 216.
63. Lazarus, 'The poet Heine', 216.
64. Lazarus, 'The poet Heine', 217.
65. Lazarus, 'The poet Heine', 217.
66. Cited in Kramer, 'The Link Between Heinrich Heine and Emma Lazarus', 257.
67. Hollander, *Emma Lazarus,* 59.
68. In many modern Jewish tributes to classical statues – in Saul Tchernichovsky's poem 'Before the Statue of Apollo' of 1899, and Freud's essay 'The Moses of Michelangelo' of 1914 – Jewishness is denigrated. In 'Before the Statue of Apollo' (Lenokhah pessel Apollo), the poet kneels before the Greek god, 'the noble and the true', praising the god of light at the expense of his forefathers' god of old.
69. Bialik, *The Hebrew Book,* 198–9.
70. Bialik, *The Hebrew Book,* 198–9. For the complete passage in Hebrew, see Tanny, 'Who's afraid of Heinrich Heine', 321.
71. Morris, *The Translated Jew.*
72. Tuvia Ruebner's phrase.

Bibliography

Adler, Cyrus and Henriette Szold. 'Emma Lazarus'. *The Jewish Encyclopedia,* 1906.
Bialik, H.N. 'The Hebrew Book'. (Hebrew: *Ha-Sefer ha'ivri*) *Kol Kitvei H. N. Bialik.* Tel Aviv, 1953. 198–9.
Biemann, Asher D. *Dreaming of Michelangelo. Jewish variations on a modern theme.* Stanford University Press, 2012.
Devine, Luke. '"I Sleep, but My Heart Waketh": Contiguity between Heinrich Heine's "Imago" of the Shulamite and Amy Levy's "Borderland".' *AJS Review,* vol. 40, no. 2, 2016, pp. 219–240.
Farrell, Mary Cronk. 'The story behind the poetry of lady liberty.' https://www.marycronkfarrell.net/.
Gelber, Mark, editor. *The Jewish Reception of Heinrich Heine.* De Gruyter, 1992.
Grossman, Jeffrey. 'Heine and Jewish Culture: the poetics of appropriation'. *The Companion to Heinrich Heine,* edited by Roger F. Cook. Camden House, 2002, pp. 251–82.
Ha-Levi, Judah and Abraham Geiger. *Divan Des Castiliers, Abu'-l-Hassan Juda HaLevi.* J.U. Kern, 1851.
Heine, Heinrich and Emma Lazarus. *Poems and Ballads of Heinrich Heine.* R. Worthington, 1881.
Heine, Heinrich and Louis Untermeyer. *Poems of Heinrich Heine: three hundred and twenty-five poems. Revised Edition.* Harcourt, Brace, 1923.
Hollander, John. 'Introduction'. *Emma Lazarus. Selected poems,* edited by Emma Lazarus and John Hollander. The Library of America, 2005, pp. xiii–xiv.
Jacobs, Adriana X. *Strange Cocktail: translation and the making of modern Hebrew poetry.* Michigan UP, 2018.
Kramer, Aaron. 'The Link Between Heinrich Heine and Emma Lazarus'. *Publications of the American Jewish Historical Society,* vol. 45, no. 4, 1956, pp. 248–257. www.jstor.org/stable/43059871.
Kühne, Jan. 'Nathan Alterman's Bilingual Adaptation of Heinrich Heine's "Lorelei". Hebrew-German homophony as parody.' *Zukunft der Sprache – Zukunft der Nation,* edited by Carmen Reichert, Bettina Bannasch and Alfred Wildfeuer. De Gruyter, 2022.
Lazarus, Emma. *Admetus and Other Poems.* Hurd and Houghton, 1871. [Reprinted by Literature House. NJ: The Gregg Press, 1970].

Lazarus, Emma. *Songs of a Semite: the dance to death and other poems*. The Office of the American Hebrew, 1882. Facsimile edition printed by Literature House / Gregg Press, N.J, 1970.
Lazarus, Emma. 'The Poet Heine'. *The Century*. 1884, pp. 210–17.
Lazarus, Emma. *An Epistle to the Hebrews*. Centennial edition. Jewish Historical Society of New York, 1987. [Reprinted from the edition published by the Federation of American Zionists, 1900]
Lazarus, Emma and John Hollander, editors. *Emma Lazarus. Selected poems*. The Library of America. American Poets Project. 2005.
Lazarus, Emma, Victor Hugo and Heinrich Heine. *Poems and Translations*. Hurd and Houghton, 1867.
Lichtenstein, Diane and Esther Schor. 'Emma Lazarus'. *Shalvi/Hyman Encyclopedia of Jewish Women*. 23 June 2021. Jewish Women's Archive. https://jwa.org/encyclopedia/article/lazarus-emma. Accessed on 20 January 2022.
Magnus, Katie (Lady). *Jewish Portraits*. [1888] fourth (memorial) edition. George Routledge and Sons, 1925.
Morris, Leslie. *The Translated Jew. German Jewish culture outside the margins*. Northwestern University Press, 2018.
Omer-Sherman, Ranen. *Diaspora and Zionism in Jewish American Literature: Lazarus, Syrkin, Reznikoff, and Roth*. Brandeis University Press, 2002.
Rokem, Na'ama. *Prosaic Conditions. Heinrich Heine and spaces of Zionist literature*. Northwestern University Press, 2013.
Ruebner, Tuvia. 'Tuvia Ruebner', *Poetry International Archives*. http://www.poetryinternational.org/pi/poet/21413/Tuvia-Ruebner. Accessed 20 January 2022.
Sammons, Jeffrey L. *Heinrich Heine. A modern biography*. Princeton University Press, 1979.
Schor, Esther. *Emma Lazarus*. Nextbook / Schocken, 2017.
Tanny, Shlomo. 'Who's afraid of Heinrich Heine?' (Hebrew: מי מפחד מהיינריך היינה) *Moznaim* vol. 5/6, 1972, pp. 381–2.
Untermeyer, Louis, *Poems of Heinrich Heine: three hundred and twenty-five poems*. H. Holt, 1917.
Wall, Joshua Logan. "'Talking Hebrew in every language under the sun': Emma Lazarus, Charles Reznikoff, and the origins of documentary poetics'. *Modernism/modernity*, vol. 27, no. 1, 2020, pp. 27–49. *Project MUSE*. doi:10.1353/mod.2020.0001.
Wolosky, Shira. 'Emma Lazarus Transnational'. *Oxford Handbook of the Bible in America*, edited by Paul Gutjahr. Oxford University Press, 2018, pp. 396–405.
Young, Bette Roth. *Emma Lazarus in Her World: life and letters*. Jewish Publication Society, 1997.

4
City of the Dead or The Dead City? Yitskhok-Leybush Peretz as Self-Translator

Efrat Gal-Ed[1]

I.

In 1773, the scholar, lexicographer, poet and critic Samuel Johnson travelled to Scotland and the Hebrides. Two years later appeared his *Journey to the Western Isles of Scotland*. In a chapter called 'Sky. Armidel' Johnson criticizes the historical stories he heard on the journey as a muddle, composed of the traditions of ignorant people, who muddled up past events and the persons involved in them beyond repair. His critique culminates in this observation: 'But such is the laxity of Highland conversation that the inquirer is kept in continual suspense, and by a kind of intellectual retrogradation, knows less as he hears more.'[2]

Did something similar happen to the writer Yitskhok-Leybush Peretz when for six months in 1890 he travelled through the central Polish region of Tomaszów? It was only a few months after his move from Zamsość to Warsaw that he joined an expedition commissioned by the philanthropist, banker and railroad magnate Jan Bloch, the expedition's purpose being to put together a statistical account of the social and economic condition of the Jewish populations there.[3] The literary distillations of this statistical field study – 'looking for numbers', as he mockingly called it in Hebrew – are his 1891 quasi-journalistic fictions, which he, alluding to Heine, called *Rayzebilder* or *Bilder fun a provints-rayze* (scenes from a journey, scenes from a provincial journey).[4] We know that Peretz encountered, in the course of the journey, numerous *Luftmenschen*,[5] which is to say an impoverished population that through the socioeconomic and political upheavals of the last third of the nineteenth century had lost its traditional way of living as intermediaries between country and city.

The Tomaszów region around Zamość was not new to him; still, the confrontation with its hopeless destitution set a transformation in motion in him. The year 1890 marks a step not only in his writerly reorientation, but also in his political and literary radicalization.[6] In 1891, Peretz, together with Yankev Dinezon, founded the *Yudishe bibliotek* (the Yiddish/Jewish Library), in which he published his *Rayzebilder*. The same period saw the beginning of his crucial work with Hasidic themes, and of his gradual shift from realistic methods of composition to symbolist and romantic ones.

My focus here is on the story called '*Ir ha-metim, Di toyte shtot* ('the city of the dead', 'the dead city'), which Peretz wrote immediately after the works just mentioned. The narrator is a traveller who reveals himself to be Yitskhok-Leybush Peretz the statistician; he gives a ride in his wagon to a man who looks ill. As is typical in such stories, the two engage in conversation, alternating between questions and answers. The traveller asks where the other, wearing traditional Jewish clothing, might come from; he answers, *fun der toyter shtot!* ('from the dead city!'). From that point on, the conversation centres on this 'dead city', with the passenger attempting to convince the sceptical narrator that the city actually exists. When he sees that he has succeeded in making himself credible to his more modern host, and thus in confusing him, he leaps from the wagon and disappears into the woods.

Johnson's observation is precisely true of this primary, diegetic narrator;[7] the inquiring traveller (and the reader) is kept in constant tension by the narrative of the passenger, and 'the more he hears, the less he knows'.

The short story was published in Hebrew with the title '*Ir-hametim* ('City of the Dead'), on 5 and 7 August 1892, in the weekly review *Hatsefirah* ('The Dawn'). On Friday 5 August, Peretz wrote a long letter to Yankev Dinezon,[8] in Kiev, expressing his mood that summer:

מיר זענען אלע געזונט, א דאנק דעם אייבערשטן, וועלכער שפייזט די נפשות אין די זומער־טעג אין ווארשע אויך אויף נאלעווקעס און פראנציסקאנער. אין אוונט גיי איך ארויס, ווי אלע ווארשעווער געפאנגענע פונעם קעסל, און איך וווּנדער זיך, וואָס איך בין נישט אינגאַנצן צעקאָקט געוואָרן און וואָס איך האָב נאָך א נשמה איבערצוענטפערן זי אין די הענט פון הקדוש־ברוך־הוא 'אויף א גאנצע נאכט'. און אינדערפרי: כאָפּ איך זיך ארויף און איך ווּנדער זיך אויף גאָט, וואָס ער האָט אין אָט דער צייט נישט פארלאָזט און פארגעסן זיין פּיקדון.

בײַ מיר עסן סאָקאָלאָוו און דר. מינץ, וועלכע האָבן געשיקט זייערע ווייבער 'פאַשען זיך אין פעלד'... זיי עסן ווייניק, רעדן געלאסן, לאכן זייער זעלטן, פירן וויכוחים בנוגע

דער כאָלערע, וואָס שטייט הינטער אונזערע ווענט, און דערציילן נייעס, וואָס איך לייען צומאָרגענס אין ה׳צפירה׳.

We are all well. All thanks to the Highest, who during these summer days in Warsaw gives nurture even to those living on Nalewki and Franciszkańska Streets. In the evenings I go out walking, like all Warsaw-dwellers trapped in this boiler and marvel that I have not entirely boiled away, and that I still have a soul that I can commit to God's hands 'for all the long night'. And in the morning I awake and marvel at God, that He in this time has neither abandoned nor forgotten His pledge.

Sokolow and Dr. Minz[9] are boarding with me; they have sent their wives 'out to pasture'. They eat little, speak calmly, seldom laugh, have discussions about the cholera beyond our walls, and recount what I will read on the following day in *Ha-tsefirah*.

I've started to write in *Ha-tsefirah* to pay the cost of the ads.[10]

Peretz tells Dinezon what he has composed in exchange for the ads: a book review, a column that responds to the reviewed author's 'insolent' reaction, and an additional piece: *'Ir hameytim / Di meysim-shtot* ('The City of the Dead') in Hebrew and Yiddish.[11]

We learn from this letter that people are suffering in Warsaw's summer heat, that they fear an outbreak of cholera, that the *Yudishe bibliotek* is not selling well, which is why Peretz is placing ads for it in *Ha-tsefirah*. He is paying for the ads by contributing pieces in Hebrew. He is also hampered by writer's block, as he indicates in a later part of the letter:

די ׳ביבליאָטעק׳ גייט נישט, די ׳קליינע׳ קריכן נישט; כ׳האָב צוגעזאָגט אָנצושרייבן פֿאַר אביגדורן, נאָר אַזוי ווי כ׳האָב צוגעזאָגט, פֿאַלט מיר די פעדער אַרויס פֿון האַנט און איך קאָן גאָרנישט שרייַבן.

The Library isn't going well,[12] the little ones not prospering. I told Avigdor I would write for him, but hardly had I done that and the pen falls from my hand and I cannot write a thing.[13]

Towards the letter's end he mentions the ambivalent state of mind in which he wrote the earlier letter, a state of mind that illustrates not only a particular occasion but also Peretz's self-perception and self-reflection at this time:

מיין האַרץ [איז] געווען ווייך ווי בוימל אין איין אָרט, און שטאַרקער פֿון אַ פֿעלדז אין אַ צווייטן אָרט.

איך בין אַ קנעכט פֿון מײַנע נערוון, און אַלץ, וואָס איך לאָז אַרויס פֿון מײַן האַנט, איז אַ פּראָדוקט פֿון די נערוון.

> My heart was in one place soft as oil and in another stronger than rock.
>
> I am the slave of my nerves, and everything my hand sets down is the product of my nerves.[14]

Also significant for the author's state of mind was the fact that in May 1892 the discriminatory laws in Congress Poland, which Bloch had tried to hinder with his statistical surveys, came into effect. Nachum Sokolow reported in his memoir *Yosl ha-meshuga'* ('Yosl the Madman') that both he and Peretz had participated in the expedition because of their own interests in exploring the region, which was for them a goal in itself and not a means to an end. Neither thought much of Bloch's idea that a statistical survey could be a means of defending against anti-Semitism – such a survey would be as useful 'as spectacles for the blind or cupping-glasses for the dead'. Sokolow further writes that 'the poet Peretz got first agitated, then angry, then stiff with rage'.[15] They were looking for Jewish farmworkers, but instead ran into countless small-scale merchants, struggling in their desperate competition with one another simply to survive.[16] These strong impressions of misery and hopelessness in Polish-Jewish *shtetl* life seem to have kept their grip on Peretz even after the publication of the *Rayzebilder*.[17] In 1892, he found in *'Ir-hametim* a way of shaping the impressions more radically.

In 1901, Peretz published the story a second time, now as a part of his Yiddish *Shriften*, under the modified title *Di toyte shtot*.[18] Whether Peretz was translating an unpublished Yiddish version into Hebrew for *Ha-tsefirah* or wrote the story first in Hebrew and later translated it into Yiddish cannot be determined. The original publication in Hebrew, and the dating of the Yiddish version in the later edition of his complete works (*Ale verk*, 1947–8) to the years 1895–1900, argue for a first version in Hebrew.[19] But since both in the real and in the narrated worlds Yiddish was the language spoken, the Hebrew first version represents a self-translation, though perhaps only an inward one. (More on this in Part III.)

When Peretz in his letter to Dinezon calls *'Ir ha-metim* a *feuilleton*, he is classifying the story as belonging to a particular journalistic-literary text-type, which 'critically and entertainingly emphasises, reflects on and evaluates' social questions of immediate and contemporary relevance.[20] Is this in fact the case?

II.

To the title *'Ir ha-metim* the author adds a subtitle: *Ma'aseh nora' be-'emet* ('a truly terrifying incident'). By choosing the multivalent word *ma'aseh* – it can mean deed, work, event, incident, occurrence and fact – the author presents his story as a real happening. This first paratextual, exegetical indication, which suggests the narrative perspective and is understood to offer an early proof of the primary narrator's reliability, is followed by several others.[21] With the modifiers *nora' be'emet* ('truly frightening') the author brings his story nearer to its actual genre, since *'Ir ha-metim* and *Di toyte shtot* both show the characteristic marks of fantastic literature. The story interweaves the realistically communicated world of the frame story with the reality-incompatible events of the inner story. The status of the quoted world remains unclear (is there a city of the dead, a dead city, or not?). The characters seem to act in accordance with the customs and conventions of Jewish *shtetl* life; as ghosts, however, they evoke a quite divergent world of reference. Narrative sequences of the inner story are interpolated into the dialogue of the frame story; these then radiate out into that story and its reality-comparable world. This strategy of narrative boundary-crossing creates tension, affirms the divergent character of the quoted world, heightens both in the primary narrator and in the reader the degree of hesitation and unease, and culminates in an uncanny uncertainty: was the passenger a living man or a ghost?[22]

In the very first sentence the primary narrator reveals himself to be the biographical author, who has travelled through the provinces as part of a statistical mission, and he confirms that revelation in a footnote that contains a paratextual reference to his book *Rayzebilder*:

אַרומפֿאַרנדיק אויף דער פּראָווינץ וועגן דער ייִדישער סטאַטיסטיק[1] ‏[זע רייזע-בילדער]. ‏
(הערה פֿון מחבר)], האָב איך אונטער וועגנס געטראָפֿן אַ מאָל אַ ייִד, וואָס האָט זיך ‏
געשלעפּט טריט בײַ טריט אין שווערן זאַמד.

When I was traveling about the provinces collecting Jewish statistics [see *Rayzebilder* (author's note)], I happened once on a man who was dragging himself step by step through the heavy sand.[23]

The speaker thus introduces himself as a diegetic, explicit, strongly marked and personal narrator, and anchors the narrated events in real temporal and spatial frames of reference, in order to present himself and the narrated world as reliable. Then, in the second sentence, the tense changes to the present; this suggests a greater immediacy in the narrated material, and leads into the dramatic narrative, the conversation of two travellers during their ride on a horse-drawn wagon through the late afternoon and early evening.

דער ייִד זעט אויס קראַנק, קוים וואָס ער גייט, קוים וואָס ער שלעפּט די פֿיס. איך קריג אויף אים רחמנות און נעם אים אויף, אויף דער פֿור. ער זיצט אויף, שטעקט מיר אָפּ ,,שלום עליכם", פֿרעגט מיך אויס וועגן אַלערליי נײַעס. איך ענטפֿער און פֿרעג צום סוף:

– און איר פֿון וואַנען זײַט, ר׳קרובֿ?

– פֿון דער טויטער שטאָט! – ענטפֿערט ער געלאַסן.

איך מיין ער שפּאַסט.

– וווּ איז עס, – פֿרעג איך, – הינטער די הרי-חושך?

– אי! – שמייכלט ער, – דווקא אין פּוילן.

The man looks sick, can hardly walk, hardly lift his feet. I feel sympathy with him and bring him onto the wagon. He sits up, says *sholem aleichem*, asks me about all sorts of news. I answer, then finally ask:

'And where are you from, my friend?

'From the dead city', he answers calmly.

I think he's joking. 'Where is it?' I ask. 'Beyond the mountains of darkness?'

'Well', he smiles, 'right here in Poland'.[24]

It is here that the 'dead city' is named for the first time; even the mere act of naming commands attention and creates tension. The primary narrator and the author of the *Rayzebilder* is already functioning as a perceiving entity, who not only sets out his own scepticism and unease regarding the reality-compatible character of the city named by the secondary narrator, but also reflects those of the reader.

What follows the curiosity and tension thus evoked is the validation of this divergent reality as a legitimate system. As regards narrative technique, Peretz concentrates on incorporating the distinctive traits of a typical *shtetl*'s daily life. He thus ornaments the secondary narrator's speech with an abundance of Hebrew and Aramaic terms and idioms, in order to make the fantastic plot elements seem more possible and credible.

– איר גלייבט נישט? – פֿרעגט ער װײַטער.

איך שװײַג.

— און דאָך איז אַזוי! אונדזער מרא־דאתרא שרײַבט זיך דורך מיט אלע גאונים פֿון דער וועלט! עס גייען שאלות־ותּשובֿות וועגן אלע די וויכטיקסטע זאַכן... און אַלץ וועט פֿאַרזאָרגט... איז נאָך דער צײַט! נישט לאַנג, למשל: האָט מען מתּיר געווען אַן עגונה, וואָס האָט שוין לאַנג אויסגעלעבט אירע יאָרן; נו, וואָס איז? דער עיקר איז דער שׂכר פֿון פּילפּול, נישט די עגונה!

'You don't believe me?' he asks further.

I say nothing.

'But it's true! Our rabbi exchanges letters with all the Talmud scholars of the world! Questions and answers about the most important things go back and forth … and everything's being taken care of, though too late. Recently, for example, an *agune*[25] was allowed to remarry. Of course, she'd been dead for a long time, but what of that? The main thing is the gain from the debate, not the *agune*!'[26]

This mix of incredible but plausible-sounding content with a guileless, colloquial tone reveals the author's irony and critical perspective. The secondary narrator is not only eloquent because of his adroitness with idiom; his readiness of speech also has to do with the seamless transition between the concrete case and the generalization, which marks a culture-specific convention or a trait of Jewish self-awareness. Here the general statement is joined to the narrated case, which declares the oversubtle deliberations of Jewish scholars to be an activity that is beyond usefulness and more important than life itself. A bitter view, which modern readers can be counted on to smile at and assent to.[27] The narrative is constructed from lively dialogues, interrupted by a few passages of affect-laden nature description and inner monologue. Peretz here draws on a process of conversation that is familiar to readers of the *Rayzebilder*,[28] as when the primary narrator (in the *Rayzebilder*, the statistician) asks what people live on:

— פֿון וואָס?

— פֿון וואָס? ווי דער סדר־עולם איז! אַן אָרעמאַן האָט בטחון; אַ סוחר שלינגט לופֿט, און דעם ערד־אַרבעטער, דעם קבֿרן מיין איך, דעם פֿעלט אַוודאי נישט...

'On what?'

'On what? It's the way of the world! The poor man has his faith, the merchant lives on air, and as for the earthworker, I mean the gravedigger, why, he lacks for nothing.'[29]

Critical distancing is avoided by structuring the narration as a dialogue between the primary and secondary narrators. Immediacy and familiarity are evoked. Peretz thus fits plot elements together in an ordering that feels free and unforced, as when the traveller interrupts his passenger:

– איר לאַכט פֿון מיר, ר׳קרובֿ, – פֿאַל איך אים אין די רייד, – עס איז דאָך ציאַחנאָװקע! ציאַחנאָװקע מיט איר מיסחר, צדקות און מעשׂים־טובֿים! פֿאַר װאָס זאָגט איר: די טויטע שטאָט?

'You're making fun of me, my friend', I say, interrupting him. It's Tsyakhnovke with its buying and selling, its alms and charities. Why are you calling it 'the dead city'?[30]

There is no Tsyakhnovke, but there is the similar-sounding town name Ciechanów.[31] The suffix *ke* with fictitious town names also turns up in Abramovitsh's Dalfoynevke and Sholem Aleichem's Kasrilevke; it is, from a literary standpoint, common. Unlike Abramovitsh, however, Peretz is not attempting to coin symbolic names; rather he invents a name that through its dependence on a real town name, and its familiar suffix, sounds unremarkable.[32] But his passenger insists that the dead city is a different city altogether:

איך רעד פֿון אַ שטאָט, װאָס באַלד אין דער התחלה, װען זי האָט זיך געבױט, איז זי געהאַנגען אױף אַ האָר, און הײַנט, אַז די האָר האָט זיך איבערגעריסן, הענגט זי אין דער לופֿט. אױף גאָר נישט האַלט זי זיך. און װײַל זי האַלט זיך אױף גאָר נישט און שװעבט אַרום אין לופֿט, איז זי געװאָרן אַ טױטע שטאָט...[33]

I'm talking about a city that right from the beginning, when it was built, hung by a hair; and today, with the hair broken, it hangs in the air. It holds tight to nothing. And because it holds tight to nothing, and hovers in the air, it became a dead city …

Validation[34] is followed by augmentation. Before the secondary narrator unveils the strange story of the city's origin and development, and its precarious current condition, an exegetical event is interpolated, an inner monologue of the primary narrator; it begins with an account of the now falling darkness, described simply as a vivid nature tableau, then goes further, and through its self-reflective elements creates a mood of fear.

עס פֿאַלט דערװײַל צו די נאַכט... דער הימל װעט אין אַ זײַט בלױטיק, פֿײַערדיק; דאָרט גײט אונטער די זון. פֿון דער צװײַטער זײַט דאַגעגן, פֿון אַ קלאָרן, לײַכטן נעפֿל שװימט אַרױס די לבֿנה, װי אַ כּלהס פּנים פֿון אונטער אַ װײַסן שלײער. די בלאַסע שטראַלן, װאָס זי זײַט אױף איבער דער ערד, ציטערן און מישן זיך אױס מיט די ציטערדיקע שאָטן פֿון דער טרױעריק שטילער נאַכט...

עס װעט אומהײמלעך.

מיר פֿאָרן אַרײַן אין אַ וועלדל. [...]

איך וואַרף אַ בליק אויפֿן אורח, ער האָט שוין, דאַכט זיך, גאָר אַן אַנדער פּנים... עס איז
אַזוי טרויעריק און ערנסט; דער בליק, דאַכט זיך, איז אַזוי ערלעך און פּראָסט...

זאָל דאָס אַ ל ץ אמת זײַן?

הא...איך וועל הערן!³⁵

> Meanwhile it has now become night … On one side the sky is blood-red, full of fire; the sun is going down there. On the other side the moon is coming out, from a clear, light mist, like the face of a bride beneath her white veil. The pale beams that it scatters over the earth are trembling, and mix together with the trembling shadows of the sadly silent night …
>
> It is eerie.
>
> We are driving into a small wood …
>
> I have a look at the passenger; he now has, it seems to me, a wholly different face. It is altogether mournful and earnest; his gaze seems so honest and simple …
>
> Is *all* of that supposed to be true?
>
> Well … I'll hear soon enough!

Peretz was familiar with psychological texts, among them those of Théodule Ribot and Wilhelm Wundt,[36] and in this dark romanticist passage makes use of what Freud will later call transference. In an adroit inversion of the transference dynamic, he allows the doubts of the reader to speak along with those of the narrator. Thus thematized, readers' doubts are weakened, and readers can now more easily allow themselves to enter into the strange story and its divergences.

In this richly dialogical narrative process, the primary narrator takes a double role: he questions his passenger, casts doubt on his answers, and scrutinizes the passenger's further explanations, and thus directs the lively conversation. Moreover, he as the first hearer of the secondary narrator is the perceiver, and it is in his thought report that the effect of the quoted world is reflected, for himself and for the reader too.

The brief inner monologue is followed by the bewildering, absurdity-saturated recounting of the city's history, which initially seems compatible with reality, though no causal sequence is discernible. At the height of the ornate and sometimes ironic and witty inner story, the dead rise from their graves, are frightened at the appearance of the bailiff, return to their former houses, take over the businesses and oust the living. Peretz has his secondary narrator skilfully explain the peculiar laws governing the reality system of the dead city, drawing on both folkloric and modern psychological elements:

אין אונדזער שטעטל איז כמעט קיינער קיין מאָל נישט רעכט געשטאָרבן, װײַל עס האָט קיינער נישט רעכט געלעבט! נישט קיין גוטע, נישט קיין שלעכטע, קיין רשעים, קיין צדיקים... פּשוטע שלאָפֿמיצלעך אין עולם־הדמיון... לייגט זיך אַזאַ שלאָפֿמיצל אין קבֿר אַרײַן, בלײַבט עס שלאָפֿמיצל, נאָר אין אַן אַנדערע דירה, – װײַטער נישט...³⁷

> Hardly anyone in our *shtetl* has properly died, because hardly anyone has properly lived! None are good and none are bad, none are sinners or saints – just simple sleepyheads in the dream world ... And if a sleepyhead lies down in a grave, he remains a sleepyhead, just in a different dwelling, nothing more than that ...

The predominance of mimetic discourse determines both the duration of the narrative and the ordering of events, and heightens the fictive reliability, the tension and the reader's resulting indecisiveness. The apparently familiar character of the Jewish world increases the attractive power of the fantastic events; both narrator and reader are at first ironic and at the end horrified, left hanging in uncertainty.

The subtle infusing of the ordinary with the unreal, the real with the grotesque, along with the highly ornamented presentation of the quoted world, full of Jewish scholarly elements, suggest that Peretz did not consider this short story simply a literary *feuilleton*. His undertaking was rather the shaping of a fantastic story. This genre allowed him an innovative fusing of realistic, grotesque, darkly romantic and symbolist themes and formal devices. The story also allowed Peretz, in his disappointment at the meaninglessness of his statistician's task in the face of the *shtetls'* hopeless destitution, to respond to that disappointment with the literary construction of an alternative world. He captured the unbearable liminal state of Jewish existence in the Polish province in the non-reality-compatible *toyte shtot*, presented as plausible by being embellished with culturally specific grotesque elements.[38]

What were his literary models? His field of reading – he read Russian, Polish and German[39] – was broad and diffuse. Probably he read Gottfried August Bürger's 'Lenore' (1773), Kleist's 'The Beggar Woman of Locarno' (1810), E.T.A. Hoffmann's 'The Golden Pot' (1814) or 'The Uncanny Guest' (1810). Perhaps he had also read Poe's 'The Fall of the House of Usher' (1839) and surely he knew the satirically fantastic stories of Gogol.

An astonishing coincidence demonstrates that the literary reshaping of the decadence of European cities was a trait of the *Zeitgeist*: 1892 saw the publication of *Bruges-la-morte*, by the Belgian author Georges Rodenbach, a book usually considered the archetype of the symbolist novel. It was translated into German in 1903; in German, it became the source of Erich Wolfgang Korngold's opera *The Dead City*.

'Ir hametim/Di toyte shtot was read by Shmuel Werses as an allegory,[40] and by Khone Shmeruk and other scholars as a grotesque.[41] The allegorical and grotesque features are evident; I, however, would also read Peretz's story as one of the early modern fantastic stories of world literature, appearing six years before James' 'The Turn of the Screw' and twenty before Kafka's 'Metamorphosis'. With its textual procedures based on the particularity of historical strata in Hebrew and Hebrew-Yiddish diglossia, this fantastic story undermines both the cultural conventions and discursive paradigms of its own community and the relation between the minority and the hegemonic systems it lived in.[42]

III.

Since we have no drafts or manuscripts of the story, we cannot determine the genesis of the text, nor know in which language the first version was created, or for that matter whether the creative process took place in the two languages simultaneously. If we attend to the time of publication of 'Ir ha-metim (1892) and *Di toyte shtot* (1901), then we are dealing with two time-delayed translation processes. The Hebrew version appeared a year or so after the first publication of the Yiddish *Rayzebilder*. The Yiddish version is not part of the second printing of that longer work (1894);[43] which would mean that Peretz considered that version, if it existed already in Yiddish, not as a part of the cycle but as an independent story, which he included in the first volume of the *Shriftn*, published in 1901 but submitted to the censors as early as 1900.

The spatial centre of the described world is the Polish provinces; the scene of the plot of the inner narrative, with the town Jews have built there in defiance of all law, is in the same region. The day-to-day language of that Jewish world was Yiddish.[44] Speakers in the represented world converse in that language. Writing the short story in Hebrew extends the process of literary construction by adding to it the translation of a depicted world – a world presented by the author – that speaks Yiddish, into a world represented in Hebrew; the outer (read) text for the inner (represented) voices is already the product of a cognitive linguistic recoding.

Thus, in the process of the Yiddish literary compression of the story, two components are interwoven: a translation back into the language of the portrayed world, and a reworking of diverse passages. Modifications in the form of corrections, rewriting and re-creation during the translation are common in self-translations.[45]

In 1888, eleven years after the publication of his first Hebrew poems,[46] Peretz began writing literary texts in Yiddish as well.[47] From that point on, he used both languages indifferently for the various genres of his belletristic and journalistic work.[48] His self-translation of several works, as in the case being discussed here, was a part of his integrative way of working, in which Hebrew and Yiddish functioned as literary languages of equal value.[49] Peretz translated in both directions and appeared not as self-translator but as author;[50] accordingly, both versions of the present story were read as original texts.

Peretz's competence in Jewish and non-Jewish languages[51] was variously assessed by his contemporaries. The physician, author and culture activist Gershon Levin, for example, who had heard Peretz lecture in the Warsaw branch of the *Safah Berurah* (clear language) Society, stated in his memoirs that Peretz 'fluently spoke a beautiful Hebrew'.[52] Sokolow, too, found that Peretz 'wrote wonderful Hebrew', that he 'moved freely in that language', but also that the idiomatic fullness of his Yiddish sounds 'translated' in Hebrew.[53]

Whether or not Peretz's Hebrew works sounded 'translated' to his contemporaries,[54] his practice of self-translation raises questions about the translation of his artistic intentions into literary works in both languages. All the more because Yiddish, at this time, could look back to a long oral tradition, but only a short literary one.[55] Hebrew, on the other hand, was being used chiefly as a literary language, but hardly at all as a language of everyday life.[56] Can we discern differences of textual production between the two languages? What part do correction and revision have in the translation process, what role does self-translation have in the creative process?

Even the subtle difference between the titles of the two versions bears witness to Peretz's self-awareness as a self-translator, acting as an author, as someone for whom the Hebrew version does not occupy the hierarchically superior position of an original text, determining translational norms such as fidelity. When Peretz translates, he creates anew, the shifts being sometimes subtle and sometimes substantial.

Table 4.1 Interlinear comparison of עיר המתים (City of the dead) and די טויטע שטאָט (The dead city)

the dead city	די טויטע שטאָט	city of the dead	עיר המתים
–	–	(a truly terrifying incident)	(מעשה נורא באמת)

In both languages, the title consists of the same lexeme, 'city'; a word meaning 'dead' (a nominalized adjective in Hebrew, an adjective in Yiddish); and the definite article. The decomposition of the Hebrew compound through the use of an adjective shifts the accent from the dead and their actions to the city itself as the chief character. By the adjectival translation of the compound, the condition of the city changes; no longer does it belong to the dead, to its inhabitants, or to those who have taken possession of it; rather, it is itself lifeless. To dissolve compounds in this way is not, to be sure, unusual, but in this case, a more literal rendering would have been possible in Yiddish, with *di meysimshtot* or *di toytnshtot*. Peretz's decision for 'the dead city' entails a shift in effect. The Hebrew title suggests the genre of the horror story, its plausibility, as noted, affirmed by the subtitle that the Yiddish lacks; the Yiddish title evokes an atmosphere of decay and destruction.

Peretz as self-translator shapes the Yiddish version alongside the Hebrew one, retains structure and events and themes of the narration; but as author he allows himself omissions, additions and transpositions, which have linguistic and stylistic functions and suggest a change in his poetics.[57] The question of Peretz's translational procedures must then be considered through close comparative readings, though in the scope of this article that can be done only in a few cases.[58]

That the Yiddish version is not a literal translation is evident even at the story's beginning:[59]

Table 4.2 Interlinear comparison of עיר המתים (City of the dead) and די טויטע שטאָט (The dead city)

'What are you saying?' 'What you hear! You're of course familiar with geography, and think that everything is recorded there. No way! We Jews live without geography ... not recorded, and they come to us from near and far and then go. Why geography? Every coachman knows the way . . .'	— וואָס רעדט איר? — וואָס איר הערט! איר קענט אַוודאי געאָגראַפיע און מיינט, אַז אַלץ איז דאָרט פֿאַרשריבן; אַז אַסור! מיר יידן לעבן אָן געאָגראַפיע... נישט פֿאַרשריבן און פֿון נאָענט און ווייט קומט מען צו אונדז און מע פֿאָרט פֿון אונדז. נאָך וואָס געאָגראַפיע?.. יעדער בעל־עגלה ווייסט דעם וועג...	'The thing is extraordinary'. 'In my eyes not at all extraordinary! Our people don't live by geography! People from near and far know of our town without it, know its exits and entrances.'	— נפלא הדבר! — בעיני לא יפלא! אנשי־שלומנו אינם חיים על פי הגיאוגרפיה! קרובים ורחוקים ידעו בלעדיה את העיר, מוצאיה ומובאיה.

The double length of the Yiddish version results not only from the synthetic morphology of Hebrew, but also from Peretz's additions. The passenger claims that in this familiar region there is a 'dead city' that the traveller is unaware of; the traveller reacts with sceptical astonishment. This is expressed in both languages equivalently, albeit in different registers. The Yiddish phrase is colloquial, the Hebrew biblical.[60] The Yiddish exchange, 'what are you talking about?' / 'what you're hearing!' is idiomatic, earnest and witty. Both sentences begin with the pronoun 'what', followed by a predicate: 'talking' then 'hearing' – a beginning indicating the contrasting perspectives of the speakers. The primary narrator doubts not that he has heard correctly, but that the claim he has heard is true. The secondary narrator, in his turn, stresses his opposite position regarding the same set of facts, by answering, provokingly, that his interlocutor has indeed heard him correctly, that is to say, with understanding, and in the subtext implies that his utterance is true.

The Hebrew answer again draws on biblical idiom; but since it is embedded in a short conversational exchange, we get the impression of a spoken back-and-forth. In Hebrew, too, the exchange is both earnest and witty. There is a revelation of the adversarial relationship between the two speakers, in their affirming or denying application of the same lexeme, nifla'/ yippale', 'unbelievable'.

This rhetorical figure, the repetition of a single lexeme in utterance and reply, is used in the conversations between the traveller and his passenger with a considerable number of variations.[61] The repetition turns up in both versions of the text, and suggests a translational strategy that seeks a sufficiently precise rendering of the mode of speech, as well as the importance of that mode in the repertoire of artistic means and the intention of the author to deploy it in both languages. The repeated word binds statement and counter-statement, gives a rhythm to the exchange and functions as a *Leitwort*, motivating the response of the secondary narrator.

In the Hebrew, what follows this first, brief exchange is just two sentences. The first refers back to the content of the previous paragraph: the existence of the dead city was never, is not now anywhere attested in works of geography such as atlases and maps.[62] The formulation is ambiguous: the people of our community (Jews) do not live according to (the rules of) geography (a science); they live without geography, that is, without their own land; their existence hangs 'by a hair', as the passenger will later report, a phrase that indicates their extraordinary condition, their life outside of law. The Yiddish phrase 'we Jews' corresponds to the Hebrew phrase *'anshey shelomenu* (our people), an expression of biblical origin, common since the eighteenth century as a Hasidic idiom.[63]

To link that phrase to 'geography', to a lexeme from a secular domain of knowledge, emphasizes, in a witty undertone, the contrast between 'us', Jews, and 'them', Gentile scholars, and between the disparate modes of life experienced by those with and those without geography.

In the second sentence, a claim is made that Jews from near and far all know the roads that lead to and from the city, without depending on the help of geography. Which also means that Jews know their way around and can orient themselves without a need for secular knowledge. The sentence begins with one rabbinic pairing of opposites: *'qerovim u-rekhoqim'* (people from near and far)[64] and ends with another: *'motsa'eyha u-mova'eyha'* (exits and entrances). The second pairing, given its biblical connotations, extends the competence of those travelling into or out of the city, despite their ignorance of geographical works, from a mere knowledge of place to an unrestricted competence in life (and survival).[65] The rhyming, acoustically similar pairings bracket off the idea of a competence not dependent on secular technical knowledge, and affirm its finality by onomatopoeia. Putting the paronomasia at the beginning and end of the sentence both dynamizes and rhythmicizes the speech.[66] In the whole exchange, the embedding of biblical or rabbinic phrasing in a more modern semantic environment, and also the syntactic ordering of the sentence, allow the discourse to sound colloquial and spoken.

In the Yiddish version too the joke comes from the double message, now conveyed in separate sentences: 'Obviously you know about geography, and you think that everything is recorded there. No way! We Jews live without geography …'. In the first sentence the concrete statement is made, that not everything is recorded in geographical works (notably the dead city). The second, almost philosophical sentence, can mean 'we Jews live without maps', but also, 'Jewish life takes place outside of geographical coordinates', whereby in the Yiddish text, too, an existential statement is smuggled in. The second half of the reply mocks scientific findings as useless, given that every coachman, with his knowledge of local place, gets along just fine. The extended passage in the Yiddish text contributes to the literary shaping of spoken discourse. The sentences are short, contain ellipses and an evaluative interjection – *az oser* (absolutely not; or no way) – that develops the emotion of the statement, and thus replicate the course and dynamic of spoken speech.[67] To this original rhetoric of oral discourse a further artifice is added: the speaker verbalizes the presumed thoughts of his silent interlocutor, so as to contradict them immediately and to adduce his counterarguments. This device not only contributes to animating the dramatic speech, it also enriches it with the psychodynamically familiar and thus authentic-sounding traits of verbal duels.

A key word of both versions is 'geography'. In the briefer Hebrew version it appears just once, in the longer Yiddish one three times. In the repetitions, the *Leitmotiv* of geography ends up the object of sarcasm: the traveller has knowledge of it, but Jews live without it, so what use is this science to anyone? That geography here stands for other secular methods of knowledge and exploration and their causal interpretations, statistics among them, is clear. And just as one cannot by statistical means grasp the nature of Jewish existence, nor hinder the effects of discriminatory laws, so too is there no non-Jewish name for the dead city, and it cannot be found on any map. The city does not call into question either science or reason, or their capacities for exploration; rather it constitutes a symbolic, subversive alternative to the dominant systems of power.

In the two versions Peretz moves in opposite directions: in Yiddish, he makes oral discourse literary; in Hebrew, he makes literary language colloquial. It is as if he wanted, not to make the speech registers of the two versions equal, but at any rate to bring them closer to each other.

Among the features of Peretz's style is discourse in parallel clauses; this shapes the two versions of the story both semantically and rhythmically. When, for example, the passenger is asked how the city inhabitants earn their bread, he answers by resorting to biblical parallelism, as in Proverbs:[68]

Table 4.3 Interlinear comparison of עיר המתים (City of the dead) and די טויטע שטאָט (The dead city)

'How?'	— פֿון וואָס?	'How?'	— במה?
'How? The way the world is! The poor man has his trust in God, the merchant lives on air, and the earthworker, the gravedigger that is, he of course lacks for nothing.'	— פֿון וואָס? ווי דער סדר-עולם איז! אַן אָרעמאַן האָט אַ בטחון; א סוחר שלינגט לופֿט, און דעם ערד-אַרבעטער, דעם קברן מײַן איך, דעם פֿעלט אַוודאי נישט...	'The poor man lifts his eyes to the heavens, the merchants "live on air", and the earthworker too has plenty of bread – that is, the gravedigger…'	— הרש עיניו נשואות השמימה, הסוחרים ,,חיים מן האוויר", וגם עובד אדמתו ישבע לחם, זהו – הקברן...

In the Yiddish text, the author and translator does not wish to miss the chance of repeating the interrogative word; accordingly, he fits into this characteristic feature of spoken discourse a witty, lapidary observation on the ordinary course of things in the world, which then introduces the actual answer. In both versions, this is formed as three parallel, semantically comparable clauses. The first concerns the social category of paupers, and stipulates 'the poor man hopes for God's help'. The Hebrew *rash* (poor man; masculine singular), evokes through its biblical connotation the poor man as deprived of rights.[69] The metonymic expression for the man's hope for God's help refers to a biblical idiom as it is used in rabbinic, liturgical and Hasidic literature.[70] The Yiddish clause similarly uses a common idiom, formed from the German-origin *oreman* (poor man), and the Hebrew-origin *bitokhn* (trust in God). In both languages the second phrase introduces a new idiom: 'to live on air'.[71] It is translated into Hebrew with the verb 'live', in the sense of 'feeding oneself on air', and set apart with quotation marks. In Yiddish, Peretz creates, with his phrase *shlingen luft* (gulping air), a new meaning for its use.[72] The third clause asserts that 'the earthworker has his fill'. In the Hebrew, this works by means of a biblical quotation, of Proverbs 12:11: *oved 'admato yisba' lehem* (he that tilleth his land will be satisfied with bread); in the Yiddish the word *erdarbeter* (earthworker), instead of the usual *poyer* (peasant), is a modern translation of the beginning of the biblical verse, which foregrounds the social dimension of being a peasant and alludes to the ethnographic project.[73] The remainder of the biblical quotation is paraphrased; in place of 'will be satisfied' Peretz gives in free translation 'he lacks for nothing', an inversion of *hasar-lehem* (he lacks bread), Proverbs 12:9.[74] The irony in the clause is in calling the gravedigger an earthworker, and thus equating agriculture with burial. In the parallel enumeration of social groups – paupers, merchants, peasants – the last group is replaced by gravediggers, whose services, as we later learn, are in this city in high demand.

Peretz thus creates in both languages a biblically inspired *parallelismus membrorum*, which in its rhythmic, ironic discourse of sequential utterances portrays not a means of earning bread but an image of systemic unemployment. The author's focus, the translator's focus, is equally on the shaping of the rhetorical figure and the maintaining of meaning.

The speeches of the eloquent passenger are full of effervescent life, and contrast sharply with his appearance. After the reply that was just discussed, the narrative flow is halted. The next section begins with the traveller's inner monologue, which in the Hebrew text's first publication, in 1892, is not present, but which was added in the book version of 1900. It is also present in the first publication in Yiddish, in 1901, where it is somewhat longer than in the Hebrew. We cannot say for certain whether the Yiddish version was an intermediate step on the way to the Hebrew version of 1900. Some passages are briefer in the Yiddish; others, though, are expanded, sometimes on a small scale, sometimes more substantially.[75]

Table 4.4 Interlinear comparison of עיר המתים (City of the dead) and די טויטע שטאָט (The dead city)

| Is he making fun of me, this emaciated little man, this heap of bones with the strangely flashing fire in his deep-set eyes? In the sharply lined face, as if overlaid with yellow parchment, there isn't even the trace of a smile ... But his voice ... somehow it sounds strange! | צי מאַכט ער חוזק, דאָס אויסגעדאַרטע ייִדל, דער גל־עצמות, מיטן מאָדנע פֿײַערל, וואָס בליצט אים אין די טיף אײַנגעפֿאַלענע אויגן? אויפֿן שאַרפֿבײַניקן פּנים, וואָס איז אַרומגעצויגן ווי מיט אַ געל שטיק פּאַרמעט, באַוויַיזט זיך דאָך קיין מינדסטן שמייכל... נאָר דאָס קול זײַנס ...עפּעס קלינגט עס מאָדנע! | Is he making fun of me? In his eyes is a strange fire, he is generally a heap of bones ... On his cheeks, white as chalk and creased as parchment, not the slightest smile is shown, and yet in his voice – mockery! | היתקלס בי האיש? בעיניו אש זרה כולו גל של עצמות... על לחייו, הלבנות כסיד והנקמטות כגוויל, לא יראה אף צחוק קל, ובכל זאת בקולו – לעג! |

What are the differences in literary design between the two versions?[76]

Though the versions are of different length, they convey the same meaning: the man is very pale, gaunt as a skeleton, a disquieting light shines from his eyes, his skin is wrinkled and the tone of his voice does not correspond to his facial expression. The introductory question, in free indirect thought, 'is he making fun of me?' is expressed in both languages with appropriate phrases. The phenomena (eyes, skin, smile, voice) and the imagery revealing them (fire, heap of bones, parchment) are the same in both languages. In both versions, the word translated as 'voice' is *kol*, since Peretz uses the Hebrew-origin lexeme in the Yiddish text as well. The same is true for the Hebrew-origin *gal-atsomes* (boneheap) in the Yiddish, and for the more common prepositional phrase, *gal shel atsamot* (heap of bones) in the Hebrew.[77]

The greater length of the Yiddish translation comes from added details providing additional imagery. The man is both thin *and* a heap of bones; his eyes are now 'deep-set'; instead of 'cheeks' there is reference to sharply defined facial features; the face is not, as in the Hebrew, chalk-white like the cheeks, but as if overlaid with a piece of yellow parchment. The extended description contributes to the visual vividness, and works well with the Yiddish oral discourse. The thought report in the Hebrew is energized by ellipses and short syntactical units, and reflects an inner flow of speech.

But the two versions are also sharply distinguished. The Hebrew begins with a question and ends with a clear answer – the passenger's speech expresses mockery. His physical appearance is indicated matter-of-factly and precisely. Especially conspicuous is the 'strange fire' in his eyes, indicating the *'esh zarah* (literally: strange fire / a fire of strangers) of Leviticus 10:1, a fire ritual not in accordance with the laws of divine worship, figuratively indicating an evil passion. In the Yiddish text, the fire is called *modne* (strange), and the sound of the passenger's voice is too. The repetition of the adjective at the end of the thought report gives it, despite its vividness, a diffuse character – because, as a result, the initial question remains unanswered. Can the traveller not discern the nature of the fire, that is, not assess the disposition of his passenger? Can he not assign to the tone a precise mood? Is the primary narrator too confused to draw clear conclusions, or are his interlocutor and the described facts clearer than he admits – in which case he would be revealed as an unreliable narrator? The diffuse attribute creates the reader's hesitation.

In what follows, the divergence between the narrations increases, in particular in the colourful account of causality and of the ideational framework of the events leading to the takeover of the city by the dead.[78] Here (Table 4.5), there are differences both in the content and in the organization of the narrative sequence. The explanatory comment at the beginning of the Hebrew paragraph, explaining why those who have died are not dead, is, in the Yiddish version, set out at length in an earlier passage. The formulation of individual notions and ideas is more abstract in the Hebrew, more concrete in the Yiddish. The visual component of the narrative is, in the Yiddish version, richer in imagery and substance. The dead behave like ordinary people, do not always keep accounts, forget things, live according to Jewish customs and fear being 'deterritorialized' by the bailiff. The interpolation of particular bits of real life (prayer house, bathhouse, barley soup) bring the daily life of the *shtetl* and the psychological state of the dead into the foreground and thus contribute to the normalization of the fantastic. The close sense of actual life produced by this narrative strategy balances, moreover, the philosophical passages. Peretz brings that sense into the Hebrew version as well, but to a lesser extent, with the result being that the reflective components, with the truth claims inherent in them, are more dominant.

The speech of the passenger, gradually revealing himself as a perfect informant with a broad knowledge of detail, is full of wit and irony in both languages. In the Hebrew, the interpolation of exact or altered biblical quotations as predicates for various subjects creates an estrangement. The incongruence between the embedded quotation and the embedding clause allows the critical perspective to be heard. Thus the relation between soul and body is described by the biblical

Table 4.5 Interlinear comparison of עיר המתים (City of the dead) and ד׳ שמעו שטאט (The dead city)

… The same dream, the same dream world…. It's like that in many cities…. And sometimes it happens, and it happened to us too, when a dead man creeps out of his grave, he doesn't at all remember that once he said the confession of sin, wrestled with death, and died … And hardly, when he has arisen, do the scales fall from his eyes, but he goes straight to the house of study or the bath-house, or goes home to eat barley soup – he doesn't know a thing! I do not know whether the moon was responsible, or perhaps I was not as usual – I hear, I believe, I go on to ask: – 'So, have *all*, all the dead arisen?' – 'Who knows? Are books being kept?' Maybe there were secret atheists there, who thought it was about the resurrection of the dead, and out of spite went on lying down there… But a community of the dead, a whole congregation, has arisen! Arisen, and fled from the bailiff into the forest.'	[Yiddish text column]	… Therefore our inhabitants are dead only seemingly … The soul and the body, the beloved and the companions, unseparated in their lives and in their deaths, there is no difference between this world and the world to come except for the transition, the hour of death, the liberation from commandments and from the need for bread winning … The dream goes on … Or man goes from one dream world to the next dream world … So when, as in our case, it happens that a dead man gets up from his grave, he does not remember his death or his grave, he again goes about, without knowing, how he lies down and gets up … I do not know whether it was by the storyteller's beautiful words or the charms of the luminous moon that I was so impressed, but the truth is, I began to believe the story was possible, and asked: – 'And have *all* the dead risen up?' – 'Maybe the ones eaten by worms stayed there. … But many of the dead rose up!' Rose up and ran into the forest.'	[Hebrew text column]

84   IN THE FACE OF ADVERSITY

predicate 'in their life and their death [they are] not separated' (2 Sam. 1:23); but what is referred to here is not the love and friendship between David and Jonathan, but rather the fatal clinging of soul to corpse. And when the dead man himself does not know how he 'lays himself down and rises up', his self-forgetfulness is in sharp contrast to the commemoration of Israel's loving relationship to God that is commanded in the *Shema'* (Deut. 6:7), though the freely cited predicate is drawn precisely from that prayer. From this intertextual fabric of relations, with its inversions of relational patterns, arises the linguistic dimension of the uncanny.[79]

In the Yiddish, the irony comes into being through the tension between the fantastic character of what is shown and the normalizing way of showing it – when the scales fall from the eyes of the dead, he goes immediately to the house of study or the bathhouse. In both versions, the comic aspect has a subversive note as well, because it arises not only through plays on words (calling gravediggers 'earthworkers'), through the situational comedy of particular scenes (the mechanical repetition by the dead of the routines of daily life) and through the absurd linkages of ideas and casualties (because people live a dead life, they live on in death), but also through the superiority felt by a minority and its dead who live on in spite of all circumstances opposing them.

Peretz's poetics in the two languages are composed of similar and different elements. The goal is the aesthetic shaping of a narrative core, which presents an unstable notion of the world, and is motivated by the 'horrifying intrusion of the uncanny'[80] into a system of reality. Peretz strongly criticized the unreflective acceptance of artistic 'isms', instead letting himself be led by the inner laws of his artistic intentions, and links in both versions of the story dark-romantic, realistic and symbolist motifs and traits. This allows him to describe his ghosts and their natural-law-shattering behaviours in realistic ways, ways that are deepened psychologically by dreams, stirred-up feelings, passion, fantasy. The embedding of the events within the narrative and reflective conversation of the two travellers allows, in the context of the philosophical exchanges, the heightening of what is morbid and lurid to seem plausible. What unfolds before the reader's eyes is a richly detailed tableau of decay, lacking any prospect of healing and repairing.

The same stylistic means are at work, regardless of which language is in question. The modelling of orality in the dialogue and in thought report draws chiefly on associative leaps, short sentences, rhythmically ordered clauses, repetitions, ellipses and onomatopoeia.

What is dependent on the language being used, however, is Peretz's various uses of internal code-switching. In the Hebrew, he mixes fragments from diverse historical repertoires (biblical, rabbinic, liturgical, Hasidic), and creates, through divergent frames of reference, parody, irony, estrangement and critical distance. The close proximity of historically quite disparate linguistic elements leads to their de- and recontextualization, and creates, in this modernist way, a substantially modified idiom.[81] Yiddish is a fusion language with a Hebrew-Aramaic component; Peretz moves it beyond the familiar use of these components, often by means of Hebrew and Aramaic lexemes of scholarly idiom.[82] This change in the use of internal diglossia, applied to particular themes, is not only lexical, but extends the semantic field by creating ambiguity. In both languages, by means of the polyvalent code of conceptually and contextually unequal language worlds, Peretz forms richly varied leaps of thought, authentic speech and categorizing distinction, which together maintain the indeterminate status of the narrated world.

As author and self-translator, Peretz not only translates his text from one language to another, he also pours into two languages a single literary conception.

Translated by Lawrence Rosenwald

Notes

1. My heartfelt thanks to Astrid Blees, Almut Seifert, and Daria Vakhrushova for stimulating conversations during my seminar, 'Self-Translations by Yiddish-Hebrew authors', in the winter semester of 2015–16, in which the present investigation had its beginning; to Natasha Gordinsky, Jan Kühne, and Fin Westerkamp for their help in getting hold of Hebrew and Yiddish scholarship; and Annelen Kranefuss, Daria Vakhrushova, and Akiñcano M. Weber for critical readings of the manuscript. Thanks also to Larry Rosenwald for the English translation of the present contribution.
2. Johnson, *Journey to the Western Isles of Scotland,* 112.
3. Cf. Lewin, *Perets,* 31f; Mayzil, 'In der statistisher ekspeditsye'; Wisse, *Peretz and the Making of Modern Jewish Culture,* 17–19.
4. Cf. for example Peretz, 'Rayzebilder' or 'Bilder fun a provints-rayze'. 'For a while I was under the influence of Heine and Börne – my first Yiddish poems' (Peretz to Zinberg, 3 December 1911, Peretz, *Ale verk,* vol. X–XI, 282f). On the stories cf. Niger, *Y.L. Perets,* 200–3; Mayzil, 'In der statistisher ekspeditsye'; Blank and Hein, 'I.L. Peretz's Blick auf das Shtetl' (2001); Mahalel, *The Radical Years of I.L. Peretz,* 71–85; Caplan, 'The fragmentation of narrative perspective in Y.L. Peretz's 'Bilder fun a Provints-Rayze''; Miron, 'I.L. Peretz as the poet of the Jewish age of sensibility', 14f.
5. 'Persons without a definite occupation', says the Beinfeld-Bochner dictionary, but the word has connotations of irresponsibility. (Translator's note.) On the history of the metaphor see Berg, 'Luftmenschen'.
6. Cf. Rozntsvayg, 'Der radikaler period fun peretses shafn'; Moss, 'Isaac Leib Peretz', 232–4; Mahalel, *The Radical Years of I.L. Peretz,* 24 and 30.
7. Wolf Schmid uses 'primary' to refer to the narrator of the frame story (Schmid, *Elemente der Narratologie,* 81). The 'diegetic narrator' tells 'about himself – rather his earlier self – as a figure in the narrated story', and thus is 'both in the narrating and in the narrated story [present], on the two levels of the represented world, the level of the narrated world, or *diegesis*, and the level of the narration, or *exegesis*' (Schmid, *Elemente der Narratologie,* 82, emphasis in original).

8. Undated in the edition of the letters.
9. Both men were also members of the expedition's staff; cf. Mayzil, 'In der statisher ekspedisye', 110–12; Sokolow, 'Yosl ha-meshuga", 61f.
10. Quoted from the translation of the Hebrew original in Peretz, *Ale verk*, X–XI, 257f.
11. Peretz, *Ale verk*, X–XI, 258.
12. The two first volumes of the *Yudishe bibliotek* were published in 1891.
13. Peretz, *Ale verk*, X–XI, 260.
14. Peretz, *Ale verk*, X–XI, 260.
15. Sokolow, 'Yosl ha-meshuga', 62. Since Bloch lent all the materials of the expedition to Theodor Herzl, and since beyond that point the trail of the materials is lost (see Shatski, 'Af die shpurn fun di materialyen fun Yan Blokhs statistish-ekonomisher ekspeditsye'), the 'Rayzebilder' and 'Yosl ha-meshuga" are the final witnesses of the enterprise.
16. Sokolow, 'Yosl ha-meshuga", 62f.
17. Cf. Mayzil, 'In der statistisher ekspeditsye', 118; Roskies, 'I.L. Peretz', 104; Moss, 'Isaac Leib Peretz', 232.
18. Peretz, *Shriften*, 1, IV, 138–48. Warsaw 1901.
19. Cf. the Table of Contents in Peretz, *Ale verk*, vol. III; this temporal order is the one proposed by the volume's editor, Shmuel Niger.
20. Porombka, 'Feuilleton', 264.
21. Shmuel Werses notes the frequent use, in Peretz's early prose in the 1890s, of a 'fictional reliability' (Werses, "Al 'omanut ha-sippur shel y. l. perez', 293).
22. Cf. Todorov, *Einführung in die fantastische Literatur*, 34, discussed critically in Brittnacher and May 'Phantastik-Theorien', 190f, and Dunker, 'Fantastische Literatur'.
23. Peretz, 'Di toyte shtot', 319. For lack of space, only the Yiddish version is quoted in this part of the chapter.
24. Peretz, 'Di toyte shtot', 319.
25. *Agune*, hebr. *aguna*: a women whose husband cannot be located, so that she, neither widowed nor divorced, cannot remarry.
26. Peretz, 'Di toyte shtot', 319.
27. Such comments on Jewish practices and concepts are abundant in the story, and help in the contextualization of the fantastic and also to its relativization, by setting the events, incompatible with the laws of logic, in a familiar cultural frame of reference. At the same time they bear subversively on patterns of religious discourse. 'The religious and religion-critical dynamics of modernity, the pluralization and differentiation of religion are a fundamental condition for the development of fantastic themes and genres' (Frenschkowski, 'Phantastik und Religion', 553).
28. On Peretz's creation of an 'interview-like atmosphere' with its rhetorical and situational characteristics, cf. Werses, "Al 'omanut ha-sippur shel y. l. perez', 293; also Y. Mark, 'The language of Y.L. Peretz', 65, and Finkin, 'Y.L. Perets's conversational art in Yiddish and in Hebrew'.
29. Peretz, 'Di toyte shtot', 320.
30. Peretz, 'Di toyte shtot', 321.
31. My thanks to Daria Vakhrushova for this reference.
32. Peretz seems to have devised the name earlier. See his letter to Sholem Aleichem (1888), though in a divergent spelling, tshakhnovke (Perets, *Ale verk*, Bd. X–XI, 244). Peretz also uses the name in the 1890 story 'Der meshugene batlen' (Peretz, *Ale verk*, II, 17–20). The name has an acoustical similarity to the Russian *čaxnut'* (wasting away) and may have been chosen by Peretz as a name for its sonority.
33. Peretz, 'Di toyte shtot', 321.
34. Here through the apparently logical deduction.
35. Peretz, 'Di toyte shtot', 321f.
36. Cf. Peretz's 1888 letter to Sholem Aleichem (Mayzil, 'In der statistisher ekspeditsye', 145).
37. Peretz, 'Di toyte shtot', 325.
38. Sokolow, 'Yosl ha meshuga',' 62–4, describes and comments at length on the characteristics of Jewish collective life in the villages and small towns of the Polish provinces, oppressed and threatened by the hegemonic system of state order.
39. Cf. Peretz's 1888 letter to Sholem Aleichem (Perets, *Ale verk* X–XI: 236).
40. Werses, *Mi-lashon 'el lashon*, 293.
41. Shmeruk writes, the story 'is a grotesque synthesis of 'realism' and popular fantasy' (Shmeruk, *Peretses yiesh-vizye*, 9).
42. Especially interesting in this context is Sokolow's perspective on the interplay between diglossia and Yiddish in the world that he and Peretz both came from (Sokolow, *Perzenlekhkaytn*, 41).
43. Cf. Shmeruk, *Peretses yiesh-vizye*, 9.

44. See n. 42 above
45. See for example Anselmi, *On Self-Translation*, 20–6. Cordingley comments on the complexity of this 'hybrid writing, locating it at the intersection of original creation and authorial rewriting' ('Self-Translation' 253). Oustinoff foregrounds the simultaneity of two processes: self-translation is 'notably *at the same time* translation and writing' (emphasis in the original, cited in Cordingley, 'Self-Translation' 359).
46. *Sippurim be-shir ve-shirim shonim, me'et sheney ba'aley 'asuppot* ('Stories in verse and various poems by two learned authors', Y.L. Peretz and Gabriel Judah Likhtenfeld. N. Shriftgisser, 1877. Cf. Malochi, 'Y.L. Peretz, der hebreisher shrayber'.
47. On Peretz's life and work in Hebrew and Yiddish there is an abundant literature. His movement between Hebrew and Yiddish, however, in particular his praxis of self-translation – as compared with, say, the case of Abramovitsh – has received little scholarly attention. Shmuel Niger touches on the theme of bilingualism in his essay 'Peretz u-khetavav ha-'ivriyim' (1946) and in his Peretz book of 1952. Cf. also Friedlander, *Beyn hawaya le-khavayah*; Adler, 'The psychodynamics of Y.L. Peretz's bilingualism'; Finkin, 'Y.L. Perets's Conversational art in Yiddish and Hebrew'. Shmuel Werses in 1956 noted the biased perceptions of Peretz as a literary figure, and traced the distortions to, among other things, the response to Peretz's social engagement and his publicly stated positions in the struggles between Hebrew and Yiddish (Werses, *Mi-lashon 'el lashon*, 290). For revised perspectives on Peretz's character and work see, for example, Miron, 'I.L. Peretz as the poet of the Jewish age of sensibility', and Holtzman, 'The Harp' by I.L. Peretz and the Controversy over Hebrew Love Poetry', and the literature cited there. On Abramovitshs's shifts between Yiddish and Hebrew see, for example, Sadan, 'Mendele beyn shetey ha-leshonot'; Raskin, 'Mendele in yidish un hebreish'; Perry, 'Thematic and structural shifts in autotranslations by bilingual Hebrew-Yiddish writers'; Miron, 'Sh'Y Abramovitsh beyn yidish le'ivrit'; Frieden, 'Yiddish in Abramovitsh's Literary Revival of Hebrew'.
48. This mode of bilingual literary production is what Miron calls 'integral bilingualism' (Miron, 'Sh'Y Abramovitsh beyn yidish le'ivrit', 58f). Unlike Peretz, Abramovitsh had before 1886 a differentiated bilingual system, in which the author used one or the other language only for set artistic needs and genres (Miron, 'Sh'Y Abramovitsh beyn yidish le'ivrit', 35, 44–7, 51–3). Cf. also Miron, *From Continuity to Contiguity*. On Berdyczewski's call for a differentiated praxis cf. Werses, *Mi-lashon 'el lashon*, 58–102.
49. Cf. Peretz's 'Hebreish un – yidish'; also Miron, 'Literature as a Vehicle for National Renaissance', 27f. On Abramovitsh's different stance cf. Miron, 'Sh'Y Abramovitsh beyn yidish le-'ivrit', 62. On bilingualism in the Yiddish and Hebrew literary systems cf. also Shmuel Niger, *Di tsveyshprakhikayt fun undzer literatur*; Sadan, 'Vegn tsveyshprakhikayt'; Werses, *Mi-lashon 'el lashon*; Miron, *From Continuity to Contiguity*; Brenner, *Lingering Bilingualism*. On Peretz's Yiddish literary language cf. Mark, 'The Language of Y.L. Peretz'; Spivak, 'Perets un die yidishe literarishe shprakh'; Finkin, 'Y.L. Perets's Conversation Art in Yiddish and Hebrew'.
50. We have neither peritexts nor epitexts for the story, nor for the actual translational practice.
51. On the differentiation in Jewish multilingualism between internal and external bilingualism, see Weinreich, *History of the Yiddish Language'*, 247: 'Only within the context of internal bilingualism can we understand the fact that so many writers wrote in both Yiddish and Hebrew ... It can be said that both literatures were essentially created by the same writers, and the readership was to a certain extent the same as well. We may be able to find out what each of the writers contributed from his Hebrew to Yiddish and vice versa' (Weinreich, *History of the Yiddish Language'*, A285). Cf. also Harshav, 'Multilingualism'.
52. Lewin, *Perets*, 17. On Peretz's Hebrew lectures in 'Safah berurah' see Mayzil, *Briv un redes fun Y L. Perets*, 359–61.
53. Sokolow, *Perzenlekhkaytn*, 37. Sokolow's judgment was that Peretz's education and formation in Zamość, and also the impulsive approach of his writing, had as a result that 'he was a great master chiefly in Yiddish', and 'only secondarily a writer and poet in Hebrew' (Sokolow, *Perzenlekhkaytn*, 37).
54. In his profound analysis of rhetorical phenomena in 'A shmues', 'Sichat chasidim', Jordan Finkin reveals Peretz's linguistic and stylistic accomplishments in both languages (Finkin, Y.L. 'Perets's Conversational art in Yiddish and Hebrew' and, in particular, the summarizing accounts on 132f and 146).
55. Peretz, 'vos felt unzer literatur?', *Ale verk* VI–VII, 270–9.
56. Cf. Harshav, *The Meaning of Yiddish*, 143–8.

57. In an article on Abramovitsh's self-translations, Menachem Perry differentiates some of the functions of divergent self-translation: 'because it is possible to treat auto-translation, particularly if it contains considerable shifts, as a re-writing by the author, one should check whether these shifts are really the consequence of the act of transferring from one literature to another, or whether they are changes that occurred in the poetics of the writer himself, changes that are also discernable in his works within the frame of one language' (Perry, 'Thematic and structural elements in autotranslations by bilingual Hebrew-Yiddish writers', 181).
58. The comparison is based on the following editions: for the Hebrew, the publication in *Ketavim* (1900), which is a re-working of the first publication in 1892; the posthumously published *Kol kitvey* contain some dubious changes. For the Yiddish, the scholarly edition of 2021, whose primary text is drawn from the 1901 *Shriftn*.
59. Peretz, *Ketavim*, 183; 'Di toyte shtot', 319.
60. For *nifla'* see, for example, Psalm 139:14.
61. Mark, 'The Language of Y.L. Peretz', 71f, had already noted Peretz's frequent use of this figure.
62. In the Hebrew version there is talk of the *hakhmey 'umot ha-'olam*, the learned of the world who have not included the city in their chronicles and geographical books. In the Yiddish version, we are told that the city is there, though 'the people of the world know nothing of it, and to this day have given it no Gentile name ... It is a Jewish, a truly Jewish city!'
63. Cf. Jeremiah 38:22. For the Hasidic use of *'anshey shelomenu*, see the frequent occurrences in the 1808 *Liqqutey Moharan* by Nachman of Bratslav.
64. Devarim Rabbah 5:15.
65. For 'exits and entrances' cf. Judges 1:24, Ezekiel 43:11; for 'competence in life' see the figurative verbal phrase 'to have care of every need', 2 Samuel 5:2.
66. To investigate the formation of rhythmic figures by accentuation, Peretz's Polish pronunciation of Hebrew should be taken into account; within the scope of this article, this aspect can only be hinted at.
67. Cf. Mark, 'The Language of Y.L. Peretz', 67–72.
68. Peretz, *Ketavim*, 184; 'Di toyte shtot', 320.
69. For the base meaning cf. Proverbs 22:2; for *kivsat ha-rash*, the poor man's lamb, see 2 Samuel 12:1–4.
70. Cf. Psalm 123:1; Midrash Aggadah Gen. 22:4:1; *Khayey moharan* 579:1.
71. The phrase at the time is also attested in Polish and Russian: żyć powietrzem, cf. *powietrze* in Krasnowolski, *Słowniczek frazeologiczny*, 148 (1899/1900); жить воздухом (žyt' vozduchom), cf. 'vozdychat'' in Dal', *Tolkovyj slovar' Dalja* (1863–1866).
72. Peretz uses the expression in this sense also in the nearly contemporary work *Der lets* (The Clown): Peretz, *Ale verk*, VIII, 25.
73. Cf. Sokolow, 'Yosl ha-meshuga', 61.
74. Cf. Yehoyesh's Yiddish translation of Proverbs 12: 9: 'un im felt broyt', 'and he lacks bread', and 12:11, 'der vos baarbet zayn erd, hot broyt tsu zat', 'he who tills his field has his fill of bread'. In Peretz's translation the lexeme *broyt* is the common denominator, presumed as familiar and therefore omitted: 'un dem erd-arbeter ... dem felt avade nisht'.
75. For example, Peretz, *Ketavim* 188f; 'Di toyte shtot', 326f.
76. Peretz, *Ketavim*, 184; 'Di toyte shtot', 320.
77. Peretz uses the phrase as a metaphor for an extremely thin person, with a reference to the rabbinic metaphor for the entire destruction of a human being, cf. Shabat 34a.2: 'he directed his eyes toward him and turned him into a piles of bones'.
78. Peretz, *Ketavim*, 188f; 'Di toyte shtot', 325.
79. Cf. Brittnacher and May, 'Phantastik-Theorien', 191f.
80. Wilpert, *Die deutsche Gespenstergeschichte*, 34.
81. In his comparative analysis of the Hasidic story 'A shmues' ('A Conversation'), *Sichat chasidim* ('A Conversation of Hasids'), Finkin observes: 'Perets' Hebrew works represent a too seldom recognized 'proto-anti-*nusach*', and the Hebrew version of this story develops a more naturalistic style, organized around the rabbinic stratum as the unmarked foundation of the language. This attempt at a more unified tone and language at the same time allows for subtle irony and critique. The proto-anti-*nusach* here is an important early shift away from Abramovitsh, though focused on a different linguistic center of gravity from the later anti-*nusach* writers in Hebrew' (Finkin, 'Y.L. Perets' conversational art in Yiddish and Hebrew', 146).
82. Cf. Mark, 'The Language of Y.L. Peretz', 74f. On the language of the scholar see the chapter 'The language of the way of the SHaS' in Weinreich, *History of the Yiddish Language*, 213–25.

Bibliography

Adler, Ruth. 'The Psychodynamics of Peretz's Bililngualism'. *Yiddish*, vol. 11, no. 1–2, 1998, pp. 119–124.
Anselmi, Simona. *On Self-Translation. An exploration in self-translators' teloi and strategies*. Edizioni Universitarie di Lettere Economia Diritto, 2012.
Berg, Nicolas. *Luftmenschen. Zur Geschichte einer Metapher*. Vandenhoeck & Ruprecht, 2008.
Blank, Inge and Heidi Hein. 'I.L. Peretz' Blick auf das *shtetl*. Die Provinzreise in historischer Perspektive'. *Ashkenas. Zeitschrift für Geschichte und Kultur der Juden*, 11, 2001, pp. 497–513.
Brenner, Naomi. *Lingering Bilingualism. Modern Hebrew and Yiddish literatures in contact*. Syracuse University Press, 2016.
Brittnacher, Hans Richard and Markus May. 'Phantastik-Theorien'. *Phantastik. Ein interdisziplinäres Handbuch*, edited by Hans Richard Brittnacher and Markus May. Metzler, 2013, pp. 189–97.
Caplan, Marc. 'The fragmentation of narrative perspective in Y.L. Peretz's "Bilder fun a Provints-Rayze"'. *Jewish Social Studies*, vol. 14, no. 1, 2007, pp. 63–88.
Cordingley, Anthony. 'Self-translation'. *The Routledge Handbook of Literary Translation*, edited by Kelly Washbourne and Ben Van Wyke. Routledge, 2019, pp. 352–68.
Dal', V. I. *Tolkovyj slovar' Dalja*. 1863–1866. https://dic.academic.ru/contents.nsf/enc2p/. Accessed 31 January 2022.
Dunker, Axel. 'Fantastische Literatur'. *Handbuch der literarischen Gattungen*, edited by Dieter Lamping. Alfred Kröner Verlag, 2009, pp. 240–7.
Finkin, Jordan D. 'Y.L. Perets's conversational art in Yiddish and Hebrew'. Finkin, *A Rhetorical Conversation: Jewish discourse and modern Yiddish literature*. The Pennsylvania State University Press, 2010, pp. 109–46.
Frenschkowski, Marco. 'Phantastik und Religion'. *Phantastik. Ein interdisziplinäres Handbuch*, edited by Hans Richard Brittnacher and Markus May. Metzler, 2013, pp. 553–61.
Frieden, Ken. *Classic Yiddish Fiction: Abramovitsh, Sholem Aleichem, and Peretz*. State University of New York Press, 1995.
Frieden, Ken. 'Yiddish in Abramovitsh's Literary Revival of Hebrew'. *Leket: Yiddish Studies Today*, edited by Marion Aptroot, Efrat Gal-Ed, Roland Gruschka and Simon Neuberg. Düsseldorf University Press, 2012, pp. 173–88.
Friedlander, Yehuda. *Beyn hawayah le-khawayah. Masot al yetsirato ha- ivrit shel Y.L. Perets*. Dvir, 1974.
Harshav, Benjamin. *The Meaning of Yiddish*. University of California Press, 1990.
Harshav, Benjamin. 'Multilingualism'. *The Polyphony of Jewish Culture*. Stanford University Press, 2007.
Holtzman, Avner. 'The Harp by I.L. Peretz and the Controversy over Hebrew Love Poetry'. *The Trilingual Literature of Polish Jews from Different Perspectives. In memory of I.L. Peretz*, edited by Alina Molisak and Shoshana Ronen. Cambridge Scholar Publishing, 2017, pp. 22–43
Johnson, Samuel. *Journey to the Western Isles of Scotland*. 1775. https://www.gutenberg.org/files/2064/2064-h/2064-h.htm. Accessed 23 December 2021.
Krasnowolski, Antoni. *Słowniczek frazeologiczny. Poradnik dla piszących*. N.p., 1899/1900.
Lewin, Gershon, *Perets. A bisl zikhroynes*. Farlag Yehudiyah, 1919.
Mahalel, Adi. *The Radical Years of I.L. Peretz*. Diss., Columbia University, 2014.
Malochi, A.R. 'Y.L. Perets, der hebreisher shrayber'. *Y.L. Perets. In 19tn yorhundert*, edited by Shmuel Rozhansky. Yoysef-lifshits-fond fun der literatur-gezelshaft baym Yivo, 1962, pp. 264–8.
Mark, Yudl. 'The language of Y.L. Peretz'. *YIVO Annual of Jewish Social Science*, 4, 1949, pp. 64–79.
Mayzil, Nakhmen. *Briv un redes fun Y.L. Peretz*. Ikuf-farlag, 1944.
Mayzil, Nakhmen. 'In der statistisher ekspeditsye'. Mayzil, *Y.L. Perets. Zayn leben un shafn*. Ikuf-farlag, 1945, pp. 110–18.
Miron, Dan. 'Literature as a vehicle for a national renaissance: the model of Peretz versus that of Bialik'. *The Enduring Legacy of Yitzkhok Leybush Peretz*, edited by Benny Kraut. Queens College, CUNY, 2005, pp. 30–48.
Miron, Dan. 'Sh'Y Abramovitsh beyn yidish le-'ivrit. 'Omanut ha-neshimah bi'sheney ha-nekhirayim''. *'Itot shel shinnuy – sifruyut yehudiyot ba-tequfah ha-modernit. Qove. ma'amarim li-khevodo shel Dan Miron*, edited by Gidi Nevo und Michal Arbel. Ben Gurion University, 2008, pp. 25–72.

Miron, Dan. *From Continuity to Contiguity: toward a new Jewish literary thinking*. Stanford University Press, 2010.
Miron, Dan. 'I.L. Pretz as the poet of the Jewish age of sensibility'. *The Trilingual Literature of Polish Jews from Different Perspectives. In memory of I.L. Peretz*, edited by Alina Molisak and Shoshana Ronen. Cambridge Scholar Publishing, 2017, pp. 1–19.
Moss, Kenneth B. 'Isaac Leib Peretz'. *Writers in Yiddish*, edited by Joseph Sherman. Gale, 2007, pp. 228–39.
Niger, Samuel. *Di tsveyshprakhikayt fun undzer literatur*. Louis LaMed Foundation for the Advancement of Hebrew and Yiddish Literature, 1941.
Niger, Samuel. 'Perets u-khetavaw ha-'ivriyim', *Ha-tekufah*, 1946, pp. 30–1.
Niger, Samuel. *Y.L. Perets: Zayn lebn, zayn firndike perzenlekhkayt, zayne hebreishe un yidishe shriftn, zayn virkung*. Argentiner opteyl fun alveltlekhn yidishn kultur-kongres, 1952.
Peretz, Yitskhok-Leybush. *Ketavim*, vol. 2.5. Tushiya, 1900.
Peretz, Yitskhok-Leybush. *Shriften*, vol. 4. N.p., 1901.
Peretz, Yitskhok-Leybush. 'Hebreish un – yidish'. (First published in *Yudishe vokhnshrift* 1–2, January 28, 1909). *Di ershte yidishe shprakh–konferents. Barikhtn, dokumentn un opklangen fun der tshernovitser konferents 1908*. N.p., 1931, pp. 286–8.
Peretz, Yitskhok-Leybush. 'Rayzebilder'. Peretz, *Ale verk*, vol. 6, Farlag internatsyonale bibliotek kamp, 1913, pp. 5–124.
Peretz, Yitskhok-Leybush. 'Bilder fun a provits-rayze'. *Di yudishe bibliotek*, edited by Y.-L. Peretz. Vol. 2, Warsaw 1891, pp. 75–141; and later in Peretz, *Ale verk*, vol. II, 'CYCO' Bikher-farlag, 1947, pp. 117–209.
Peretz, Yitskhok-Leybush. *Ale verk*, vol. I–XI, 'CYCO' Bikher-farlag, 1947–8.
Peretz, Yitskhok-Leybush. 'Di toyte shtot'. *Iber der grenets | Crossing the Border. An anthology of modern Yiddish short stories*, edited by Efrat Gal-Ed, Simon Neuberg and Daria Vakhrushova. De Gruyter / Düsseldorf University Press, 2021, pp. 319–28.
Perry, Menachem. 'Thematic and structural shifts in autotranslations by bilingual Hebrew-Yiddish writers. The case of Mendele Mokher Sforim'. *Poetics Today*, 2, 1981, pp. 181–92.
Porombka, Stephan. 'Feuilleton'. *Handbuch der literarischen Gattungen*, edited by Dieter Lamping. Alfred Kröner Verlag, 2009, pp. 264–9.
Raskin, Arn. 'Mendele in yidish un hebreish'. *Sovetish heymland*, 12, 1967, pp. 13–21.
Roskies, David. G. 'I.L. Peretz'. *A Bridge of Longing. The lost art of Yiddish storytelling*. Harvard University Press, 1995, pp. 99–146.
Rozntsvag, Ayzik. *Der radikaler period in peretses shafn. Di yontev-bletlekh*. Melukhe-farlag far di natsyonale miderhaytn in uss'r, 1934.
Sadan, Dov. 'Mendele beyn shetey ha-leshonot'. *Moznayim*, 22, 1966, pp. 111–13.
Sadan, Dov. 'Vegn tsveyshprakhikayt'. Sadan, *Heymishe ksovim. Shrayber, bikher, problemen*, vol. 2, Farlag 'Ha-menorah', 1972, pp. 417–27.
Schmid, Wolf. *Elemente der Narratologie*. De Gruyter, 3rd ed., 2014.
Shatski, Yankev. 'Af die shpurn fun di materialyen fun yan blokhs statistish-ekonomisher ekspeditsye'. *YIVO bleter*, 34, 1950, pp. 296–8.
Shmeruk, Khone, *Peretses yiesh-vizye. Interpretatsye fun Y.L. Peretses bay nakht afn altn mark un kritishe oysgabe fun der drame*. YIVO bibliotek fun YIVO, 1971.
Sokolow, Nachum. 'Yosl ha-meshuga'. *Ha-Tekufah*, 26, 1930, pp. 62–145.
Sokolow, Nachum. *Perzenlekhkaytn*. Tsentral-farband fun Poylishe Yidn in Argentine, 1948.
Spivak, Elye. 'Perets un die yidishe literarishe shprakh'. *Di tsukunft*, 2, 2000, pp. 38–46.
Todorov, Tzvetan. *Einführung in die fantastische Literatur*. Verlag Klaus Wagenbach, 2013.
Weinreich, Max. *History of the Yiddish Language*. Yale University Press, 2008.
Werses, Shmuel 'Al 'omanut ha-sippur shel y. l. perez'. *Molad*, 23, 1966, pp. 290–9.
Werses, Shmuel. *Mi-lashon 'el lashon*. The Magnes Press, 1996.
Wilpert, Gero von. *Die deutsche Gespenstergeschichte. Motiv – Form – Entwicklung*. Kröner, 1994.
Wisse, Ruth R. *I.L. Peretz and the Making of Modern Jewish Culture*. University of Washington Press, 1991.

Part II
**Modes of Intervention:
Translating Dissent and Diversity**

5
How George Eliot Came to Write
Gail Twersky Reimer

Just as she was beginning to publish the fiction for which she is celebrated, George Eliot wrote an essay at the back of her journal titled 'How I Came to Write Fiction'. Her retrospective account opens with a description of her former despair over ever being able to write fiction:

> September 1856 made a new era in my life, for it was then I began to write Fiction. It had always been a vague dream of mine that some time or other I might write a novel, and my shadowy conception of what the novel was to be, varied, of course, from one epoch of my life to another. But I never went farther towards the actual writing of the novel than an introductory chapter describing a Staffordshire village and the life of the neighbouring farm houses, and as the years passed on I lost any hope that I should ever be able to write a novel, just as I desponded about everything else in my future life.[1]

As Eliot moves on to the account of how she did come to write fiction, a significant shift occurs. With a flurry of sentences beginning with he – 'He was struck with it as a bit of concrete description'; 'He began to think that I might as well try, some time, what I could do with fiction'; 'He began to say very positively, "You must try and write a story"' – George Henry Lewes takes centre stage as the prince who rescued the despairing maiden from her unhappiness and creative paralysis, believed in her potential to realize her dream, encouraged her to try her hand at fiction, and responded enthusiastically to her efforts.

With the perspective of an additional ten years, Eliot, in a letter to an American admirer and aspiring writer, tells a rather different story of how she came to write fiction. Reflecting on her own modest beginnings as a writer, she links her work as a writer of fiction to writing of another sort with which she began her professional writing career.

> I did not believe that I could do anything fine, and I did not choose to do anything of that mediocre sort which I despised when it was done by others. I began, however, by a sort of writing which had no great glory belonging to it, but which I felt certain I could do faithfully and well. This resolve to work at what did not gratify my ambition, and to care only that I worked faithfully, was equivalent to the old phrase – using the means of grace. Not long after that I wrote fiction … [2]

With her invocation of the Methodist concept of 'using the means of grace' to achieve grace, Eliot suggests that beginning with a kind of writing that she felt able to do 'faithfully and well' led to her believing that she could write something fine and, by implication, to her eventual willingness to try her hand at fiction. While others have claimed that the writing to which she refers here is her journalism,[3] the repetition of the word 'faithfully', a key term in the discourse of translation, is a powerful, if not definitive, indicator that she is referring to the writing with which she actually began – translation.

Most readers of Eliot's novels have no idea that more than a decade before adopting the pen name George Eliot and first publishing the fictional work that would make her famous, Marian Evans published her first book. Her translation of Strauss' *The Life of Jesus, Critically Examined* (*Das Leben Jesu*), like many a translation, was published anonymously. Several years later, she produced a second work of translation, Feuerbach's *Essence of Christianity* (*Wesen des Christenthums*). Advertisements for the book announced 'a new work by the Translator of Strauss' *Life of Jesus*' and the translation was published with her name on the title page. Yet a third work of translation was completed before Marian Evans made her first foray into fiction writing. Because of a dispute between George Henry Lewes and the publisher, her translation of Spinoza's *Ethics*, which would have been the first English translation of Spinoza's work, was not published in her lifetime and remained unpublished for more than a century until its official publication by Princeton University Press in 2020.

Forty years ago, as I embarked on what I believed would be a lifelong career of teaching and scholarship, I was hastily completing a dissertation focused on the opening and concluding chapters of George Eliot's artistic career. As my professional career evolved in unanticipated ways, I never found the time to further develop my thesis and what at the time was the radical claim that Eliot's artistic career begins with these translations and not, as was conventionally understood, with her first fictional work, *Scenes of Clerical Life*.

Until recently, existing scholarship on the translations focused exclusively on their significance to Eliot's intellectual development. My interest, as I attempted to define the arc of Eliot's artistic career, was in shifting the focus from the ideas of Strauss, Feuerbach and Spinoza to Eliot's practice of translation and evolving sense of herself as an author translating and (re)writing their works for an English public. To emphasize the continuity between translation and fiction writing, I used the name by which she is best known to refer to translator, essayist and novelist and will continue that practice here.

In this chapter I return to some of my long-ago thoughts about Eliot the translator, exploring them anew with the benefit of several decades of work in translation studies, a discipline that did not exist when I was writing my dissertation. My focus here will be on her translation of Strauss' *Life of Jesus*, the first of her published works; my goal to demonstrate that, far from being what Cross first described as the yoke that galled her neck,[4] *Life of Jesus* was the stage on which Eliot made her debut and launched her career as a writer. The letters she wrote while working on her translation, filled as they are with anguish, exhaustion and suffering, also reveal a young woman exercising her creativity as she translates and finding her authority and authorial voice as she writes. By foregrounding this aspect of her letters, I hope to correct the pervasive overemphasis on the 'soul stupefying labor' of translating Strauss and inspire new appreciation for this opening chapter of Eliot's writing life.

In their introductory essay to the second edition of *The Cambridge Companion to George Eliot* (2019), the editors explain that

> the twenty-first century George Eliot emerges from approaches to her novels that build on the critical movements and methodologies of the twentieth century and also from attention to works that tended to be neglected in the past, including her journalism; poetry; short fiction; and her last, generically anomalous book, *Impressions of Theophrastus Such*.[5]

Noticeably absent from this list are her translations; there is no chapter on Eliot (or Marian Evans) and translation.

The *Companion* does not ignore Eliot's translations altogether. Suzy Anger's chapter on George Eliot and philosophy includes a brief two-page section titled 'early readings and translations'[6] and Barry Qualls, in his chapter on George Eliot and religion, insists on the importance of 'understanding how she read Strauss and Feuerbach'.[7] For both scholars it is Eliot's *reading* of Strauss and Feuerbach rather than her *translating* of their works that matters, how the ideas of Strauss and Feuerbach get transmuted into her novels rather than how translating their ideas faithfully and well empowered her as a writer.

Resistance to considering Eliot's translations as the first works in her artistic oeuvre is grounded in a rigid distinction between primary and secondary forms of writing that, as Susan Bassnett explains in *Translation Studies*, took hold in the mid-nineteenth century. 'In the early nineteenth century translation was still regarded as a serious and useful method for helping a writer explore and shape his own native style, much as it had been for centuries.' Translation gradually came to be seen as a secondary activity, 'a mechanical rather than a creative process, within the competence of anyone with a basic grounding in language other than their own; in short as a low status occupation'.[8]

At times, as when in a letter written while translating Strauss, Eliot apologizes for getting agitated over 'a thing in itself so trifling as a translation',[9] or in her essay on translation when she declares that 'a good translator is infinitely below the man who produces *good* original works',[10] it appears that she, too, holds this view of translation as derivative. Elsewhere in this same essay, however, she is scornful of the 'young ladies and some middle-aged gentlemen who consider a very imperfect acquaintance with their own language and an anticipatory acquaintance with the foreign language, quite a sufficient equipment for the office of translator'.[11] Her clear rejection of translation as a dilettante pursuit aligns with the essay's emphasis on the difficulty of the translator's task and the skills, as well as moral qualities, good translating requires.

By the time she wrote 'Translation and Translators' Eliot had completed her translations of works by Strauss, Feuerbach and Spinoza and, as Pinney notes in his introduction to the essay, 'could speak with special authority on the subject'.[12] Her essay offers a host of clues to how she thought about her own practice as a translator, as well as important insights into her ideas about translation and the creativity and responsibility involved in interpreting another man's mind.

Acknowledging the seemingly random pairing of a translation of Kant's *Critique of Pure Reason* (*Kritik der reinen Vernunft*) with a miscellaneous collection of translations of German lyrics, Eliot explains that the two volumes 'happen to be the specimens of translation most recently presented to our notice'. The odd pairing, however, enables her to suggest that discussion of translations could benefit from a focus on the actual translations, as distinct from the content of the original works: 'We are concerning ourselves here simply with translation – not at all with Kant's philosophy or with German lyrics considered in themselves.'[13]

At the same time, Eliot recognizes that both the genre and quality of the original work invariably affect what is demanded of the translator:

> The power required in the translation varies with the power exhibited in the original work: very modest qualifications will suffice to enable a person to translate a book of ordinary travels, or a slight novel, while a work of reasoning or science can be adequately rendered only by means of what is at present exceptional faculty and exceptional knowledge. Among books of this latter kind, Kant's Critique of Pure Reason is perhaps the very hardest nut – the peachstone – for a translator to crack so as to lay open the entire uninjured kernel of meaning.[14]

Philosophical texts, not insignificantly the kind of texts that she had spent the previous five years translating and by which she was known following the translation of Feuerbach's *The Essence of Christianity*, require translators of exceptional talent and extraordinary knowledge, translators able 'to crack' the hard 'nut' that is the source text, 'so as to lay open the entire uninjured kernel of meaning'. With this metaphorical description of the translator's task, Eliot alludes to the creativity of the translator who, in order to lay open the inviolate (uninjured) meaning of the text, must violate (crack open) the text on which she is working. The translation she produces must convey the meaning of the original in words and sentences that are markedly different from those through which meaning was originally conveyed. The subjective and creative element in this critical distinction is alluded to later in the essay when, remarking on Schlegel's translation of Shakespeare, Eliot first draws on the fine arts, comparing the moments of 'faithful adherence to the original' to 'a fine engraving of a favourite picture' and then reinforces with a musical analogy, noting that sometimes Schlegel's German is as good as Shakespeare's English – 'the same music played on another but as good an instrument'.[15]

The successful translator must have precisely what the young ladies and middle-aged gentlemen mentioned earlier in the essay lack – an exceptional knowledge and understanding of both the author's language and her own. Knowledge of the author's language is not simply a matter of fluency. As becomes clear in Eliot's praise of Meiklejohn's translation of Kant's *Critique of Pure Reason,* it entails knowing the source language so well that one understands the intentions behind an author's particular linguistic choices, what Eliot calls 'a real mastery' of the author. Choosing the words in one's own language that will make the author's 'meaning accessible to English readers', the second reason for her praise of Meiklejohn's translation is what transforms a translation into a work of authorship in its own right, and potentially the work of genius.

Eliot concludes her essay on translation by summarily mentioning what she calls 'the moral qualities' demanded of the translator. 'We had meant to say something of the moral qualities especially demanded of the translator – the patience, the rigid fidelity, and the sense of responsibility in interpreting another man's mind. But we have gossiped on this subject long enough.'[16] This puzzling ending to a relatively short essay is often read as indicative of Eliot's ambivalence about translation.[17] An alternative reading is to see it as self-referential, a nod in the direction of the many letters she wrote while translating, letters in which she discusses her struggles to be patient, her nuanced understanding of fidelity and her agreements and disagreements with the men whose work she was translating. Though far from a coherent theory of translation, *Translation and Translators*, when read in conjunction with these letters, reveals Eliot's recognition of the importance of the translator's role as interpreter, mediator and author and, by extension, of her own importance as the translator of major cultural works.

The story of how Eliot, at age twenty-four, came to undertake the first of her published translations, warrants retelling here. In brief, upon moving to the outskirts of Coventry with her father in 1841, Eliot was introduced to Charles and Cara Bray and their circle of freethinking Unitarians, which included Cara's sister Sara Hennell and her brother Charles Hennell. A second edition of Charles Hennell's *Inquiry Concerning the Origin of Christianity* had just been published. In his new preface Hennell wrote about his belated discovery of Strauss' *Das Leben Jesu*. Shortly after the publication of the book, Joseph Parkes told Hennell of his interest in subsidizing a translation of *Das Leben Jesu* into English. Hennell first turned to his sister Sarah who, by her own account, 'told him it was quite beyond me both for its labour and difficulty'. He then asked Rufa Brabant, the woman he wished to marry (and would soon marry), to undertake the translation. According to Sara, Rufa 'at once took it up' and had translated over 200 pages when, upon her marriage to Charles, she decided she could no longer continue translating and suggested that Eliot take over the translation.[18]

The path by which Eliot came to be the translator of *Life of Jesus* raises interesting questions about Eliot's motivations for, and feelings about, becoming Strauss' translator.[19] I have deliberately stripped this oft-told story down to only the verifiable facts, eliminating the assumptions and biases that have constrained a full consideration of her motives.

Did Eliot, as Ruby Redinger suggests, experience herself as little more than a 'substitute – translator', merely completing what Rufa began,[20] or did she embrace the opportunity to become the English voice of the bold and controversial Strauss? Was she seeking, as Redinger also argues, to please Charles Hennell, or did she see the translation as a path to asserting herself as his intellectual peer? Was she interested in hiding behind Strauss as she continued to pursue the inquiries that had led to her rejection of Christian doctrine and refusal to go to church with her father or, having only recently suffered the stresses of being an outcast herself, did she feel an affinity with the author of *Das Leben Jesu*, whose quest for truth cost him his university position and academic career?

An additional piece of the story of Eliot's relationship with the Brays and Hennells sheds important light on these questions. As noted above, Eliot met the Brays and Hennells shortly after the publication of the second edition of Hennell's *Inquiry*, the one in which Hennell pays homage to Strauss. Whether the Brays introduced Eliot to Charles' *Inquiry* or she read it in anticipation of meeting the Brays is a matter of controversy but of little consequence. What matters is that within days of her first visit to the Brays' home, we find Eliot writing to her Evangelical teacher Maria Lewis that her

> whole soul has been engrossed in the most interesting of all enquiries for the last few days, and to what result my thoughts may lead I know not – possibly to one that will startle you, but my only desire is to know the truth, my only fear to cling to error.[21]

The primary result to which her thoughts led is among the best known incidents of Eliot's biography – her refusal to go to church with her father and the consequent rift with her family, which Eliot dubbed her 'Holy War'. A secondary result, rarely discussed as such because it happened several years later, was her decision to translate Strauss' *Das Leben Jesu*, a decision made just two months after she wrote Sara Hennell the unusually depersonalized and abstract letter that effectively brings her Holy War to a close. Written to Sara just weeks before Charles Hennell's marriage to Rufa Brabant, the precipitating event for Eliot becoming Strauss' translator, the letter ends by proposing a new strategy for pursuing her determination 'to know the truth':

> But it may be said how are we to do anything toward the advancement of mankind? Are we to go on cherishing superstitions out of a fear that seems inconsistent with any faith in a Supreme Being?

> ... We cannot fight and struggle enough for freedom of enquiry ... Those who can write, let them do it as boldly as they like and let no one hesitate at proper seasons to make a full confession (far better than *profession*).[22]

In her illuminating discussion of this letter, Rosemarie Bodenheimer calls attention to the 'impersonal thinking of the letter', 'the appearance of the George Eliot "we"', and Eliot's 'presentation of her experience as one in a common category'. She further observes that 'the tremendous self-distancing in this lofty perspective becomes truly baffling ... in sentences that make it grammatically impossible to know whether Mary Ann is referring to her own experience or to that of the people around her'.[23] The same confusion Bodenheimer notices in Eliot's use of 'we' occurs when she uses 'those', the demonstrative in the sentence in which she expresses admiration for writers who use their talents in pursuit of truth and suggestively signals the vocation of writer that she will soon embrace: 'We cannot fight and struggle enough for freedom of enquiry ... Those who can write, let them do it as boldly as they like.'

One month after she wrote this letter, we find Eliot sharing samples of her translation of Strauss with Sara. I am not suggesting that Eliot knew, expected or even hoped that Rufa would turn the Strauss translation over to her. But it seems that when Sara proposed to Eliot that she become Strauss' translator, Eliot already was poised, possibly even determined, to begin her career as a writer.

Sara's proposal also quite likely triggered recall of Charles' lengthy discussion of Strauss in the preface to the second edition of the *Inquiry*. Noting that since the book's initial publication he has made 'further acquaintance with modern criticism on the subject', Hennell singled out the work of Strauss' *Das Leben Jesu*:

> Since the first edition of this work was published the writer has read the celebrated Leben Jesu of Dr. Strauss, which contains a most minute and searching analysis of the various stories, anecdotes and sayings which mainly make up the Gospels; and especially a careful weighing of the probable proportion of reality and fiction in each.

The broader scope of his own work, Hennell explains, prevented him from pursuing the deep and thorough analysis of the four gospels to be found in Strauss:

> In only a few cases, and by way of example, the subject is pursued at some length; in others, for the sake of brevity, conclusions are given

without arguments. The reader, who may feel that more satisfaction is justly demanded on this head, will share the pleasure which the writer felt on becoming acquainted with the elaborate and erudite work referred to. There the most extensive theological reading is brought to bear on the subject; and this, combined with unwearied patience, and unvarying philosophical candour, leaves a strong conviction that the Gospels have been examined by minds the most competent as well as willing to give them a full and fair trial.[24]

When offered the opportunity to translate a work that provides the arguments for the conclusions presented in her brother's signature work, Sara declined, deeming the effort too difficult and demanding. Rufa took it on, but then backed out because it interfered with her new life as a wife. Yet Eliot undertakes the project without hesitation, undaunted by its difficulty or the time Strauss' 'elaborate and erudite work' would demand. Why?

Though an enthusiastic reader of German texts and an aspiring translator who had, a short while earlier, begun to translate *Mémoire en Faveur de la Liberté des Cultes* by the Swiss Protestant theologian Vinet, and dropped that venture to translate Spinoza's *Tractatus Theologico-politicus.*, Eliot had no significant experience translating a German text, let alone a text full of complex German theological terminology. Yet, when offered the opportunity, she seemed eager to be Strauss' translator and was sending Sara specimens of her translation even before Sara had informed Rufa that Eliot would be taking over the translation.

Basil Willey, I would argue, misses the point when he claims that 'Strauss with all his vastly greater learning and philosophical depth, could do little for her that Hennell had not already done'.[25] It was precisely Strauss' greater learning and philosophical depth and what Willey later describes as 'the encyclopedic range' of his book's 'erudition' and 'philosophic profundity of its basis' that would have attracted Eliot to Strauss. Work on the Strauss translation was an opportunity for her to fully explore the arguments behind Hennell's conclusions in the *Inquiry* that had so profound an influence on her beliefs and so devastating an effect on her relations with her father. It would allow her, as Barry Qualls writes, to put 'into English circulation more sophisticated and developed ideas that mirrored and expanded what she had discovered in Hennell'.[26] Moreover, given the real mastery of the author demanded of a translator, Strauss' erudition would effectively become her erudition, securing for her a place among Coventry's small circle of freethinkers as more than Hennell's equal. And with the publication of her translation, Eliot could claim a place for herself beyond that familiar circle, at the side of

Coleridge and Carlyle, the other bold writers/translators active in the introduction of German Higher Criticism to the English public.[27]

For Eliot, these aspirations were, initially, unspeakable, for they would have betrayed the immensity of the ambition she tried to conceal by hiding behind utterances about the 'triviality of translation'. Years later, however, in a letter to Cara Bray recalling her 'dreams' when she was 'four or five and twenty', the age in which she began translating Strauss, she wrote – 'I thought then, how happy fame would make me!'[28]

If Eliot had anticipated experiencing nothing other than the pleasure Charles Hennell described feeling on becoming acquainted with Strauss' elaborate and erudite work, she was undoubtedly severely disappointed. The labour of translating Strauss' 1,400 pages demanded far more than a passing acquaintance. That said, I believe too much has been made of Eliot's Strauss sickness.[29]

In a letter to Sara, written four months into her work translating, Eliot attributes her discouragement to the headaches that slow her down and impede her ability to work on the translation. 'Thank you for the encouragement you sent me – I only need it when my head is weak and I am unable to do much. Then I sicken at the idea of having Strauss in my head and on my hands for a lustrum, instead of saying goodbye to him in a year.' As the letter continues, Eliot makes clear that this is only one aspect of her experience and that translating Strauss continues to engage her, even if she is no longer sure that translation is the kind of writing she wishes to pursue in the future. 'When I can work fast, I am never weary, nor do I regret either that the work has been begun or that I have undertaken it. I am only inclined to vow that I will never translate again if I live to correct the sheets of Strauss.'[30] Of course she does translate, again and again, completing her translation of Spinoza's *Ethics* in the same year she began the first of her *Scenes of Clerical Life*.

The frequently referenced 'Strauss sickness' is reported by Cara Bray in a letter written to Sara as Eliot was reading proofs. 'She said she was Strauss sick – it made her ill dissecting the beautiful story of the crucifixion and only the sight of her Christ image and picture made her endure it. Moreover as her work advances nearer its public appearance, she grows dreadfully nervous.' Cara picks up on Eliot's anxiety about how her translation will be received, but fails to appreciate its possible connection to her 'Strauss-sickness'. As she concludes her letter, however, Cara acknowledges what too many of the critics who reference this letter ignore, which is that Eliot's Strauss sickness was not the whole of her experience translating Strauss. 'Nevertheless she looks happy and satisfied at times with her work.'[31]

Eliot certainly had her low moments, moments in which she experienced her work on the translation as 'soul stupefying labor'[32] or grew tired of her 'own garb for Strauss' thoughts'.[33] Writing for Eliot, as Bodenheimer has so eloquently demonstrated, was, from the beginning of her writing life to its end, a constant source of pain and melancholy. When understood in this context, the headaches and depression that she frequently writes about while translating Strauss set the pattern for the suffering that she experiences with each writing project she undertakes and reveal an ongoing need to conceal her ambition. 'There is little doubt about George Eliot's actual susceptibility to depression', writes Bodenheimer. 'Yet her willingness to broadcast primarily that aspect of her creativity suggests how necessary it was to her to be seen as a sufferer rather than as one of the ambitious, authoritative narrators of her book.'[34] The books Bodenheimer has in mind are the novels, but the dynamic she describes can readily be traced back to the letters Eliot wrote while working on her translation of a book whose German narrator is unquestionably ambitious and authoritative.

Significantly, the frustrations and complaints Eliot expresses while working on Strauss are often related to her worries as to whether her work will be published. Within weeks of beginning to translate Strauss, Eliot writes to Sara asking for the 'particulars' of publication, particulars that would make little difference to her had she engaged in translating Strauss solely for her own intellectual benefit. The questions she asks are those of a writer determined to see her work out in the world and equally determined to have authorial control over the work. Her first concern is with the funding that will guarantee the translation's publication. Who, she asks, 'are the parties that will find the funds'.[35] A month later, her apprehension over the possibility that the work may never see the light of day has become a source of real distress: 'I begin utterly to despair that Strauss will ever be published ... I have no confidence in Mr. Parkes and shall not be surprised if he fails in his engagement altogether.'[36]

At this early stage in the project, Eliot is also asking whether she will have final say over what gets printed, 'whether the manuscripts are to be put in the hands of any one when complete, or whether they are to go directly from me to the publisher?'[37]

The oft-quoted 'soul stupefying labor' appears in a letter that begins with yet another writerly concern that would remain a central preoccupation of Eliot's throughout her writing career: audience. 'Glad I am that someone can enjoy Strauss', she writes Sara after close to a year and half of translating Strauss. 'The million certainly will not, and I have ceased to sit down to him with relish.' Why she no longer finds translating Strauss enjoyable is not really explained, though the sentence links it to fears that the work will not find an audience. Similarly, the sentence that follows connects her soul-stupefying labour to the absence of any tangible proof that her work will ever reach the British public for whom she is writing. 'I should work much better if I had any proof sheets coming in to assure me that my soul-stupefying labor is not in vain.'[38]

When Eliot took charge of the Strauss translation, Sara continued, as she would later acknowledge, quite unnecessarily, in the role she had undertaken with Rufa, – 'to scrupulously revise her manuscript by comparing it with the original and 'as a general security against inaccuracy'.[39] A good deal of Eliot's correspondence with Sara during the years in which she is at work on the Strauss translation is focused on the corrections, revisions and emendations that Sara makes. Eliot finds most of these obvious and inconsequential matters of taste rather than of fidelity, but still does not hesitate to challenge Sara:

> I do not mind about any alterations that will satisfy your taste, though I am at a loss to know the rationale for some. According to dictionaries and grammars, '*as though*' is good gentlemanly English as well as '*as if*', and if you heard more evangelical sermons, dear, you would find that it is invariably 1stly, 2dly,3dly,4thly and lastly, not *finally* .... But about all these matters I am perfectly indifferent and quite glad to make your pencil marks ink.[40]

Yet two weeks after she claimed indifference to these matters, Eliot had still not let go of the matter. Though willing to accede to Sara's insignificant changes, she would not silence her own voice or conviction that her choices were the better ones. 'Let me assure you for the last time', she writes Sara, 'that I never stickle for a word or a phrase unless it expresses an idea that cannot be equally well conveyed by another. I like *as if* quite as well as *as though* and *lastly* as well as *finally* – indeed rather better.'[41]

An even more confident voice takes over when meaning, the fidelity of translation, is at stake. At times, Eliot's confidence is expressed with self-deprecating humour about a phrase of her choosing:

> I think on the whole, that 'the Lord's Supper' is better than 'the Sacrament'. My objection to it was the awkwardness of saying 'Jesus instituted the Lord's Supper'. It reminded me of who was the father of Zebedee's Children? But I think the grand consideration that there are many sacraments – 7 Romish and 2 Anglican – must carry the day against *the* Sacrament.[42]

At other times, she expresses her disagreement far more emphatically as in the rather long disquisition on when the Passover meal was eaten that begins with 'I have *no doubt* that Paschaabend must be translated the *evening* of the Passover, and I think if you look at the passage again you will see that it would make nonsense of it to translate *eve* of the passover'.

A curious postscript at the end of the letter offers further insight into Eliot's sense of her competence as an interpreter and integrity as a translator. 'Do not ask anybody about the meaning of Paschaabend', she adds, 'because the nature of the subject is the only evidence.'[43]

Eliot is no less confident in her rejection of revisions made by Charles than she is with those made by Sara:

> Please to tell Mr. Hennell that 'habits of thought' is not a translation of the word *partikularismus*. This does not mean national idiosyncrasy, but is a word which characterizes that idiosyncrasy. If he decidedly objects to *particularism* ask him to be so good as substitute exclusiveness though there is a shade of meaning in particularism which even that does not express. It was because the word could only be translated by circumlocution that I ventured to anglicize it.[44]

Confident in her knowledge of German as well as in her grasp of Strauss' intentions, Eliot understands that rigid fidelity often calls for flexibility and creativity. She understands that German words like *partikularismus* encapsulate complex ideas that do not translate simply into English and defends her inclination to anglicize them. On other occasions, as she explains to Sara, she translates by circumlocution or periphrasis:

> It will not do to translate the words always the same though that might seem the proper plan at first. For sometimes the introduction of them is of real and obvious use and has an influence on the sense, and at other times they are a mere pleonasm or else could not be strictly represented in English without committing an arrant Germanism. I could not say how I would translate them unless I saw the passage in which they occur.[45]

Though effusive in her gratitude to Sara for her help and encouragement, Eliot clearly has the more sophisticated understanding of translation. She regularly highlights and even delights in her own creative rewriting of Strauss' text, from additions she inserted to make a reference clear to paraphrases made to 'eke out [Strauss'] metaphor'. Reacting to one of the first reviews of her translation written by Charles Wicksteed, Eliot wrote Sara: 'Is it not droll that Wicksteed should have chosen one of my interpolations or rather paraphrases to dilate on? The expression "granite", applied to the sayings of Jesus is nowhere used in Strauss, but is an impudent addition of mine to eke out his metaphor.'[46]

Another kind of confidence expresses itself in Eliot's willingness to doubt and disagree with Strauss, to express displeasure or disinterest in one or another part of his work.[47] Her periodic shifts from interpreter to critic create a space in which she can distinguish between the author of *The Life of Jesus* and the author of *Das Leben Jesu*. When she writes Sara that the 'last few sections ... are not Strauss' best thoughts, nor are they put into his translator's best language',[48] Eliot is not simply criticizing Strauss; she is underlining the uniqueness of *his* thoughts and of *her* language, quietly asserting her independence as a writer.

Eliot's fullest declaration of independence and ownership of the text of Strauss in English is made in a letter written to Sara on the eve of publication, just days after she has approved the translation's title page from which her name is absent: 'I do really like reading our Strauss – he is so klar und ideenvoll but I do not know *one* person who is likely to read the book through, do you?'[49] In context, it is clear that the Strauss she is enjoying reading is her translation of Strauss, the book about to be published, the book she worries no one will read all the way through. It should not come as a surprise that her boldest statement of owning her work is made in the plural rather than the singular. To speak of 'my Strauss', would betray the ambition that I have suggested initially drew her to translating Strauss. It can be kept under wraps by substituting 'our' for 'my'. More significantly, even as she signals her authorship of *Life of Jesus*, she resists erasing the cultural context of the original *Das Leben Jesu* and intentionally slips into German to describe her English translation, a work that she imagined from the start as an agent for cultural change. 'She was aware of Strauss' immense importance for the progress of historical research', Rosemary Ashton writes, 'and was wise enough to see that if German transcendental philosophy and its heirs had some shortcomings, what was nonetheless needed in England was a fair welcome to such works as Strauss', which were far in advance of British notions'.[50]

George Eliot's first translation was published anonymously, just as her first works of fiction would be. But it did not take long for her to be known as the translator of Strauss. Her publisher Chapman thought that advertising her next published work – a translation of Feuerbach's *Wesen des Christentums* as a new work by the translator of Strauss' *Life of Jesus* – was sufficiently persuasive advance publicity for the book. And when the *Essence of Christianity* was published with her name (Marian Evans) on the title page, Eliot, who by then was well known for her essays, reviews and criticism, became visible as the author of the celebrated and increasingly influential English translation of Strauss, the first work of her writing life.

Now that scholars are making a case for her letters, her journals and her journalism as significant parts of her writing career, perhaps we can finally acknowledge that her translations are as well. As Eliot herself suggested in the letter quoted at the start of this essay, translation is where she began. Her desire to write something of lasting value led her to embrace the opportunity to translate Strauss. Indeed, George Eliot's translation of *Das Leben Jesu* remains the standard translation to this day. That should be reason enough for us to re-evaluate the importance of her translation work and reassess its place in her artistic career. Though translating Strauss was difficult and draining work, it was considerably more than 'a long dry process of drudgery and disenchantment'.[51] When we look beyond the complaints and distress expressed in the letters she wrote while translating Strauss, we discover a translator engaged with many of the concerns central to contemporary discourse on translation and a writer painfully but determinedly struggling, as she would throughout her artistic career, to write faithfully and well.

Notes

1. 'How I came to write fiction', Haight, *The George Eliot Letters, II*, 406.
2. Haight, *The George Eliot Letters VIII*, 383–4.
3. See Dillane, 'Marian Evans's journalism', 37.
4. Cross, *George Eliot's Life*, 110.
5. Henry and Levine, 'Introduction: George Eliot and the art of realism', 16.
6. Anger, 'George Eliot and philosophy', 216–18.
7. Qualls, 'George Eliot and religion', 198.
8. Bassnett, *Translation Studies*, 2–3.
9. Haight, *The George Eliot Letters I*, 191.
10. 'Translation and translators', Pinney, *Essays of George Eliot*, 211.
11. Pinney, *Essays of George Eliot*, 208.
12. Pinney, *Essays of George Eliot*, 207.
13. Pinney, *Essays of George Eliot*, 209.
14. Pinney, *Essays of George Eliot*, 208.
15. Pinney, *Essays of George Eliot*, 210.
16. Pinney, *Essays of George Eliot*, 211.
17. See, for example, Stark, 'Marian Evans, the translator', 136–7.
18. Haight, *The George Eliot Letters I*, 171.
19. For a related but different set of questions, posed 'in order to evaluate Marian Evans' involvement in the translation' see Stark, 'Marian Evans, the translator', 123.
20. Redinger, *George Eliot The Emergent Self*, 132.
21. Haight, *The George Eliot Letters I*, 120.
22. Haight, *The George Eliot Letters I*, 163

23. Bodenheimer, *The Real Life of Marian Evans*, 75.
24. Hennell, *An Inquiry Concerning the Origin of Christianity*, xi.
25. Willey, *Nineteenth Century Studies: Coleridge to Matthew Arnold*, 220
26. Qualls, 'George Eliot and religion', 197.
27. See Ashton, *The German Idea*, 147–55. For a general discussion of the authority in the public sphere that Eliot and other Victorian women gained by translating see Scholl's introduction in Scholl, *Translation, Authorship and the Victorian Professional Woman*, 1–8.
28. Haight, *George Eliot Letters III*, 170.
29. Avrom Fleishman, in *George Eliot's Intellectual Life*, also notes the critical emphasis on Eliot's Strauss-sickness and neglect of letters that express a broader range of feelings about translating and attitudes towards Strauss. *George Eliot's Intellectual Life*, 35–40.
30. Haight, *George Eliot Letters I*, 176.
31. Haight, *George Eliot Letters I*, 206.
32. Haight, *George Eliot Letters I*, 185.
33. Haight, *George Eliot Letters I*, 182.
34. Bodenheimer, *The Real Life of Marian Evans*, 164.
35. Haight, *George Eliot Letters I*, 172
36. Haight, *George Eliot Letters I*, 191
37. Haight, *George Eliot Letters I*, 172. Since the translation was originally commissioned from Charles Hennel, the proofs, it seems, were to be sent directly to him for correction and revision before going to the publisher. A year and a half of translating, and a growing sense of her own integrity as a translator, led Eliot to oppose this arrangement, as Sara informed her sister-in-law Rufa: 'She wishes decidedly to have the correcting of her own proofs and revises herself.' See Haight, *George Eliot Letters I*, 198.
38. Haight, *George Eliot Letters I*, 185.
39. Haight, *George Eliot Letters I*, 171.
40. Haight, *George Eliot Letters I*, 185.
41. Haight, *George Eliot Letters I*, 189.
42. Haight, *George Eliot Letters I*, 209.
43. Haight, *George Eliot Letters I*, 213–14.
44. Haight, *George Eliot Letters I*, 201
45. Haight, *George Eliot Letters I*, 198–9.
46. Haight, *George Eliot Letters I*, 227.
47. 'I am never pained when I think Strauss right – but in many cases I think him wrong, as every man must be in working out in detail an idea which has general truth, but is only one element in a perfect theory, not a perfect theory in itself'. *George Eliot Letters I*: 203.
48. Haight, *George Eliot Letters I*, 187.
49. Haight, *George Eliot Letters I*, 218.
50. Ashton, *The German Idea*, 154.
51. Davis, *The Transferred Life of George Eliot*, 89. In his otherwise uniquely sensitive reading of Eliot's writing life, Davis falls into all the old cliches when writing about Eliot's translation of Strauss – 'It was completed dutifully by rote;' 'She toiled away at a literal translation', it became ' "soul-stupefying labour" that gave her headaches and worse'.

Bibliography

Anger, Suzy. 'George Eliot and philosophy'. *The Cambridge Companion to George Eliot, Second Edition*, edited by George Levine and Nancy Henry. Cambridge University Press, 2019, pp. 215–35.

Ashton, Rosemary. *The German Idea: four English writers and the reception of German thought 1800–1860*. Cambridge University Press, 1980.

Bassnett, Susan. 'Preface to the third edition'. *Translation Studies*. Routledge, 2004.

Bodenheimer, Rosemarie. *The Real Life of Mary Ann Evans: George Eliot, her letters and fiction*. Cornell University Press, 1994.

Cross, John Walter, editor. *George Eliot's Life as Related in Her Letters and Journals*, 3 vols. Harper & Brothers, 1885.

Davis, Philip. *The Transferred Life of George Eliot*. Oxford University Press, 2017.
Dillane, Fionnuala. 'Marian Evans's journalism'. *The Cambridge Companion to George Eliot, Second Edition*, edited by George Levine and Nancy Henry. Cambridge University Press, 2019, pp. 37–56.
Feuerbach, Ludwig. *The Essence of Christianity*, translated by George Eliot. Harper and Bros., 1957.
Haight, Gordon S., editor. *The George Eliot Letters, 9 vols*. Yale University Press, 1954–78.
Hennell, Charles. *An Inquiry Concerning the Origin of Christianity, Second Edition*. T. Allman, 1841.
Levine, George and Nancy Henry. 'Introduction'. *The Cambridge Companion to George Eliot, Second Edition*, edited by George Levine and Nancy Henry. Cambridge University Press, 2019, pp. 1–19.
Pinney, Thomas, editor. *Essays of George Eliot*. Columbia University Press, 1963.
Qualls, Barry V. 'George Eliot and religion'. *The Cambridge Companion to George Eliot, Second Edition*, edited by George Levine and Nancy Henry. Cambridge University Press, 2019, pp. 195–214.
Redinger, Ruby V. *George Eliot: the emergent self*. The Bodley Head, 1976.
Scholl, Lesa. *Translation, Authorship and the Victorian Professional Woman: Charlotte Brontë, Harriet Martineau and George Eliot*. Ashgate, 2011.
Stark, Susan. 'Marian Evans, Translator'. *Essays and Studies: Translating Literature*, vol. 50, 1997, pp. 119–40.
Strauss, David. *The Life of Jesus Critically Examined*, translated by George Eliot, edited by Peter G. Hodgson. Fortress Press, 1972 (1846).
Willey, Basil. *Nineteenth-Century Studies: Coleridge to Matthew Arnold*. Columbia University Press, 1964.

6
Venture, Courage, Ruin: Karin Michaëlis in Translation Across Genre and Time

Katherine Hollander

In his ground-breaking work on pacifist literature and criticism, Lawrence Rosenwald analyses Lynn Nottage's acclaimed play *Ruined* as an adaptation and commentary on Bertolt Brecht's *Mother Courage and Her Children*. As Rosenwald argues, *Ruined* is a kind of 'translation' of *Courage*, into a new century and a different war, and it picks up many of the same threads and themes while also transforming them to make new arguments. But *Courage* is itself the same kind of translation, of the Danish feminist author Karin Michaëlis' novel, *Mette Trap og Hendes Unger* (Mette Trap and her children), which first appeared in Denmark in 1922, in Germany in 1925, and in an English edition in 1927 under the title *Venture's End*. This chapter explores *Venture's End* as an originary text for *Courage*, just as *Courage* is for *Ruined*, linking the three works in order to see their similarities and differences. This linked examination reveals that the three texts share a set of preoccupations – with the entrapments of war and capitalism and the dangers that uniquely threaten women – and shows that a careful exploration of these moments of translation can illuminate unexpected priorities and arguments.

On the surface, the three texts (one novel and two plays) are only nominally similar: all three explore the limited choices available to a strong, resourceful businesswoman entangled in a destructive system, and illuminate the consequences of those choices for her and her dependents. *Ruined* tells the story of Mama Nadi, a bar-keeper and madam trying to survive and maintain some safety and equilibrium within her small sphere of influence in the midst of a civil war. *Mother Courage* traces the progress of Anna Fierling, called Mother Courage, a canteen woman with a wagon full of goods to sell, determined to protect her daughter and two sons from war while also extracting profit from it. *Venture's End* centres on Mette Trap, an independent single mother whose addiction to gambling leads to the destruction of the life she has built for herself and her daughters as she serves a prison sentence for forgery and embezzlement.[1]

The settings are distant in time and space: *Ruined* takes place in the Democratic Republic of Congo in the 1990s, *Mother Courage* in the Holy Roman Empire of the seventeenth century, and *Venture's End* in early twentieth-century Denmark. Some commonalities are shared among only any two of the three texts: both *Ruined* and *Courage* take place in a war zones, but *Venture* plays out in peacetime; the families in *Venture* and *Courage* are biological ones (a mother and her three children, all by different fathers), while *Ruined* focuses on a non-consanguineous chosen family; *Ruined* and *Venture* both feature female families (a mother and her daughters, biological or not), while *Courage* has one daughter and two sons. And yet, there is a kind of 'family resemblance' between the three works, despite their topical differences and even their diversity of tone and argument.

This chapter excavates the three texts as if they were an archaeological site, moving downwards through the strata, beginning with the most recent work. Although this may create an uneasy sensation of moving backwards, rather than in the usual chronological manner, it will more accurately reveal the moments of translation, revision and continuity among the three works. In order to provide some scaffolding, it is important to lay out some facts about the three works and their production, before excavation and analysis begin. This might alternatively be conceived as a map of the archaeological site, starting with the lowest, oldest layer. This layer is, of course, the novel *Venture's End*, first published in Danish in 1922 by Karin Michaëlis. At this point, and already at the height of her fame, Michaëlis had produced several dozen books of fiction, non-fiction and children's literature; she was also a well-known and well-travelled lecturer and social activist. Not only a feminist, champion of girls' education and, through her novels, a critic of gender and sexual mores, she was a pacifist, anti-capitalist and prison abolitionist (though the term had not yet been coined). Michaëlis was also a vocal critic of fascism.

Five years before publishing *Venture's End*, Michaëlis had befriended a young actress named Helene Weigel who would, with her husband Bertolt Brecht, eventually go on to develop ground-breaking plays and found the Berliner Ensemble. When Brecht and Weigel fled Germany with their children in 1933, they turned to Michaëlis, and they made a home for themselves in a thatched-roof house in Svendborg, not far from her home on the small island of Thurø just off the coast of southern Fyn. Under that thatched roof, Brecht and an important collaborator (*Mitarbeiterin*), the writer, editor and dramaturge Margarete Steffin, developed the plans and early drafts of the play *Mutter Courage und ihre Kinder* (*Mother Courage and her Children*). As was typical of their working style, Brecht and Steffin drew on a wide variety of texts in developing *Courage*. Perhaps the most important of these was *Venture*, the story of an independent, resourceful and deeply flawed woman who loses all three of her children, and her own freedom, because of her addiction to gambling and speculation (translated, in *Courage*, into Anna Fierling's compulsive bargaining).[2] First performed in 1941, *Courage* would go on to become one of the most iconic and important antiwar plays of the twentieth century, translated into many languages and still performed today.

The American playwright Lynn Nottage and director Kate Whorisky discovered a mutual admiration for *Courage* some sixty years later, in 2004. Their desire to set a new version of the play amidst the civil war in the Democratic Republic of Congo sent them on a research trip to neighbouring Uganda, where they interviewed women who were victims of rape as a weapon of war. *Courage* had initially seemed to them like a dynamic vehicle for exploring women's 'complicated relationship to war', but as Nottage and Whorisky listened to women's stories, met those who had founded an organization dedicated to addressing the issue of widespread sexual assault resulting from the war, and got to know doctors who treated these women, it became clear to Nottage that in order to '[portray] the lives of Central Africans as accurately as she could', she would need to write a new play, not simply adapt the text of *Courage*.[3] *Ruined* grew out of that text – one might say even *outgrew* it – but it exists as a kind of translation, illuminating its predecessor as *Courage* does to *Venture*.

Ruined from *Courage*

The protagonist of *Ruined* is Mama Nadi; like Anna Fierling of *Courage*, Mama Nadi is a businesswoman whose main customers are soldiers and other men engaged in the war economy. In a very Brechtian way, the entanglements between the violent conflict of the civil war and the economic apparatus of mining coltan, diamonds and gold are made explicit through the identities of Mama's miner and soldier customers. Unlike Anna Fierling, Mama's business is not mobile but fixed, not a wagon but a bar, and she runs a trade not only in liquor, cigarettes and chocolate, but, as a madam, in sex. Like Anna Fierling, Mama expects to make a profit from those she protects, but she does protect and care for them, and her complaint that she keeps the eight women in her establishment fed is also a statement of pride.[4]

There are other immediate similarities between *Ruined* and *Courage*. The young woman Sophie, who becomes a daughter of Mama's, resembles Anna Fierling's daughter Kattrin in having been disfigured by the war (she is 'ruined', that is, has been repeatedly wounded through rape and genital injury), and in her initial refusal to speak – though, unlike Kattrin, she is physically capable of it, and, indeed, she sings. Sophie's songs punctuate the play like the musical interludes in *Courage*, but instead of celebrating war's eternal nature, as Anna Fierling's refrain does, Sophie sings about the war's end.[5] Yet it is an imaginary end, and the song offers no real hope for resolution or cessation of the conflict. Again, as in *Courage*, Mama Nadi has a suitor – the friendly travelling salesman Christian. But he is both more upstanding than the cowardly (yet occasionally wise and gentle) Chaplain, and kinder than the ungenerous (though quite resourceful) Cook. Acting as a surprising moral compass, Christian delivers one of the play's most passionate and convincing speeches on the futility of war, as well as a succinct and stinging critique of capitalism and Mama Nadi's involvement with it.[6]

In fact, despite its almost unimaginably brutal context, the most significant transformative move *Ruined* makes vis-a-vis *Courage* is that the small social world it creates on stage is kinder, warmer and more interpersonally humane. This is in itself surprising, since, through the speeches and experiences of its characters, *Ruined* depicts not only a vicious civil war characterized by its use of rape as a weapon, but also horrifying environmental degradation – the destruction of bush and forest, and the literal ruination of the earth through mining. Salima and Josephine, women who have been sexually assaulted and cast out of their communities, are compelled to perform sexual labour for the same sorts of soldiers who might have raped them; Sophie is exempt only because she is 'ruined'. And yet there is a warmth between the characters, a gentleness inside Mama Nadi's bar, even in her haggling with Christian or the spats between Salima and Josephine. Though he originally shunned her, Salima's husband Fortune risks his life to search for her, and she dies in his arms – while all three of Courage's children die very much alone. When Mama Nadi says, 'There must always be a part of you that this war can't touch', we believe her. We believe she has kept some essential part of herself separate, not in the deluded way of Anna Fierling, but because this untouched part is her own moral centre, one she keeps sacred not out of pure self-interest but in solidarity with other women. 'It's a damn shame', she says of a diamond she is safekeeping for someone else, though it would profit her to sell it, 'but I keep it for that stupid woman'.[7]

Rosenwald writes that Nottage's 'chief challenge is to Brecht's hopelessness, the chief alternative the presence of hope; *Ruined* is a play in which hope is possible, agency is possible, survival is possible'.[8] Unlike Anna Fierling, Mama Nadi can successfully balance her pragmatism with her generosity. Rosenwald argues,

> The people we see her taking care of are her employees and not her children, but taking care of them is what she does, she is maternal if not their mother, she cherishes them and wants to keep them safe, just as she cherishes her war-dependent business and wants to keep it profitable ... In what it borrows from Brecht's play, Nottage's play is a tribute to it. In what it alters or rejects, it is a commentary on it and an alternative to it: a challenging commentary, a fruitful alternative.[9]

Nottage offers this alternative as a translation of *Courage* that both illuminates Anna Fierling's world and improves upon it, opening up space for a different set of dramatic arguments. As Rosenwald implies, these arguments depend on frankness about violence and, specifically, sexual violence. He argues that, by contrast, the representation of war's physical violence in *Courage* 'is almost wilfully flat, in particular its representation, or its choice not to offer a representation, of systematic violence against women'.[10] Yet this violence against women is never truly absent from *Courage*. It becomes clear from a reading of *Ruined* that what is absent is not sexual assault, but the community of women in which to discuss it.

As Rosenwald writes, '*Ruined* dramatizes those horrors [of rape as a weapon of war] partly by showing us soldiers and officers hurting and threatening, partly by letting characters tell of what they have heard, above all by letting characters show or tell of what they have experienced'. One of the strengths of Nottage's work as a translation of *Courage* is the way it gathers onstage a community of women who are able to hold space for the horrors they have endured and, perhaps, eventually heal from them, both physically and emotionally. Mama Nadi, for example, makes plans to use the diamond to pay for Sophie's reconstructive surgery; she does this despite disclosing, in the play's last scene, that she herself is also 'ruined', and presumably could have used the diamond for her own surgery instead. The person she confides this in is Christian, as an argument for why they cannot be lovers; despite her initial resistance, he holds her and she weeps. Thus, at the end of the play, both romantic love and sustained female community seem possible and within reach. As Rosenwald reminds us, the play's 'penultimate long stage direction includes an indispensable one-word sentence: 'Possibility'.[11] That possibility is incipient only through and in the presence of community, and especially female community.

Female community of this kind *is* absent from *Courage* – perhaps quite deliberately, rather than as a result of what might be perceived as sexist Brechtian myopia. After all, Steffin as a *Mitarbeiterin* had considerable influence on the text, as did Weigel on the role of Courage, and, just as significantly, Michaëlis' profoundly feminist *Venture's End* exists as a kind of puissant kernel at the heart of the play. Still, most of the characters in Anna Fierling's world are male; Kattrin does not speak, and the sex worker Yvette, though a friend to Courage and Kattrin, is only intermittently present, traveling on her own journey, selling her own wares, following the war in her own way. 'Mama [Nadi] is never alone the way Mother Courage is alone, she lives in community, she builds community', Rosenwald reminds us.[12]

Courage by contrast is indeed very much alone, and always on the move. Yet she talks about sexual violence against women the way women often talk about it when their interlocutors are men – angrily and obliquely. She alludes to her own rape when introducing her daughter in the first scene; instead of playfully discussing the paramours who were her son's fathers, she says only, and abruptly, 'She's half German'.[13] Kattrin, we are to understand, has at least twice been sexually assaulted: first, as a child, when a soldier 'stuffed something in her mouth', resulting in her muteness, and then later when she once 'stayed out all night' and then 'went around like before, except she worked harder'.[14]

The tenderest Anna Fierling is with her daughter throughout the entire action of the play is when Kattrin returns wounded from an errand her mother has sent her on. The nature of the assault is suggested in Kattrin's rejection of a pair of red boots she coveted in an earlier scene: Courage had shooed her away from these boots, which belong to Yvette, as if to safeguard her daughter's respectability. Now, although she offers them as consolation, Kattrin merely creeps away into the wagon, as if ashamed and overwhelmed, unmoved or repulsed by the idea of sex or sexuality in any form. Indeed, the running discourse about whether the wound on her head will leave a scar, and whether this scar will make her unmarriageable, seems contrived to distract from, or stand in for, other questions about Kattrin's injuries and sexual future. Courage seems to comprehend; this moment is the only one in the play when she truly understands that war is not neutral, that she cannot live off it without losing to it. 'War be damned', she curses.[15] If rape occupies a central place in *Ruined*, it haunts the edges of *Courage*. By centering sexual assault as a weapon of war, *Ruined* illuminates its presence in its predecessor.

Courage from *Venture*

Some of the elements central to *Ruined* define *Courage*: the strong, sometimes necessarily ruthless businesswoman at its centre, her hard-fought freedom and prosperity, her desire to provide for her dependents, her three very different children, her flawed, somewhat bumbling suitor(s). All these elements, which Nottage translated from *Courage* to *Ruined*, in fact originate in *Venture*. The detail of Courage's three children with their three different absent (but unmissed) fathers is a feature of *Venture*, too – Mette Trapp is proud to be enough for her girls, who do not need or miss their fathers (until, as the plot unravels, all three fathers reappear). But what is largely an interpersonal and legal drama of freedom and entrapment in *Venture* is transplanted in *Courage* to a conflict as belief-defyingly brutal as that in *Ruined*: the Thirty Years War of central Europe. The violence – sexual and otherwise – described in *Ruined* is intimate, person-to-person, carried out with machetes and men's bodies (and as Whorisky points out, their imaginations), with none of the distance afforded by drones or missiles.[16] Despite the existence of firearms, cannons and even bombs, which did define the experience of sieges and some battles in the Thirty Years War, much of the violence was similarly intimate, creative and brutal.[17]

Thus, just as Nottage and Whorisky did not construct *Ruined* as a strict translation of *Courage*, so too in making *Courage*, Brecht and Steffin did not simply translate *Venture*. Indeed, topically and tonally, the play has much more in common with other sources they consulted in the process of creation. The play's protagonist is directly borrowed from Jakob Grimmelshausen's *Trutz-Simplex*, a narrative of the Thirty Years War which centres on the adventures of a self-reliant, sexually-free woman who has earned the nickname 'Courage'. Yet where Grimmelshausen's soldierly heroine gets her nickname from her fearlessness in combat, Brecht's risk-taking businesswoman is distinguished by braving a battlefield in order to sell a compliment of bread before it goes bad.[18] This minor edit signals a significant translation of thematic focus from *Trutz-Simplex* to *Courage*, as Brecht and Steffin immediately introduce the economics of war and recast bravery itself in its light. And this bravery – as much as the bravery associated with battle fever – may be perceived as a kind of madness, one that raises economic desperation, as well as the lust for profit, to an extreme that reveals a human vice as destructive as violence itself. As Marxists, Brecht and Steffin were keen to show the destruction latent in the system, but the notion of the smart woman who cannot let her own vice go feels like a pure echo of Michaëlis, much more psychologically rooted than many other Brechtian character traits.[19]

Anna Fierling also bears a close resemblance to the folk character Dulle Griet, or Mad Meg, who is said to have gone to hell to sell wares to the devil himself, and who is the subject of a 1561 painting by Bruegel the Elder.[20] In the painting, Griet strides with (perhaps slightly stunned) determination through an apocalyptic landscape, carrying her goods and wearing a metal breastplate. In another layer of influence, the characters in *Mother Courage* speak in an informal, bluntly vivid dialect, which Brecht indicated he had borrowed from Jaroslav Hašek's World War I novel *The Good Soldier Svejk*, after he and Steffin read it in German translation.[21] Other immediate influences include Runeberg's *Tales of a Subaltern* and Schiller's *Wallenstein*, a verse play set in the Thirty Years War and focusing on the famous Bohemian general.[22] These works, in their explorations of conflict, violence and the desperate, irrational, and even deranged actions war provokes in its participants, are perhaps more immediately apparent as influences than *Venture*.

By contrast, *Venture* inhabits a completely different world, neither battlefields nor trenches, but rather the stockrooms and parlours of Copenhagen in the early twentieth century. Its cast of characters are middle-class parvenus and genteel nobility rather than war-weary soldiers and terrorized peasants.

Yet in its political argumentation *Courage* hews close to *Venture's* own themes. What starts out feeling like a realist drawing room novel about an independent businesswoman and her three unconventional daughters transforms into a relentless meditation on women's autonomy, the ethics of capitalism and the carceral system. Like *Courage*, *Venture* illuminates the entanglements of capitalism, and the losses a woman incurs when she strays too close to the line between basic economic stability and the desire for real wealth and profit. Both works suggest that there is no escape from the system without a major collective change. Much as in the play, Anna Fierling loses her children to her delusion that she can profit from the war, Mette Trap's personal charisma, maternal commitments and considerable sexual and economic freedom are threatened by her addiction to gambling and speculation, and she eventually loses her daughters and finds her spirit extinguished by the humiliation and austerity of confinement in prison. Both Mette Trapp and Anna Fierling are addicted to the excitement and risk offered by bargaining and speculation – synecdoches for capitalism itself – and it is this addiction that blinds them to the consequences of their actions.

Like Brecht and Steffin, Michaëlis understood the ways in which economic and sexual freedom were entangled and, for her, the prison was a site not only ripe for real political action, but also rife with metaphorical and literary significance. If Mette Trapp is literally confined to prison by her economic actions, and, even when the cell door opens, remains spiritually imprisoned by her experience of incarceration, Anna Fierling is physically free to move about the fields and battlefields seeking profit, but actually trapped within a system in which she can only lose everything she values.[23] It is this demonstration of entrapment within the economic system created by the Thirty Years War that provides *Courage's* most piquant and powerful argument, and this theme of confinement not only corresponds to a Marxist understanding of the totalizing force of capitalism, but also to the world Michaëlis constructs in *Venture's End*. Indeed, the iconic revolving stage of the Berliner Ensemble's long-running production of *Courage* makes visible the circularity of the world in which the play takes place. Anna Fierling can pull her cart wherever she likes, traverse untold acres and miles in pursuit of profit as she follows the war, but in reality, she never goes anywhere, and always ends up where she started.[24] Here again is a translation, rather than just a simple borrowing, a kind of critical commentary we can read in the interaction of altered plot details layered with retained argumentation and motif. For Anna Fierling, tied to the war – just as for Mette Trap, tied to her crimes – there is no escape and in both cases, it is capitalism that animates the system in which they are caught.

A closer look at *Venture's End*

Venture's End is a forgotten gem. It was translated by Grace Isabel Colbron for an English edition in 1927 and has never been retranslated; once out of print, it has not been reissued. It is too bold to say Michaëlis should be as widely-read as Virginia Woolf; she lacked Woolf's originality, precision and rigorous political intellect, and certainly lacked Woolf's education and deliberate experimentation in literary form.[25] Still, similarities present themselves: she was a modernist interested in the human (and especially female) interior, and she could capture dialogue or nature in language with a few imagistic strokes. She was wildly popular and influential – when she met Brecht in the early 1930s, she was easily and vastly senior to him in fame, and her children's books about the little girl Bibi spawned untold imitations, including *Pippi Longstocking*.[26] She counted among her friends dozens of important European artists and thinkers, including Alexandra Kollontai, the novelist and sexual theorist, who was the only woman commissar in Lenin's cabinet.[27] Her best friend, the educator and *salonière* Eugenie Schwarzwald (one of the first German-speaking women to earn a doctorate), called her 'the conscience of Europe'.[28]

Though it begins as if it were just another droll middle-class novel, *Venture's End* reflects Michaëlis' intellectual sophistication and sense of urgent social problems. And it seems, at first, optimistically prepared to solve them: despite an unstable childhood with a philandering father, long-suffering mother and a variety of bizarre relatives, Mette Trapp grows up into a resourceful, brave and appealing young woman, surprisingly lacking in neuroses. She has love affairs that do not result in marriage but does not panic; when they do result in pregnancy, she does not despair, but is happy and finds herself a protector and employer in the kindly Epsen Soelberg; she goes to business school and becomes a trusted partner in his fine carpet and upholstery firm. She is independent and unashamed, and she loves and raises her three talented daughters well. She has one vice – gambling and financial speculation – but this seems to be under control, until she runs up her debt and embezzles from the firm. Ever scrupulous, she admits to the crime and insists upon standing trial and enduring her punishment: confinement in a women's prison. Despite her daughters' initial (and total) devotion to her, the secrets she kept from them about their three fathers – who one by one enter the tale – shake their faith. Mette ends the novel completely transformed by her time in prison, ready to submit and become a wife, not out of love but as a way of paying another debt, and unprepared to see any of her three daughters, who have had their small, secure and happy world of four women irrevocably broken up. 'Prøv ikke ad lede, jeg vil det helst saaledes' ('Do not search for me, I do not wish it'), she tells her eldest in the novel's last line.[29]

Very little has been written in English about this remarkable novel, though Michaëlis' devoted biographer, the scholar Beverly Driver Eddy, analyses it in connection with *Courage* – it was Eddy who first pointed out the relationship between the two works.[30] For Eddy, the main difference between *Courage* and *Venture* is not genre or setting or even emphasis, but argument. She sees the two works as embodying a spirited disagreement between Brecht and Michaëlis about the evils of human society and how many of them could fairly and systematically be blamed on capitalism. Eddy understands Michaëlis as a less-than-systematic thinker, one more interested in human psychology than political programmes: 'Mette Trap is motivated not by capitalistic urges or exploitation; she is simply an individual addicted to the excitement of the gaming table', Eddy writes. 'In her psychological novel Michaëlis looked at Mette as an individual case study; Brecht's Marxist views caused him to look at Courage as representative of larger societal forces'.[31]

It is true that Michaëlis was much more interested in psychology than Brecht, who was fundamentally opposed to the notion that illuminating individuals, rather than types, was useful in the literature he aimed to create. Michaëlis, by contrast, was intrigued by emotion and repression, had connections through Schwarzwald to Anna Freud and Marie Jahoda, and her work influenced the Austrian psychoanalyst Melanie Klein.[32] But it is not the case that a close reading of *Venture's End* suggests merely that 'money, like drink or the sex drive, can become addictive and therefore harmful to some people'.[33] Mette Trap is not a simple holiday gambler addicted to the gaming tables, she also (and for the same reasons) plays the stock market, and it is in speculation that she truly loses her way.[34] Her involvement with the larger system of the market, and Michaëlis' repeated conflation of Mette's gambling with her speculation, goes beyond a personal flaw to constitute a broader critique. Still, a number of scholars who have recognized Michaëlis' psychological astuteness have been less attentive to the keenness of her anti-capitalism.[35]

Eddy sees it as 'a superb irony' that Brecht turned to *Venture* in developing *Courage*. For her, the issue of capitalism (and, more specifically, money and the acquisition of wealth) was 'a basic bone of contention' between Brecht and Michaëlis, rather than an issue upon which they agreed in essentials but not in details.[36] Eddy suggests, moreover, that it may have been a kind of weakness in Brecht to have had to borrow from *Venture*, if indeed he so disagreed with its argumentative premise. What this reading misses, however, is that for Brecht, Steffin and Michaëlis herself, borrowing (or translation) was not perceived as a sign of creative weakness, but rather, and as Rosenwald puts it, 'a tribute[,] a challenging commentary, a fruitful alternative'.[37] It was no more a weakness for Brecht and Steffin to translate some of *Venture*'s powerful, dynamic elements into *Courage* than it was for Nottage and Whorisky to translate those in *Courage* into *Ruined*.

Eddy's reading also obscures, or perhaps flattens, Michaëlis' politics, which were central to her as an author, social activist and human being, and not nearly so rooted in 'childlike innocence' as her works for young people suggest.[38] While it is true she was never a Marxist, she was, as Eddy acknowledges, a lifelong and explicit critic of capitalism. Michaëlis was particularly aware of the way that capitalism treated women as property and transformed sex and other interpersonal relations into commodity exchanges. Her novels frequently portray women as independent beings seeking a moral centre in a world whose double standards around gender, sex and money have become untenable. Moreover, Mette's incarceration is not an apolitical plot point; Michaëlis was what we would now call a prison abolitionist, corresponding with inmates, advocating for official pardons, and even offering herself to the state as a personal guarantor for prisoners in exchange for their release.[39]

Although Denmark has come to be seen, since the advent of its robust welfare state, as an exemplar of prosperity, egalitarianism and social reasonableness, when Michaëlis was born in 1872, it was still a very poor rural country, burdened with debt and, for many Danes, a low quality of life and nutrition. Following bankruptcy and inflation resulting from the Napoleonic Wars, and because of failed agricultural reforms and falling grain prices, Denmark came to be known, in the words of the poet Poul Martin Møller, as 'poor and small', and the defeat of the navy by Prussia in 1864 was humiliating for a country that had been a significant sea power.[40] Denmark was poor, Danes were poor, and many families lived with the threat of debtor's prison or the workhouse.[41] By the late nineteenth century, legal reforms and the burgeoning cooperative movement lifted education levels and participation in local democratic economic ventures, which in turn greatly improved quality of life in the countryside; the reforms of 1920 extended this prosperity further.[42] But only in 1933 did a massive legislative package pass that cemented the welfare state and stabilized the lives of all Danes to the extent that democracy became associated with economic security – thus effectively (and by design) blocking off one avenue for the appeal of fascism.[43] For Michaëlis, however, the continuance of a punitive carceral system meant that a truly secure and just life for all Danes remained out of reach. In her long memory, which included her own very poor childhood in Randers, prison was associated with poverty and debt; through the workhouse, it was also associated with labour, further tightening the link between criminality, capitalism and confinement.

For a prolific author of imaginative fiction, these links were clearly present, not only in the external world of banks and prisons, but in the intimate ones between, and even interior to, individuals. It is not a very wide leap from the literal prison to the metaphorical – or psychological – one, and Michaëlis was preoccupied in her creative work with questions of freedom and confinement, particularly for women in their economic, interpersonal and sexual lives. She did not shy away from tackling these subjects. The book that made her famous throughout Europe was a novel called *The Dangerous Age* (in Danish, *Den Farlige Alder*, in German *Das gefährliche Alter*). Published in 1910, *The Dangerous Age* sold over a million copies, 100,000 in the French edition alone.[44] The story unfolds via letters and diary fragments and is essentially modernist in its subjectivity, sensuousness and stream-of-consciousness narration. At its core, it is about a woman's disastrous realization that her entire life has been lived, with her own active participation, in a social milieu that is crushingly, if invisibly, oppressive to women, a realization that comes just as she is losing the only currency she possesses in that system: her youth, beauty and fertility. In the first decade of the twentieth century, a popular novel whose undisguised subject was menopause was scandalous, and Michaëlis upset not just conservatives but feminists as well with her prioritization of this physiological aspect of women's experience and oppression.[45] Moreover, the protagonist's most painful revelation is her sense that, as a young woman, she had quite literally sold herself for money, by cultivating her beauty and pursuing a wealthy husband – pointing to an uneasy conclusion that, within a capitalist patriarchy, all women are necessarily whores.

By contrast, Mette Trap is determined to live outside of these structures, to keep love and money separate, to be dependent on neither a lover nor a husband, and to teach her daughters to stand on their own. But – as is also true for Anna Fierling – she cannot be satisfied with simple economic security. She always wants more – more excitement, more money, more profit. Brecht and Michaëlis both understood that this inability to be content with what one has is not simply an individual character flaw (though some individuals may indeed be more susceptible to it than others) but an inexorable attribute of capitalism itself, of economies of enrichment which always have to be expanding in order even to maintain themselves. Goods in a cart, money in an account, coltan in the ground – in *Courage*, *Venture*, and *Ruined*, what is in your hand is never enough to keep you safe, and these women know it.

Conclusions

What should we make of these three texts and their various moves of translation? The moments of translation tell us much about the priorities of those doing the translating. Nottage keeps Brecht and Steffin's unrelenting critique of war and capitalism, but gives us more hope and possibility, shedding light on sexual violence by creating a community of women on stage who can speak about it in solidarity. Brecht and Steffin retain Michaëlis' admirably tough and independent single mother, but show her flaws as more deeply fatal in an infinitely more dangerous world, heightening the critique of capitalism by showing its entanglement with war – a critique of which the pacifist Michaëlis would have approved. She would likely have endorsed, too, Nottage's presentation of hope and human community among women, although *Venture* ends with a chill that is closer to the final scene of *Courage* than to the last moments of *Ruined*. Where each text places its measure of hope is telling. Michaëlis suggests, if faintly, that Mette's daughters may do better in their own lives than their mother did, and, similarly, Nottage shows that a small community of women can restore warmth and humanity. For all these authors, but for Brecht and Steffin most of all, hope lies in the audience: the watchers and listeners who receive the story and resolve to change their world.

In Rosenwald's work on pacifist literature and criticism, that change involves nothing less than war and peace. As he argues, Nottage shows that agency and community are possible, maybe even reconciliation – in the midst of war, and, perhaps, even as a way of ending war. Brecht and Steffin, by contrast, demonstrate that the seductions of war are the seductions of capitalism; no individual, no matter how clever, can easily escape them – collective action is needed. In *Venture's End*, Michaëlis does not comment upon war, though her argument about the prison system is closer to Brecht and Steffin's in that she refuses to give the reader any comfortable indication that Mette Trap will recover from her ordeal and return to her resilient self. She is, in her own way, ruined. Yet even without its presence in the novel, Michaëlis' pacifism reaches across the three texts. Brecht was no pacifist when he arrived in Svendborg; as late as 1931 he was still actively (if perhaps somewhat ironically) endorsing political violence in arguments with his friend Walter Benjamin.[46] Yet by the end of a life filled with more than a few lively conversations with Michaëlis, he wrote the beautiful antiwar poem 'Den Krieg haben die Menschen gemacht' ('War is Made by Humankind'), which ends:

> Mutter, es geht um dein eigen Kind,
> Wehr dich und laß es nicht zu.
> Und ob wir Millionen mächtiger sind
> Als der Krieg, das entscheidest du.
> Und das ist jedermanns großer Entscheid,

Und sagen wir alle "Nein",
Dann wird der Krieg die Vergangenheit.
Und der Frieden die Zukunft sein.[47]

Mother, it's your child that's at stake
Fight back, say this cannot be allowed!
Whether we millions are mightier than
War is for you to decide.
And that's the big choice for all of us
and if we all say: no!
War will be where we've come from
And peace where we choose to go.[48]

Notes

1. Michaëlis, *Venture's End*, 120.
2. Michaëlis' Mette Trap loses her daughters in that their relationships are destroyed and contact severed. Brecht and Steffin's Anna Fierling loses her children literally, in that they are killed.
3. Nottage, *Ruined*, ix, xi.
4. Nottage, *Ruined*, 14.
5. Courage sings: 'The new year's come. The watchmen shout. / The thaw sets in. The dead remain. / Wherever life has not died out. / Staggers to its feet again'. Bertolt Brecht, *Mother Courage and Her Children* 4. The German is even more explicit: 'Das Früjahr kommt. Wach auf, du Christ! / Der Schnee schmilzt weg. Die Toten ruhn. / Und was noch nicht gestorben ist / Das macht sich auf die Socken nun'. See Brecht, *Mutter Courage und ihre Kinder*, 9. By contrast, Sophie sings: 'Cuz you come here to forget, / You say drive away all regret, / And dance like it's the ending / The ending of the war'. Nottage, *Ruined*, 24.
6. Nottage, *Ruined*, 76, 85.
7. Nottage, *Ruined*, 53.
8. Rosenwald, *Pacifist Critic*.
9. Rosenwald, *Pacifist Critic*.
10. Rosenwald, *Pacifist Critic*.
11. Rosenwald, *Pacifist Critic*.
12. Rosenwald, *Pacifist Critic*.
13. Brecht, *Courage*, 7. This detail, suggesting the brutality associated with Germanness, is not insignificant in the context of the exiled Steffin and Brecht, composing the play among their fellow refugees; in a poem written a few years later, Brecht's daughter weeps because the Finnish children with whom she is playing associate the German she spoke with 'a nation of gangsters', and Brecht comforts her by reminding her that Germany is, in fact, a nation of gangsters. That others around them thought so, too, meant that they – refugees from Germany – were in a safe place.
14. Brecht, *Courage*, 56.
15. Brecht, *Courage*, 56.
16. Nottage, *Ruined*, xi.
17. Excellent histories of the conflict include Peter H. Wilson, *The Thirty Years War: Europe's Tragedy* (The Belknap Press of Harvard University, 2009), Hans Medick and Benjamin Marschke, *Experiencing the Thirty Years War: A Brief History with Documents* (Bedford/ St Martins, 2013) and the much older but still captivating *The Thirty Years War*, by C.V. Wedgwood (NYRB, 2005). First published in 1938, it is likely Steffin read this volume as part of research for *Courage*.
18. See Jakob Grimmselshausen, *Life of Courage*. Brecht, *Courage*, 5.
19. For analysis on Michaëlis and psychoanalysis and/or psychological literature, see: Beverley Driver Eddy, 'The dangerous age: Karin Michaëlis and the politics of menopause', 491–506,

Ole Andkjaer Olsen, 'Depression and repression in Melanie Klein's Analysis of the painter Ruth Weber', 35, and Madeleine Wood, 'Centrifugal fires: consuming desires and the performative female subject in Karin Michaelis'.
20. Breugal, *Mad Meg*.
21. Parker, *Brecht: a literary life*, 411.
22. Brecht, *Werke*, 26, 424–5.
23. 'I shall leave this place in a few days. The door stands open for me. I can go wherever I will. But the cell, the uniform, the odour, the nights in here, the days in here ... will all go with me. And all those who still remain here. Their complainings, their curses, their sleepless nights. It will all follow me'. Michaëlis, *Venture's End*, 270.
24. See Wekwerth and Palitzsch, dir., *Mutter Courage und ihre Kinder*.
25. Woolf makes an excellent case for the inadequacy of that education in the magnificent *Three Guineas*, but nevertheless she was the daughter and sister of educated men; Michaëlis' schooling was extremely limited and mostly dedicated to training her to be a pianist, a career intended to give her a way out of poverty. See Eddy, *Karin Michaëlis*, 31.
26. James K. Lyon noted in 1996 that, during her collaboration with him in the 1930s, Michaëlis 'was more widely published than Brecht', and this is certainly the case. See Lyon, 'Collective productivity: Brecht and his collaborators'. See also Phyllis Lassner's preface to the 1991 edition of Michaëlis' *Dangerous Age* (Northwestern University Press), which reiterates this fact. See also von Eyben, 'Karin Michaëlis', 223.
27. Michaëlis and Soresby, *Little Troll*, 242.
28. Eugenie Schwarzwald, 'Karin Michaëlis'.
29. Michaëlis, *Mette Trap og hendes Unger*, 217; *Venture's End*, 270.
30. Eddy, 'Brecht in dialogue with Karin Michaëlis', 246.
31. Eddy, 'Brecht in dialogue', 246.
32. See Jahoda, *Ich habe die Welt nicht verändert*, 27. Olsen, 'Depression and repression in Melanie Klein', 37.
33. Eddy, 'Brecht in dialogue', 246.
34. Michaëlis, *Venture's End*, 62, 105, 164.
35. Madeleine Wood's article, 'Centrifugal fires', offers an insightful literary critical analysis, especially in that it connects Michaëlis to her contemporary, Sigmund Freud, but unfortunately it does not take the anti-capitalism of the novel particularly seriously. See also Eddy, 'The dangerous age', 491–506.
36. Eddy, 'Brecht in dialogue', 246, 243.
37. See Katherine Hollander, 'Brecht and collaboration'.
38. Eddy, 'Brecht in Dialogue', 243.
39. Nielsen, *Karin Michaëlis*, 27.
40. Møller, 'The joy of Denmark', 153. For the complete poem in a different translation, see *A Book of Danish Verse*, trans. S. Foster Damon and Robert Silliman Holyer, selected and annotated by Gluf Triis (The American-Scandinavian Foundation, 1922), 63–5.
41. See Larner, 'Gender discrimination does both ways in 18th century Danish prisons'. Though Larner's work specifically focuses on the eighteenth century, workhouses persisted well into the nineteenth.
42. Jespersen, *History of Denmark*, 157, 154, 150. See also Jens Christiansen, *Rural Denmark: 1750–1980*, trans. Else Buchwald Christensen (Central Cooperative Committee of Denmark, 1983).
43. See Lidegaard, *A Short History of Denmark in the Twentieth Century*, 114, and Christiansen and Petersen, 'The dynamics of social solidarity', 182.
44. Michaëlis, *Little Troll*, 142. The English translation, published in 1911, was made from this French edition, which in turn was translated from the German version.
45. Eddy, 'Brecht in dialogue', 250.
46. Wizisla, *Walter Benjamin and Bertolt Brecht*, 37–8.
47. Brecht, *Gedichte und Gedichtfragmente 1940–1956*, 239.
48. Brecht, *The Collected Poems of Bertolt Brecht*, 986.

Bibliography

Brecht, Bertolt. *Werke: Große kommentierte Berliner und Frankfurter Ausgabe*, Bände 1–30, edited by Werner Hecht et al., Aufbau Verlag, 1992.
Brecht, Bertolt. *Gedichte Bd. 5, Gedichte und Gedichtfragmente 1940–1956*. Aufbau, 1993.
Brecht, Bertolt. *The Collected Poems of Bertolt Brecht*, translated by David Constantine and Tom Kuhn. Liveright, 2018.
Brecht, Bertolt. *Mother Courage and Her Children*. Methuen Drama, 2022.
Breugal, Peter I. *Mad Meg*, oil on board, 1561, Museum Mayer Van der Bergh, Antwerp. https://museummayervandenbergh.be/en/page/mad-meg.
Christiansen, Finn and Klaus Petersen. 'The dynamics of social solidarity: the Danish welfare state, 1900–2000'. *Scandinavian Journal of History*, 2001, pp. 176–96.
Eddy, Beverley Driver. 'The dangerous age: Karin Michaëlis and the politics of menopause'. *Women's Studies*, vol. 24, no. 4, 1992, pp. 491–506.
Eddy, Beverly Driver. 'Brecht in dialogue with Karin Michaëlis'. *Brecht Unbound*, edited by James K. Lyon and Hans-Peter Breuer. University of Delaware Press, 1995.
Eddy, Beverly Driver. *Karin Michaëlis: Kaleidoskop des Herzens*, translated by Vibeke Munk and Jörg Zeller. Edition Praesens, 2003.
Grimmelshausen, Jakob. *Life of Courage: the notorious thief, whore, and vagabond*, translated by Mike Mitchell. Dedalus Books, 2015.
Hollander, Katherine. 'Brecht and collaboration: new directions, new discussions'. *Communications of the International Brecht Society*, 2017, p. 2. https://e-cibs.org/issue-2-2017/#hollander.
Jahoda, Marie. *Ich habe die Welt nicht verändert: Lebenserinnerungen einer Pionierin der Sozialforschung*, edited by Steffani Engler and Brigitte Hasenjürgen. Beltz Taschenbuch, 2002.
Jespersen, Knud J.V. *A History of Denmark*. Bloomsbury, 2018.
Larner, Anette. 'Gender discrimination goes both ways in 18th century Danish prisons'. Paper and poster presented at 'Gender in the European Town: medieval to modern', University of Southern Denmark, May 2013.
Lidegaard, Bo. *A Short History of Denmark in the Twentieth Century*. Gyldendal, 2009.
Lyon, James K. 'Collective Productivity: Brecht and his collaborators'. *The Brecht Yearbook 21: Intersections*. University of Wisconsin Press, 1996, pp. xii–19.
Michaëlis, Karin. *Venture's End*, translated by Grace Isabel Colbron. Harcourt, Brace, and Co., 1927.
Michaëlis, Karin. *Mette Trap og hendes Unger*. Lindhardt og Ringhof Forlag, 2017.
Michaëlis, Karin and Lenore Soresby. *Little Troll: the reminiscences of Karin Michaëlis*. Creative Age Press, 1946.
Møller, Poul Martin. 'The joy of Denmark'. *A History of Denmark*, edited by Knud J.V. Jespersen, translated by Ivan Hill and Christopher Wade, second edition. Palgrave Macmillan, 2011.
Nielsen, Birgit S. *Karin Michaëlis: En Europaesk Humanist*. Museum Tusculanums Forlag, Københavns Universitet, 2002.
Nottage, Lynn. *Ruined*. Theatre Communications Group, 2009.
Olsen, Ole Andkjaer. 'Depression and repression in Melanie Klein's analysis of the painter Ruth Weber'. *The Scandinavian Psychoanalytic Review*, vol. 27, 2004, pp. 34–42.
Parker, Stephen. *Brecht: a literary life*. Bloomsbury, 2014.
Rosenwald, Lawrence. *Portrait of a Pacifist Critic*. Unpublished manuscript, 28 October 2021, electronic copy.
Schwarzwald, Eugenie. 'Karin Michaëlis'. *The Living Age*, June 1932, reprinted from *Vossiche Zeitung*.
von Eyben, Merete. 'Karin Michaëlis: famous Danish novelist and humanitarian rebel with a cause'. *The Bridge*, vol. 29, no. 2, p. 223.
Wekwerth, Manfred and Peter Palitzsch, directors. *Mutter Courage und ihre Kinder*. DEFA, 1961.
Wizisla, Erdmut. *Walter Benjamin and Bertolt Brecht: the story of a friendship*, translated by Christine Shuttleworth. Yale University Press, 2009.
Wood, Madeleine. 'Centrifugal fires: consuming desires and the performative female subject in Karin Michaelis' *The Dangerous Age*'. *Orbis Litterarum*, vol. 68, 2013.

7
Lu Xun's Unfaithful Translation of Science Fiction: Rewriting Chinese Literary History

Mingwei Song

In 1903, when Lu Xun 魯迅 (1881–1936, known as Zhou Shuren 周樹人 at that time; his original name that was replaced by Lu Xun, his nom de plume, in 1918) was still studying Japanese in Tokyo and planning to get into medical school, he published a translation of Jules Verne's (1828–1905) *De la Terre à la Lune* 月界旅行 based on a secondhand Japanese translation that was itself based on an English translation. Through the same complicated detour, Lu Xun also translated Verne's *Voyage au centre de la Terre* 地底旅行, the first two chapters of which were published in 1903 in a magazine edited by Chinese students in Japan, *Tides of Zhejiang* 浙江潮.[1] The entire book of this second translation was printed in Nanjing in 1906 and signed with the pen name Zhijiang Suozi 之江索子, the second part of which Lu Xun used as the pen name for 'The art of creating humanity' 造人術, his third extant translation of science fiction. This third translation provides some clues that have long been overlooked, but can be very useful for scholars to understand Lu Xun's ground-breaking vernacular story 'A madman's diary' 狂人日記 (1918) from a new perspective. When it was written, 'A madman's diary' was an audacious, genre-less experiment that had never before happened in Chinese literature. Only later did scholars define it as 'realism' of its rich references to China's harsh reality. The long history of Chinese scholarship that focuses solely on the story's cultural symbolism may be missing part of the story of the origins of Chinese literary modernity.

Can we read 'A madman's diary' as science fiction?

Can we read 'A madman's diary' as science fiction? This provocative question does not yield a simple or certain answer. Rather, it aims to inspire a new understanding of the relationship between science fiction and the modern Chinese literary tradition that Lu Xun helped create. Lu Xun's first vernacular fiction, 'A madman's diary', has long been considered a foundational text of the mainstream literary realism of twentieth-century China. My argument is that this short story can also be viewed as a pioneering experiment, which not only keeps alive an avant-garde spirit and a perpetual resistance to constraining conventions but also serves as a major inspiration for the subversive new wave emerging in twenty-first century Chinese science fiction.

Lu Xun looms large in the new wave of Chinese science fiction. I gave this name to this cutting-edge new trend of literary experiment in the form of science fiction, and I have regarded the new wave of science fiction as the single most important literary phenomenon in twenty-first-century China.[2] Science fiction captures the anticipation and anxieties of China's new epoch as one filled with ever-accelerating changes in technology, moral sensibilities, political culture and everyday life. In previous publications, I have expressed the central argument that this new wave of Chinese science fiction illuminates the 'invisible' aspects of reality. The invisible is a key element in the poetics of the new wave. As a symbolic trope, it points to realms beyond what we can ordinarily perceive, allows for the representation of our fears and dreams, and challenges moral conventions and political doctrines. The invisible is a category that includes those unknowable and inexplicable phenomena that bring into question the validity of our knowledge and belief systems, make our sense of reality uncertain and, more importantly, present possibilities for building alternative images of the world. In the context of contemporary China, the invisible also includes all that is not available for conventional literary representations due to artistic constraints or political prohibitions. The representation of both the epistemologically and politically invisible functions as the centre of gravity for the contemporary Chinese science fictional imagination.

Yet, seeing the invisible also means that one needs to overcome the fear of seeing. 'Fear of seeing' is a central theme in the stories and novels by Han Song 韓松 (b. 1965). Han Song's characters are often forced into a conundrum: to see, or not to see. Seeing leads to terrifying discoveries at odds with the fabricated smooth surface of reality represented in mass media and state propaganda. The design of the plot is therefore closely intertwined with the ethics of storytelling – that is to say, the moral question of seeing or not seeing drives the narrative towards a moment of truth-claiming Enlightenment. Science fiction allows contemporary Chinese authors to overcome the fear of seeing and behold a truth that is otherwise invisible.

With respect to cultural politics, the representation of the invisible leads to serious reflections on Enlightenment ideals and revolutionary teleology. In depicting the looming, menacing future of modernity, science fiction casts shadows upon some of the key notions of Chinese modernity, such as progress, development, nationalism, scientism and humanism. The poetics and politics of the new wave are particularly timely in this political moment as the Chinese government works to engineer the 'Chinese dream'. The new wave has shed light upon the nightmarish unconscious of the Chinese dream that subjects all individual citizens to a seductive, overarching vision. The new wave experimentations have made science fiction a distinctive literary genre that cuts sharply into the popular imagination and influences intellectual thinking of alternatives to our current way of life. Deeply entangled with the politics of a changing China, the new wave complicates visions of the nation's future. It introduces a strong discord into the triumphant rhetoric of historical determinism and tempers political consciousness with scientific discourse on uncertainty. Its acute awareness of both the potential and menace of technological revolution sharpens social criticism, and invites rethinking of the fate of individuals and nations in an age of relentless, ever accelerating technologization.

My efforts to explore the connections between Lu Xun and the new wave have led me to investigate the epistemological, ethical and cultural turns that have shaped both the earlier May Fourth literary revolution (1915–19) and the aesthetics of Chinese new wave science fiction (1999–2011). I consider the new wave a literary experiment heavily indebted to Lu Xun rather than to earlier science fiction. My purpose is not just to claim the genre's legitimacy as a part of modern Chinese literature, but also to appreciate science fiction's textuality in the larger literary context. I take this as a practice in 're-writing literary history' with the hope that 're-writing' leads to a more diverse, inclusive and democratic way of elucidating Chinese literary modernity.[3] This is also a way of illuminating invisible paths in literary history, which allows us to recollect how Lu Xun's largely overlooked earlier dedication to science and science fiction contributed to his later literary ideas, aesthetic style and cultural visions.

The aesthetics of the new wave offer us a new interpretation of 'A madman's diary'. The madman's discovery of a never-before-seen truth through reading 'between the lines' and investigating things as they are is a subversive move to detach his mind from the moral and epistemological codes of Confucian China. The madman overcomes the fear of seeing and observes the invisible, deep structure of reality that is too evasive and elusive to fit into conventional views. Such an unusual question as 'Is it right to eat people?'[4] calls into question all conventional references to a moralized and clearly regulated reality. It leads to a revolt in linguistic certainty, logical inference, narrative orientation and the structure of feeling, and projects a revelation about the dark and invisible depths in humanity beyond accustomed social behaviours. If we read 'A madman's diary' as science fiction, it estranges the familiar reality and inspires an insurgence in our knowledge about what is real. The alternative, disruptive truth-claiming discourse of 'A madman's diary' resonates with new wave science fiction's challenge to the fixed cultural values and ethical notions of contemporary China.

Reading 'A madman's diary' as science fiction requires repositioning Lu Xun's early engagements with science fiction within his lifelong career as a modern writer. His practice as a translator of Western science fiction and his devotion to Western sciences can be traced to the inception of his literary vision. How does 'A madman's diary', which contains an epistemological paradigm shift that attempts to discredit and rebuild the hermeneutics regarding reality, create an alternative conception of the real? How is it related to Lu Xun's knowledge of modern sciences and his practice of science fiction? After addressing these questions, I will re-examine Lu Xun's impact on the new wave of Chinese science fiction. Even though the history of Chinese science fiction is not continuous, several new wave authors claim to have received their inspiration from Lu Xun. For them, Lu Xun's unique vision created an alternative to realism through which they can perceive the invisible, see the gleams of the darkness and reach a larger imaginary realm that includes more than can be represented in literary realism.

Translating science fiction in the last decade of the Qing dynasty

Lu Xun undertook his translations during the 1902 'Revolution in Fiction' that was launched by Liang Qichao 梁啟超 (1873–1929) and began when the exiled leader of China's reform movement realized that fiction contains an immensely magical power to enlighten common readers.[5] Liang Qichao learned from Japanese politicians who used popular fiction to gain political influence during and after the Meiji Restoration and promoted a dozen new genres that prevailed in Japan, including science fiction. The genre had existed there since 1886, coined by the politician and writer Yukio Ozaki 尾崎行雄 (1858–1954).[6] Liang became a translator of Western literature through secondhand Japanese translations. The first volume of *New Fiction* 新小說, which Liang launched in Yokohama in 1902, featured the first instalment of Liang Qichao's own translation of Verne's *Two Years of Vacation* 十五小豪傑 as well as a translation of Verne's more famous *Twenty Thousand Leagues under the Sea* 海底旅行. This was the beginning of science fiction in China, when the genre was first introduced to Chinese readers. Translations of science fiction became popular, particularly the works of Jules Verne; twenty of Verne's novels were translated into Chinese within ten years. This eventually motivated Chinese authors to write China's own science and utopian fiction, which led to the first, short-lived golden era of the genre in the decade between 1902 and 1911.

Lu Xun was obviously under the influence of Liang Qichao. He wrote a concise, persuasive preface to his first translation of Verne, depicting how people overcame obstacles to communicate with each other across mountains and oceans, and how humans, with a hope for progress and evolution, will eventually have interplanetary travel. He makes it clear that his mission is to promote the value of science in order to reform China, and because science writings are not appealing to common readers, he resorts to the genre of science fiction to encourage people to learn about science. Lu Xun concludes: 'If we are to guide the Chinese people to progress, we must begin with writing science fiction.'[7] The preface echoes Liang Qichao's mission of a 'revolution in fiction', and Lu Xun also used vernacular Chinese to translate the two Verne novels, which was his earliest literary writing in the vernacular.

Like many other translators in the late Qing, Lu Xun was what might be called 'unfaithful'. He often indulged in emotional outbursts and added his own words to enhance and embellish the expressions in the original text. For example, Jules Verne's *From the Earth to the Moon* originally begins with a simple sentence: 'Pendant la guerre fédérale des États-Unis, un nouveau club très influent s'établit dans la ville de Baltimore, en plein Maryland.'[8] The standard English translation is: 'During the War of the Rebellion, a new and influential club was established in the city of Baltimore in the state of Maryland.'[9] Lu Xun's translation reads:

> Anyone who has studied world geography and history knows of a place called America. As for the American War of Independence,

even children know that it was an earth-shattering event, a deed that ought to be recalled often and never forgotten. Now, among all those states that participated in the war, one of them was called Maryland, whose capital, Baltimore, was a famous city teeming with crowds and packed with the traffic of horses and carriages. In this city was a club, magnificent in appearance, and as soon as you saw the high-flying American flag flapping in the wind in front, you naturally felt a sense of awe.[10]

As Lu Xun later confessed in a letter to Yang Jiyun 楊霽雲 (1910–96), he would rather characterize his translation method as rewriting 改作, which was not unusual at the time when Lin Shu's 林紓 (1852–1924) unfaithfully creative but beautifully 'enhanced' translations of classic Western novels were making a deep impact on Chinese intellectual readers.[11] In addition to some explanatory words about the geography and history of the United States, Lu Xun added descriptions of the street scenes of Baltimore and the details of the American flag, which create an awe-inspiring effect – estranging and sublime. This serves to enforce Lu Xun's own nationalist sentiment; throughout the text, he adds allusions to classical Chinese literature, such as the poems of Tao Yuanming 陶淵明 and the mythical figures of Jingwei 精衛 and Xingtian 刑天,[12] as well as Taoist and Buddhist terminology to bring the estranging images home. What stands out in Lu Xun's translation is a sweeping optimism that certainly originated in Verne's novels, but also applied the utopian vision of the nineteenth-century industrial revolution to an imaginary realm of China's future.

Lu Xun's translations of Western science fiction are not limited to the above-mentioned two Verne novels. In the 1930s, Lu Xun mentioned his early passion for translating science fiction: 'Because I studied science, I also favoured science fiction. When I was a youth, I was ambitious and arrogant, so I was never a faithful translator, and now it is too late for regrets.'[13] He then mentioned that he had translated four science fiction stories, including one titled 'The adventures at the North Pole' 北極探險記, which was lost after being turned down by the Commercial Press. But he did not mention the title of the fourth piece.

This fourth piece was not known to Lu Xun scholars until the 1960s. Lu Xun translated it in classical literary Chinese and published it in 1905. Titled 'Zaorenshu' 造人術, it is a translation of a science fiction story by the American female writer Louise Jackson Strong.[14] The original story is titled 'An unscientific story' and was published in *The Cosmopolitan* in February 1903. This translation, signed with the pen name 'Suozi', was rediscovered in 1962 alongside his brother Zhou Zuoren's 周作人

(1885–1967) commentary, both originally published in a double issue of the Shanghai magazine *Women's World* 女子世界 in 1905 (though the actual publication date was 1906). Lu Xun's younger brother Zhou Zuoren verified that this was indeed Lu Xun's work.[15] Research has confirmed that Lu Xun's translation, much shorter than the original story and with important modifications, was actually based on a Japanese translation by Hara Hôitsu-an 原抱一庵 (1866–1904), published in June and July 1903, just one year after the original story's publication. Hara's Japanese translation was serialized in a Japanese magazine, but only the first part was included in an anthology of Western fiction published in September 1903. It appears that Lu Xun only saw the anthologized part of the translation, so his version was only based on the first part of Hara's translation, thus creating a text that is only about one-seventh of the original length of Strong's story. However, Lu Xun's Chinese translation is largely faithful to Hara's Japanese translation.[16]

Like the majority of writings about science and science fiction of the late Qing, this translation is marked by a sweeping optimism: it depicts a scientist experimenting with creating lives. The 1,000-word translation by Lu Xun is filled with excitement over the process of creation. The scientist successfully creates 'sprouts of humanity' 人芽, which makes him feel like a god:

> Hooray! Have I not succeeded in unlocking the world's secrets? Have I not succeeded in explaining humanity's mysteries? If the world has a primal creator, then am I not the second? I can create life! I can create worlds! If I am not the creator of everything under the sun, then who is? I beget all, peopling the peopled people. I rule over all, as the king of the king of kings. What a wondrous thing it is for a mortal to become a creator![17]

The translation ends with tears of gratitude rolling down the cheeks of this new creator. Compare to Strong's original text that sticks to third-person narrative:

> Life! Life, so long the mystery and despair of man, had come at his bidding. He alone of all humanity held the secret in the hollow of his hand. He plunged about the room in a blind ecstasy of triumph. Tears run unknown and unheeded down his cheeks. He tossed his arms aloft wildly, as if challenging Omnipotence itself. At this moment, he felt a very god! He could create worlds, and people them![18]

Lu Xun's translation resonates with his belief in science. When he translated this story, he was still a student obsessed with Darwinist notions of progress and evolution. Scientific optimism deified a scientist as a god, the maker of life, which Lu Xun seems to have celebrated.

Translating science fiction synchronized Lu Xun's interests in literature and science while strengthening his belief that science could motivate larger social progress.[19] Jing Jiang's analysis of Lu Xun's translations of science fiction confirms that 'Chinese men of letters pinned their hopes for a strengthened nation on a brand-new species of man that had no ties whatsoever to the Chinese people's biogenetic past. In Lu Xun's imagination, this new species of man boasted of a new man-made body, a new physiology'.[20] This belief in the making of the new man, body and soul, continued in Lu Xun's later reflections on reforming national characteristics, a cultural motif that repeatedly re-emerged in the mainstream of modern Chinese literature throughout the twentieth century.[21]

When Lu Xun's translation was published in *Women's World*, two commentaries were printed at the end of the story, one by Zhou Zuoren (under the pen name Lady Pingyun 平雲女士) and the other by the editor, Ding Chuwo 丁初我 (1871–1930). Both commentaries derive a pessimistic message from Lu Xun's story and condemn it as being 'mythical' or evil fallacy. The critics denounce this art of creating humanity as inhuman behaviour, claiming that the true creators of life are women, or the nation's mothers. Ding Chuwo states that the art of creating humans actually 'disseminates evil causes and spreads deviants seeds, which is scary'.[22] Lydia Liu questions how the editors 'could have correctly predicted the dystopia of Louise Strong's original on the basis of partial knowledge'.[23] Yoojin Soh proposes, through a contrast between the commentaries and the text, that 'Lu Xun's translation does not showcase the omnipotence of science but motivates pessimistic interpretations; carrying out reforms through scientific means does have great potential, but it is also likely that this will further worsen the problems with the national character'.[24] The way that the story was presented foregrounds both its thesis and antithesis. While the commentaries view science, or scientism, as counternatural and unethical, the tension between the text and the commentaries predicts the later debate on science and metaphysics 科學與人生觀. If Lu Xun was on the same page with the two commentators, this translation actually could be viewed as an ironic portrait of the mad scientist, who is a violator of nature and an enemy of an organic society. In terms of biopolitics, it is clear that the textuality or intertextuality created by the two commentaries shows a tendency toward treating life as organic rather than a product of technology. In other words, the commentaries amount to a disbelief in science, contrary to Lu Xun's advocacy for scientific progress. The scientific discourse leads to the 'illusion' or 'myth' that turns back into 'reality', and scientific truthfulness is discounted by its ethical ambiguity. But on the other hand, ethics is defined by conventions, and human nature is shaped by accustomed cultural habits. The truthfulness defined by the commentators may not be less 'organic' or 'natural' than the unaccustomed scientific views.

These scholars point out the paradoxical questions that highlight the uncanny resonance between the commentaries and the untranslated other half of the story. The anti-science commentaries and the original 'unscientific story' share the suspicion of the scientific optimism expressed in the first half of the story, which forms the entirety of Lu Xun's text. The untranslated part of Louise J. Strong's 'An unscientific story' contains the scary message that Ding Chubo implies, while the second half of the story is even more important than the first half. The lives that the scientist creates mutate into cannibals, which quickly turns this glorious moment of creation by scientific means into an apocalyptic event threatening the order of human society. Louise J. Strong may have followed Mary Shelley in depicting the Frankenstein-like scientist, through which a scepticism about science, based in Romanticism, is presented to counter 'Baconian optimism and Enlightenment confidence that everything can ultimately be known and that such knowledge will inevitably be for the good'.[25] Strong's story, written after H.G. Wells (1866–1946), is even more sharply contrary to the Enlightenment belief in scientific progress represented by Jules Verne. The living creatures that the professor creates in Strong's original story are more hideous than Frankenstein's monster. They are not romantic and sensitive; they are cannibals. The creation of life turns out to be a detriment to science. The scientist has no choice but to lock all the devilish creatures in the laboratory to destroy but, before he does so, the creatures destroy themselves in an accident. The surviving scientist tells his wife that he is not going to rebuild the laboratory and now belongs to her and their children, indicating his intention to return to the normative society and his submission to the conventional ethical codes.[26]

Written before the genre became pulp fiction as defined by Hugo Gernsback (1884–1967), Strong's story casts doubt on science. Labelled as a scientific story, it is unscientific, or rather, counterscientific. The self-contradictory title 'An unscientific story' almost lays bare that this tale could be read as a self-parody of 'scientific story'. Its deeply dystopian suspicion of the benefits of science for humanity continues a sentiment that H.G. Wells expressed in *The Time Machine* (1895), *The Invisible Man*

(1896) and, in particular, *The Island of Doctor Moreau* (1897). As an 'unscientific story', Strong's text epitomizes the questioning of science in both natural and ethical terms, a perpetual motif that defines science fiction as a genre that engages with science in both its positive and negative aspects.

'A madman's diary' was written twelve years after Lu Xun published 'The art of creating humanity', and he never mentioned this translation again in any writing or recorded conversation. However, 'A madman's diary', including the diary entries together with the prologue, shares three crucial elements with 'An unscientific story', particularly the second half that Lu Xun did not translate. Because he may not have read the second half at all, the three elements discussed here are not proof of American science fiction's influence on Lu Xun, but rather manifestations of the potential for science fictionality in Lu Xun's text. Cannibalism is the most obvious. By including cannibalism, 'An unscientific story' turns a scientific story into horror fiction, rendering science as a threat to humanity. 'A madman's diary' turns cannibalism into a cultural metaphor that constitutes an allegory about the national character and, on the surface of the text, the allegory of cannibalism creates a truthful discourse supported by a reconfiguration of scientific knowledge and epistemological paradigm. 'A madman's diary' can be read as 'an unscientific story' full of illusive moments about 'eating people' and 'being eaten', a fear that dismantles the orderly structure of the entire civilization. But it is also a 'scientific story', which presents a medical case and represents its abnormal manifestation as a new method to apprehend and interpret the social reality. By revealing 'cannibalism' in the Chinese nation, the story produces a medical report on the disease in the body, mind and culture of an entire nation.

The thesis shared by both stories is to use science to create humans or to use Enlightenment ideas to create the true humans, which embodies the dual hopes invested in scientific optimism and social progressivism. 'An unscientific story' begins here, but this thesis collapses as the plot evolves – the scientist's ecstasy soon turns into agony when he tries to imprison the cannibals in the laboratory. 'A madman's diary' also ends with the collapse of this humanist thesis. Lu Xun's writings are more revealing about the predicament of the project of Enlightenment, represented in his metaphor of the iron house, the image he conceived right before the story for 'A madman's diary'. When Qian Xuantong 錢玄同 (1887–1939) invited him to contribute 'something' to the progressive magazine *New Youth* 新青年, Lu Xun presented the allegory about an iron house in which people were confined and about to suffocate to death. Lu Xun argues: 'Is it right to cry out, to rouse the light sleepers among them, causing them inconsolable agony before they die?'[27] The iron house where the people are imprisoned, if they are cannibals as described in 'A madman's diary', bears some resemblance to the locked laboratory in Strong's story, in terms of the containment of the living, whether the intention is to sympathize with or condemn them. Thus, the second shared element between the two stories is the confinement of the cannibals. Both the laboratory in Strong's story and the iron house in Lu Xun's writings represent the failure of science and Enlightenment, which opens the gate to darkness, the irrational and inhuman.

Both stories constitute the antithesis to scientism, Enlightenment and modernization of humans in both body and mind. 'An unscientific story' shows the failure of science straightforwardly. 'A madman's diary' is much more sophisticated in expressing doubt about science and Enlightenment. The preface, written in classical literary Chinese, and the following diary entries, written in vernacular Chinese, each represent a claim to truthfulness. While the madman's discovery of the cannibalism in Confucian society can be understood as a truth-claiming moment, the madman's pathological status both enlarges and limits the power of this truth, depending on how much the reader gives credit to the assumed orthodoxy and scientism in the preface. But, at the same time, the truth evokes the fear of seeing. In the first diary entry, the madman reaches enlightenment but also says, 'I have reason to be afraid'.[28] The fear may be a totalistic feeling about the entire environment as the iron house that suffocates the imprisoned souls; while awaking from the illusive dream can be liberating, seeing the truth of the world can be more terrifying, for it also enlightens the disillusioned to despair. The fear also comes from the awareness that the madman, the awakened and enlightened, is not only surrounded by the cannibals but also one of them: 'With the weight of four thousand years of cannibalism bearing down upon me, even if once I was innocent, how can I now face real humans?'[29] Who are the real humans? 'A madman's diary' ends with a famous quote: 'Save the children'. It echoes Strong's scientist's last words to his wife. This moment marks the third shared element between the two stories. In 'A madman's diary', self-reflection leads to a profound suspicion of the enlightened subject, which inserts themselves ahead of the emergence of modern Chinese consciousness; this moment is characterized by a sweeping darkness. Science, Enlightenment, progress and the change that each will bring about are subject to the same denial that is imposed upon modern subjectivity. There is no hope here and now; hope can only be reserved for the future: 'saving the children' from becoming cannibals (like Lu Xun's generation) represents the last and only hope.

The richness of Lu Xun's textual techniques and implications makes 'A madman's Diary' far superior to the straightforward narrative in 'An unscientific story' in literary terms. But reading 'A madman's diary' alongside 'An unscientific story' helps illuminate Lu Xun's doubt about scientific progressivism in the larger context of the twentieth-century intellectuals' sophisticated attitudes toward science, Enlightenment and progress when the world was about to turn modern. Furthermore, 'An unscientific story' helps connect Lu Xun's earlier views on science and science fiction to his later literary practice, such as what he does in 'A madman's diary'. Science fiction can serve as one of the many gates through which to enter Lu Xun's literary world.

Lu Xun in the matrix

In April 1918, Lu Xun wrote 'A madman's diary', a text that resists definition and released phantoms and strange images to haunt Chinese literature. This story caused an earthquake in the literary field of modern China, and the aftershocks are still being felt today. 'A madman's diary' is a work that cannot be repeated or imitated. It is Lu Xun's second short story, 'Kong Yiji' 孔乙己 rather than 'A madman's diary' that sealed Lu Xun's position as the master of literary realism. But the black-body radiation of 'A madman's diary' would extend to Lu Xun's entire oeuvre and define his artistic strength. Now, 100 years later, new wave science fiction writers have illuminated that invisible darkness again, and their writings caused a new revolution to change worldviews, just like 'A madman's diary' did in the past.

Lu Xun's literary talent went far beyond writing a national allegory and social criticism. He later wrote more personal, lyrical stories about childhood, his hometown, nostalgia, disillusionment, despair, regret, self-deception and self-questioning. Lu Xun was a writer with a profound self-consciousness. He questioned the notion of progress and doubted the utility and validity of his own writing together with its 'poisonous' effects in enlightening youths but driving them to a spiritual limbo where they have no way out.

Many decades later, his darker, cannibalistic, morally ambivalent literary vision found echoes in *The Three-Body Problem*, which, together with its two sequels, depicts the epic journey of humans into deep space where they see the real truth of the universe, swirling above the tombs of those perished civilizations. It is a truth based in chaos and amorality: the universe, once a hyperdimensional paradise, has been ruthlessly reduced by competing intelligent species to three-dimensional ruins, and further to a two-dimensional flat world, and ultimately to nothing. The universe has been consumed by its populations, which have first cannibalized each other. Ironically, this novel bases its world building on concepts and theories drawn from the quantum revolution,[30] which dismantled the Newtonian universe. When the new wave of Chinese science fiction began to emerge, the quantum revolution had become widely accepted in the scientific community. The virtual reality game featured in *The Three-Body Problem* renders the physicists into game players to explore the chaotic, lawless universe of the Trisolarans, though their speculations about that invisible world are not related to how the world appears to be; like the madman, they look through the appearance to capture the hidden truth beneath the surface of reality.

Cannibalism also returned as a salient motif. Liu Cixin's 劉慈欣 (1963–) *The Three-Body* trilogy depicts cannibalism as a reasonable means by which the survivors continue to live in the isolated Starship Earths; Han Song's many stories and novels depict cannibalism prevailing in all sorts of worlds. If Liu Cixin tries to use science fictional speculation to justify cannibalism as a necessity for survival, Han Song continues Lu Xun's method to create a truth-claiming literary discourse that goes beneath the surface reality, illuminating the invisible darkness where dream is sleepwalking, utopia is dystopian, life is dead, human is machine. The quantum chaos has turned from a metaphor into one kind of (virtual) reality in the writings of Liu Cixin, Han Song, and younger writers such as Fei Dao 飛氘 (b. 1983). Which is more science fictional, Han Song asks, China's reality or science fiction? Contemporary Chinese science fiction, when situated outside the mainstream paradigm of Chinese realism, is a hyperrealist effort to capture the truth about China's invisible reality. In this sense, the nightmarish, the cannibalistic and the surreal all answer to Lu Xun's first outcry in 'A madman's diary', a story that has become like Planck's constant, moving through all variations of its own positions or states and still there, invisible, uncertain, inexplicable – whether you believe it or not.

Finally, I will examine Lu Xun's appearance in new wave science fiction. Fei Dao's appropriation of Lu Xun's own strategy of 'Old Chinese tales retold' 故事新編 as a narrative device in the making of the so-called 'Chinese sci-fi blockbusters' 中國科幻大片 creates one particular scenario that is borrowed from the American sci-fi film *Cube* (1997) but more immediately concerns Lu Xun.[31] In this story, Zhou Shuren is a physician who uses his own blood to make some red pills, which he feeds awakened youths so that they can see the true reality of the Cube world, a dark world plagued by cannibals, zombies, monstrous creatures and all sorts of demons. Though he tries very hard to lead those trapped in the Cube to escape to the outside world, this is a hopeless battle. Zhou Shuren knows that this is a predesigned game, and reality is nothing but virtual, and the game designer did not create any exit.

Fei Dao's story playfully showcases Lu Xun's bewildering position in China's modernity project: though a leading intellectual in modern China, he never stopped doubting the results of the Enlightenment. This narrative can also be read as an allegory that implies an intensely entangled relationship between Lu Xun's role in the rise of literary realism and his devotion to science studies and science fiction. His fight and his despair, his gaze into the darkness and his insightful understanding that this is a hopeless game heightens this chapter's major concern about how we can read Lu Xun's works, particularly 'A madman's diary', in light of the aesthetic innovations of science fiction.

Lu Xun's, Han Song's and Liu Cixin's texts all make us feel that something is wrong with the world. It is no longer what it appears to be. A deeper revolution happens to reconfigure the textual world. What is real? The madman discovers cannibalism – such a subversive claim makes a virtual truthful world above the surface reality. One hundred years later, Han Song shows us the cannibalism in the underground world beneath Beijing's subway system, and Liu Cixin's characters debate the legitimacy of eating people in outer space. Is cannibalism a symptom of disease, the malady of civilization, a true event in its literal meaning, or a cultural metaphor that transcends time? Lu Xun uses this unsettling image to subvert our reality. One hundred years later, new wave science fiction has done the same. Back to the future, we find the world is no longer what it appears to be.

Notes

1. Lu Xun, 'Didi lüxing', 151–60.
2. Song, 'After 1989'.
3. For 'rewriting literary history', I have borrowed the ideas from Chen Sihe 陳思和, who first conceived this strategy together with Wang Xiaoming王曉明 in 1988. See Chen, 'Rewriting literary history', 797–803.
4. Lu Xun, *The Real Story of Ah-Q and Other Tales of China*, 27.
5. Liang 1996, 74–81. The piece was originally published in *Xin xiaoshuo*新小說 vol. 1:1 (1902). The same inaugural issue featured a column dedicated to 'science fiction' 科學小說.
6. Yasuo, *Riben kehuan xiaoshuo shihua*, 53.
7. Lu Xun *Yuejie lüxing*, vol. 11, 10.
8. Verne, *From the Earth to the Moon* (online access).
9. Verne, *From the Earth to the Moon*, 7.
10. Lu Xun, *Yuejie lüxing*, 13. The English translation is Ken Liu's. See Liu, *The Dark Forest*.

11. For a systematic study in Lin Shu's translation strategies and their cultural significance in the making of modern Chinese culture, See Hill, *Lin Shu, Inc.*
12. Lu Xun, *Yuejie lüxing*, 13–15.
13. Lu Xun, 'Suoji', vol. 13, 99.
14. Louise J. Strong was an author of several adventure novels written for children, active at the beginning of the twentieth century. But nothing more is known about her life.
15. In a letter to the Lu Xun scholar Chen Mengxiong 陳夢熊, Zhou Zuoren verified that the translation was Lu Xun's work, which he brought to the magazine *Nüzi shijie* 女子世界 to which Zhou Zuoren contributed numerous translations and original works. As for the story's original author, Zhou Zuoren called her an 'obscure literatus'「無名文人」. See Chen, 'Zhitang laoren tan "Aichen," "Zaorenshu" de sanfengxin', 40.
16. Soh 'Cong kexue dao chiren: Lu Xun 'Zaorenshu' fanyi yu yeman de qianzai shuxie', 70.
17. Lu Xun (as Souzi) 'The art of creating humanity', 74–5.
18. Strong, 'An unscientific story', 411–17.
19. Jones 2011, 7–8.
20. Jiang, 'From the technique for creating humans to the art of reprogramming hearts', 138.
21. Liu 1993, 138–16; Liu, *Translingual Practice*, 45–76.
22. Deng, 'Lu Xun yi Zaorenshu he Bao Tianxiao yi Zaorenshu', 28.
23. Liu, 'Life as form', 21–54.
24. Soh, 'Cong kexue dao chiren', 67–83.
25. Haynes, *From Faust to Strangelove*, 94.
26. Strong, 'An unscientific story', 417.
27. Lu Xun, *The Real Story of Ah-Q and Other Tales of China*, 19.
28. Lu Xun, *The Real Story of Ah-Q and Other Tales of China*, 22.
29. Lu Xun, *The Real Story of Ah-Q and Other Tales of China*, 31.
30. Liu Cixin heavily relies on quantum physics in his creation of the alien world as well as the universe beyond human knowledge. The entire chapter 33 'Trisolaris: Sophon' is a scientific, or at least seemingly scientific, description of the quantum-like sophon that is used by the alien civilization to experiment with spatial dimensional adjustment. Liu, *The Three-Body Problem*, 357–83.
31. Fei Dao, *Zhongguo kehuan dapian*, 177–9.

Bibliography

Chen, Mengxiong 陳夢熊. 'Zhitang laoren tan "Aichen," "Zaorenshu" de sanfengxin' 知堂老人谈<哀尘>、<造人术>的三封信. *Lu Xun yanjiu dongtai* 鲁迅研究动态, vol. 12, 1986. pp. 39–42.

Chen, Sihe. '"Rewriting literary history" in the new era of the liberated thought'. *A New Literary History of Modern China*, edited by David Der-wei Wang, Harvard University Press, 2017, pp. 797–803.

Deng, Tianyi 鄧天乙. 'Lu Xun yi Zaorenshu he Bao Tianxiao yi Zaorenshu' 鲁迅譯〈造人術〉和包天笑譯〈造人術〉, *Changchun shifan xuebao* 長春師院學報 (社科版), vol. 4, 1996, pp. 26–30.

Fei, Dao 飛氘. *Zhongguo kehuan dapian* 中國科幻大片. Qinghua daxue chubanshe, 2013.

Haynes, Roslynn D. *From Faust to Strangelove: representations of the scientist in western literature*. Johns Hopkins University Press, 1994.

Hill, Michael Gibbs. *Lin Shu, Inc.: translation and the making of modern Chinese culture*. Oxford University Press, 2013.

Jameson, Fredric. 'Third-world literature in the era of multinational capitalism'. *Social Text*, vol. 15, 1986, pp. 65–88.

Jiang, Jing. 'From the technique for creating humans to the art of reprogramming hearts: scientists, writers, and the genesis of China's modern literary vision'. *Cultural Critique* 80 (Winter), 2012, pp. 131–49.

Jones, Andrew. *Developmental Fairy Tales: Evolutionary Thinking and Modern Chinese Culture*. Harvard University Press, 2011.

Lee, Leo Ou-fan. *Voices from the Iron House: a study of Lu Xun*. Indiana University Press, 1987.

Liang Qichao. 'On the Relationship Between Fiction and the Government of the People.' *Modern Chinese Literary Thought: Writings on Literature, 1893–1945*, edited by Kirk Denton, translated by Gek Nai Cheng. Stanford University Press, 1996, pp. 74–81.

Liu, Cixin. *The Three-Body Problem,* translated by Ken Liu. Tor Books, 2014.

Liu, Cixin. *The Dark Forest*, translated by Joel Martinsen. Tor Books, 2015.

Liu, Ken. 'The "heroic translators" who reinvented classic science fiction in China'. *Gizmodo*. https://io9.gizmodo.com/the-heroic-translators-who-reinvented-classic-science-1696944844. Accessed 8 November 2020.

Liu, Lydia 劉禾. "Yige xiandaixing shenhua de youlai: guominxing huayu zhiyi" 一个现代性神话的由来：国民性话语质疑, edited by Chen Pingyuan. *Wenxueshi congkan* 文学史丛刊 Beijing daxue chubanshe, 1993, pp. 138–56.

Liu, Lydia. *Translingual Practice: literature, national culture, and translated modernity, 1900–1937.* Stanford University Press, 1995.

Liu, Lydia. 'Life as form: how biomimesis encounters buddhism in Lu Xun'. *The Journal of Asian Studies*, vol. 68., no. 1, 2009, pp. 21–54.

Lu, Xun 鲁迅. 'Didi lüxing' 地底旅行, *Zhejiang chao* 浙江潮, vol. 1, no. 10, 1903, pp. 151–60.

Lu, Xun 鲁迅. *Yuejie lüxing* 月界旅行. *Lu Xun quanji* 鲁迅全集, Renmin wenxue chubanshe, vol. 11, 1973, pp. 7–119.

Lu, Xun 鲁迅. *Xuwai xiaoshuo ji* 域外小說. *Lu Xun quanji*, vol. 11, 1973, pp. 185–231.

Lu, Xun 鲁迅. 'Suoji'. 瑣記. *Lu Xun quanji* 鲁迅全集, Renmin wenxue chubanshe, vol. 2, 2005, pp. 301–312.

Lu, Xun 鲁迅. '340515 zhi Yang Jiyun' 340515致楊霁雲. *Lu Xun quanji*, vol. 13, 2005, pp. 99–101.

Lu, Xun. *The Real Story of Ah-Q and Other Tales of China: the complete fiction of Lu Xun*, translated by Julia Lovell. Penguin. 2009.

Lu, Xun. 'Diary of a madman'. *The Real Story of Ah-Q and Other Tales of China*. Penguin, 2009, pp. 21–31.

Lu, Xun (as Suozi) 'The art of creating humanity', translated by Carlos Rojas, *Renditions*, vol. 77/78, 2012, pp. 70–7.

Soh, Yoojin 徐维辰. 'Cong kexue dao chiren: Lu Xun 'Zaorenshu' fanyi yu yeman de qianzai shuxie' 从科学到吃人：鲁迅'造人术'翻译与野蛮的潜在书写. *Wenxue* 文學 (Spring/Summer), 2017, pp. 67–83.

Song, Mingwei. 'After 1989: the new wave of Chinese science fiction'. *China Perspectives*, vol. 1, 2015, pp. 7–13.

Strong, Louise J. 'An unscientific story'. *The Cosmopolitan*, vol. 34, no. 4, 1903, pp. 411–17.

Teruo, Tarumoto 樽本照雄. 'Lu Xun 'Zaorenshu' de yuanzuo, buyi' 鲁迅〈造人术〉的原作·补遗. *Lu Xun fanyi yanjiu lunwenji* 鲁迅翻译研究论文集, ed. Beijing Lu Xun Museum 北京鲁迅博物馆, Chufeng wenyi chubanshe, vol. 201, pp. 186–7.

Yan, Fu 嚴復 and Xia Zengyou 夏曾佑. 'Benguan fuyin shuobu yuanqi' 本館附印說部緣起. *Guowenbao* 國聞報, 10, 13 November, 8, 11 December, 1897.

Yasuo Nagayama 長山靖生. *Riben kehuan xiaoshuo shihua: cong mufumoqi dao zhanhou* 日本SF精神史 幕末・明治から戦後まで (translated into Chinese as 日本科幻小說史話——從幕府末期到戰後). Nanjing daxue chubanshe, 2012.

Verne, Jules. *From the Earth to the Moon, and a Trip Around It*. Scribner, Armstrong & Company, 1874.

Verne, Jules. *De la Terre à la Lune*. Project Gutenberg. http://www.gutenberg.org/files/799/799-h/799-h.htm. Accessed 8 November 2020.

8
Translating Chinese Science Fiction into English: Decolonization and Reconciliation on a Cultural Battlefield

Emily Xueni Jin

Introduction

Following the growing presence of translated Chinese science fiction (SF) on the international literary market in the past decade,[1] a question emerges as Chinese SF engages extensively with a readership beyond its own mother tongue: what makes Chinese SF Chinese? Over the past years, this has been the million-dollar question from which writers, translators and scholars could barely escape. Truly, when non-Chinese readership speaks about Chinese SF, which in itself is an amalgamation of subgenres, influences and cultural representations, it appears that the indicator 'Chinese' is reinforced as the primary – if not the sole – point of focus. In his essay 'China dreams: contemporary Chinese science fiction', Ken Liu[2] asks American readers to 'imagine asking a hundred different American authors and critics to characterise "American SF" – you'd hear a hundred different answers. The same is true of Chinese authors and critics, and Chinese SF'. As Liu summarizes, the only thing that makes Chinese SF Chinese is that it is written for a Chinese audience.[3] Liu Cixin 刘慈欣 addresses this question by stating in an interview with NPR (National Public Radio) in 2015, 'I hope that one day, American readers will buy and read Chinese SF because it's sci-fi, not because it's Chinese. The calamities we face in SF are faced by humanity together.'[4] The writers quoted here reiterate a similar approach: the writers' subjective creative identity should be reinforced instead of their relationship with an implied 'Chineseness'.

Instead of furthering the writers' responses, I wish to answer the question by posing one of my own: does Chinese SF have to be 'Chinese'? It is important to interrogate the Chineseness of Chinese SF, as it presents itself as a space of ambiguity. Deconstructing the question down to its core, I argue, is that the particularization of a certain Chineseness implies the existence of a point of comparison, a calibration against a global system defined by national borders. In other words, the categorization of Chinese SF is contingent on the perceived presence of a readership that is linguistically and culturally non-Chinese. It is such a linguistic and cultural relativity that inevitably leads us to examine the role of translation in the formulation of the idea of Chinese SF. It is precisely the translation of Chinese SF – primarily into English – that engenders the debates surrounding its Chineseness. The Chineseness of Chinese SF, hence, is conceivably induced via translation. The interdependence between China's future-oriented vision of development, technological prowess and 'soft power' output further complicates the scenario, placing the specific genre of science fiction – defined by its intricate ties with science, technology and future imaginations – in a peculiar position that warrants disproportionally great attention from both the Anglophone world and the Chinese state, leading to further speculations of the relationship between Chinese SF and China. Translation enables a contact zone, which, given the increasing tension between China and the West, could also be described as a cultural battlefield.

I suggest that the particularization of Chinese SF's Chineseness coalesces from its peripheral status and a bilateral orientalism that impacts China just as much as the West. However, I by no means wish to pigeonhole the case of translated Chinese SF as yet another example of victimization, highlighting its vulnerability in the face of the palimpsest of colonialism and the global literary market's iron-clad hierarchy. Instead, I devote this chapter to discussing the potential for empowerment that arises from translation, which I optimistically believe is aiding Chinese SF down the toilsome path of decolonization. Translation, in this case, is a pharmakon with the inherent duality of oppression and emancipation: the kind of translation-induced Chineseness as viewed through the eyes of Chinese SF's Anglophone readers, embedded with orientalist essentialization, could be undone through the very act of translation. Buttressed by my own translation experience and the changes that I have observed, I propose that nearly a decade after Ken Liu's article, his definition of Chinese SF, 'written for a Chinese audience', is now due for re-examination.

One of the greatest changes that Chinese SF has seen in recent years is the number of practising translators and the amount of Chinese

SF demanding to be translated. Engaged in a strong symbiosis, they now constitute an integral part of Chinese SF's production and reception, both domestic and international. Meanwhile, a generation of younger writers born after 1980 are beginning to occupy centre stage. Born in the time of China's economic reform and opening, influenced by the massive amount of translated works entering China just as much as canonized Chinese literature, this generation is characterized by their openness to translations and the idea of a global community. Additionally, most of these writers are fluent in English, which means that they can directly engage with the English editions of their stories as well as the translators' working process, blurring the line between the traditionally distinct roles of the writer and the translator. In general, due to the increased accessibility of translators and the marrying of the writer and the translator, the boundaries between the domestic and the international are also undergoing erasure; the writer, who now expects the attention of more than one readerships, may tailor their work to appeal to a global audience or create translingual texts with support from the translator. In an epoch of translatability and multilingualism, traditional concepts of semantic equivalence, authenticity and target audience are continually scrutinized by the writer and the translator. Together, they are actively engaged in a process that Italian SF writer Francesco Verso denotes as 'decolonize the future'.[5] Chinese SF, no longer necessarily written for a Chinese audience or in the Chinese language in its most narrow definition, demonstrates its agency in resisting the illusion of a unified 'Chineseness' constructed substantially from orientalist preconceptions.

Finally, my peculiar role, wedged between a scholar and a translator working on the forefront of rendering Chinese SF in English, determines that my perspective will be a synthesis of detached academic criticism and subjective personal involvement. I also acknowledge that my approach is nowhere near a comprehensive analysis of translated Chinese SF in general. It is grounded in my own familiarity with the Chinese–English translation scene, primarily between China and America, and is therefore constrained within these parameters.

Orientalization of Chinese science fiction

The case of the three-body problem may shine light on the explicit and implicit manifestations of orientalism in the case of translated Chinese SF. As early as 2014, a week before the official English publication of the book, *The Wall Street Journal* already addressed its critical acclaim in a news report, describing it as 'China launches a sci-fi invasion of the US',[6] On 3 December 2019, *The New York Times* published an article on contemporary Chinese SF, 'Why is Chinese sci-fi everywhere now? Ken Liu knows'. Composed from a series of interviews conducted by Alexandra Alter, the article is primarily centred on Ken Liu, describing how he came to be in touch with the Chinese SF community and details Ken Liu's collaboration with Liu Cixin. However, only two days after, *The New York Times* changed the article's title to 'How Chinese sci-fi conquered America'.[7] On top of the deliberate highlighting of Chineseness, the usage of words like 'conquer' and 'invasion' evoke war-like images that imply an underlying antagonism towards Chinese SF. We can observe an immediate equation of Chinese SF with the Chinese state, in which Chinese SF is politicized as a token of China. Existing scholarship has also critically pointed out the underlying orientalism behind this common perspective from the West. Gwennaël Gaffric warns that it would be dangerous to embrace such a reductionist perspective and agrees that the attempts taken by the American press are markedly a result of xenophobia.[8] Similarly, Cao Xuenan argues that it is an inherently orientalist position to take, 'in suggesting that Liu's novels reflect the changing political order of China and that they appeal to Western sensibilities about Chinese politics'.[9]

Orientalism manifests in not only the antagonization of the current nation-state China, as illustrated by the case of 'The three-body problem' which takes place in modern and future China, but also the fetishization of a temporally distant China. The genre of SF and fantasy has a history of borrowing from non-Western cultures for the purpose of world-building. As a culturally disparate 'other', China appears different enough from the lived reality of writers with a Western-centric perspective, hence a mosaic of over-simplified fragments of Chinese history and mythology is often conjured up in the fantastical imagination in the form of Eastern mysticism and native purity. Chinese cultural elements are either appropriated to suit the needs of the writer, or negligently described as rough equivalences of prominent Western cultural symbols. Scholars in the volume 'Techno-orientalism: imagining Asia in speculative fiction, history and media' tease apart the orientalist stereotypes that litter speculative fiction, ranging from popular media like *Star Trek* to prominent authors including Neal Stephenson, William Gibson and Philip K. Dick.[10]

In the same vein, an ethnocentric 'welcoming' from the West that encourages Chinese SF to self-represent may also bring about essentialization in a way that is more implicit than blatant antagonism or fetishization. For instance, as Verso delineates eloquently in a recent article, he staunchly rejects the use of the word 'diversity' because it implies the existence of a heteronomous standard of reference, a not-so-conscious measure of comparison that a privileged 'gatekeeper' (an English-speaking editor, a marketing director of a multinational corporation, or a publishing group executive) has imposed as a method of compensating for a deeper problem and masking a predetermined point of view by which to evaluate every other identity, narrative, cultural history, and, ultimately, vision of the future.[11]

From Verso's perspective, the global market's demand for diversity betrays and further perpetuates its own ethnocentrism. Postcolonial theorist Robert Young elucidates the same dilemma, 'the politics of recognition is once again a self-fulfilling paradigm that only seeks to cure the illness that it has itself created'.[12] In my case, by pigeonholing translated Chinese SF into a representation of Chineseness and parading it around as a spectacle, the American market stamps Chinese SF with the qualification to meet its diversity requirement – it is not Anglophone and not white. At various conventions and conferences that I have attended, Chinese SF writers and translators were rarely grouped with professionals from other linguistic and cultural backgrounds based on thematic interest or specialized skill. Instead, writers and translators distinct in creative content and style were often assembled into a single panel based on the sole characteristic of being Chinese instead of their professional identity. In order to comply with the kind of diversity that the American market prescribes, translated Chinese SF had to forego another kind of diversity – the geographic, linguistic and cultural diversity *within* China.

Moreover, the dominant culture's celebration of a particularized Chineseness that is 'diverse' relative to themselves fails to acknowledge the myriad of influences on Chinese SF from translation: Nicoletta Pesaro and Gaffric both highlight the substantial inspirations that Chinese SF has drawn from works translated into Chinese from English, Russian, Japanese and more, which ultimately coalesced into the genre's vibrance.[13] This approach embalms Chinese SF so that it is solely defined by an ossified indigenousness, depriving it of its fluidity, transformational potential and arguably cosmopolitan nature. In the words of Naoki Sakai,

> what is heterogeneous to the West can be organised into a kind of monolithic resistance against the West, but within the nation homogeneity must predominate ... exactly the same type of relationship as that between the West and the non-West will be reproduced between the nation as a whole and heterogeneous elements in it.[14]

When the West lauds Chinese SF in the name of diversity, the result may be an erasure of the heterogeneity of Chinese culture – an ever-evolving symphony composed of a plethora of cultures within China and external influences translated into China.

However, it would be reductionist as well to pinpoint the West as the sole perpetrators of the construction of 'Chineseness' in Chinese SF. In the same vein, I will refrain from the usage of 'self-orientalism' in this chapter, as it would totalize the responses of Chinese writers into mere passive reactions to the West. The reality is, China is just as complicit in the construction of Chinese SF's Chineseness. After Liu Cixin rose to global fame, the Publicity Department of the Chinese Communist Party celebrated 'The three-body problem' as an integral part of contemporary China's success in cultural exportation, canonizing the work as one of the seventy most influential literary works of China's seventy years. Pesaro attributes the thriving of new Chinese SF to four reasons, three of which speak to how the genre's inherent characteristics coincide with the Chinese state's future blueprint of technological advancements,[15] hence SF is 'a tool for Chinese soft power aimed at building up strategic narratives suitable to China's present day domestic and international policies'.[16] The elevation of Liu's status from obscure pulp fiction writer to literary hero signifies a state-supported attempt to cultivate a national literature of China that is specifically translated to showcase China's own cultural and technological achievements. Hence, we can read the prescription of essentializing Chineseness as China's deliberate agenda to promote an exportable version of contemporary Chinese culture defined primarily by national borders.

Yet, we must also recognize that the West's approval is weighted heavily in determining the choices of both the Chinese government and the Chinese market. The Chinese state's critical emphasis on translation may inadvertently reveal another consequence of orientalism: the valorization of Chinese literature is relative to its prestige in the global market, which is underlain with Western-centrism. Hence, success of the English translation of a Chinese work may be sufficient in determining its domestic reception. Shih Shu-mei's critical analysis of early twentieth-century Chinese literature continues to be relevant in the case of contemporary China, that is, the particularization of Chineseness is a result of an orientalizing Western endorsement of certain aspects of Chinese culture. As Shih states, 'it was still the West that determined what could be granted the virtue of universalism'.[17] Thus, the China that wishes to enter literary universalism and achieve global cultural recognition in the twenty-first century must first particularize its Chineseness in exchange for an opportunity to acquire the rest of the world's attention.

Decolonizing the future through translation

Chinese SF writers and translators, now at the forefront of Chinese literature in translation, are sailing across treacherous seas with prevailing orientalism, which constrains them to straddling the line between antagonism, exotification and a state-induced particularization. However, I believe that uncritical pessimism and overemphasis on victimization would only lead to a reductionist theorization that deprives the writer and the translator of their agency and subjectivity. In the subsequent section, I will demonstrate that the *awareness* towards Chinese SF's translatability is key to the active decolonization that has emerged in the creative efforts of Chinese SF writers and translators. Here, to decolonize consists of both neutralizing the Anglocentric hierarchy of the global literary scene and counteracting various forms of orientalism that manifest through the production and reception of the text's 'Chineseness'. Examples from my own practice of translating Chinese SF into English illustrate the empowering potential of translation in the face of orientalism's omnipotence. It should be noted, however, that my personal case is not generalizable to other Chinese SF translators; with both Chinese and English as mother tongues and having spent equal years in China and Anglophone countries, my ease in accessing cultural connotations and forming personal bonds with writers is rather peculiar than commonplace.

Pascale Casanova acerbically acknowledges the current dominating, 'universal' position of English upon its replacement of French as the new lingua franca and points to the consequent ignorance of the Anglophone world towards peripheral languages and cultures. As Casanova extrapolates, Italian poet Giacomo Leopardi 'accuses the French of systematically appropriating as their own the foreign literary texts that they translate, forgetting, in a way, the works' provenance in order to transform them into French texts';[18] the same could be said for the contemporary international literature scene in the case of translating from any given language into English, in which the Anglophone reader's arrogance often demands the translator to actively forego cultural particularities of the source text to appeal to its new audience that is situated high up in the hierarchy of cultural power due to the wide circulation of the English language. Endowed upon the Anglophone world is the gatekeeping authority to evaluate literature from peripheral cultures and languages according to its own ethnocentric standards, for it holds the power of determination over the global market's taste. Echoing Casanova's criticalness towards the hierarchy of the global circulation of texts, Lawrence Venuti criticizes the phenomenon of valorizing translations that read seamlessly like a text produced in the target language, which he refers to as the translator's invisibility.[19] Contextualizing translation in the age of Anglophone superiority, Venuti delineates the idea of domestication. He expounds on domestication in translation as adherence to the dominant target language's syntactical, narrative and cultural norms, by which the source work's provenance is sacrificed for 'the illusion of transparency produced in fluent translation',[20] and further coins it as an 'ethnocentric violence'.[21]

However, though Casanova's illustration of the central–peripheral model is helpful in providing a toolkit to dissect the Anglocentric hierarchy, it is insufficient to account for the specific case of translated Chinese SF. As I had previously discussed, in addition to the peripheral status of Chinese language relative to English, translated Chinese SF bears another layer of complexity from the prevailing orientalism, which manifests itself simultaneously as antagonism towards the modern Chinese state, alongside its cultural products, and exotification of various facets of Chinese culture and society. Venuti propagates that foreignization, a practice that '[resists] dominant target-language cultural values so as to signify the linguistic and cultural difference of the foreign text',[22] is an effective solution to the implicit rule of domestication that permeates through the act of translating into English, hence making the translator visible. However, I argue that the translator's *visibility* is just as concerning as the translator's invisibility in the case of translated Chinese SF. Neil Clarke, editor-in-chief of *Clarkesworld Magazine*, in a 2019 essay that refutes the proposal of establishing a separate category within the Hugo Awards for translations, contends that 'Anglophone SF is something of an invasive species in many markets ... breaking off translated works on their own reinforces the negative perception that Anglophone SF is the king of the hill and that they aren't welcome or as worthy'.[23] Clarke's rationalization exposes Anglophone readership's tendency to ostracize translated works once the translator's presence is made conspicuous by prioritizing their 'foreignness' over genre, style and length. For translated Chinese SF in particular, such a heightened visibility may be further fused with a demand to showcase Chineseness. Nonetheless, for translators of Chinese SF, an undiscriminating adoption of the foreignization method may inadvertently participate in the othering of Chinese culture and thus perpetuate exotification. Therefore, they must strike a delicate balance between invisibility and visibility on a case-by-case basis and apply foreignization with caution.

My translation of Wu Shuang 吴霜[24]'s short story, *The Facecrafter* 捏脸师,[25] is an example of the writer and the translator's mutual effort in executing the technique of foreignization. Aware of the translatability of her works, Wu considers both Chinese and non-Chinese readership as her target audience. Wu's oeuvre is an active exploration of ways in which she could deploy the future-oriented genre of SF to revivify Chinese classics and strive for an authentic representation of Chinese culture. In *The Facecrafter*, she depicts a post-apocalyptic world deprived of civilizations, where mythological deities and creatures emerge to reconstruct the Chinese tradition. Specifically, she introduces the lóng 龙 and the fèng 凤, a pair of mythological creatures that are translated respectively into 'dragon' and 'phoenix' by custom. However, I have always found this translation problematic because these creatures only bear the most superficial resemblance to the dragon and the phoenix in Western culture. Furthermore, the trope of the dragon and phoenix has had a historical presence in Anglophone literature as a means to exotify Chinese culture, hence reiterating the questionable translation would only reinforce orientalism linguistically. Therefore, I eschewed the most common translations and preserved the pinyin. As a joint decision between Wu and I, we fine-tuned the translation to offer supplementary in-text explanations of the creatures' significance to Wu's Anglophone readers: 'Storm clouds gathered in the sky, shrouding the outline of a giant beast: half indigo and half purple, antlers like a stag, claws like a hawk and body like a snake. It was the *long*, the guardian of emperors and bringer of prosperity in mythology.'[26] By deliberately detaching 'lóng' from 'dragon', I have foreignized the translation, so that it generates a cognitive distance between Anglophone readers accustomed to such a symbolic equivalence and the story itself, undoing the misleading impacts of the inaccurate translation by reintroducing the lóng's image and definition under a new name. This example, I suggest, illustrates a case in which *literal* faithfulness may hinder the delivery of *literary* faithfulness, which further calls for a re-examination of the way that translation studies define 'faithfulness'. Arguably, my reworking of the text is more representative of Wu's creative intentions of rendering the authenticity of classical Chinese culture than a domesticated translation that would escalate the exotification of certain cultural symbols.

An alternative approach to foreignization is to dismantle the preconception of an essentialized Chineseness, that is, to underscore the heterogeneity of Chinese culture. While Wu explores temporal heterogeneity by turning to the classics, writer Chen Qiufan 陈楸帆, who grew up under the influence of both Cantonese culture and the local Teochew culture of his hometown Shantou, eastmost of Guangdong, renders spatial heterogeneity by highlighting the significance of regional culture to his work. His short story *The Ancestral Temple in a Box* 匣中祠堂[27] introduces the gold-lacquered wood carving, an art native to Teochew, and speculates the possibility of utilizing virtual technology as a means to revolutionize traditional handicraft. Chen firmly reinforces his creative subjectivity against the expectation to showcase a generalized Chineseness by anchoring his narrative within a specific cultural environment most tangible to himself. He strives for accurate representation by foregrounding the relationship between the art, technology and Teochew family traditions, describing the lacquer craft in lavish details instead of reducing the cultural elements to mere embellishments. As much as I am translating the original Chinese version into English for an audience with little to no previous exposure to Chinese culture, Chen is translating the culture specific to his home region into a narrative enhanced by descriptive language and empathy for a larger Chinese audience. My translation takes the route opposite from that of *The Facecrafter*: in this case, preserving literal faithfulness is imperative to literary faithfulness. Therefore, I painstakingly reproduced the descriptive language in English, retaining details that Anglophone editors may find too tedious and pace-slowing and occasionally resorting to footnotes, in order to honour Chen's endeavour of representing *a particular aspect* of Chinese culture instead of a slapdash sketch of China-in-a-nutshell.

On the other hand, this example also demonstrates cautiousness towards foreignization: the story focuses on the depiction of a father–son relationship characterized by incommunicability against a backdrop of traditional filial piety and clanship. Though a literal translation of Chen's original content would better represent the background in which the story takes place and thus generate a foreignizing effect on the readers, I also recognize that it is susceptible to be criticized in partiality by Western readers as backwards and thus a dichotomic opposition to the modern idea of the nuclear family; it would, at best, end up as a major misreading that would hinder their reception of the text. Hence, adhering to literary faithfulness again, I deliberately toned down the language that may give rise to that interpretation, domesticating the description as I see fit, as it would in fact be a deviation from the thematic and emotional content that Chen portrays.

As illustrated by previous examples, my translations of Wu and Chen resist a homogenized idea of Chineseness by deploying foreignization to varying degrees. However, with the ever-evolving writer–translator paradigm in Chinese SF and the prevalence of multilingualism, I suggest that we should also look past Venuti and conjecture alternative approaches to translation. Inspired by Rita Felski's overture that interprets translation in light of Bruno Latour's Actor-Network Theory, 'not as an oscillation between oppressive sameness and radical singularity, but as chains of association and mediation that have no predetermined politics',[28] I propose that the renewed working relationship between a generation of SF writers who are perfectly fluent in English and their translators undermines the orthodox model of translation, which regards the translation as inferior to the original. In current translated Chinese SF, translation is no longer a linear process in which the translator, secondary to the writer, simply poses as a static filter through which the sacred original passes. A writer fluent in English may access their translator's work and mind with unprecedented rapport, forming a relationship that Venuti dubs as *simpatico*, that is, a bond shared by the writer and translator in which they vicariously experience each other's creative process.[29] The ideas of authenticity and authorship are due further scrutiny in this case as the writer is as involved with the English edition as with the Chinese, and the translator is endowed with more creative authority over the content and rhetoric of the text. As the line separating the writer from the translator grows ambiguous, the dichotomy of the translated and the translation, the Chinese language and English and consequently China and the Anglophone world becomes disintegrated. Translation thus poses a liminal space of indeterminacy that engenders robust and dynamic discourse, where the neither invisible nor entirely visible translator acts as a medium of empathy and cultivation. Locked in a symbiosis with my writers, I am engaged in a bilingual, bilateral working model that signifies not merely a passive reaction to the intrusive force of orientalism, but also an active attempt of erasing boundaries and redefining the creative process as a whole. It is time to return to the question that I had proposed at the beginning of this chapter: does Chinese SF have to be Chinese?

AI2041: ten visions for the future, co-authored by Chen Qiufan and Dr. Kaifu Lee 李开复, is a collection of ten SF stories respectively set in ten cities around the world twenty years from now, paired with essays on artificial intelligence technology.[30] This case illustrates an innovative model of collaboration for writers and translators who are of peripheral languages and cultures. From the beginning, the book set itself apart from other works of translated Chinese SF in that it is primarily contracted to Penguin Random House, an American publisher. Lee wrote in English; though Chen's stories were drafted in Chinese, they arose out of the expectation that the book would have its first contact with Anglophone readership. Additionally, the making of the book involves a myriad of creators: aside from the two authors, there are four translators, including myself, and a cohort of scholars that synthesize AI research in reality with fictional imagination. I was the first to comment on Chen's drafts before producing preliminary translations into English, which we fine-tuned together, then finalized the stories after rounds of feedback from Lee and the chief editors – who edited the work in the exact same way that they would edit a text written originally in English, except that they communicated with a hivemind instead of a single voice of authority. Chen, fluent in English, would occasionally make direct edits to the English version, which I then polished and perfected.

As I had elucidated, *AI2041* subverts the traditional writer–translator paradigm and offers a radical erasure of the stark boundaries between those roles, complicating the disputation of authenticity. Moreover, utter awareness towards the fact that the primary audience of *AI2041* is Anglophone has significantly impacted Chen's style of writing. Unlike in the aforementioned *The Ancestral Temple in a Box*, which is principally written for Chinese readers while bearing its translatability in mind, Chen chose to render his stories in *AI2041* with simple syntax and a plot-driven narrative, prioritizing clarity and storytelling over poeticness. The translation in this case is more or less of direct equivalences, as we had already modelled the Chinese draft based on the structure of English and standard Anglophone narrative structures. Authenticity in *AI2041* is thus in constant oscillation: the Chinese language functions as the vehicle by which Chen's storytelling crystallizes, which undoubtedly impacts the work's overall delivery, yet the underlying grammar and logic of the narrative is arguably English-inspired. This is a result of the close collaboration between Chen and I, as well as Chen's own unique, cosmopolitan background and artistic endeavour. *AI2041* questions the conventional idea of translation as a whole: it is an amalgamation in which every agent is a translator, a multi-input idea reified into a tangible creation by 'chains of association and mediation' perpetually engaged in circulation. In a way, as the 'translatedness' of the text becomes diluted, it simultaneously displaces concerns of power imbalance and orientalism that overshadow translating Chinese into English. Perhaps the translator is made invisible, but such an invisibility is primarily due to the disintegration of the traditional role of the writer and the translator, instead of the partiality of domestication. *AI2041*, translingual and transauthorial at its heart, written by a Chinese SF writer yet primarily for an Anglophone audience, gives rise to a new framework that we can deploy to recalibrate comparative literature and translation studies: what is authenticity? Should we judge the first language of a work by the language in which it is drafted, or language of final publication? What becomes of the translator when a translated work is no longer regarded as a translation? Furthermore, it urges multilingual Chinese writers to consider the experimental potential of translating the syntax, logic and rhetoric of other languages into Chinese, establishing a space in which the Chinese language and narrative repertoire may evolve vigorously.

I wish to conclude with *AI2041* as well, as I believe that this project embodies my central argument in manifold ways. The making of the book was a transnational and translingual creative process that spanned the entity of Covid-induced global isolation and strife. The first translated story of the collection, 'The holy driver', was produced by Chen and me as a duo, both in quarantine on separate continents, in March 2020, a time when Covid-19 had stricken the entire world. In a rather sci-fi manner, it was the prevalence of virtual communication software that enabled such a consistent creative engagement. Its success suggests an emerging potential of bridging languages, minds and rifts – both physical and ideological – via a much more complex model of translation that encourages creative reformation as much as deconstruction of ossified frameworks, augmented by technology. The significance to decolonization that *AI2041* poses is articulated by a critical question that has emerged five years from when 'The three-body problem' rose to the stage: to what extent would the global literary community take off their orientalist lens and readily embrace a version of the future world that is conjured up by a Chinese writer and canonized in English? Chinese SF can be about China on any given temporal and spatial scale; Chinese SF can also be about fundamental concerns shared across the globe from the perspective of a writer who lives in China and writes in the Chinese language. This book, though rudimentary in many aspects, dismantles the illusion of a particularized Chineseness by partaking in a new framework of authorship, readership and translation. Perhaps Chen's own words, said in personal correspondence, are adequate in responding to my question: 'I consider myself a world writer who writes in Chinese, rather than a "Chinese" writer.'

Notes

1. For a comprehensive overview of the history of translated Chinese SF, see Regina Kanyu Wang's article published by *Clarkesworld Magazine*. Wang, 'Another word'.
2. Ken Liu, American writer and translator. Liu translated over fifty short stories and five novels, including the three-body problem by Liu Cixin, the first book of a trilogy which was awarded the Hugo Award for Best Novel in 2015, the first translated work to have received a prize in the highly competitive category.
3. Liu categorically rejects a generalized idea of 'what is Chinese SF' upon contemporary Chinese SF's introduction to American readers and introduces major writers. My chapter is, in many ways, in dialogue with Liu's main viewpoints. Liu, 'China dreams: contemporary Chinese science fiction'.
4. Kuhn, 'Cultural revolution-meets-aliens: Chinese writer takes on sci-fi'.

5. The title of FutureCon 2021, a convention spearheaded by Verso that strives to decentralize SF and promote SF from around the world equally, is 'Decolonize the future', which I attended virtually as a guest speaker.
6. Bako, 'Chinese sci-fi novel, the three-body problem, touches down in US'.
7. Alter, 'How Chinese sci-fi conquered America'.
8. Gaffric, 'Chinese dreams', 121–4.
9. Cao, 'The multiple bodies of the three body problem', 186.
10. See this title for more examples. Roh et al., *Techno-Orientalism*.
11. Verso, 'From the sense of wonder to the sense of wander'.
12. Young, 'Postcolonial remains', 39.
13. Pesaro, 'Contemporary Chinese science fiction', 18–23. Gaffric, 129.
14. Sakai, *Translation and Subjectivity*, 174.
15. Pesaro, 'Contemporary Chinese science fiction', 24–5.
16. Pesaro, 'Contemporary Chinese science fiction', 32.
17. Shih, *The Lure of the Modern*, 374.
18. Casanova, 'What is a dominant language?', 393.
19. Venuti, *The Translator's Invisibility*, 1–2.
20. Venuti, *The Translator's Invisibility*, 43.
21. Venuti, *The Translator's Invisibility*, 61.
22. Venuti, *The Translator's Invisibility*, 23.
23. Clarke, 'Hugo proposal for best translated novel'.
24. Referred to as Anna Wu as well.
25. First published in *Clarkesworld Magazine* as a part of Clarkesworld's translated Chinese SF column in partnership with Chinese SF agency Storycom, October 2018.
26. Wu, 'The Facecrafter', translated by Jin.
27. First published in *Clarkesworld Magazine* as a part of Clarkesworld's translated Chinese SF column in partnership with Chinese SF agency Storycom, January 2020.
28. Felski, 'Comparison and translation', 754.
29. Venuti, *The Translator's Invisibility*, 274.
30. Chen was in charge of writing the stories, and Lee the accompanying essays.

Bibliography

Alter, Alexandra. 'How Chinese sci-fi conquered America'. *The New York Times Magazine*, 3 December 2019. https://www.nytimes.com/2019/12/03/magazine/ken-liu-three-body-problem-chinese-science-fiction.html. Accessed 4 January 2022.

Bako, Zachary. 'Chinese sci-fi novel, the three-body problem, touches down in US'. *The Wall Street Journal*, 4 November 2014. https://www.wsj.com/articles/chinese-sci-fi-novel-the-three-body-problem-touches-down-in-u-s-1415122369. Accessed 4 January 2022.

Cao, Xuenan. 'The multiple bodies of the three body problem'. *Extrapolation*, vol. 60, no. 2, 2019, pp. 183–200. https://doi.org/10.3828/extr.2019.12.

Casanova, Pascale. 'What is a dominant language? Giacomo Leopardi: theoretician of linguistic inequality'. *New Literary History*, vol. 44, no. 3, 2013, pp. 379–99.

Clarke, Neil. 'Hugo proposal for best translated novel'. *Neilclarke.com*, 9 July 2019. http://neil-clarke.com/hugo-proposal-for-best-translated-novel/. Accessed 4 January 2022.

Felski, Rita. 'Comparison and translation: a perspective from actor-network theory'. *Comparative Literature Studies*, vol. 53, no. 4, 2016, pp. 747–65.

Gaffric, Gwennaël. 'Chinese dreams: (self-)orientalism and post-orientalism in the reception and translation of Liu Cixin's *Three-Body* trilogy'. *Journal of Translation Studies*, vol. 3, no. 1, 2019, pp. 117–37

Kuhn, Anthony. 'Cultural revolution-Meets-Aliens: Chinese writer takes on Sci-Fi'. *NPR*, 9 April 2015. https://www.npr.org/sections/parallels/2015/04/09/398519222/cultural-revolution-meets-aliens-chinese-writer-takes-on-sci-fi. Accessed 4 January 2022.

Liu, Ken. 'China dreams: contemporary Chinese science fiction'. *Clarkesworld Magazine*, December 2014. https://clarkesworldmagazine.com/liu_12_14/. Accessed 4 January 2022.

Pesaro, Nicoletta. 'Contemporary Chinese science fiction: preliminary reflections on the translation of a genre'. *Journal of Translation Studies*, vol. 3, no. 1, 2019, pp. 7–43.

Roh, David S., Betsy Huang and Greta A. Niu. *Techno-Orientalism: imagining Asia in speculative fiction, history and media*. Rutgers University Press, 2015

Sakai, Naoki. *Translation and Subjectivity: on 'Japan' and cultural nationalism*. University of Minnesota Press, 2008.

Shih, Shu-mei. *The Lure of the Modern: writing modernism in semicolonial China, 1917–1937*. University of California Press, 2001.

Venuti, Lawrence. *The Translator's Invisibility: a history of translation*. Routledge, 1995.

Verso, Francesco. 'From the sense of wonder to the sense of wander'. *Apex Magazine*, 7 December 2021. https://apex-magazine.com/from-the-sense-of-wonder-to-the-sense-of-wander/. Accessed 4 January 2022.

Wang, Regina Kanyu. 'Another word: Chinese science fiction going abroad – A brief history of translation'. *Clarkesworld Magazine*, May 2018. https://clarkesworldmagazine.com/another_word_05_18/. Accessed 4 January 2022.

Wu, Anna. 'The Facecrafter', translated by Emily Jin. *Clarkesworld Magazine*, October 2018. https://clarkesworldmagazine.com/wu_10_18/. Accessed 4 January 2022.

Young, Robert. 'Postcolonial remains'. *New Literary History*, vol. 43, no. 1, 2012, pp. 19–42.

9
Whose Voice(s)?: Authorship, Translation, and Diversity in Contemporary Children's Literature

Isabelle Chen

In 1965, educator and author Nancy Larrick published her article 'The all-white world of children's books' in the *Saturday Review*. She advocated for a greater representation of people of colour in children's literature, both in text and illustration, by citing statistics about the presence of Black characters. Most notably, in a survey of over 5,000 trade books published in a three-year period (1962–4), 6.7 per cent included at least one Black character, and only four-fifths of 1 per cent featured a Black character in a contemporary setting.[1] Larrick's forceful call for textual representation of ethnic difference is widely considered the forerunner of contemporary diversity movements in children's literature.

Particularly in the last decade, children's publishing has seen a shift from this 'all-white world' to a more robust representation of race, gender, sexuality, ability and language.[2] Movements such as We Need Diverse Books and #OwnVoices, both started on Twitter, have taken Larrick's work a step further by calling for diversity not only in the books themselves, but on the level of the authors, illustrators and other industry professionals who create and mediate them.[3] Proponents of these movements maintain that since experiences of marginalization are highly personal and rooted in a specific cultural context, they are best written by someone who has lived them herself, or who belongs to the identity group represented in the work.

Evolving in parallel to this diversity discussion is one about translation in children's books and how it facilitates movement across literary and cultural borders. Recent scholarly work and individual practices of translation have put a spotlight on who can and should translate certain texts, whether certain ideas are translatable between cultures, and what the ethical implications are for the translation of books for young readers. While these questions are intimately linked to diversity movements by considerations of authorship, voice and cultural context, the two areas are rarely studied together.

This chapter aims to put the two into dialogue: to consider translation in children's book publishing through the lens of the industry's evolving values and its current emphasis on diverse voices. In a field increasingly concerned with the metaphorical untranslatability of lived experience, what is the place of translation in the literal sense, a transition from one language to another? What are the ways in which a translator, #OwnVoices or not, can strike a balance between linguistic understanding of a text and recognition of the unique cultural context in which it is rooted? After providing an overview of diversity movements and translation studies with regard to English-language and multilingual children's literature published in the United States, I will consider how both spheres approach the intersection of language and cultural identity, and to what extent these textual elements are translatable in either a literal or a metaphorical sense. Finally, I will examine their relationship with the help of a case study: Elizabeth Acevedo's young adult novel-in-verse, *The Poet X*, and its translations into French and Spanish. Analysis of the original text alongside its translations will provide further insight into the sociocultural implications, and even the ultimate feasibility, of translating a bilingual and #OwnVoices text for international audiences.

The call for diverse representation and authorship

In March 2014, two *New York Times* op-eds made clear that little had changed in the five decades since Larrick's 'All-white world'. In his 'Where are the people of color in children's books?', Walter Dean Myers uses anecdotes from his childhood and professional life to highlight the importance of diverse representation, while his son Christopher Myers, in 'The apartheid of children's literature', points to the emptiness of the industry's promises to diversify its material:

> The mission statements of major publishers are littered with intentions, with their commitments to diversity, to imagination, to multiculturalism, ostensibly to create opportunities for children to learn about and understand their importance in their respective worlds

... But there are numbers and truths that stand in stark contrast to the reassurances.[4]

It was after the publication of the Myers' articles, as well as the subsequent founding of the non-profit organization We Need Diverse Books, that the industry began to see a steady, albeit slow, uptake in ethnically diverse representation. According to data from the Cooperative Children's Book Center of the School of Education at the University of Wisconsin-Madison, 73.3 per cent of children's books published in the United States in 2015 across the three primary age categories (picture book, middle grade and young adult) featured White protagonists; 12.5 per cent featured non-human characters such as animals or personified objects; 7.6 per cent featured Black characters; 3.3 per cent Asian; 2.4 per cent Latinx; and 0.9 per cent Native American.[5] By comparison, out of the 3,134 children's books published in 2018, there was a significant decline in the overall percentage of White protagonists: 50 per cent. Yet, while the per centage of Black characters increased to 10 per cent, Asian characters to 7 per cent and Latinx characters to 5 per cent, the greatest increase was in that of non-human characters, which jumped to 27 per cent.[6]

Over this three-year period, White and non-human characters together made up between 77 per cent and 85.8 per cent of all children's books published; these oft-cited statistics have been a driving force behind recent calls for diverse *representation*, or the textual presence of characters from diverse backgrounds regardless of the author's own identity. Representation continues to hold a central place in many theories of children's literature: for instance, Rudine Sims Bishop emphasizes the importance of 'seeing' oneself in a book in her 'windows and mirrors' theorization, in which books either mirror a reader's own experience or offer a window into an unfamiliar experience, and 'all children need both'.[7] In a 2014 article, Ebony Elizabeth Thomas highlighted the relevance of Bishop's work for representation today, warning of an 'imagination gap' in children that can stem from the lack of diverse depictions in books and other media.[8]

Despite the continued importance of representation in scholarly and industry discourse, there has been a more recent focus on literary creators of diverse backgrounds. In 2015, author Corinne Duyvis coined the Twitter hashtag #OwnVoices, which would be used 'to recommend kidlit about diverse characters written by authors from that same diverse group'.[9] The term has become, in the words of its creator, 'an integral part of the publishing lexicon', used in agent and editor wish lists, publication announcements and book reviews.[10] The concept of #OwnVoices, like that of identity, is not always clear-cut, and its use has thus at times been controversial. The term is indeed difficult to apply in all certainty – and when it cannot be applied, it serves as a reminder to tread carefully and write responsibly, while not necessarily discouraging authors from writing outside of their own experience or background.

In order to consider the place of translation in the #OwnVoices context, it is first necessary to recognize the complex role that multilingualism already plays in the representation of diverse cultures. Code-switching and translanguaging have become common in children's literature across age groups, and are often a mark of a text's #OwnVoices linguistic particularity. On a textual level, authors employ a range of strategies to represent interactions between English and another language. In his book *Multilingual America,* Larry Rosenwald outlines several of these by applying Meir Sternberg's concept of 'translational mimesis' to multilingual American literature.[11] Sternberg's terms, such as 'selective reproduction' (in which dialogue is quoted directly in the non-English language used by the characters) and 'explicit attribution' (which involves a narrative statement about the language being spoken, even if dialogue is not reported directly in this language), form a useful framework for analysing textual representations of multilingualism in largely monolingual contexts, which Rosenwald takes further by considering how its application varies across narrative prose, theatre and poetry.[12] I would propose that books aimed at younger readers, given their often simpler language and heavier-handed textual explanations, may privilege certain strategies over others, and therefore constitute another literary genre that fits differently into Sternberg's system. Ed Lin's *David Tung Can't Have a Girlfriend Until He Gets into an Ivy League College,* for instance, relies heavily on selective reproduction, as it includes Mandarin and Cantonese phrases transliterated via pinyin into the Latin alphabet, followed by in-text narrative explanations: 'She then turned to YK and said, "jia you." This literally meant, "add oil," but figuratively it meant, "let's go."'[13] Kelly Yang's *Parachutes*, on the other hand, often reverts to English and indicates via explicit attribution the translation taking place: '[S]he turns and yells at Mrs. Wallace in Mandarin, "Hey, woman, it's a free country! Why you think we came here?"'[14] Elizabeth Acevedo's *The Poet X,* by comparison, switches more spontaneously between English and Spanish. At times, key words are translated for emphasis ('"Cuero," she calls me to my face. / The Dominican word for *ho*'[15]), but at others, no translation is offered; a bilingual reader will be exposed to an additional layer of textual richness without the monolingual English reader losing the passage's overall meaning. Multilingualism in all its stylistic variations is thus a key mode of expressing cultural identity in children's literature and, for this reason, it also calls into question who has the right to use a certain language or dialect. Indeed, authors have faced backlash for writing in language variations different from their own, and for irresponsibly representing the cultures associated with them. e.E. Charlton-Trujillo, a Mexican American author, had the publication of their novel *When We Was Fierce* postponed in 2016, not only for its apparently stereotypical representations of Black communities, but also for its African American vernacular English slang, some of which was entirely invented and rang false to Black readers.[16] The idea of an author's 'own voice' is therefore concerned as much with the linguistic untranslatability of language as it is with the metaphorical untranslatability of culture: both suggest limitations on the languages an author should employ, the points of view they should adopt and the groups for whom they should speak.

Translating children's literature: practices and debates

This intersection of textual diversity and multilingualism provides us a new lens through which to consider how cultural context might affect who can, or should, translate. In translation studies, these questions have been increasingly pertinent since the field's 'cultural turn' of the late twentieth century; Susan Bassnett and André Lefevere's *Translation, History, and Culture* posits translation as a highly contextualized mode of cultural construction, irreducible to the notion of a simple shift from one language to another, let alone to that of linguistic equivalence.[17] Going further into the implications of cultural identity in a postcolonial context, Gayatri Chakravorty Spivak considers translation as the most intimate act of reading, caring for and thereby understanding not only the text's language and logic, but also, and more importantly, its rhetoricity, which operates 'in the silence between and around words'.[18] The danger, particularly when translating a text with non-Western linguistic or cultural elements, is that the translator may be insufficiently equipped to care for and understand the original text's rhetoricity, which refers not simply to what is written on the page, but to that which can be grasped only through a deeper, more personal connection to what Spivak terms 'the specific terrain of the original',[19] including the language's history and the author's background. The cultural rootedness of any given text thus inevitably gives way to the question of the suitable translator: one with not only mastery of the source and target languages, but also an intimate understanding of the contexts in which these languages are produced, and who can thereby avoid speaking for, or over, another culture via translation.

Current conceptions of children's literature likewise focus on the cultural insight a young reader may gain or lose from reading in translation. Generally, children's stories have long been conceived in terms of their pedagogical role. Cecilia Alvstad notes that what some consider the earliest forms of children's literature in many countries – fairy tales and folktales – are in themselves 'a translated phenomenon', with many translations altering the tales' content for didactic purposes and cultural accessibility.[20] While children's literature today is considered less as a means of imparting an overt message, questions of how to adapt material from one culture into another remain a cornerstone of its translation. Many theorists evoke, for instance, Lawrence Venuti's foreignization–domestication dichotomy, which points to the choice a translator must make between emphasizing the foreign and thus translated nature of the text, and 'localizing' certain textual elements to make the work more easily understandable to readers in the target culture. Venuti himself advocates for foreignization, citing it as a method that 'send[s] the reader abroad', while domestication would be an 'ethnocentric reduction of the foreign text to the target-language cultural values'.[21] Such a balance between foreignization and domestication becomes more pertinent and precarious when it comes to young readers, for whom translators and editors have specific ideas about what material is appropriate. Some scholars of children's book translation claim that since readers in various cultures have different ways of interpreting a text, domesticating strategies on the part of the translator are often warranted or even necessary.[22] Others conceive of their work as more of a balancing act between two risks: too many textual changes could lead to cultural appropriation and a denial of the author's original intent, while not enough changes could render a text culturally inaccessible to young readers.[23]

Reading in translation already poses ill-defined boundaries between translating and authoring. As Larry Rosenwald writes in his essay 'On Not Reading in Translation', if we are unfamiliar with the source text's linguistic and cultural idiosyncrasies, then when we read in translation, 'we do not know whose work we are reading, interpreting, savouring, judging; we expose ourselves to dizzying uncertainty, we are making a profession of faith'.[24] The potential for children's books to require heavier mediation, both linguistically and culturally, further blurs the distinction between the two levels of textual creation. Alvstad, for instance, cites a 'grey zone'[25] in which translation is paradoxically situated between authorship and itself, suggesting the need for a separate term to represent the in-between role of the translator – simultaneously literary, linguistic and cultural. Author and translator David Bowles considers himself a 'co-creator of the translated text ... because ultimately, that's what translations are: new works that are co-created by the author and the translator to do essentially the same job as the original, but with a wholly different audience'.[26] Indeed, this author–translator amalgam does provoke a 'dizzying uncertainty': one that can be clarified only through more explicit indications of whose message, whose voice and whose values are put forth in a given translated text. Gillian Lathey, a scholar of translated children's literature, cites the need for 'a more precise and broadly based account of relative degrees of paratextual mediation in blurbs, prefaces or child-friendly translator biographies'.[27] Indeed, this would not only help researchers compare domestication and foreignization strategies in translated children's literature, but it would also aid in specifying the boundary between author and translator. An uptake in translation-oriented paratext would alert young readers to the fact of reading in translation, which, despite children's translator Anthea Bell's assertion that 'the function of a translator is to be invisible',[28] might help name more precisely, as well as justify, the cultural role of the translator.

Diversity in translation

If an author's voice is increasingly called into question with regard to what they write – on what topics and in which languages – then the same can naturally be said for the translator, whose textual voice is equally, if not more, tangled up in questions of language and culture, of authorship and mediation. When it comes to translating multicultural children's books, the central question therefore fluctuates between 'Who can and should write certain material?' and 'Who can and should translate it?'[29]

First, the translation of diverse children's books comes with undeniable advantages for both readers and authors, regardless of the translator's cultural identity. Translator Ruth Ahmedzai Kemp cites the benefits of spreading multicultural works across geographical borders: 'Sharing diverse children's books with young children ... can foster more outward-looking perspectives and critical thinking about language, identity, and the way we interact and empathise with people from other countries and backgrounds'.[30] As we will see, this is also the case for Elizabeth Acevedo's *The Poet X*, given its mix of English and Spanish, as well as the Dominican American culture of both its author and protagonist. By translating this identity-oriented book for French readers – many of whom may have grown up with France's universalist values, which tend to minimize personal identity, particularly racial difference – Clémentine

Beauvais exposes readers not only to Acevedo's Afro-Latina heritage, but also to the greater emphasis placed on ethnic identity more generally in the United States. For children's literature, therefore, translation can promote cultural visibility and inclusivity in the same way that diversity movements promote multicultural representation. Translations therefore serve as, in Bishop's terms, textual 'windows' that expose readers to a culture previously unfamiliar to them, inspiring greater awareness and sensitivity. In addition, prominent translators can use their position in the publishing industry to help elevate marginalized voices. Regardless of who mediates it, translated children's literature expands the international and cultural reach of its author; in turn, greater profit and greater renown allow the author more opportunities to share their stories and to lift up other marginalized voices in the process. In cases like these, the positive results of translation perhaps outweigh any discrepancy between the cultural backgrounds of the author and translator.

At the same time, the translator's background can pose difficulties for both the practice and the sociocultural implications of translation. It is necessary first to consider the question of who profits from textual mediation. Some might argue that multicultural texts should be edited, illustrated and/or translated by someone from a similar background to the author's, not necessarily because this will affect the quality of work, but because a diverse book creates the possibility of diversifying publishing on levels beyond simply authorship.[31] In recent years, this debate has been especially pressing for illustrators. A 2018 study examined all 337 recipients of the Caldecott Medal, the most prestigious United States-based award for picture books. The study found that white authors and illustrators made up over 86 per cent of prize winners, and that even for books featuring main characters of colour, illustrators from that same identity group were in the vast minority.[32]

In addition to imbalances in industry access and profit, translators must navigate sensitive cultural issues within the practice of translation itself. Lawrence Schimel has recounted his experience as a White American man translating an African woman of colour writing in Spanish. Instead of translating the term *curandero*, whose common English translation of 'witch doctor' Schimel cites as 'a very loaded colonialist term' and 'not appropriate' for him to use, he decided to leave the word in its original Spanish and gloss it with an in-text description, thereby preserving the 'same texture of the Spanish' while avoiding a potential cultural blunder.[33] Another approach to cultural limitations is Sarah Ardizzone's English translation of the French young adult series *Golem*. Since *Golem* features French-language slang used in certain communities of colour,

Ardizzone spent three months in an Algerian community in Marseille in order to familiarize herself with the source language's idiosyncrasies. She then recruited Afro-Caribbean 'slang advisors' in London to verify that her translation of these passages into English-language slang was responsible and respectful.[34]

In these two instances, the translator acknowledged their sociocultural position and translated accordingly. However, both raise questions about the thorny intersection of literary voice and cultural background. If a translator alters their methods according to their own cultural limitations – for instance, choosing not to translate a word altogether due to its questionable connotations in the target language – could this be considered a form of domestication, even if it stems from a place of sensitivity and care? If a translator does linguistic or cultural research, at what point do they decide that they have learned enough to accurately represent non-standard language between the source and target cultures – particularly if working with different communities of colour in each, as was the case for Ardizzone? There are as many approaches to translating multicultural literature as there are translators: practising exclusively #OwnVoices translation; supplementing a non-#OwnVoices translation with research; maintaining the 'foreign' nature of a non-#OwnVoices translation in order to minimize the possibility of cultural appropriation; or more cleanly separating language and culture in order to focus largely on linguistic transformation. In all of them, however, it is difficult to know how cultural difference may impede the resulting translation, and to what extent the translator herself can be the judge of this.

Case study: *The Poet X, Poet X* and *Signé, Poète X*

In order to consider the practice of multicultural children's book translation in addition to its politics, it will be helpful to study the example of one contemporary novel alongside its translations. Elizabeth Acevedo's award-winning young adult novel-in-verse *The Poet X* embodies the language- and identity-based diversity that poses difficulties, and sometimes barriers, to translation. It follows fifteen-year-old Xiomara Batista, who uses written and spoken-word poetry to reckon with her cultural background, her femininity and sexuality, and her turbulent relationship with her mother. The novel's narrative voice is grounded in the Dominican roots shared by author and protagonist: an identity conveyed especially through frequent code-switching between English and Spanish, in both narration and reported dialogue. This section will explore how the multilingualism and multiculturalism inherent in *The Poet X* are represented in its Spanish and French translations, and to what extent these adaptations diverge from the original. As the Spanish translation can be called #OwnVoices and the French cannot, we will examine in particular the potential influence of a translator's cultural identity on the transformation of an #OwnVoices text.

Poet X is the Spanish translation by Silvina Poch, published in 2019 by Puck, a Madrid-based press for young readers. Poch hails from Argentina, and her translation can therefore be considered #OwnVoices due to the Latina and Spanish-speaking identities (though, of course, a different variety of Spanish) shared by Acevedo and herself. Perhaps unexpectedly, certain parts of Poch's translation diverge quite significantly from Acevedo's original on syntactic and semantic levels. Linguistically, the first challenge posed to the Spanish-language translator is the fact that *The Poet X* is written in both English and Spanish. How can one maintain the semblance of bilingualism in an entirely Spanish-language text? At times, Poch uses quotation marks or italics to set apart the Spanish of the original from her Spanish translation. For instance, she translates 'Marina from across the street told me you were on the stoop again talking to los vendedores'[35] as 'Marina, la que vive enfrente, me ha dicho que has estado afuera hablando con "los vendedores"'.[36] At others, she keeps phrases from the original English with some added modifications, such as when '"Pero, tú no eres fácil". / You sure ain't an easy one'[37] becomes '"Pero tú no eres fácil". / *You sure ain't an easy one*'.[38] Between English interjections and punctuative and stylistic changes, *Poet X* reads like a text set in an Anglophone environment but told in Spanish, which indeed maintains a sense of bilingualism even in this more monolingual text.

At other moments, Poch's language choices create quite a vast cultural divergence from Acevedo's original, despite similarities in the two creators' linguistic background. In an instance of intralingual translation, Xiomara's mother's sharp 'Oíste?' in the original[39] becomes the more formal, drawn-out '¿Me has oído?' in Poch's version,[40] indicating a change in register between Spanishes. Moreover, 'Twin', Xiomara's nickname for her brother, is rendered as 'Melli', short for the Spanish 'mellizo', or 'fraternal twin'. This abbreviation, arguably unfeasible in English, perhaps implies more endearment and closeness than would 'Twin'. Both instances of translation, whether inter- or intralingual, ultimately add new meaning to Acevedo's text. In a final example, Poch alters a key scene toward the novel's conclusion, in which Xiomara expresses resentment toward her mother for trying to silence her poetic voice. In the original, this poem is given an English title, 'A Poem Mami Will Never Read', yet is written in Xiomara's mother's native Spanish – a gesture, despite the poem's title, of shared heritage and a hidden desire for connection. On the next page comes 'In Translation', which offers Xiomara's (and Acevedo's) own English translation of the previous poem.[41] In Poch's Spanish translation, the order of these poems is reversed: first, a poem entitled 'A poem my mom will never read', written this time entirely in *English*, and then followed by the Spanish-language 'Un poema que mi madre nunca leerá'.[42] Poch makes several small lexical and grammatical changes to Acevedo's original Spanish version. To name just one, 'Cómo tus labios son grapas' ('How your lips are staples') changes from metaphor to simile with the shift in placement and grammatical form of just one word – 'Tus labios son como grapas' ('Your lips are like staples').[43] Whether a question of stylistic preference or a different variation of Spanish, Poch's translation differs from Acevedo's original voice even in such moments when linguistic translation is arguably unnecessary. Perhaps most importantly, the reversed order of the English and Spanish versions of the poem alters quite significantly their textual meaning. In the original, Xiomara first writes in her mother's native language, thus implying a sense of hope that her mother might indeed read and understand her words; in the Spanish version, writing in English suggests that Xiomara truly does hope that her mother will not read the poem, and bars her from doing so by writing in a language less accessible to her. Overall, while Poch's Spanish translation can be categorized as #OwnVoices, this certainly does not prevent linguistic decisions from at times altering the cultural meaning of Acevedo's original text. It is precisely *The Poet X*'s bilingualism – part of what makes the text #OwnVoices – that both makes a Spanish translation the most culturally relevant one, yet poses the ultimate linguistic challenge for this translation.[44]

Signé, Poète X, the French translation, was published in 2019 by Éditions Nathan and translated by Clémentine Beauvais, a French author and academic. On her personal blogs and in interviews, Beauvais has written and spoken extensively about her philosophy of translation. In an interview about *The Poet X,* she elaborates upon the notion of the translator as co-creator: 'Quand on traduit, on n'est jamais dans le littéralisme. On est toujours dans une interprétation, on est toujours dans un processus d'adaptation. C'est vraiment un travail de créer une œuvre originale à partir d'un matériau existant. Et c'est un défi, mais c'est aussi énormément de liberté.'[45] In a similar vein, she has also expressed belief in the separability of a work from its author: for instance, in a blog post, she justifies her decision to translate J.K. Rowling's *The Ickabog* in light of the author's transphobic comments on social media. While affirming that she does not agree with J.K. Rowling's views, Beauvais writes that the multivocality of a certain text – what different readers gain from their individual interpretations of it – transcends the singular, personal voice of the author.[46]

The notions of translator as author and of a work's separability from its writer, alongside a non-#OwnVoices translator, might suggest a more radical departure from the original work.[47] However, in the case of *Signé, Poète X*, Beauvais maintains most structural elements of the original, including its bilingualism. Because French is not present in the source text and therefore does not pose the same challenges as Spanish, shifts between the two languages remain largely the same, with the addition of occasional in-text explanations. What goes untranslated in Acevedo's original is at times accompanied by the same sentence in French (the original sentence 'Te estoy esperando en casa', for example, is included in full but followed by the French 'Je t'attends à la maison').[48] In terms of register, Beauvais adopts a casual voice, with many abbreviations, contractions and dropped negation particles. These are strategies typical of spoken French which, if not always equivalents of English or Spanish slang and rhythm, reflect the oral nature of Xiomara's slam poetry.

It is important to note that some of the greatest differences in Beauvais' translation stem from domestication, to use Venuti's term. When Xiomara's poetry club teammate uses complicated vocabulary in a poem, she narrates, 'I think he's studying for the SAT'.[49] In French, this becomes, 'je crois qu'il est en L, un truc comme ça' ('I think he's in L, or something like that').[50] 'L' stands for literature, one of the three paths of study in the French high school system. An American standardized test therefore becomes a more relevant cultural reference in French, bypassing the need for a translation not specific to French, such as 'concours d'entrée' ('entrance examination'). At another moment, when it comes to dating rules, Xiomara narrates in English, 'The thing is, / my old-school / Dominican parents / *Do. Not. Play*'.[51] In Beauvais' version, this becomes: 'Le truc c'est que / pour mes parents, / Dominicains traditionnels, / on ne badine pas avec l'amour'[52] ('The thing is / For my parents, / Traditional Dominicans, / There's no trifling with love') – a nod to the title of Alfred de Musset's nineteenth-century play. While this reference is relevant to the theme at hand, it does move away from Dominican references and English-language slang by anchoring the text in the French literary canon. In these domesticating departures from Acevedo's original, Beauvais' own cultural background becomes evident, but does not result in a sweeping divergence from the original text overall, nor an unjust representation of Dominican American culture.

Conclusion

The pressing call for diverse children's literature adds a new challenge to the already complicated nature of linguistic and cultural translation. Because the use of the term #OwnVoices presents many conflicts despite its best intentions, very few works would end up translated if precise identity affiliation were the rule for translation. A White French translator will perhaps not have deep insight into Afro-Latina ethnic identity and culture, but neither will, perhaps, a Black French translator, who may be of an entirely different national origin, linguistic background, or family upbringing than the book's author. A Dominican Spanish-speaker and a South American Spanish-speaker might, likewise, see bilingual English–Spanish material in vastly different ways; this would seem to be the case for Silvina Poch's translation of *The Poet X*, which departs from Acevedo's original even at the potential loss of the author's 'own voice' in Spanish. It would be difficult to find a translator whose identity and vision for the translated work corresponded entirely to that of the author, unless, of course, the author were in a position to translate her own work. Yet even in this case, her decisions regarding how to alter her language and story would vary greatly depending on the source and target cultures.

This is not to say that translators should translate indiscriminately, nor that readers should forget the essential but at times precarious role of the translator. As Spivak writes, 'Without a sense of the rhetoricity of language, a species of neocolonialist construction of the non-western scene is afoot'.[53] Keeping with Spivak's definition of translation as a form of cultural care, the translator of a multicultural and/or multilingual work must recognize the risk of glossing over linguistic particularities, minimizing important cultural details and infusing their own cultural biases or innate presumptions about the source text into her interpretation and adaptation. On the reader's end, it is necessary to continue to read translations with a critical eye. Ebony Elizabeth Thomas puts forth several questions meant to point to 'previously hidden metaphors' that have long guided our reading practices.[54] Questions such as 'What (or whose) view of the world, or kinds of behaviours are presented as normal by the text?' and 'What are the possible readings of this situation/event/character?' are equally useful when applied to translated work, particularly in instances in which it departs greatly from the original.

Finally, the case can still be made for the importance of the #OwnVoices translator. Just as it is significant for a young reader to see their unique culture represented in a book – a cornerstone of current diversity movements – it could be just as impactful for an author to have their work translated by someone with whom they share a cultural connection. It could mean a new opportunity not only for the book and the author on international markets, but also more room for diverse voices among textual mediators, particularly those such as translators who are responsible for transmitting authorial voice itself. When it comes to translation, we might take up the same notion of #OwnVoices that Corinne Duyvis herself suggests: '#OwnVoices should be a tool, not a blunt weapon'.[55] Indeed, while the debate around literary diversity does exert a challenge upon the translator, this challenge need not be seen solely as a limitation; instead, it is one that, if answered, can create greater accessibility throughout the publishing field as a whole by opening the door to a wider range of voices in all their cultural complexity.

Notes

1. Larrick, 'The all-white world of children's books', 64.
2. The website of the non-profit organization We Need Diverse Books defines 'diversity' as 'including (but not limited to) LGBTQIA, Native, people of colour, gender diversity, people with disabilities and ethnic, cultural and religious minorities' ('About WNDB'). For the purposes of this chapter, I will focus on ethnic diversity.
3. #OwnVoices is now such a widely recognized phrase that it has evolved into an adjective, which I will use in this chapter. For instance, an #OwnVoices book is one written by an author of the same traditionally marginalized background as the main character(s); an #OwnVoices author is one whose characters share her cultural identity.
4. Myers, 'The apartheid of children's literature'.
5. Huyck and Dahlen, 'Diversity in children's books 2018'.
6. Huyck and Dahlen, 'Diversity in children's books 2018'.
7. Bishop, 'Reflections on the development of African American children's literature', 9.
8. Thomas, 'Stories still matter: rethinking the role of diverse children's literature today', 112.
9. Duyvis, *Twitter*, 6 September 2015, 1:55 p.m.
10. Duyvis, 'Q&A with Corinne Duyvis'.
11. Rosenwald, *Multilingual America*, 2–3.
12. Rosenwald, *Multilingual America*, 13.
13. Lin, *David Tung Can't Have a Girlfriend*, 175–6.
14. Yang, *Parachutes*, 208.
15. Acevedo, *The Poet X*, 205.
16. Flood, 'Publisher delays YA novel amid row over invented black "street dialect"'.
17. Bassnett and Lefevere, *Translation, History, and Culture*, 3–6.
18. Spivak, 'The politics of translation', 314.
19. Spivak, 'The politics of translation', 320.
20. Alvstad, 'Children's literature', 159–60.
21. Venuti, *The Translator's Invisibility*, 20.
22. Oittinen, *Translation for Children*.
23. Alvstad, 'Children's literature', 175.
24. Rosenwald, 'On not reading in translation', 313.
25. Alvstad, *The Translator's Invisibility*, 165.
26. Kantor, 'Building bridges: the art of children's book translation'. Bowles also claims that his own experience as a writer helps him take on this role of translator and co-creator. Indeed, as Alvstad notes, it is common practice for children's literature to be translated by other authors rather than trained translators, precisely because in children's literature, the translator's responsibility extends from language mediation to a more immersive textual composition.

27. Lathey, '"Only English books": The mediation of translated children's literature in a resistant economy', 51.
28. Lathey, *The Role of Translators in Children's Literature*, 192.
29. It is worth noting that the polemical notion of a 'right to translate' goes well beyond children's literature. A recent example is the translation of Amanda Gorman's inaugural poem 'The Hill We Climb'. Many questioned whether this text associated with 'a significant cultural moment for Black people' should be translated into Dutch by Marieke Lucas Rijneveld, a White author. (See Marshall, 'Amanda Gorman's poetry united critics. It's dividing translators'.)
30. Kantor, 'Building bridges: the art of children's book translation'.
31. A survey by Lee & Low books found that in 2019 the publishing industry was at least 74 per cent White at the levels of editors, agents, book reviewers and marketing teams (see Jiménez and Beckert, 'Diversity in Publishing 2019').
32. Koss, Johnson and Martinez, 'Mapping the diversity in Caldecott books from 1938 to 2017', 12–14.
33. Schimel and Hahn, 'Translating for the future: children's literature in translation'.
34. Lathey, *Translating Children's Literature*, 80–1.
35. Acevedo, *The Poet X*, 6.
36. Poch, *Poet X*, 14.
37. Acevedo, *The Poet X*, 10.
38. Poch, Poet X, 14.
39. Acevedo, *The Poet X*, 6.
40. Poch, Poet X, 14.
41. Acevedo, *The Poet X*, 233–34.
42. Poch, Poet X, 231–32.
43. Acevedo, *The Poet X*, 233; Poch,Poet X, 232.
44. Larry Rosenwald, in *Multilingual America*, very aptly describes the 'new language fun' – the joy and the challenges – of translating a multilingual text into a language or culture already present in it: '[I]t is often the case that the language into which we want to translate a multilingual text is one of the languages it represents. We are more likely to want to translate immigrant-language American immigrant fiction into English than into any other language, because American anglophone readers have more reason to read American non-anglophone fiction than do the reading publics of Europe.'
45. Beauvais, 'Interview de Clémentine Beauvais, la traductrice de Poète X'. 'When you translate, it's never literal. You're always interpreting, always adapting. It's really about creating an original work from material that already exists. And it's a challenge, but also an enormous amount of freedom.' Translation my own.
46. Beauvais, 'Sur' ma traduction de l'Ickabog dans le contexte des propos de J.K. Rowling".
47. Of course, the opposite could be true as well: a translator with a poststructuralist background might discount the author as a source of meaning for a text, and therefore keep her translation grounded in what she reads on the page, resulting in a less notable divergence.
48. Acevedo, *The Poet X*, 299; Beauvais, *Signé, Poète X*, 323.
49. Acevedo, *The Poet X*, 257.
50. Beauvais, *Signé, Poète X*, 280.
51. Acevedo, *The Poet X*, 90.
52. Beauvais, *Signé, Poète X*, 99.
53. Spivak, 'The politics of translation', 314.
54. Thomas, 'Stories still matter: rethinking the role of diverse children's literature today', 116.
55. Duyvis, 'Q&A with Corinne Duyvis'.

Bibliography

'About WNDB'. *We Need Diverse Books*, diversebooks.org/about-wndb/. Accessed 18 April 2021.
Acevedo, Elizabeth. *The Poet X*. HarperCollins Publishers, 2018.
Acevedo, Elizabeth. *Poet X*, translated by Silvina Poch, Puck, 2019.
Acevedo, Elizabeth. *Signé, Poète X*, translated by Clémentine Beauvais, Éditions Nathan, 2019.
Alvstad, Cecilia. 'Children's literature'. *The Routledge Handbook of Literary Translation*, edited by R. Kelly Washbourne and Van Ben Wyke. Routledge, 2019, pp. 159–80.

Bassnett, Susan and André Lefevere. *Translation, History, and Culture*. Pinter Publishers, 1990.
Beauvais, Clémentine. 'Interview de Clémentine Beauvais, la traductrice de Poète X'. *YouTube*, uploaded by lireenlive, 4 October 2019. https://www.youtube.com/watch?v=Lp5uyRDN GL0&t=189s. Accessed 18 April 2021.
Beauvais, Clémentine. '"Sur" ma traduction de l'Ickabog dans le contexte des propos de J.K. Rowling." *Mais pourquoi tu fais pas de la vraie littérature?'*, Clémentine Beauvais, 15 July 2020. http://clementinebleue.blogspot.com/2020/07/sur-ma-traduction-de-lickabog-dans-le.html. Accessed 18 April 2021.
Bishop, Rudine Sims. 'Mirrors, windows, and sliding glass doors'. *Perspectives*, vol. 6 no. 3, 1990, pp. ix–xi.
Bishop, Rudine Sims. 'Reflections on the development of African American children's literature'. *Journal of Children's Literature*, vol. 38 no. 2, 2012, pp. 5–13.
@corinneduyvis (Corinne Duyvis). '#ownvoices, to recommend kidlit about diverse characters written by authors from that same diverse group'. *Twitter*, 6 September 2015, 1:55 p.m. https://twitter.com/corinneduyvis/status/640584099208503296.
Dahlen, Sarah Park. '"We need diverse books": diversity, activism, and children's literature'. *Literary Cultures and Twenty-First Century Childhoods*, edited by Natalie op de Beeck. Palgrave Macmillan, 2020, pp. 83–108.
Duyvis, Corinne. 'Q&A with Corinne Duyvis'. Interview by Claire Kirch. *Publishers Weekly*, 15 September 2020. https://www.publishersweekly.com/pw/by-topic/childrens/childrens-authors/article/84336-q-a-with-corinne-duyvis.html.
Flood, Alison. 'Publisher delays YA novel amid row over invented black "street dialect."' *The Guardian*, 16 August 2016. https://www.theguardian.com/books/2016/aug/16/delays-ya-row-over-invented-black-vernacular-when-we-was-fierce. Accessed 18 April 2021.
Huyck, David, Sarah Park Dahlen and Molly Beth Griffin. 'Diversity in children's books 2015 infographic'. *sarahpark.com* blog, 14 September 2016. https://www.slj.com/?detailStory=an-updated-look-at-diversity-in-childrens-books.
Huyck, David and Sarah Park Dahlen. 'Diversity in children's books 2018'. *sarahpark.com* blog, 19 June 2019. Created in consultation with Edith Campbell, Molly Beth Griffin, K. T. Horning, Debbie Reese, Ebony Elizabeth Thomas, and Madeline Tyner, with statistics compiled by the Cooperative Children's Book Center, School of Education, University of Wisconsin-Madison: http://ccbc.education.wisc.edu/books/pcstats.asp.https://www.slj.com/?detailStory=an-updated-look-at-diversity-in-childrens-books.
Jiménez, Laura M. and Betsy Beckert. 'Diversity in publishing 2019: diversity baseline survey 2.0 by Lee & Low Books'. *blog.leeandlow.com*, 28 January 2020. https://blog.leeandlow.com/2020/01/28/2019diversitybaselinesurvey/.
Kantor, Emma. 'Building bridges: the art of children's book translation'. *Publishers Weekly*, 17 September 2020. https://www.publishersweekly.com/pw/by-topic/childrens/childrens-industry-news/article/84362-building-bridges-the-art-of-children-s-book-translation.html. Accessed 18 April 2021.
Koss, Melanie D., Nancy J. Johnson, and Miriam Martinez. 'Mapping the Diversity in Caldecott Books From 1938 to 2017: the changing topography'. *Journal of Children's Literature*, vol. 44, no. 1, 2018, pp. 4–20.
Larrick, Nancy. 'The all-white world of children's books'. *Saturday Review*, 11 September 1965, pp. 63–5.
Lathey, Gillian. '"Only English books": the mediation of translated children's literature in a resistant economy'. *Children's Literature in Translation*, edited by Jan Van Coillie and Jack McMartin. Leuven University Press, 2020, pp. 41–54.
Lathey, Gillian. *The Role of Translators in Children's Literature*. Routledge, 2010.
Lathey, Gillian. *Translating Children's Literature*. Routledge, 2016.
Lin, Ed. *David Tung Can't Have a Girlfriend Until He Gets into an Ivy League College*. Kaya Press, 2020.
Marshall, Alex. 'Amanda Gorman's poetry united critics. It's dividing translators'. *New York Times*, 26 March 2021. https://www.nytimes.com/2021/03/26/books/amanda-gorman-hill-we-climb-translation.html. Accessed 18 April 2021.
Myers, Christopher. 'The apartheid of children's literature'. *The New York Times*, 15 March 2014. https://www.nytimes.com/2014/03/16/opinion/sunday/the-apartheid-of-childrens-literature.html.
Myers, Walter Dean. 'Where are the people of color in children's books?' *The New York Times*, 15 March 2014. https://www.nytimes.com/2014/03/16/opinion/sunday/where-are-the-people-of-color-in-childrens-books.html.

Oittinen, Riitta. *Translation for Children*. Garland, 2000.

Rosenwald, Lawrence. *Multilingual America: language and the making of American literature*. Cambridge University Press, 2008.

Rosenwald, Lawrence. 'On not reading in translation'. *The Antioch Review,* vol. 62, no. 2, Spring 2004, pp. 308–18.

Schimel, Lawrence and Daniel Hahn. 'Translating for the future: children's literature in translation'. Conversation with Lyn Miller-Lachmann. *HowlRound,* 2 June 2020. https://howlround.com/happenings/translating-future-childrens-literature-translation. Accessed 18 April 2021.

Spivak, Gayatri Chakravorty. 'The politics of translation'. *The Translation Studies Reader*. 3rd ed, edited by Lawrence Venuti. Routledge, 2012.

Thomas, Ebony Elizabeth. 'Stories still matter: rethinking the role of diverse children's literature today'. *Language Arts*, vol. 94, no. 2, November 2016, pp. 112–19.

Venuti, Lawrence. *The Translator's Invisibility. a history of translation*. Routledge, 1995.

Yang, Kelly. *Parachutes.* Katherine Tegen Books, 2020.

Part III
Modes of Remedialization: Translating Beyond the Text

10
Seeing Images, Thinking of Words: Visual Art as Translation

Werner Sollors

When images are described with words in literary works, such as the shield of Achilles in Homer's *Iliad*, we call that 'ekphrasis'. There is no technical term for the transformation of texts into images, or for images that evoke words, and Sigrid Weigel suggested that we should call that process 'reverse ekphrasis'.[1] If we think of visual art as a kind of second language (as Pope Gregory the Great did when he supported the use of imagery in Christian churches) then we could also call the transformation of words into pictures 'translation'. And as is the case with all translations, a word rendered into an image involves ambiguities and uncertainties, questions of 'serving two masters', source language and target language and may make apparent the limits of any translation.[2] Of course, one could pursue this line of inquiry in many different works of art in which the presence of implied or inscribed texts plays a crucial role. Here I have chosen works from different time periods and in different media to illustrate some of the issues in word-to-image translation: an explicitly political contemporary painting, a Baroque sculptural installation, a nineteenth-century oil painting of Moses and a woodcut and an engraving from the Renaissance representing St Jerome as translator.

I. Mawande Ka Zenzile

An explicitly political contemporary painting may serve to illustrate some of the issues in word-to-image translation. The South African artist Mawande Ka Zenzile (born 1986) was one of three artists selected for the South African Pavilion at the 2019 Venice Biennale.[3] Among his work

Figure 10.1 Mawande Ka Zenzile, 'Calling a Spade a Spade' (2016, cow dung and oil on canvas, 154 × 172cm). © Stevenson, Amsterdam, Cape Town, Johannesburg.

that was exhibited there, against the darkened brick wall of the Arsenale, was the painting 'Calling a Spade a Spade' (Figure 10.1).

Mawande Ka Zenzile included a personal manifesto with his artwork, evoking the new world order that has emerged with 9/11 and the assassination of Osama Bin Laden, while old political ideologies and forms of religious fanaticism have been reinvented. 'I dedicate my work', Zenzile writes, 'to denouncing and debunking hegemonic ideologies, and explore how these global events contribute to a jaundiced view of the world'.[4]

What the viewer sees in the painting looks at first like it was taken from a deck of cards: sharply outlined against a light background, the centre of the image is taken by a black inverted heart-shaped figure with a short stalk, the symbol of the suit of spades (♠). Yet superimposed over the centre of that symbol is an image of a spade in the primary sense of 'tool for digging, paring, or cutting ground'. Its handle is upright and reaches the top of the card symbol, its silvery metal blade is shining just a little below the centre of the painting. We notice that the shape of the card symbol resembles its upside-down namesake or, rather, name-giver.

Because the word's two literal meanings are visually represented, looking at Zenzile's painting, even without regarding the title, almost *forces* us to think, and perhaps say, 'spade'. That, however, evokes yet another meaning of the word beyond the colour of a playing card or the gardening tool. It is, as the *Oxford English Dictionary* puts it, 'a term of contempt or casual reference among white people: a black person, esp. a black man'; originally an American slang term, it has gone global in the English-speaking world, and it is used here, in its translation into visual art, as a political statement against 'depreciative and offensive' language (*OED* again).[5] Though the painting represents a gardening tool and the suit of a playing card, it should probably be understood as a summons against racist slurs that the ironic title 'Calling a Spade a Spade' makes more urgent.[6] The use of the unusual material of cow dung intensifies the painting's ironic activism.

The source language, English, of the word we are made to think of is so strongly inscribed into this painting that the target audience of a painting, without any additional inscription or text beyond its title, is also imagined to be an English-speaking one. Few other languages are likely to have a single word that not only denotes the two major meanings of English 'spade' but also uses that word as a racial epithet. European languages, for example, now tend to use words for the suit of cards that are derived from French *Pique* (♠): German *Pik*, Italian *Picche*, Spanish *Picas*, or Russian Пики. The corresponding words for the spade that is used for digging out earth are French *bêche*, German *Spaten*, Italian *pala*, Spanish *vanga* and Russian лопата or заступ. In several languages, the word for the tool is also applied to the suit of cards (as in German *Spaten* for *Pik*), but it is unlikely that the three meanings of the English word *spade* – two of which Zenzile's 'Calling a Spade a Spade' shows, thereby evoking and challenging the third one – would coalesce into a single word in too many other languages. Non-Anglophone viewers of the painting probably need an explanation of the English word that contains the meaning and carries the message of its visualization.

II. Heinrich Meyring

When visual art 'translates' a word into an image, it may in many instances carry over the specific meaning of that word in the source language from which the artist proceeds. In other cases, artists may also have to make the choice of which of a word's multiple meanings to visualize. Because I am in Venice, I shall now take the Baroque sculptor Heinrich Meyring (or Enrico Marengo) (ca. 1638–1724) as an example. He was born in

Westphalia and worked in Venice for most of his lifetime. One of his first big assignments was work on the modernization of the church of San Moisé. (In Venice, figures from the Hebrew Bible, like the prophets Job and Jeremiah, could become Catholic saints to whom churches are dedicated, as San Moisé is to Moses).

Meyring's high altar has a title, like a work of art in a museum: 'Moses receiving the Law on Mount Sinai' (1684). It is a massive and quite theatrical installation in the church of San Moisé that Meyring created together with the architect Alessandro Tremignon. It includes a bearded God, angels with trombones, Aaron, Miriam and Joshua, as well as two Israelites who are ready to worship the golden calf, all on a huge Mount Sinai, made out of sand-coloured marble slabs on which the figures are mounted. My focus is only on the statue of Moses himself (Figure 10.2).

In clear view is the Hebrew script on the two black tables of the law, on one of which Moses is writing with his left hand, as he is kneeling below God on a rock of the mountain and the trombones of God's angels. Looking at the altar from the pews, Moses appears sharply outlined in profile against a nineteenth-century mural that replaced an earlier

Figure 10.2 Heinrich Meyring, 'Moses receiving the Law on Mount Sinai' (1684. Carrara marble, High Altar front. San Moisè, Venice. Werner Sollors).

window and light source. The figure has some features that distinguish Meyring's approach to sculpture: a part of Moses' coat is bulging out over his bare right knee, his curly hair and long beard are very finely sculpted, the ends of the twirled strands of the beard lie on the folds of the part of the gown covering his upper arm. What is not a Meyring idiosyncrasy is that on top of Moses' forehead, his hair seems twirled into two hornlike cones, for that was, by the late seventeenth century, a traditional representation of Moses with horns, most famously in Michelangelo's marble statue (1513–15), but present in numerous other sculptures and paintings as well.[7]

As is well known, these horns in Christian representations of Moses owe their presence to a translation problem of Exodus 34:35. In the King James Version, this verse is rendered: 'And the children of Israel saw the face of Moses, that the skin of Moses' face shone: and Moses put the vail upon his face again, until he went in to speak with him.'[8] The version of the Greek Septuagint had a similar sense.[9] But when St Jerome translated this verse, he went back to the Hebrew original and translated it into Latin as follows: 'qui videbant faciem egredientis Mosi esse cornutam sed operiebat rursus ille faciem suam si quando loquebatur ad eos.'[10] According to Jerome's translation, when Moses came out, the children of Israel saw that his face was *horned* (*facies cornuta*), and he had to veil it when he spoke to them. The reason is that the decisive Hebrew word here consisted only of the three consonants k, r and n that could be read as *keren* (glowing, shining) or as *qā-ran* (horn), and Jerome chose the latter meaning.[11] His Latin Vulgate influenced the visual choices of many artists, including Meyring's, even long after the translation had been changed in official use by the Church.

III. Moritz Daniel Oppenheim

Representing a horned Moses meant that viewers had to think of only one meaning of that original Hebrew k, r and n, for its ambiguity could not be rendered visually. Or could it? The Hanau-born German Jewish painter Moritz Daniel Oppenheim (1800–82) would seem to have been able to accomplish just that (as did other artists who took up the theme). His 'Moses mit den Gesetzestafeln' (1817–18, Jüdisches Museum Frankfurt), painted when Oppenheim was still a young art student, represents the tall, stern-looking, bearded, toga-and-sandals-clad Moses seated on a rock at Mount Sinai, with a staff on his left and in front of an encampment of Israelites far down behind him on the right. Holding the tables with the Hebrew commandments with his left arm upright on his left thigh, he points his right index finger at a line of the first table of the law, 'like a rabbi and teacher'.[12] The skin on his face, and especially his forehead, is shining, and two sets of rays are emanating from his temples. One could think at first that one sees horns before realizing that these are beams of light. Did Oppenheim intend his representation of the horn-like rays as a correction or completion of Jerome's translation and of earlier artwork that derived from it? Oppenheim's very large image of a 'life-sized' Moses (217 × 149 cm) was the first work that he painted 'of his own design'.[13] In his memoirs, Oppenheim states that he painted Moses the way he imagined him, reports that his two Munich Academy teachers – Peter Langer, father and son – disapproved, and adds sarcastically, 'the Holy Ghost was missing'.[14]

In portraying a heroic Moses figure that fits into the then new trend of historical painting, was the artist who later became famous for his portraits of the Rothschilds, of Heinrich Heine, of Ludwig Börne, and for his genre paintings of Jewish life in nineteenth-century Germany also calling attention to the issue of the emancipation of Jews? Since his later work often includes specific visual clues that suggest that he was keenly aware of painting for a double audience of Jews and non-Jews, are there any visual codes in this early painting, too?[15] Seeing Oppenheim's Moses raises many questions, but we are looking at an image that renders Moses' shining rays in such a way that they could also be taken for horns.[16]

IV. Albrecht Dürer

It may not be surprising that Jerome, the patron saint of translators, should be a persistent presence here. He was of great importance to Albrecht Dürer (1471–1528) who devoted six works in different media to Jerome. I would like to conclude these brief remarks with a few comments on two of these representations. In 1492, Dürer, at age twenty-one, created a woodcut as a frontispiece for a Basel edition of Jerome's letters (Trier City Library), in which Jerome is honoured as translator and Dürer reveals his linguistic proficiency as woodcutter.[17] As Michael Embach writes, this woodcut is an early example of how a realistic spatial reproduction that was true to perspective could be achieved in this medium, too, as had already happened in painting and copperplate engraving.

On the left, the background shows, behind a partly drawn curtain, Jerome's bed chamber and, on the right, a view onto a street through an arched window. The prominent middle ground displays to the viewer three lecterns with three different bibles, each of which is open at the beginning page of the Book of Genesis. They are clearly legible and probably constitute the first pictorial element that catches the viewer's attention. One is in Hebrew, one in Greek and the third one is in Jerome's own Latin translation. Dürer thus visualizes the translation process *textually* by showing the viewer the same passage in three languages and fonts, and the rendering of the various typefaces is impressive, all the more so if one remembers that they had to be cut as mirror images. The Hebrew Bible has the highest position and the Latin version is directly below it, as though Dürer wanted to show that Jerome's Latin followed the Hebrew original and not the Greek Septuagint that is separated from the other two by Jerome himself, who has turned his back to the Greek translation. He is seated in the foreground, wearing his cardinal's hat and flowing robe. He has apparently interrupted his work of translating. Instead, following an old legend that had become one of Jerome's visual attributes, he is shown in the foreground pulling a thorn out of a lion's paw. It is a scene that has been read as an indication of Jerome's fearlessness and kindheartedness, for he is not afraid of a lion, and to relieve a suffering animal's pain he even takes a break in his important work as translator – which is, of course, the central theme of the woodcut.[18]

Dürer's much better-known copper engraving 'Hieronymus im Gehäus' (Jerome in his study) (Kupferstichkabinett Berlin) followed in 1514. Together with 'Melencolia 1', it is considered one of his masterpieces in this genre. If Jerome's study seems smaller here, it is because the slice of the room shown excludes its continuation to the right and to the foreground.[19] It is also a wooden structure – Dürer pays meticulous attention to the wood grain – inserted in such a way into a larger monastic-seeming hall that the second window of the former hall is now cut in half by a beam.[20] Unlike in the earlier frontispiece, no bedchamber is portrayed. Jerome is bent over his lectern, and his cardinal's hat is hanging on the wall behind him. Though his figure, seated on the bench at the back wall, may seem relegated to the background,[21] the viewer's attention is drawn to him right away, and for at least two reasons. Dürer employs a sharply regular perspective, the vanishing point of which is to the right and on the level of Jerome's head.[22] The halo that surrounds his bald pate is most unusual in that it is not shown as a disk but as a light aureole emanating from his head.[23]

The central part of the halo is the only completely white area in the engraving, creating the sense of a second source of light, even brighter than that flowing in through the slug windows and casting its patterned shadows that help to give the room its friendly appearance.[24] Seated behind his desk, close to the back wall, Jerome appears to be writing into a small notebook that he is holding down on the lectern with his hand. The tabletop is empty, except for the lectern, an inkwell and a small crucifix. Under the elegantly constructed table, one sees that Jerome is wearing slippers. The domestic feeling is enhanced by the four cushions on a chair and a bench running along the wall under which there is a second pair of slippers. A good number of objects are familiar from the 1492 woodcut: candlesticks and flasks, books on a shelf, a rosary hanging from the back wall and, of course, the lion, again in the foreground. Yet now the scene clearly is set at the time after Jerome has pulled the lion's thorn, and the lion shares the foreground with a sleeping dog. They project the sense of domestic animals at peace with each other, which has suggested to some observers the promise of a paradise-like state.[25] (It may also evoke one of the meanings of *Gehäus*, 'abode for animals', another sense of the word being 'temporary, provisional home', which might go along with the wooden structure mounted for Jerome inside a larger hall.[26]) Lion, cardinal's attire and books are Jerome's attributes, but dog, pillows and slippers are not, and they help to create the atmosphere of a German interior.[27] Dürer's Jerome has been regarded as a typical 'Stubengelehrter'.[28] (Dürer has made not even the slightest gesture toward a representation of Jerome's setting in Bethlehem and makes the room appear like a prior's or abbot's chamber.[29]) New are the still-life-like evocations of mortality and vanity – a half-run hourglass hangs next to the cardinal's hat, and a jawless skull rests on the windowsill, with its empty eye sockets facing the room. Also new are a bunch of letters, a scroll and a pair of scissors, all fastened to the back wall with a ribbon. The scissors seem to point down toward a letter 'D' engraved on the cabinet below that is, in fact, also the vanishing point of the perspective. Dürer's classic 'AD' initials and year also appear on a board that has been prepared to be hung up with a string, but that is instead lying on the floor, behind the lion's tail. Under the lion is a downward step, a threshold that gives the engraving a border below and creates, together with the supporting pillar on the left and the doubly grooved ceiling beam on top, a frame for the whole scene which resembles a stage set.[30] It is a frame, however, that remains open on the right: it invites the viewer to imagine a continuation of the room to the right, toward which the perspectival lines direct us to look in any event.[31]

Dürer's 'Gehäus' thus contains Jerome together with several of his familiar attributes as scholar and hermit and with other objects that have a symbolic significance. Also present are things that may not symbolize anything but evoke a particularly domestic mood. But what are we to make of the large bottle gourd that is fastened tight with a double knot to the eyelet of a hook on the grooved ceiling beam on the top right of the engraving? Modern viewers may be anachronistically reminded of ceiling lamps, but the hanging gourd is an object that seems to fit in neither as an attribute of Jerome nor as a symbol in its own right.[32] It also does not look like a common part of a sixteenth-century study and has been viewed as the only superfluous decoration there and a botanical curiosity.[33] It is big, calls attention to itself, and seems to radiate light.[34] At its bottom, the gourd shows a ring within its circular shape, and it is as large as the round cardinal's hat that also is rendered as a circle within a circle. With its narrower neck on top of its round belly, the gourd furthermore resembles the shape of Jerome's upper body. While one of its elaborately etched shoots curves upward, echoing the lion's tail's downward curve, the other vines stand out in their corkscrew twists and elaborate spirals that find no parallel in the engraving. The vines reminded one scholar of musical clefs and inspired him to imagine a concert of the objects in the room, while the dry stalk of the pumpkin with its bony hand impatiently taps the beat on the wood.[35] Ignored for a long time, Dürer's gourd has generated some attention in recent years and inspired whole essays devoted to the 'pumpkin question'.

Structurally, the presence of the gourd was interpreted as a kind of curtain or a *repoussoir* that, together with the lion and the dog on the bottom, opens the image and directs the viewer to it.[36] Only, does it not rather call attention to itself and thus have the function of blocking, rather than opening, the view?[37] A dried gourd could signify vanity, but does the gourd not look freshly picked, like it was just put up?[38] If it was freshly picked, was it a symbol of the harvest season and autumn, or a reminder of Jerome's saint's day, 30 September, also the day of his death in 420?[39] Could drying a gourd and later using it as a flask refer to Jerome's mortification of all sinful bodily desires so as to become God's vessel, like a calabash?[40] Was the gourd meant as a parallel to the skull on the windowsill, as 'caution against the vanity of all temporal pursuits'?[41] Could the light that the pumpkin seems to emanate be the light of Christ, of God's word, of Jerome himself inside the *Gehäus* of the Church, in embryonic bliss inside its and the Virgin's maternal womb – at peace, not unlike the dog in the engraving?[42] Or might the gourd simply be dangling from that ceiling beam as a decorative curiosity and not be a symbol of anything in particular?[43]

Larry Rosenwald and other readers may wonder at this point what this page on a gourd has to do with translation. But there is a connection between the mysterious presence of the gourd and the problem of translation or, more precisely, a problem in Jerome's translation of the Book of Jonah, and a subsequent dispute about it. Adolf Weis and Peter

W. Parshall are among the scholars who have looked at 'Hieronymus im Gehäus' through this lens.⁴⁴ The argument goes like this: Jerome is not translating in this image. He has no books on his table, but only a little notebook on his lectern and behind him a small collection of letters on the wall. He may thus be drafting one of his letters to St Augustine. There was a translation dispute between Jerome and Augustine concerning Jonah 4:6, set after Jonah has come out of the big fish and grieves when God changes his mind and does not destroy the city of Niniveh, whose inhabitants Jonah had exhorted and warned. The King James Version has the verse as follows: 'And the Lord God prepared a gourd, and made it to come up over Jonah, that it might be a shadow over his head, to deliver him from his grief. So Jonah was exceeding glad of the gourd.'⁴⁵

At issue is the Latin equivalent of the Hebrew name of the shrub that God sends Jonah to shade him and to teach him that since he can grieve for a plant that withers when attacked by a worm, he should also have pity on the city of Niniveh. Jonah's shrub must be a plant that grows fast without needing support, has wide leaves like wine so that it can give shade, and also withers quickly. While the Hebrew name of the plant that climbs up – הַקִּיקָיוֹן (or haq qî qā yō wn)⁴⁶ – does not allow for an exact botanical assignment, it was most likely the castor oil plant. The Septuagint translated it as κολόκυνϑα (bottle gourd or pumpkin), of which *cucurbita* was the Latin equivalent. However, the castor bean plant was not a pumpkin, but Jerome did not know a good Latin term for it. He had apparently forgotten that Pliny (whom he knew well) had in his *Natural History* used the word *ricinus*.⁴⁷ So what could Jerome do? As he explains in his commentary on Jonah, transcribing the Hebrew word as *ciceion* would have been unintelligible to readers of Latin. Had he chosen *cucurbita* he would have departed from the Hebrew original. Hence he chose *hedera* (ivy), which he had found in another translation by Aquila. He weighed his options very carefully and saw the pros and cons of both gourd and ivy, neither of which grows fast without needing support. In the literal sense, 'ivy' made more sense, on the level of 'mystical' comprehension of redemptive history, 'gourd' would also work from a semiotic and botanical perspective.⁴⁸

Ultimately, Jerome chose ivy. This created an uproar, and Jerome found himself vilified by adversaries, one of whom he satirically called cucurbophile (φιλοκολόκυνϑο) and ridiculed another one whom he called Asinius Pollion for supposedly believing that 'if ivy were taken instead of gourds that there would not be anything to drink in his secret place and his shade'.⁴⁹ Jerome defended his choice in his correspondence with Augustine, who was concerned that this deviation from the choice of words of the Septuagint could lead to confusion, disputes and potential divisions within the Church and therefore advocated keeping 'pumpkin' for unity's sake. And indeed, in Byzantine art, the scene of Jonah lying under ivy prevailed, whereas in Western art it was a gourd.[50] Seen against this background, Dürer's engraving may thus show Jerome drafting one of his letters to Augustine in which he defended his use of ivy, while the cucurbophiles still loomed large, like a big pumpkin hanging over Jerome's study.[51]

Of course, there is a counterargument. Kuder writes forcefully that the thesis that Dürer, alluding to Jerome's translation controversy with Augustine, had put a splendid pumpkin over the Church father's head in the engraving dedicated to him is downright ludicrous.[52] If Dürer had wanted to allude to that dispute, would he not have shown Jerome's ivy instead of the Septuagint's gourd? Others have seconded Kuder. Yet in the absence of a more convincing explanation of the bottle gourd hanging from the ceiling of Jerome's study, is it not possible that Dürer's 'Hieronymus im Gehäus' contains, among its many other themes, a visualization not just of a biblical word, but of a translation problem of the word, a problem that the presence of the gourd signals?

When looking at Mawande Ka Zenzile's 'Calling a Spade a Spade', showing a spade and the pattern of a playing card, we realize that we are being asked to think of an English word in its derogatory sense. In sculpting his Moses, Heinrich Meyring visualized only one meaning of an ambiguous Hebrew word and gave Moses horns. Moritz Daniel Oppenheim rendered the more plausible meaning of the word and painted Moses with a glowing face, but also added rays extending from his temples as if they were horns and thus may have tried to find a visual equivalent for two meanings embedded in a term. Dürer produced a woodcut that served as the frontispiece of an edition of Jerome's letters and, in it, he visualized the translation process textually by displaying three versions of Genesis 1:1, in the original Hebrew, in the Greek of the Septuagint, and in Jerome's Latin. Is it not possible that Dürer added a big gourd to his *Hieronymus im Gehäus* in order to remind viewers of the antagonism Jerome met when, in translating Jonah, he had chosen 'ivy' and not the word that now claims our visual attention?

Notes

1. Weigel, 'Die Richtung des Bildes', 457. Her term is 'umgekehrte *Ekphrasis*'.
2. Rosenzweig, 'Scripture and Luther', 47.
3. It was curated by Nomusa Makhubu and Nkule Mabaso under the title *The Stronger We Become*.
4. From a manifesto-like page displayed at 2019 Venice Biennale.

5. 'Spade, n.1' and 'Spade, n.2', *OED* online.
6. See also the recent collection of Zenzile's work at https://issuu.com/stevensonctandjhb/docs/mawande_ka_zenzile_uhambo_luyazilawula_issuu, p. 160.
7. See Wolff, 'Der Hochaltar von S. Moisé in Venedig', 178–82 and Costantini, *Chiesa di San Moisè*.
8. At https://www.kingjamesbibleonline.org/Exodus-Chapter-34/.
9. At https://en.katabiblon.com/us/index.php?text=LXX&book=Ex&ch=34: καὶ εἶδον οἱ υἱοὶ Ισραηλ τὸ πρόσωπον Μωυσῆ ὅτι δεδόξασται καὶ περιέθηκεν Μωυσῆς κάλυμμα ἐπὶ τὸ πρόσωπονἑαυτοῦ ἕως ἂν εἰσέλθῃ συλλαλεῖν αὐτῷ.
10. At https://vulgate.org/ot/exodus_34.htm.
11. See https:// de.cat holi cnew sage ncy.com/ story/ warum- hat- moses- hor ner- auf- dem-kopf- 1708. The Hebrew text is at https:// www.mec hon- mamre.org/ p/ pt/ pt0 234.htm: {ס .וְאֵתוֹ לְדַבֵּר בָּאוֹ-עַד ,פָּנָיו-עַל הַמַּסְוֶה-אֶת מֹשֶׁה וְהֵשִׁיב עוֹר פְּנֵי מֹשֶׁה כִּי קָרַן ,אֶת-פְּנֵי מֹשֶׁה ,אֶת-יִשְׂרָאֵל בְּנֵי וַיִּרְאוּ לה}. The three-consonant word qā-ran could also be read as 'keren' and rendered 'horn'.
12. See the phrase 'Mosche rabbenu' at https://sammlung.juedischesmuseum.de/objekt/moses-mit-den-gesetzestafeln/.
13. Merk, 'Die künstlerische Entwicklung von Moritz Daniel Oppenheim', 16–17.
14. Berankova and Riedel, 'Moritz Daniel Oppenheim', 341.
15. Graf, *Die jüdische Genremalerei der voremanzipatorischen Zeit*, 121: Graf mentions that Oppenheim inserted 'codes' into his genre paintings that could be deciphered only by 'insiders'.
16. I wonder what Larry Rosenwald would make of Meyring's and Oppenheim's renditions of the Hebrew writing on the tables of the Law. Is the prohibition of graven images shown in very large, life-sized images?
17. Embach, *Hundert Highlights,* 184–5. I am following Embach's commentary on p. 184.
18. See Richter, 'Hieronymus Tinctus', 281–2, and Kummer, 'Der einsame Gelehrte', 125–6.
19. Großmann, 'Das 'Gehäus' des Hieronymus von Albrecht Dürer', 129–31, criticizes past readings that found the room small and stresses that the right limit of the room is not indicated. He believes that the actual room must be extraordinarily large, four times the size of the piece of it that Dürer shows.
20. See Weis, '" ... Diese lächerliche Kürbisfrage", 195, and Jeon, *Meditatio Mortis,* 117, n. 545.
21. Strümpell, 'Hieronymus im Gehäuse', 179 where Strümpell speaks of 'Staffage'.
22. Weis, '" ... Diese lächerliche Kürbisfrage", 195.
23. Kummer, 'Der einsame Gelehrte', 127, and Richter, 'Hieronymus Tinctus', 284.
24. Strümpell, 'Hieronymus im Gehäuse', 228.
25. Weis, '" ... Diese lächerliche Kürbisfrage", 195.
26. See 'Gehäus' im Deutschen Wörterbuch von Jacob Grimm und Wilhelm Grimm. Jeon, *Meditatio Mortis,* 117, finds that the reference to 'Gehäus' distinguishes this engraving from Jerome portraits as a hermit in nature.
27. See Strümpell, 'Hieronymus im Gehäuse', 175, who stresses the element of growing bourgeois individualism.
28. Wölfflin, quoted by Jeon, *Meditatio Mortis,* 116
29. Kummer, 'Der einsame Gelehrte', 116.
30. Jeon, *Meditatio Mortis,* 114.
31. The perspective lines of ceiling beams, wall shelf and windowsill meet, as we saw, to the right of Jerome, exactly in the cabinet with the letter D, and direct our glance from left to right, which calls attention to the fact that the right vertical has no frame. However, Wölfflin, 'Über das Rechts und Links im Bilde', 86–7, finds, " ... dass in Dürer's *Hieronymus im Gehäus* 'alle lauten und unruhigen [Formen] links bleiben und rechts die Erscheinung ins Klare, Begrenzte, Durchgebildete mündet', wobei die rechte Seite 'schon durch den Löwen und den eckfüllenden Kürbis ... für den Eindruck des Beschlossenen sorgen'.
32. Behling, 'Eine "ampel"-artige Pflanze', emphasizes the lantern-like quality of Dürer's plant.
33. Kuder, *Dürers 'Hieronymus im Gehäus',* 229. Weis, '" ... Diese lächerliche Kürbisfrage", 197. See also Kummer, 'Der einsame Gelehrte', 117, who sees the gourd as a 'schmückende Kuriosität'.
34. Jeon, *Meditatio Mortis,* 114.
35. Richter, 'Hieronymus Tinctus', 285, reads like an ekphrastic prose poem on the gourd that is compared to a spinning bell and an Atlas figure.
36. Jeon, *Meditatio Mortis,* 114–15.
37. Jeon, *Meditatio Mortis,* 114.

38. Jeon, *Meditatio Mortis*, 117, mentions emblem books that associate the pumpkin with 'vain pride' and 'fleeting pleasure'. Richter, 'Hieronymus Tinctus', 276, sees in the big leaf that has not yet withered proof that the bottle gourd was hung up only recently.
39. See Richter, 'Hieronymus Tinctus', 278, about the freshly harvested gourd, fall season, and Jerome's name day.
40. See Schuster, *Melencolia I.*, 344–5, quoted by Kuder, *Dürers 'Hieronymus im Gehäus'*, 233. Jeon, *Meditatio Mortis*, 118, also mentions that the gourd alludes to Jerome himself as a vessel ('Gefäß') for God's will. There may be an analogy between 'Gefäß' and 'Gehäus'.
41. Parshall, 'Albrecht Dürer's St. Jerome in his study', 305.
42. Kuder, *Dürers 'Hieronymus im Gehäus'*, 261–2.
43. Kummer, 'Der einsame Gelehrte', 117.
44. Weis, " … Diese lächerliche Kürbisfrage", 197–200; Parshall 'Albrecht Dürer's St. Jerome in his study', 303–5.
45. At https://www.kingjamesbibleonline.org/Jonah-4-6/.
46. From https://biblehub.com/text/jonah/4-6.htm.
47. See Fürst, 'Kürbis oder Efeu', 15.
48. Fürst, 'Kürbis oder Efeu', 18–19. For Jerome's reasoning, see https://sites.google.com/site/aquinasstudybible/home/jonah/st-jerome-on-jonah/chapter-1/chapter-2/chapter-3/chapter-4.
49. Fürst, 'Kürbis oder Efeu', 16, on the Cucurbophile.
50. According to Kuder, *Dürers 'Hieronymus im Gehäus'*, 238.
51. Schauerte, *Albrecht Dürer. Das große Glück*, 189, concurs with the approach taken by Weis and Parshall.
52. Kuder, *Dürers 'Hieronymus im Gehäus'*, 238: 'geradezu aberwitzig'.

Bibliography

Behling, Lottlisa. 'Eine "ampel"-artige Pflanze von Albrecht Dürer. Cucurbita lagenaria L. auf dem Hieronymus-Stich von 1514'. *Pantheon*, vol. 30, 1972, pp. 396–400.

Berankova, Ljuba and Erik Riedel. 'Moritz Daniel Oppenheim. Biographie sowie Selbstzeugnisse und Erinnerungen seiner Zeitgenossen'. *Moritz Daniel Oppenheim. Die Entdeckung des jüdischen Selbstbewußtseins in der Kunst*. Wienand Verlag, 1999.

Costantini, Attilio. *Chiesa di San Moisè*. 2007.

Embach, Michael. *Hundert Highlights: Kostbare Handschriften und Drucke der Stadtbibliothek Trier*. Schnell und Steiner, 2013.

Fürst, Alfons. 'Kürbis oder Efeu. Zur Übersetzung von Jona 4, 6 in der Septuaginta und bei Hieronymus'. *Biblische Notizen*, vol. 72, 1993, pp. 12–19.

Graf, Esther. *Die jüdische Genremalerei der voremanzipatorischen Zeit als Motivquelle für Moritz Daniel Oppenheims Zyklus zum altjüdischen Familienleben. Eine gattungs- und motivgeschichtliche Untersuchung*. Diss., Heidelberg, 2004.

Grimm, Jacob and Wilhelm Grimm. 'Gehäus'. *Deutsches Wörterbuch*. https://woerterbuchnetz.de/?sigle=DWB#1.

Großmann, G. Ulrich. 'Das "Gehäus" des Hieronymus von Albrecht Dürer'. *Beständig im Wandel. Innovationen – Verwandlungen – Konkretisierungen*, edited by Christian Hecht. Matthes & Seitz, 2009.

Hebrew Bible. The Book of Exodus, *Mechon Mamre*. https://mechon-mamre.org/p/pt/pt0234.htm.

Hebrew Bible Online, *Bible Hub*. https://biblehub.com/text/jonah/4-6.htm.

Jeon, Hanho. *Meditatio Mortis. Zur Ikonographie des heiligen Hieronymus mit dem Totenschädel unter besonderer Berücksichtigung des Lissabonner Gemäldes von Albrecht Dürer*. Diss., Münster, 2005.

King James Bible. https://www.kingjamesbibleonline.org/Exodus-Chapter-34/.

Kuder, Ulrich. *Dürers 'Hieronymus im Gehäus'. Der Heilige im Licht*. Verlag Dr. Kovač, 2013.

Kummer, Stefan. 'Der einsame Gelehrte – Der hl. Hieronymus im Gehäuse'. *Kulturen der Einsamkeit*, edited by Ina Bergmann and Dorothea Klein. Königshausen & Neumann, 2020, pp. 115–46.

Latin Vulgate Old Testament Bible, The Book of Exodus 34. *Vulgate*, https://vulgate.org/ot/exodus_34.htm.

Oppenheim, Moritz Daniel. 'Moses mit den Gesetzestafeln', 1817–1818. Jüdisches Museum Frankfurt. https://sammlung.juedischesmuseum.de/objekt/moses-mit-den-gesetzestafeln/.

Merk, Anton. 'Die künstlerische Entwicklung von Moritz Daniel Oppenheim'. *Moritz Daniel Oppenheim. Die Entdeckung des jüdischen Selbstbewußtseins in der Kunst*, edited by Georg Heuberger and Anton Merk. Wienand Verlag, 1999.

New Testament, Greek Septuagint and English edition. *Kata Biblon*. https://en.katabiblon.com/us/index.php?text=LXX&book=Ex&ch=34.

Parshall, Peter W. 'Albrecht Dürer's St. Jerome in his study: a philological reference'. *The Art Bulletin*, vol. 53, no.3, 1971, pp. 303–5.

Richter, Leonhard G. 'Hieronymus Tinctus'. *Dürer-Code: Albrecht Dürers entschlüsselte Meisterstiche*. J.H. Röll Verlag, 2014, pp. 275–87.

Rosenzweig, Franz. 'Scripture and Luther'. *Scripture and Translation*, edited by Martin Buber and Franz Rosenzweig, translated by Lawrence Rosenwald with Everett Fox. Indiana University Press, 1994.

Schauerte, Thomas Ulrich. *Albrecht Dürer. Das große Glück. Kunst im Zeichen des geistigen Aufbruchs*. Rasch, 2003.

Schuster, Peter-Klaus. *Melencolia I. Dürers Denkbild*. Mann, 1999.

Strümpell, Anna. 'Hieronymus im Gehäuse'. *Marburger Jahrbuch für Kunstwissenschaft*, vol. 2, 1925–6, pp. 173–252.

'Warum hat dieser Moses Hörner auf dem Kopf?'. *Catholic News Agency Deutsch*, 19. August 2020. https://de.catholicnewsagency.com/story/warum-hat-moses-horner-auf-dem-kopf-1708.

Weigel, Sigrid. 'Die Richtung des Bildes. Zum Links-Rechts von Bilderzählungen und Bildbeschreibungen in kultur- und mediengeschichtlicher Perspektive'. *Zeitschrift für Kunstgeschichte*, vol. 64, no. 4, 2001, pp. 449–74.

Weis, Adolf. '" … Diese lächerliche Kürbisfrage" … Christlicher Humanismus in Dürers Hieronymusbild'. *Zeitschrift für Kunstgeschichte*, vol. 45 no. 2, 1982, pp. 195–201.

Wolff, Silvia. 'Der Hochaltar von S. Moisé in Venedig'. *Heinrich Meyring, Bildhauer in Venedig*. Diss., Freiburg, 2006, pp. 178–82.

Wölfflin, Heinrich. 'Über das Rechts und Links im Bilde'. *Gedanken zur Kunstgeschichte*. Schwabe & Co., 1941, pp. 82–90.

Zenzile, Mawande Ka. *Uhambo luyazilawula*. https://issuu.com/stevensonctandjhb/docs/mawande_ka_zenzile_uhambo_luyazilawula_issuu.

Zenzile, Mawande Ka. 'Calling a Spade a Spade'. https://issuu.com/stevensonctandjhb/docs/mawande_ka_zenzile_uhambo_luyazilawula_issuu.

11
Theatre Without Theatres: Performance Transmission as Translation[1]

Sarah Bay-Cheng

In September 2021, designer, director and theatre professor Jared Mezzocchi posed a question to his Twitter followers: 'Why is labelling this form of performance "theatre" so important? Like film, radio and television, should it just be named differently? Or is it a site-specific pageant play w [sic] a different type of wagon?' Mezzocchi's question referred to the increased attention to and discussion of digitally broadcast theatre, virtual reality (VR) and other mediated performances that had proliferated during the hard times of the Covid-19 pandemic when performing arts venues suddenly shuttered. Mezzochi's query sparked a lively discourse, leading to claims of 'It's theatre because I called it theatre', and more nuanced discussions of theatre and theatricality within vocabularies and practices closely tied to funding and economic regimes shaped by union rules, available government support and so on. Of course, as any theatre artist knows all too well, economic concerns underlie the entirety of theatre's history across all cultures and historical periods. As a materialist art reliant on collective labour in public spaces, issues of money, audiences, government, politics and culture have always been at the heart of theatrical enterprise and practice. But, amid the unprecedented constraints of a global lockdown on performance arts and culture, there is something else at stake in Mezzocchi's question. As theatre artists, students, critics and scholars continue to assess the circumstances of the 2020 pandemic and its aftermath, we find ourselves looking at a distinctly transformed environment for theatre. What was already precarious for many has been devastating, but like the incredible shift to online learning (for better or worse), the attention to theatre transmission via digital media, or *digital theatre,* has radically shifted the field of production and reception for theatre in ways that are likely to endure and evolve.

This chapter explores how we might understand theatre and theatricality amid an ongoing media convergence that began more than 100 years prior to the pandemic but has accelerated within it. Clearly, we need finer distinctions for contemporary performance forms than the binary of 'theatre' and 'not theatre'. We might be served better by a conceptual framework that facilitates our understanding of the spectrum of *theatricality* across media, transformed in the era of *Annos Coronavirus* (ACV). One way is to view digital theatre, or 'theatre without theatres' (to repurpose Alain Badiou's derisive phrase), as a kind of *translation* of the mimetic, integrated space-time-action of traditional live forms into digital forms that, like their textual equivalents, simultaneously offer the original theatre (whether actual or imagined) and its mediated echo. Precisely because both translations and digital theatre have been dismissed as inherently inferior, inaccurate and flawed in comparison to an elevated original, this framing of translation as a function of mediated theatre offers both a way to understand contemporary theatre within and as media and, more importantly, to draw attention to the overlooked labour and aesthetics that shape performance transmissions on screen. Because of its inherent gaps and echoes, translation provides a framework in which we can appreciate the ironic impermanence of digital theatre and its position in performance and media in the post-pandemic era.

The *Oxford English Dictionary* defines translation as 'the expression or rendering of a thing in another medium or form; the conversion or adaptation of a thing to another system, context or use'. Amid all of the discussions of theatre and media since the 1980s, I am hard pressed to find a more apt definition of theatre on screens. The nuances of translation and how it has been understood in literary contexts further correspond to contemporary debates about the role and function of *theatre* as performances that occur both in and beyond the conventions of live co-presence. Translations have the sometimes awkward and often disparaged feature of presenting an original aesthetic object (either text or performance) in a form that is both more accessible and fundamentally distorted from that original. For example, a text translated from its original language into the vernacular of the reader provides wider access, as does the circulation of a live theatre production viewable online. In this sense, the original is simultaneously present and not. A translation suggests that an audience (either reader or viewer) may have perceived and maybe even understood a *thing*, even if that perception has relied on a mediator, whose work often may not be fully acknowledged or appreciated. If I say that I have read Badiou, mentioned above, have I read *Éloge du théâtre* or *In Praise of Theatre* as translated by Andrew Bielski? Both? If I have read Rilke's *Letters to a Young Poet* only in translation, can I appreciate the work that the translator has done in carrying the text from the author's original ideas to me? And how does this relation in textual translation emerge in considerations of live theatrical performances rendered on screens?

Engagement of translation as a term to connect genre across media and performance is not new. Considerations of translation's indeterminacy appear in Nietzsche's *Birth of Tragedy Through the Spirit of Music*, threaded between the Apolline and the Dionysiac. Ralph Manheim (the iconic translator for Brecht's work in English and the experimental director Richard Foreman's father-in-law) famously remarked that 'translators are like actors: we speak lines by someone else'. Alex Gross elaborated the analogy from the other side, seeing theatre as translation:

> The proscenium arch, along with the entire theatrical architecture underlying the conjuror's tricks, can readily be likened to the totality of shared cultural history between the two peoples and cultures being subjected to such alleged acts of translation. And the audience for this stage illusion, those desperately ready and willing to witness the fulfilment of this fraudulent wonder, are none other than those (often ourselves) already convinced that such a miracle can and must take place.[2]

Gross' notion of the 'fraudulent wonder' recalls Walter Benjamin's widely cited but notably problematic essay 'The task of the translator', in which he describes translation as a process that, not unlike the staging of drama, simultaneously reproduces and destroys the original:

> Finally, it is self-evident how greatly fidelity in reproducing the form impedes the rendering of the sense. Thus no case for literalness can be based on a desire to retain the meaning. Meaning is served far better – and literature and language far worse – by the unrestrained licence of bad translators.[3]

Benjamin posits translation as an interpretive and repetitive, if flawed, enactment of the original, one that develops in time, much like the performance of a play or its recording. Is this not the relation of recorded performances in the minds of their critics? Carol Jacobs, for instance, argued that Benjamin's 'task' for the translator is ultimately one of surrender, what she called a 'monstrous loss'.[4] How many playwrights confronted with the opening night of their plays have felt the same?

This gap between the 'original' ideal and its flawed copy in performance further aligns with the contested relations among theatre and other media, the so-called 'rivals' that Susan Sontag perceived when she drew distinctions between them, and cited in the work of philosophers like Badiou, who argued for the centrality of the theatrical *text* as 'symbolic treasury' that is necessary to prevent theatre from disappearing into either dance or cinema.[5] Translation in this sense is an open-ended process that evades any final realization and holds open the opportunities and space between fixed entities. Digital theatre as translation may offer similarly irreconcilable meanings, or rather theatrical experiences without physical theatres.

Jacobs' sense of 'monstrous loss' in Benjamin's translation captures the attitude of many theatre critics, scholars and historians, who even amid the pandemic explicitly rejected the value of theatrical performances on screen. Prominent among these was Peter Marks, theatre critic of the *Washington Post*, who spent much of his newfound time in the early months of the pandemic broadly dismissing online performances on Twitter: 'As margarine is to butter, theatre online comes across as an artificial substitute, with less flavour'.[6] German scholar Erika Fischer-Lichte similarly announced during an interview at the Belgrade International Theatre Festival in September 2020 that 'Something like digital theatre does not exist'.

> I have to say that I am grateful to theatres for granting us the possibility to see some old productions again. This, more or less, gives you an idea of what has happened. But, of course, this is not theatre. As you said, for me, there must be an audience. Without spectators there is no theatre. I am not talking about spectators who sit somewhere else, at home, watching it on television. The audience has to be in the same space as the performers; this is what I mean by bodily co-presence. It is this flow, back-and-forth, between performers and actors that is important. That is what counts because, in my opinion, it is what distinguishes theatre art from all the other art forms.[7]

Both the interviewer, Ivan Medenica (who subsequently declared 'digital theatre' an ignorant term) and Fischer-Lichte speak as those well-versed in theatre's original language. Attending the digital translation of the 'real thing' to which she has dedicated a long and distinguished career, Fischer-Lichte can observe the inherent failure of the digital version to convey the full sensibility of the original theatre experience better than most. Her dissatisfaction with digital theatre thus echoes the multilinguist's reading in translation. As Lawrence Rosenwald has observed in translation, 'The better we know the original, the more aspects of it we are experiencing, the more we see and feel how wrong we are getting it'.[8] Viewing digital theatre as translation reflects similar disparities in reception. Audiences split between those familiar with the original who can observe the omissions clearly and those who are content to 'read' the digital because the original is inaccessible, unfamiliar or even potentially alienating in not only its live presentation, but also the requisite customs that are aligned with particular class, race and other cultural performances by the viewer. Such formulations create a distinct hierarchy of theatrical experience among those who *know* the original and those who are ignorant and therefore content with the diminished version of theatre on screen. As Marks might have said, 'if you've never had butter, perhaps margarine will suffice'.

Rosenwald offers us a more useful framing of translation as a practice that we can apply as a more nuanced understanding and appreciation of theatre on screen. In his 2004 essay 'On not reading in translation', he distinguishes the practice of reading *in* translation from reading *of* translation: 'It's important to distinguish reading *in* translation, where translation takes the place of the original, from reading *of* translation, where the translation is read in relation to the original.'[9] Could we, perhaps, consider a mode of digital theatre viewing in which we attend to the mediated version as akin to viewing *of* theatre's medial translation? In what follows, I make the case that digital theatre is more properly understood as a kind of *translated theatre* rather than simply a flawed rendition of theatrical performance on screen. In both the live venue and the recorded versions, theatre's inherent assumption of the audience as present creates a shared 'space' between audiences and performers, even when these entities may not be visible to each other. In the context of mediated theatre, the 'shared air' of the past has been translated into new digital spaces that replicate the same communal relations in new languages and across new media. These relations apply both to stage performances recorded for screens and to novel performances created exclusively for this purpose.

Take the musical *Hamilton* (2015), which began as an off-Broadway show drawing from tropes and techniques of musical theatre, American history and hip hop. Perhaps the most successful theatre production in the history of the world, the Broadway production received eleven Tony awards in 2015, winning every category in which it was nominated except for two. *Hamilton* premiered again on the Disney+ streaming platform in July 2020. Described as 'a live stage recording', the *Hamilton* video was named as one of the best *films* of 2020 by the American Film Institute and nominated for Best Motion Picture in the category Musical or Comedy at the Seventy-Eighth Golden Globe Awards, where Lin-Manuel Miranda was nominated for Best Actor in a Motion Picture in the category Musical or Comedy. His co-star Daveed Diggs was nominated for Screen Actors Guild Award for Outstanding Male Actor in a Limited Series or Television Movie. Most recently, the show received twelve Primetime Emmy Award nominations in 2021. Whereas we might look at musical productions based on films as adaptations – films turned musicals turned films such as *The Producers* or, more recently, Miranda and Quiara Hudes' musical *In the Heights* – *Hamilton*, having been recorded with the original cast live on its Broadway stage and streamed into millions of homes and televisions via the Disney streaming platform, is a kind of transmedial translation. The musical as digital theatre followed the original staging, choreography, music and rhythms of the stage performance and marketed itself as the opportunity to 'Experience the original Broadway Production of Hamilton, now streaming exclusively on Disney+'. As in Rosenwald's translation, the viewer's experience of attending the original production in the theatre affects the perception of the screen version's accuracy to the original. However, by some measures, it may be that the screen version is much better.

By moving cameras upstage of the performers, shooting them in close-ups and in rapid editing sequences, Disney+ audiences can see *more* of the original performance than those who attended the production in the Broadway houses. This is especially true if your seats were further away, but close-ups in key scenes reveal nuance that even those seated in the front row of a Broadway house will miss. To wit, one of the most discussed effects from the screen version of *Hamilton* was the amount of saliva that Jonathan Groff generated in his performance of the song 'You'll Be Back' as King George III. Perhaps done intentionally to reflect the monarch's historic physical and mental ailments and coincidentally in the midst of a global pandemic spurred by viral transmission in respiratory fluids, Groff's spittle caused widespread commentary. For the first time, even dedicated fans of the show could attend to this minor part of the performance blown up to fill millions of Disney+ subscribers' screens. The impact was so great that Groff's performance launched its own meme across multiple social media platforms.[10]

The screen viewer is likely to be aware of the original, regardless of whether or not they have seen it themselves. But who after watching the recording on Disney+ would say that they have *not* seen *Hamilton*? Like Benjamin's distinction between the good translation and the accurate translation, the screen version of Miranda's musical was not necessarily the most *accurate* to the experience of attending the original production in New York – sitting in the audience, surrounded by strangers, perhaps with an obscured view, all in varying proximity to the events on stage. However, the media embellishments, including camera movements, close-ups, shifting focus, lighting and editing reveal much more of the performance and create entirely new meanings, effects and understandings of the original show (for example Groff's spittle as historical reference to King George's illness). The screen version of the musical illuminates the show's debt to not only musical hip hop culture, but also to rap's circulation via music videos seen on 'MTV Raps' in the 1980s and 1990s and in films like Spike Lee's iconic *Do the Right Thing* (1989), which itself brought a stylized (and perhaps even theatricalized) vision of Brooklyn street culture to global cinema audiences. Contrary to the claims that theatre on screens is a reduction or diminishment of the original, *Hamilton*'s medial translation both literally and figuratively shows us more by presenting the original production enlarged by perspectives not visible to any member of the audience in the stage version. In this sense we might even say that (again, per Benjamin) the 'meaning' of the original show was more effectively conveyed through the inaccurate and distorting media than perhaps many of the live touring shows could offer. Or, to return to Benjamin and what he called the 'dialectical image':

> If one looks upon history as a text, then one can say of it what a recent author has said of literary texts – namely, that the past has left them images comparable to those registered by a light-sensitive plate. 'The future alone possesses developers strong enough to reveal the image in all its details'.[11]

In the event of *Hamilton*, the historian as photographic developer is all the more apt (perhaps embarrassingly so) as the video camera becomes a documentary device perpetually documenting and replaying previously unseen images of a live event long ago concluded.

But what about the audience? And community? What of the flow of energy back and forth between the audiences and the performers that Fischer-Lichte and many others cite as the essence of theatre? That, too, has been translated into another language: social media. Historically, theatre has been defined by its shared space and time as the essential conditions of *theatre*. Referring to theatre as the 'hypermedium', theorist Chiel Kattenbelt described a stage of intermediality capable of holding all the other arts without fundamentally altering them. 'Unlike film and television', he argued, 'theatre always takes place in the absolute presence of here and now. The performer and spectator are physically present at the same time and the same space. They are there for each other.'[12] Kattenbelt's essay appeared in 2006, the same year that Facebook first became available to the wider public, forever changing our notions of both media and 'friends'. In 2003, Diana Taylor had already begun questioning the meaning of performance presence in the context of the digital: 'The repertoire requires presence', she wrote, 'people participate in the production and reproduction of knowledge by "being there" being a part of the transmission.'[13] In writings by Peggy Phelan, Philip Auslander and Steve Dixon, among others, the ontological liveness of theatre was vigorously debated prior to the pandemic. As many have observed over the past twenty years, the widespread circulation of performances online and the emergence of social media have upended what it means to be there or, indeed, anywhere. But now, in the age of ubiquitous smartphones and social media, it is possible to be virtually everywhere.

No longer limited to the exclusive interactions of the Broadway theatre, *Hamilton's* audiences actively engage with its creators via collaboratively annotated lyrics on Genius.com, where the original cast album lyrics have been viewed and annotated 64.7 million times and counting. The engaging antics by the cast outside the theatre on #Ham4Ham brought interactive parodies of the show to both online audiences and those gathered outside the theatre, hoping for a ticket inside. Miranda, among others, often responded directly to audiences gathered outside the theatre's stage door with the exchanges captured and circulated on YouTube and reposted and replayed on other platforms. In the wake of *Hamilton's* release on Disney+, downloads of the Disney+ mobile app increased 72 per cent between 3 July and 5 July 2020 when the show was released, with over 80 per cent of Disney's subscribers watching the show and millions of posts circulating on social media. In other words, the engagement with a show and its performers clearly does not end with the closing of the live performance venues and 'being there' includes not only physical presence but also multiple forms of digital engagement across platforms. The opportunities for live theatre to reach mass global audiences before, during and after the run of a show will not diminish as the pandemic fades. Such experiments and explorations set the stage for future endeavours and the proliferation of new platforms and tools suggest that this transition to digital performances of formerly live performance will continue even after the worst effects of the pandemic have receded. Indeed, even as previously live theatrical performances were being translated into digital forms, 2020–1 also witnessed new creations that translated *media* into highly theatricalized stagings online, including new explorations of VR and a variety of hybrid forms working at the intersection of theatre, film, television and social media.

One of the leading companies in this area is Fake Friends, a small company of playwrights, directors, actors, performers and dramaturges working to create new forms of theatre both online and off. In the fall of 2020, they created *Circle Jerk*, an explicitly medial livestream theatre experience translated from earlier workshop productions aimed at live theatre audiences. Quickly adapted to the non-space of the internet, the show satirized the phenomena of White gay men, like Milo Yiannopoulos and Peter Thiel, in right-wing movements perpetuated on social media platforms. True to its origins in live theatre (and the collaborators' training at the Yale School of Drama), the play was explicit in its theatrical sources. The opening sequence introduced a troll (played by Patrick Foley) speaking in rhymed couplets. For the 2020 online adaptation, *Circle Jerk* was filmed and performed live with simultaneous streaming from a small performance space in Brooklyn outfitted with green screens. Co-produced by playwright Jeremy O. Harris, who also promoted and provided live commentary during the show on Twitter, *Circle Jerk* was performed by a small cast of three with the two male leads playing several roles each. Drawing on both commedia and social media tropes, the actors ran from scene to scene and camera to camera while live audiences peered in through their screens. Although one could record and rewatch the show, the show was streamed in real time and performed live for each of its shows with a robust and simultaneous presence engaged in real-time chat via Twitter. This para-theatrical activity is where the real show took place: in an online community that chatted, repeated lines, registered emotions, picked favourites and virtually laughed and cheered throughout the show. There were brief comments from the cast and crew to the Twitter commentary throughout *Circle Jerk*, but their next two shows built even more vibrantly on this early experiment by including extensive contributions from audiences to create an entirely new vocabulary for theatrical productions online.

The company further extended these experiments and influences in *This American Wife*, a self-proclaimed 'livestreamed multi-camera internet play' broadcast live 20–29 May 2021 and subsequently offered on demand. The title of the show punned both National Public Radio's popular programme *This American Life* with its unusual and compelling true stories of everyday Americans, and the *Real Housewives of ...*' television programme produced on Bravo. One of the show's central themes is the ubiquity of reality-themed entertainment in the United States, though stratified by class hierarchies defined by taste as much as money. Hosted by Ira Glass, the NPR radio show offers a middlebrow version of America's obsession with reality entertainment, a preoccupation realized in perhaps its gaudiest and most excessive form on the *Real Housewives of ...* series. Like the roaming narrative of *This American Life*, the *Real Housewives* series is based in various cities, including *The Real Housewives of Beverly Hills*, *The Real Housewives of New York* and *The Real Housewives of Atlanta*. The *Real Housewives* series began in 2006 on the cable channel Bravo (a channel known in the 1980s for screening productions by Pina Bausch and other contemporary performances of the period). *The Real Housewives of Orange County* was the first in a series described as a

> riveting series exploring the complicated daily lives of five privileged women and their families ... From *Peyton Place* to *Desperate Housewives*, viewers have been riveted by the fictionalised versions of such lifestyles on television. Now, here is a series that depicts real-life 'desperate' housewives with an authentic look at their compelling day-to-day drama.

Like all great satires, *This American Wife* is fundamentally an homage from devoted fans of the show. The show roughly follows a three-act structure with interstitial dramaturgical elements that anchor viewers who are unfamiliar with the original series in the theatricality of reality television and the *Real Housewives* in particular. The introduction, for instance, is carefully couched in theatrical references to Brecht, among others, as the cast drives up to a large suburban mansion on Long Island. The first act of the play introduces the three main cast members, all men, each of whom metonymically stand in for the 'wives' of three of the series' locations: Beverly Hills, New York and Atlanta. As they and camera operators skilfully navigate the mansion's gaudy interiors, they recite verbatim lines from their respective 'housewives' show. The second act features the core cast in intimate close-ups with other cast members holding the cameras and asking each other personal questions. Even for those familiar with the original show, there is too much nuance – historically, dramaturgically, sociologically – to effectively detail here, so I will focus only on act three, which breaks out of the house frame (literally) and presents a real-time, live interaction among the cast (one of whom adamantly insists that he is an 'actor'; the other who refuses to be called an actor, but is a 'performer') and the online Twitter audience watching the show.

Physically situated in a two-car garage transformed and lined with a green screen, Patrick Foley and Jakeem Dante Powell play themselves, invoking yet another trope of reality performance found in downtown New York solo performances and the lecture-demonstrations ('lec-dem') engaged by performance artists. These performances of the self are set in relief against backgrounds digitally superimposed behind the performers. A third cast member, Michael Breslin, interviews the other two and operates a moving camera. There are at least four cameras in the space, two fixed directly on the actor/performers sitting opposite each other, a camera that pivots between them and a small Go-Pro camera fixed above the space from which the audience can look down. Breslin not only interviews and works one of the cameras with his right hand, he also engages with the show's real-time Twitter feed with his left, responding to audience questions, tweets and suggestions and retweeting hashtags. Here, the tropes of reality TV confessionals – direct address to the camera as virtual audience with off-screen social media following – are translated into a Brechtian theatre onscreen, where we can see the full construction of the video apparatus. The audience is engaged in a robust back-and-forth flow with the actor/performers, who respond to the spectators even as they translate the housewives and their own personae parodically into the mediated performance space that is simultaneously part house, part theatre, part television … and all digital. It is the quintessence of Benjamin's translation as perpetual immanence; simultaneously translating the original 'text' of the *Real Housewives* series, perpetuating its performances and destroying it simultaneously. In this sense, *This American Wife* is neither adaptation nor parody, neither film nor television, but not obviously theatre in the way that Fischer-Lichte might describe it. Instead, this is digital theatre, a unique and distinct entity that translates theatrical texts (*pace* Badiou) and co-presence into new media to reach new and radically expanded audiences. Here we may be again reminded of Benjamin when he invokes the notion of translation as *Überleben*, or 'survival', though most often translated as 'afterlife' suggesting a metaphysical durability.[14]

Certainly throughout the pandemic of 2020, digital theatre as translation has been inextricably connected to theatre's survival and the continued vitality of its artists, many of whom imaginatively turned to creating new work in virtual reality (for example The Under's *The Tempest* for the Oculus platform) or YouTube (for example Joshua William Gelb's Theatre in Quarantine).[15] Theatre is perhaps the artform most obsessed with its own imminent and ever-approaching demise, but in 2020 these fears for the death of theatre suddenly seemed more possible than any time since the dark ages. What ensured theatre's survival during this time was the translation of performance from in-person venues to online platforms. It would not be hyperbole to say that digital theatre saved theatre amid ongoing uncertainties and, as such, will almost certainly remain an essential part of theatre's future of performance post-pandemic. This is not to say that digital theatre will replace or negate other historical forms of drama or theatre, any more than film, television, videogames and other media have eliminated theatre and other live arts in the late nineteenth and twentieth centuries. These and other emerging forms will continue to circulate as related phenomena on spectra of media, adapting to new platforms and genres and remediating pre-existing forms. Unlike remediation, which aims at a transparent, immersive and frictionless media experience, the translation of digital theatre retains and foregrounds its problems, gaps and failures. It is a performance genre perpetually marked by 'monstrous loss', even as it perpetuates its source material in new and ever-changing forms.

To return to Mezzocchi's question at the opening of this chapter, it is clear that performance post-Covid requires new terminology, if only to stake out distinct economic opportunities among competing media and related labour laws and contracts. More significant, however, is that these new translations of theatrical form have the capacity to reach new and increasingly diverse audiences, both within and outside the theatre's walls. Translations require very particular receptive audiences; to endure, theatre must continue to present in the contemporary vernacular of media communications. Just as English translation directs itself to English readers, so too does *This American Wife* translate theatre performance for reality television audiences, reality television for social media audiences and social media back to theatre audiences. Across its multiple perspectives and modes of engagement, Fake Friends addresses the multiple 'literacies' of varied audiences across geographic and cultural boundaries.

It is probably no coincidence that their first pandemic-era show was titled *Circle Jerk*, a vulgar reference to communal stimulation and experience that captures the ways in which new forms and audiences are caught in ongoing affective, pleasurable and implicitly queer loops with others. (The company's name of 'Fake Friends' further comments on the tenuousness of contemporary social relationships created and conducted overwhelmingly through social media and the lens of reality television realism.) Of course, each translation or transfer is almost always a degradation, like the eroding quality of a videotape rewound and replayed too many times. But like the bootleg VHS tapes of experimental performances that used to circulate in academic theatre departments, these flaws, mistakes and imperfections are what makes translation so appealing as the *sine qua non* of digital theatre. There is no question that theatre artists today are still struggling in the wake of the pandemic, but this is not the first plague that the theatre has survived. In its digital failures, theatre may find again the opportunity for post-pandemic survival and perhaps even success.

Notes

1. This chapter was first presented as a keynote lecture at the conference 'Post-Covid art worlds: viral theatre, precarity and medical humanities' at Schloss Herrenhausen Hannover (and online), 21 July 2021. I am grateful to the conference organizers, Dr Heidi Liedke and Prof. Dr Monika Pietrzak-Franger, for their kind invitation to present and to the conference participants for their generous feedback and contributions. I am also deeply indebted to Prof. Larry Rosenwald, who first introduced me to the ideas, questions and key texts that have informed my research here and elsewhere for the past twenty-five years.
2. Gross, 'Some images and analogies for the process of translation', 33.
3. Benjamin, 'The task of the translator', 78.
4. Jacobs, 'The monstrosity of translation', 765.
5. Sontag, 'Film and theatre', 24.
6. Marks, @petermarksdrama.
7. Medenica, 'A digital talk about an analogue art'.
8. Rosenwald, 'Reflections on translators and authors, 351.
9. Rosenwald, 'On not reading in translation', 309.
10. Golder, 'People can't get over Jonathan Groff's spit during "Hamilton"'.
11. Benjamin, *Selected Writings, 4: 1938–1940,* 405.
12. Kattenbelt, 'Theatre as the art of the performer and the stage of intermediality', 33.
13. Taylor, *The Archive and the Repertoire.*
14. See: Disler, 'Benjamin's 'Afterlife': a productive (?) mistranslation in memoriam Daniel Simeoni, 83–221.
15. Gelb's 'Theatre in Quarantine' may be found here: https://www.youtube.com/channel/UCqMhCVLpToyrC9Xj1-WWSfg.

Bibliography

Badiou, Alain. *In Praise of Theatre*. John Wiley & Sons, 2015.
Benjamin, Walter. 'The task of the translator'. *Illuminations: essays and reflections*, edited by Hannah Arendt, translated by Harry Zohn. Schocken, 1968.
Benjamin, Walter. *Selected Writings, 4: 1938–1940,* edited by Howard Eiland and Michael W. Jennings. Belknap Press: An Imprint of Harvard University Press, 2006.
Disler, Caroline. 'Benjamin's 'Afterlife': a productive (?) mistranslation in memoriam Daniel Simeoni'. *TTR: Traduction, Terminologie, Rédaction*, vol. 24, no. 1, 2011, pp. 183–221. www.erudit.org.https://doi.org/10.7202/1013259ar.
Golder, Andy. 'People can't get over Jonathan Groff's spit during "Hamilton"'. *BuzzFeed*. https://www.buzzfeed.com/andyneuenschwander/jonathan-groff-hamilton-spit. Accessed 12 November 2021.
Gross, Alex. 'Some images and analogies for the process of translation'. *Translation Theory and Practice: tension and interdependence*, edited by M. L. Larson. State University of New York Press, 1991, pp. 27–37.

Jacobs, Carol. 'The monstrosity of translation'. *MLN*, vol. 90, no. 6, 1975, pp. 755–66. *JSTOR*. https://doi.org/10.2307/2907018.

Kattenbelt, Chiel. 'Theatre as the art of the performer and the stage of intermediality'. *Intermediality in Theatre and Performance*, edited by Freda Chapple and Chiel Kattenbelt. Rodopi, 2006, pp. 29–39.

Marks, Peter. *@petermarksdrama*. 10 April 2020. https://twitter.com/petermarksdrama.

Medenica, Ivan. 'A digital talk about an analogue art: interview with Erika Fischer-Lichte'. *Critical Stages/Scènes Critiques*, 18 December 2020. https://www.critical-stages.org/22/a-digital-talk-about-an-analogue-art-interview-with-erika-fischer-lichte/.

Miranda, Lin-Manuel. *Hamilton: an American Musical (Original Broadway Cast Recording) Lyrics and Tracklist. Genius.* https://genius.com/albums/Lin-manuel-miranda/Hamilton-an-american-musical-original-broadway-cast-recording. Accessed 19 July 2021.

Rosenwald, Lawrence. 'On not reading in translation'. *The Antioch Review*, vol. 62, no. 2, 2004, pp. 308–18. *JSTOR*. https://doi.org/10.2307/4614646.

Rosenwald, Lawrence. 'Reflections on translators and authors'. *Translation & Interpreting Studies: The Journal of the American Translation & Interpreting Studies Association*, vol. 11, no. 3, 2016, pp. 344–60. *EBSCOhost*. https://doi.org/10.1075/tis.11.3.02ros.

Sontag, Susan. 'Film and theatre'. *The Tulane Drama Review*, vol. 11, no. 1, 1966, p. 24.

Taylor, Diana. *The Archive and the Repertoire: performing cultural memory in the Americas*. Duke University Press, 2003.

12
From Miami to Hong Kong: Sounding Transnational Queerness and Translation in *Moonlight*

K. E. Goldschmitt

When *Moonlight* was released in 2016, music critics praised the film for its inventive soundtrack. Composer Nicholas Britell famously drew from Southern hip-hop's chop and screw tradition to slow down the orchestral strings for dramatic effect.[1] That approach was complemented by pre-existing popular music recordings culled from a deep catalogue of soul and hip-hop. Barry Jenkins, who directed and co-wrote the screenplay, specified many of the pre-existing songs that shape the film's narrative world; both as source music and within the score, or as diegetic and non-diegetic music respectively (and spanning the blurry space between them).[2] In so doing, he joined a growing tradition of auteur directors attempting to position themselves as DJs as well and, like other Black directors before him, Jenkins uses his position to highlight popular music worlds mostly left untouched by white filmmakers.[3] In this sense, Jenkins' approach is closer to that of a hip-hop DJ, featuring rare cuts and manipulated samples rather than that of a radio DJ who plays all of the hits – an approach much closer to what white directors have generally taken. Each song featured in the soundtrack has a deep history and can be read at multiple levels of interpretation, providing depth for those who pay attention to the film's sonic aspects.

This chapter discusses two of the songs in *Moonlight* that link into different strains of Black queer identity during the climax of the final act, 'Black': Aretha Franklin's 'One Step Ahead' and Caetano Veloso's 'Cucurrucucú Paloma'. These two tracks appear back to back, with 'Cucurrucucú Paloma' preceding 'One Step Ahead'. Through their example, I argue that pop music cues can link a film's themes to other minority filmmaking traditions, translating them across cultural contexts. While these references may seem innocuous to a general cinematic audience, they do important affective work for publics for whom these musical codes are much more meaningful.

Tracking minority identities in film music has been best theorized by Anahid Kassabian, whose *Hearing Film* and *Ubiquitous Listening* demonstrate some interpretive possibilities for understanding what different audiences might bring to a mass medium such as mainstream or art-house cinema.[4] As Kassabian notes, film music is at least as significant to the narrative of a film as the visuals in the way it 'draws filmgoers into a film's world [...] It conditions identification processes, the encounters between film texts and filmgoers' psyches'.[5] However, one major lacuna in English language scholarship is how placing a rare track by a well-known artist, or a vaguely familiar recording entirely in a foreign language, in a prominent soundtrack can transform the meaning of that recording among differing publics across different markets. The result is an iterative process where each text (film and song) informs the reception of the other. The meaning-making in films using pre-existing music occurs at different registers depending on the audience member's familiarity with the musical text in question.[6] What happens when we take account of minority readings and interpretation? Through performance, fan engagement and the expansion of niche tastes in digital media more generally, it has become increasingly clear that audiences are identifying with film music from multiple vantage points, sometimes coloured by mistranslations across national lines, and sometimes due to the strength of subcultural codes separating 'insiders' and 'outsiders' – a distinction that, although blurry, still holds sway in how demographics and subjectivity influence interpretation. This seems to be the case even when talking about transnational affiliating identifications. When talking about transnational queerness, in particular, the discussion tends to be about the tension between reaching a large-scale international audiences and localized understandings of musical codes. As I show in the rest of this chapter, that tension is at play in some of the musical choices in *Moonlight*.

Film music studies have had a productive discussion of well-known musical tropes and the collapse of musical referents.[7] In the case of art-house films (and prestige television) with explicitly queer content, the circuits of meaning change due to the niche tastes of the community. At the most experienced and knowledgeable register, the depth of references to a well-known song or artist has the potential to elicit the pleasure of recognizing other uses or settings within that tradition. It also has the potential of being so successful as a musical placement as to realign the values attached to the song. In those cases, the original context of the song (and sometimes previous recordings of the same song) lessens in influence compared to a famous placement in film and television. What occurs is not only a type of translation but also redefinition for viewers tracking the use of music in queer film.

This chapter analyses two songs that appear prominently in the climax of *Moonlight*. I base these interpretations in my own subject position as a white, queer, gender non-conforming scholar with an investment in how filmmakers working in independent and art-house cinema choose to represent sexual and gender minorities. Above all, I am interested in how the messages in a film soundtrack convey meanings at different registers and to different niche audiences. I ask: what kind of cultural translation is at work when audiences unfamiliar with the web of meanings attached to the song see the same scene? What aspects of this should be understood as insider knowledge? This chapter is an extension of my previous work on how soundtrack choices translate differently depending on the knowledge of the audience.[8] It is part of a project that has developed out of my interest in the role that the intermediation of music and sound plays in minority community identity. It builds off my research into what happens to musical codes in contexts when audience attention is pulled in multiple directions. What interests me about the music in *Moonlight* is that all evidence points to multiple routes for Jenkins and audiences finding a queer meaning in musical codes based in popular music.

Black queer temporalities and Aretha Franklin

The strains of Aretha Franklin's 'One Step Ahead' serve as diegetic music at two crucial moments in the narrative for *Moonlight*. The first instance occurs in the opening chapter, 'Little', when the audience first learns that Chiron's mother has a drug problem. The second instance is in the final chapter, when Kevin and Chiron lay eyes on each other for the first time in twelve years. The significance of Franklin's song is tied up in both how these two scenes are edited as well as the legacy of Franklin's music in film.

In cinema, Franklin's music has generally accompanied scenes of joy and celebration geared towards a white, mainstream audience. From the 1980s through the early 2000s, for example, it was common to see characters enjoying her big hits like 'Respect' and 'Natural Woman' on-screen. In the highest-grossing versions of these, the characters are white and straight, speaking to the crossover success that her music has achieved, to the point that it no longer indexes Blackness in film soundtracks.[9] Given that, what does it mean to queer the Queen of Soul? Given her broad popularity, placing Aretha Franklin's music in scenarios that often do not get represented on film and television, especially Black queer ones, is a bold statement. Most audiences would hear Franklin's placement in a film soundtrack as an everyday occurrence. Indeed, judging by Franklin's 287 soundtrack credits, many of them since 2015, hearing the Queen of Soul is a mainstream affair. In *Moonlight*, however, Franklin's music is part of the world of two queer men, making it function in a fundamentally different manner.

Aretha Franklin's 'One Step Ahead', first released as a single in 1965 (two years before her first full-length album and crossover success), plays as diegetic music when Chiron and Kevin see each other for the first time as adults. The first notes of the song start when Chiron walks into the diner where Kevin is working, just as the bell above the entrance rings. There are many clues that this song is supposed to be playing on a jukebox in the diner. It is at a relatively low level in the mix compared to ambient sounds, in what film sound scholar Michel Chion describes as off-screen on-the-air sound: the source of the music is not in the frame but we, as audience members, presume we can hear it along with the characters.[10] There are a few hints that this song is playing in the diner – the fidelity of the song muffles the low- and high-end frequencies, making the chicken scratch guitar accompaniment and backing vocals harder to hear.

Since this is the first music in the soundtrack following the long-shot of Chiron entering the diner after parking his car, it is also disorienting. While time in the film was previously suspended by the unaccompanied long shots, the song is moving things forward again.[11] However, that progression of time stops again as Chiron and Kevin pause to look at each other. First, we see a close-up of Chiron gazing at Kevin, followed by a close-up of Kevin gazing back. The audience hears Kevin say, 'Chiron?' without actually seeing either of them move their lips. It is the audiovisual equivalent of a gasp before the tension breaks with dialogue. 'Damn, man! Why you ain't say nothin'?' Kevin says with a laugh. And then later, 'There you go with that damn nod again. You ain't changed one damn bit. You still can't say more than three words at a time, huh.' Nicholas Brittell's score re-enters as Kevin goes to the diner's kitchen to make Chiron a 'Chef's Special'. Franklin's voice provides an important emotional foundation for this interaction, giving it the expressive depth that neither character is saying aloud. That it is also part of the film's diegesis gives the song's relative rarity added heft in the narrative. Indeed, the off-screen on-the-air sound sutures it to the everyday lives of these two Black men, and both are made more vulnerable by its appearance.

The only referent for this song is earlier in the film, in the first chapter, 'Little', when Chiron comes home after his swimming lesson with Juan, the local drug dealer. The opening strains of the song are manipulated to sound like they are coming from a portable stereo as his mother, Paula, clears what sounds like a glass pipe before disappearing into her bedroom with a male guest. This is the first time that the audience learns that Paula is a drug user. It is the only song in the film that appears twice and indicates that Jenkins used it to punctuate two important developments in Chiron's story.

There is something queer about the diner setting and the music played there that links to what many queer theorists have described as a type of queer temporality. Scholars and critics speak of the ways queer time is different from straight time, especially as regards how queer people have different expectations for the future and how that translates to representations of queerness in film and television.[12] Often these representations defy linearity or 'fail' in presenting successful narratives in a traditional sense.[13] In this instance, the rare Aretha Franklin record from 1965 on a jukebox seems at once entirely improbable – how many traditional jukeboxes have rare singles? – and in keeping with the ways that Black artists push the bounds of what is possible in art. This is especially the case when discussing the intersection of Blackness and queerness. Cinema studies scholar Kara Keeling extends queer temporalities to anti-colonial and anti-racist possibilities in Black art, especially with regards to futurity (future speculation).[14] In this example in *Moonlight*, the combination of the play with time and the rupture with what is probable in the ambient music of the diner scene opens up the potential that the music is actively repairing the damage committed to Chiron in his childhood. It opens up the potential for a misremembering of his childhood, or even a rerememembering.[15] Through its play with the expectations of linear time in film, the use of 'One Step Ahead' in this scene is not just in keeping with queer representation in cinema, but also Black queer cinema.

One major precedent for queering Aretha Franklin was when the Wachowskis featured 'I Never Loved a Man (The Way I Love You)' – Franklin's first major hit with Atlantic Records from 1967 – as diegetic music in *Bound* (1996). This is when the butch, Corky, visits a lesbian bar called The Watering Hole towards the beginning of the film. In that case, the song is rich in subtext, suturing on a lesbian meaning to the 'you' in the lyrics where it was never intended. Like the scene in *Moonlight*, the music in *Bound* is diegetic in an explicitly queer reunion in a public place, albeit one that is much less joyful.

Of course, 'One Step Ahead' as a reference is also occurring at other registers. Some might recognize it from the world of hip-hop sampling, since the song memorably appeared in Mos Def's 'Ms. Fat Booty' from his 1999 album *Black on Both Sides*. Or there is the possibility that the audience member in question is a lover of Aretha Franklin's music, including her pre-1967 singles. The interpretive possibilities vary widely, but it is clear that the scene is more meaningful in part because the track is not among Franklin's most familiar recordings. Jenkins chose a deep cut from her back catalogue, which means that audiences are less likely to attach the song to previous cinematic scenes featuring her music. In that way, he has detached Aretha Franklin from her extensive history in film soundtracks and remade her in the service of Black cinema.

Like much of the film, this scene barely has any dialogue. Franklin's voice provides the depth and ambiance for adult Chiron's quiet and powerful emotional reactions to seeing Kevin, in an important build-up to the vulnerabilities expressed later in the film's final chapter. That backdrop affords more emotional weight to the moment of connection and exposure. In contrast, the next section discusses how a musical choice explicitly connects the film to a broader world of transnational queer cinema through a cover that slows and turns down the volume of the film.

The transnational queerness of 'Cucurrucucú Paloma'

Unlike Aretha Franklin, Brazilian pop megastar Caetano Veloso has not regularly appeared in English-language film and television soundtracks. Yet, one of his recordings has had a profound impact on queer cinema. In this section, I discuss the links between the use of one of his recordings in *Moonlight* and other examples in transnational queer cinema. Since Veloso's music is based in the music of Latin America, I take some space to elaborate on how this music works.

In keeping with the film overall, the third chapter of *Moonlight* is filled with emotion. In the sequence of events just before Chiron meets Kevin in Miami, he visits his mother at her rehab facility. The mother-son reunion is emotionally intense. She tries to apologize for how she raised him, repeating both that she loves him and that she had not loved him the way he needed. Chiron stands up to hug her, and then the opening strains of Caetano Veloso's recording of 'Cucurrucucú Paloma' function as a musical dissolve to Chiron driving on U.S. Route 41, the southernmost east–west highway in Florida. After the first verse of the song, we see another dissolve, this time to children playing on the beach. The moment ties *Moonlight* to a rich tradition of queer cinematic uses of that song, a tradition so deep that sometimes scholars, filmmakers and critics talk past each other about what it means.

For example, in a 2016 interview published in the online music magazine *Pitchfork*, Matthew Schnipper asked Jenkins about the song in the context of the soundtrack. Schnipper was curious if it was a reference to Pedro Almodóvar's *Talk to Her* (*Hable Con Ella*) from 2002. Jenkins responded:

> it's the same song used in Wong Kar-wai's *Happy Together*. It's a direct homage. Even the way we framed the car driving down the highway is the same. I remember watching *Happy Together* a long time ago. It was the first movie I would say that I saw that was outright a queer film. One of the first films I saw that had subtitles, even. *Moonlight* is worlds away from *Happy Together*–it's a movie about two Asian men living in Argentina, and here we have these two black men from fucking Liberty City, Miami. The world is very big and also very small, because they're experiencing the same things. I feel like film has given so much to me and I just wanted for 30 seconds to show how small the world is. It doesn't carry any thematic impart, but hopefully it will introduce a certain audience that has been going to see this film but who has maybe never heard Caetano Veloso–the same way that when I watched *Happy Together*, I got to Asia by way of Argentina and discovered Caetano Veloso.[16]

This was clearly not the response that Schnipper was expecting, and it reveals an important layer to how the use of pre-existing music can operate at multiple registers; in this case, different references to transnational queer cinema.

It turns out that many people, especially queer people, have much to say about this song. Early in 2019, I saw it performed live as part of my effort to alleviate some culture shock I was experiencing on a preliminary research trip to Portugal. As a gender non-conforming foreigner in a country with progressive LGBTQ policies paired with conservative cultural expressions, I was elated to learn about Fado Bicha, a local duo that queers famous fado songs as a form of social activism. Over the last few years, Fado Bicha has become the literal poster group for Lisbon's gay circuit. I attended a January show at a hotel that caters to gay tourists in Lisbon. Imagine my surprise when Fado Bicha chose to close their performance set with the same song, 'Cucurucucú Paloma', as a type of lullaby. In fact, when they began to play it, a man in the audience said in English, 'This one is my favourite!' Indicating that, at least for him, it was familiar enough to hold that kind of elevated status.

When I talked to the musicians about that choice in an interview later that month, they mentioned Almodóvar's *Talk to Her* as their inspiration, but they mentioned that they did not really like how the song was used in the film (including Veloso's cameo). They described the film's aesthetic as rather aggressive, even too butch for their liking. However, the film introduced them to a song that they liked for its emotional tone, that they then felt free to adapt to their set. Like many musicians who change, translate and adapt songs they like, Fado Bicha's initial exposure to the music was less important than what they thought they could make of it as artists. While they were happy that I recognized the connection to *Moonlight*, they were explicit in their love of Almodóvar. Spanish cinema is popular in Portugal and Almodóvar appeals to the LGBTQ community. Regardless of my reaction, they did not see the song as especially remarkable for its queer content and seemed to think my knowledge of it was cool since they understood me as a queer music scholar. Yet, the next time they played the song, they happily announced its queer connections to the audience. They were proud.

Since the late 1990s, scholars, critics and music fans have taken note of the particular affective power of Caetano Veloso's recording of 'Cucurrucucú Paloma' in international queer cinema. Veloso recorded the song in question in 1995 as part of *Fina Estampa Ao Vivo*, the live album from the tour for his 1994 album-length tribute to Spanish-language songs from Latin America.[17] While the recording has appeared on a few international compilations, it has reached a much wider audience through its use in award-winning films and that have had an extended life in the LGBTQ film festival circuit. What is more, the creative choices that have gone into featuring the song in key moments of emotional gravitas on screen are often latching onto fragments of the song's extended meaning in audiovisual media, one that functions differently to what happened with Aretha Franklin's 'One Step Ahead'.

What interests me in the song's use by Barry Jenkins in *Moonlight* (as well as its use by Fado Bicha, Wong Kar-Wai's *Happy Together* and Pedro Almodóvar's *Talk to Her*) is that the song's transnational queerness was explicit in the song's selection while also being multivalent. Yet despite that multiplicity, the emotional effect of the song does not change. In the case of the Caetano Veloso recording, I believe that there is something unique about the combination of Veloso's interpretive choices, especially how he chooses to use his voice, and the important work of homage in filmic citation.

In soundtrack choices, filmic citation is especially complicated for pre-existing music. Elsewhere I have shown how film music is especially complicit in the perpetuation of musical stereotypes through a case study of the uses of the Brazilian song 'Aquarela do Brasil' (published as 'Brazil' for its English translation) in film soundtracks and trailers. Sometimes film music does this work by taking a musical sign that previously conveyed one idea and transforming it through memorable repurposing.[18] This repurposing changes in context, depending on audience and filmmaker strategy. Sometimes this occurs when a purportedly serious song is used to elicit extreme affect in context – such as soundtracking something utterly ridiculous or, by contrast, something deeply emotional – which can go on to mark the music in question. In soundtrack use, in particular, filmic citation is far from straightforward, which is perhaps why so many musicians and filmmakers disagree on how they came to Veloso's recording in particular.

It is curious that Caetano Veloso transformed this song into a ballad. It was originally composed by Mexican musician Tomás Mendez in 1954 as a song of lost love using the metaphor of the cuckoo dove weeping in sorrow. The song appeared one year later on screen when iconic Mexican Golden-Age actor and musician Pedro Infante sang it for the film *Escuela de Vagabundos* (1955) as an up-tempo serenade to his love interest. Stylistically, the Mexican recordings of this song treat it as a mariachi canción ranchera based in the huapango. Ranchera songs are topical in nature and often address themes of love, patriotism and the natural world. The huapango is a rhythmically complex style with a compound metre and switches between duple or triple metre. For readers unfamiliar with this kind of switching, imagine a song switching between a waltz rhythm (in three) and a straight-ahead march (in two). Its Mexican roots are clear in the lyrics when Infante sings 'ay-ay-ay-ay-ay-yi', a common melodicization of the mariachi's cry. All of these features are common to the rancheras that appeared in Golden Age Mexican cinema, and many of the films from this period had an extended cultural life in Mexico when they were broadcast on television decades later. This song was so popular that it appeared in another Mexican film just ten years later as the finale with the same name sung by Lola Beltrán. The extended circulation of these Golden Age Films after their heyday has lent songs like this some campy appeal.[19]

Caetano Veloso did not include 'Cucurrucú Paloma' when he made the studio album tribute to Hispanic songs, *Fina Estampa,* in 1994. Rather, he first began playing the song as part of the tour for that album. Like the other songs in the *Fina Estampa* project, Veloso uses the string quartet to accompany his voice and guitar. He also chooses to use his highest register, way up in his falsetto, when singing the chorus – well above the range that Pedro Infante and Lola Beltrán used in their versions for Mexican film decades before. The metre for the song is strictly in a duple feel which leaves the only traces of the mariachi roots of the song in the ay-ay-ay-ay-ay-yi chorus. Because he uses his falsetto, it is perhaps too tempting to reduce his vocal approach to a type of queering of the song. Of course, some gay men who love Golden Age Mexican cinema could argue that the song does not need queering since Mexican Golden Age cinema is already rife with queer readings of Mexican masculinity.[20] Or even that Lola Beltrán's version is the essence of an iconic diva performance. However, due to the limits of media circulation from Golden Age Mexican cinema, it seems that those codes do not reach beyond the Mexican and Mexican–American queer counterpublics that watched these films on television.[21] And, like other non-Portuguese songs in Veloso's repertoire, he does not translate it for his audience.[22] Veloso's recording begins with the sound of audience applause, maintaining the connection to liveness that is so prized in Brazilian live recordings.[23] Notably, most audiovisual uses of Veloso's recording remove the sound of applause that opens the track, opting instead to begin with the steady rhythm of the string quartet. That has the effect of removing the traces of live performance tied to a time and place from the recording, rendering it more timeless and pliable.

When Wong Kar-Wai's *Happy Together* was released in 1997, it made a big impact in the film festival circuit. Wong Kar-Wai won 'Best Director' at the Cannes Film Festival and competed for the Palme d'Or, becoming the first director from Hong Kong to achieve such a feat. The film centres on a dysfunctional relationship between two displaced men from Hong Kong, Ho Po-Wing and Lai Yiu-Fai, who have relocated to Argentina to 'start over'. 'Cucurrucucú Paloma' appears in the opening scene which begins in black and white. In a flashback, we learn that two men have gotten lost on their road trip to Iguazu Falls. Once Lai Yiu-Fai realizes that things are over, he covers his face with his hand. Then the palette switches to colour as we see Iguazu Falls and the strains of Veloso's recording take over. Wong gives the waterfalls and Veloso's voice ninety seconds, an evocative and sentimental gesture. On a narrative level, the use of this song in an early scene makes a big impact as the representation of an attempt to rekindle their love that never materializes due to the two men breaking things off. Wong's choice to show the strife in black and white helps to communicate that it is a flashback while also contrasting with the colour of the waterfalls.

In contrast, Pedro Almodóvar did not have to work to communicate a queer aesthetic in *Talk to Her*. He is well known for portraying women, especially hysterical women, in his films to dramatic and comedic effect. His work is inherently portraying a gay aesthetic. 'Cucurrucucú Paloma' appears in the film when Veloso himself performs in the film. Apparently, the choice to feature him had nothing to do with Wong Kar-Wai. He was already Caetano Veloso's friend, and the story goes that he received an unedited version of the song. Almodóvar also said that he was trying to bring some more 'masculine' energy into the world of his films. In fact, the film was his attempt to *not* feature hysterical women or campy subject matter and instead approach more serious topics. It is in many senses his least overtly gay film, which is likely why the musicians in Fado Bicha loved the song and not the setting.

Talk to Her brings this discussion back to the question of emotion, intelligibility and sentiment. *Talk to Her* is the only filmic setting of the song where the primary audience is likely to understand what the song is about. In the rest of these contexts, the lyrics go unknown and untranslated and their sentimental significance is instead expressed by the context of the film.[24] In that sense, then, it seems that untranslated, falsetto vocals help communicate the emotional rawness of a fragmenting relationship that is far from being about semantic meaning and instead zeroes in on effect. The aesthetic comes from an attempt to portray queer sentimentality from a director who, by all accounts, is not gay.

That same lack of shared gay identity between director and filmic subject is also a factor in Barry Jenkins' biography. Yet, in the case of *Moonlight*, the music comes just after Chiron leaves the home where his mother is convalescing to drive to Miami. In contrast to the heartbreak of *Happy Together*, the use of the song in *Moonlight* conveys hope and beauty, as visually expressed by footage of children playing in the sea. The choice of these two directors to use this song to soundtrack such emotionally weighty moments is an investment in transnational queer sentiment. That Jenkins chose to index this aspect is simply remarkable and pushes the story of *Moonlight* beyond the setting of gay Black men surviving in poverty to a much broader, hopeful, transnational vision of queer solidarity.

In that sense, Veloso's recording has turned into the type of cover song so influential that it is now the new referent for other performances rather than the 'original' settings that made the song famous in the first place. In a new twist on the queer connections among different settings of this song, a version by the Guatemalan pop musician Gaby Moreno appeared in the final sequence of the series finale for *Orange is the New Black,* the most successful TV show to feature queer women to date. Moreno's recording emulates nearly every aspect of Veloso's recording, from the tempo to the arrangement. The choice to complement the resolution of many of the stories within the show, including the love story between the main protagonist and her female love interest, with that song further reinforces the song's queer meanings.

This chapter opens new avenues for discussing the different ways that Black directors can position themselves as soundtrack DJs. In this case, Jenkins' deep knowledge of Black music and music with transnational queer meanings demonstrates a deft hand. In just those two scenes, he uses music to play with audience perceptions of time and space, affording a wider bandwidth for audiences to consider how they relate to Chiron and Kevin's relationship with sound and time. While many Black songs from the past appear on the soundtrack, Arethan Franklin's 'One Step Ahead' stands out for being a song with few available cultural references. The lack of previous iterations of this song in popular culture gives Jenkins a blank canvas on which to suture queer meanings; in this case, meanings about Black queer temporality. In an opposite move, Jenkins' use of 'Cucurrucucú Paloma' deliberately taps into a lengthy tradition of using that song in queer audiovisual contexts. The previous references are the point.

Through these two vivid examples, I have attempted to show how pop songs in film soundtracks can express multiple layers of meaning and identification for different audiences. Barry Jenkins' *Moonlight* (2016) is an excellent case study in how these different readings develop. Through my discussion of 'Cucurrucucú Paloma' specifically, I attempted to show how that meaning is palpable even when different people disagree and there are contrasting interpretations. There were many opportunities for these two songs to get lost in translation or to inspire readings at the most basic registers for a general audience. Even when the politics behind such a choice rely on repurposing existing material and on perhaps knowing a completely different reference, such a placement does not lose its community building power so long as community members are familiar with one reference or another. In fact, in the case of both of these songs, whatever baggage the audience brings to the song's performance can only lend the song more power in forging a broader community.

Notes

1. This happens most memorably in the scene where young Chiron learns to swim in the first act of the film. Chop 'n' screw is a technique most associated with the hip-hop scene in Houston, Texas, originating with DJ Screw (Robert Earl Davis, Jr) and later becoming one of the defining techniques of Southern hip-hop.
2. This is a critical shorthand for describing whether the characters 'hear' what the audience hears as part of the film's diegesis. There has been considerable scholarly debate about the utility of these two concepts since many filmmakers deliberately blur the lines between the two. That blurring happens in *Moonlight*. For the most cogent critique, see Robynn J. Stilwell, 'The fantastical gap between diegetic and nondiegetic', 184–202.
3. In recent decades, white directors such as Wes Anderson, Cameron Crowe, Martin Scorsese, Quentin Tarantino and many others have staked a claim to being tastemakers in music as well as in film. Many Black directors have a patented approach to soundtracks. For example, Ryan Coogler always works with the same composer (Ludwig Göransson). Spike Lee has long directed films that have been guided by music. For a good discussion of the 'director as DJ' phenomenon, see Todd Decker, 'The Filmmaker as DJ: Martin Scorsese's Compiled Score for Casino (1995)', 281–317.
4. Anahid Kassabian, *Hearing Film*; Anahid Kassabian, *Ubiquitous Listening*.
5. Kassabian, *Hearing Film*, 1.
6. Here, I borrow from Michael Long's discussion of how familiar classical music works at differing registers depending on the experience of the audience. Michael Long, *Beautiful Monsters*.
7. K.E. Goldschmitt, *Bossa Mundo*, 52–75; Melanie Lowe, 'Claiming Amadeus', 102–19. See also musicologist Alex Ludwig's catalogue of the 'Dies Irae' trope in film music, best summarized in Vox, *Why This Creepy Melody Is in so Many Movies*.
8. K.E. Goldschmitt, 'Favela Chic in Action', 1–17.
9. As of this writing in early 2022, Aretha Franklin has 287 soundtrack credits on film and television, according to the Internet Movie Database (IMDB.com). 'Respect' alone has eighty-four credits, including *Bridget Jones' Diary* (2001), *Two Weeks' Notice* (2002), *Forrest Gump* (1994), and a 1998 episode of *Sex and the City*. 'Natural Woman' appeared in *The Big Chill* (1984) and on numerous television shows in the 1990s such as *Northern Exposure* (1991) and twice on *Murphy Brown* (1988 and 1991).
10. Michel Chion, *Audio-Vision*.
11. In an interview with Michael Boyd Gillespie, Jenkins asserted that the progression of time from the first two chapters is deliberately suspended for the third. Michael Boyce Gillespie, 'One step ahead', 52–62.
12. For the most widely cited examples of this, see Lee Edelman, *No Future: Queer Theory and the Death Drive*; Jack Halberstam, *In a Queer Time and Place*. The best discussion of Black queer temporality is Kara Keeling, *Queer Times, Black Futures*, although that text is mainly concerned with how these issues intersection with Afro-Futurism.
13. See Jack Halberstam's discussion of queer failure in *The Queer Art of Failure*.
14. Kara Keeling, 'Looking for M—', 565–82.
15. Special thanks to Lauron Kehrer for helping me think through this point.
16. Barry Jenkins quoted in Matthew Schnipper, 'The pitch'.
17. In his interview with Lorraine Leu, Veloso contextualized his *Fina Estampa* project as part of the context in which he wrote his memoir, *Verdade Tropical* (*Verdade Tropical*) and his desire to record a similar album of popular songs from the United States. See Lorraine Leu, *Brazilian Popular Music*, 156.
18. K.E. Goldschmitt, 'From Disney to dystopia', 363–74.
19. Jacqueline Avila, *Cinesonidos*, 234–6.
20. Sergio de la Mora, *Cinemachismo*.
21. Donald Henriques, 'Mariachi reimaginings', 85–110. For more on queer publics and counterpublics, see Michael Warner, *Publics and Counterpublics*.
22. In her book-length study of Veloso's album of the United States songbook, *A Foreign Sound*, Barbara Browning argues that Veloso's resistance to translation is part of a career-long trajectory. See Barbara Browning, *Caetano Veloso's A Foreign Sound*.
23. In Brazil, 'ao vivo', or 'live', recordings outsell those of the studio albums on which they are based.
24. Rey Chow's discussion of Wong Kar-Wai's style has focused on the intense sentimentality of *Happy Together*. See Rey Chow, 'Sentimental returns', 639–54.

Bibliography

Avila, Jacqueline. *Cinesonidos: film music and national identity during Mexico's Época de Oro*. Oxford University Press, 2019.

Browning, Barbara. *Caetano Veloso's A Foreign Sound. 33 1/3 Brazil*. Bloomsbury Publishing USA, 2017.

Chion, Michel. *Audio-Vision: sound on screen*. Columbia University Press, 1994.

Chow, Rey. 'Sentimental returns: on the uses of the everyday in the recent films of Zhang Yimou and Wong Kar-Wai'. *New Literary History*, vol. 33, no. 4, 2002, pp. 639–54.

Decker, Todd. 'The filmmaker as DJ: Martin Scorsese's compiled score for Casino (1995)'. *The Journal of Musicology*, vol. 34, no. 2, 2017, pp. 281–317. https://doi.org/10.1525/jm.2017.34.02.281.

Edelman, Lee. *No Future: queer theory and the death drive*. Duke University Press, 2004.

Gillespie, Michael Boyce. 'One step ahead: a conversation with Barry Jenkins'. *Film Quarterly*, vol. 70, no. 3, 2017, pp. 52–62.

Goldschmitt, K.E. 'From Disney to dystopia: transforming "Brazil" for a US audience'. *The Routledge Companion to Screen Music and Sound*, edited by Miguel Mera, Ron Sadoff, and Ben Winters. Routledge, 2017, pp. 363–74.

Goldschmitt, K.E. *Bossa Mundo: Brazilian music in transnational media industries*. Oxford University Press, 2020.

Goldschmitt, K.E. 'Favela chic in action: soundtracking urban violence in Rio de Janeiro, Brazil'. *Music in Action Films: Sounds like action!*, edited by James Buhler and Mark Durrand. Routledge, 2021, pp. 1–17.

Halberstam, Jack. *In a Queer Time and Place: transgender bodies, subcultural lives*. New York University Press, 2005.

Halberstam, Jack. *The Queer Art of Failure*. Duke University Press, 2011.

Henriques, Donald. 'Mariachi reimaginings: encounters with technology, aesthetics, and identity'. *Transnational Encounters: Music and performance at the U.S.–Mexico Border*, edited by Alejandro L. Madrid. Oxford University Press, 2011, pp. 85–110.

Kassabian, Anahid. *Hearing Film: tracking identifications in contemporary Hollywood film music*. Routledge, 2002.

Kassabian, Anahid. *Ubiquitous Listening: affect, attention, and distributed subjectivity*. University of California Press, 2013. http://www.ucpress.edu/book.php?isbn=9780520275164.

Keeling, Kara. 'Looking for M—: queer temporality, Black political possibility, and poetry from the future'. *GLQ: A Journal of Lesbian and Gay Studies*, vol. 15, no. 4, 2009, pp. 565–82.

Keeling, Kara. *Queer Times, Black Futures – Sexual Cultures*. New York University Press, 2019.

Leu, Lorraine. *Brazilian Popular Music: Caetano Veloso and the invention of tradition*. Ashgate, 2006.

Long, Michael. *Beautiful Monsters: imagining the classic in musical media*. University of California Press, 2008.

Lowe, Melanie. 'Claiming Amadeus: classical feedback in American media'. *American Music*, vol. 20, no. 1, 2002, pp. 102–19. https://doi.org/10.2307/3052244.

Mora, Sergio de la. *Cinemachismo: masculinities and sexuality in Mexican film*. University of Texas Press, 2006.

Schnipper, Matthew. 'The pitch: director Barry Jenkins on the music that made *Moonlight*'. *Pitchfork*, 29 November 2016. https://pitchfork.com/thepitch/1377-director-barry-jenkins-on-the-music-that-made-moonlight/. Accessed 10 January 2022.

Stilwell, Robynn J. 'The fantastical gap between diegetic and nondiegetic'. *Beyond the Soundtrack: representing music in cinema*, edited by Daniel Goldmark, Lawrence Kramer, and Richard D. Leppert. University of California Press, 2007, pp. 184–202.

Vox. *Why This Creepy Melody Is in so Many Movies*, 2019. https://www.youtube.com/watch?v=-3-bVRYRnSM. Last accessed 13 January 2022.

Warner, Michael. *Publics and Counterpublics*. Zone Books, 2005.

13
Crowd Noise: Collective Turbulence in Modern Opera

Martin Brody

Introduction: 'A huge, wild, full-blooded, warm animal'

A scream and a shout.[1] These eruptions of vocal turbulence frame a story that I want to tell about vowels and consonants; noise and pitch; structure and colour; cognition and sensation; modernism and crowds. The scream is from Schoenberg's opera, *Moses und Aron*; the shout from Bach's *St Matthew Passion*. My primary concern will be to construct a phenomenology and semiotics of the scream. I will consider how this noise was defined as music – or perhaps as a rendering of music's Other, and specifically, an anti-music latent in Schoenberg's atonal structures. Screaming, I will argue, is a threshold condition that falls within the purview of the modern opera chorus, a frightening collective with a knack for splitting the difference between pitch and noise, vowel and consonant, meaning and mayhem. When a chorus turns into a mob before our ears (and eyes), it turns on music itself and violates the representational conventions of opera.

In this chapter, I will focus on the moment when the chorus in *Moses und Aron* turns into a mob. I will describe how this transformation is rendered in musical sonorities and structures and how it reflects the composer's ideas about artistic subjectivity, psychoacoustics and the social environment of modern music writ large. I will juxtapose the roar of Schoenberg's Volk with the composer's anxious ideas about the sensation of tone and the emancipation of dissonance. I want to suggest that for Schoenberg, among others, the collective voice became a medium for projecting unsettling thoughts about the physicality and structure of music, and the sound/meaning boundary in language. With this in mind, I will juxtapose a few sentences in which Elias Canetti describes the mass drive (or instinct) with the turbulent voices of a few opera choruses. Finally, I will compare the scream with Bach's shout, an example that can be understood as the complement under inversion, so to speak, of the Schoenberg example – a performance of collective empathy that remediates the pathology of the mob. The purpose of these juxtapositions is to consider some of the interactions (between semantics, textual translation, intermedial transformation and drastic vocalization) that occur when modern opera choruses become rowdy. I do not aim to produce a unified theory, nor do I wish to treat Schoenberg's brilliant rendering of passages from the Hebrew Bible as a case study in the adaptation of texts into music. Rather, I wish to focus on the passage from semiosis into sound, especially in extreme cases, and what the mapping of this borderline might suggest about social relationships and musical experience.[2]

There are plenty of rowdy, operatic choruses, but only a few operas represent modern crowds or convey their noisiness. When the supplications of the sixteenth-century Russian peasants in the opening of Mussorgsky's *Boris Godunov* turn from a submissive performance of a generic folk chorus into a raw, ensemble cry, we may momentarily hear the discharge of a modern mob. The peasants' high register, quasi-yodelling and intense melisma strain the larynx and stretch the unison voice of the crowd to a physical limit. The embodied medium of communication becomes distressed. The codes of identity dissolve into a collective shriek. Music momentarily exceeds itself.[3]

The furious crowd in *Turandot* presents a more ambivalent modernism and a different kind of boundary condition. The opera begins with a cascade of exotic orchestral sound, a Mandarin's sober incantation announcing a public execution and a flash of choral turbulence. The bloodlust that is forecast in the orchestra's portentous introduction, with its battery of exotic percussion instruments, spills into the instrumental music that accompanies the baritone voice of the Mandarin. Then it erupts into a flurry of intense collective emotion in the chorus. Excited by the baritone's announcement, the chorus performs a tight, bloodthirsty vocal paroxysm. Even as its members roar in unison and bump up against the top of their *tessitura*, however, this exotic chorus maintains a degree of vocal decorum that the Godunov crowd has lost. Its succinct homicidal cries show off the chorus' good diction. The fury of the mob is compressed into a sequence of breathless mini-phrases, terse melodic fragments and unstable harmonies that nonetheless erupt in neat, two measure units. After less than twenty seconds of this stylized collective agitation, a bunch of tenors, the imperial guards, appear. Order is restored in the tonal universe, the harmonic markers and rhetoric of orientalism subside, the music sinks into a stable key and the fairy tale mob suddenly seems more like a *verismo* crowd. The sopranos discharge full-throated sighs, as they implore the tenors to show them mercy in the unembellished object language of Italian realism: *crudeli, I miei bambini, o madre mia*, and so forth.[4]

Mixing *verismo* with the opera's signature orientalism modulates the sound of the crowd from the realm of remote myth to the representation of a more immediate world. However unsympathetic he might have been with workers' movements surging in the factories of Turin during the 1920s, Puccini marshalled the expressive force of crowds and power for theatrical effect. The affective transferences from the orchestra to the Mandarin to the chorus parallel the transaction between a composer, performers and an audience that has quite suddenly been urged to identify with a chorus of Chinese citizens from a legendary past.

In both the Mussorgsky and Puccini examples, choral music presents a stratified and dynamic representational structure – a downshifting from rarefied or conventional modes of theatrical representation to a raw kind of collective vocal presence: a sound that evokes indeterminacy and physical stress and a musical rhetoric that conveys immediacy. In both examples, a shift in the mode of vocalization or the apparatus of representation enacts a phenomenon of dissolving individuality and merging into a crowd – an artistic expression of what Elias Canetti called the 'full-blooded, warm animal in all of us'. Here is his description of the 'mass-soul,' from his 1935 novel *Auto-da-Fé*.

> We wage the so-called war of existence for the destruction of the mass-soul in ourselves, no less than for hunger and love. In certain circumstances it can become so strong as to force the individual to selfless acts or even acts contrary to his own interests. 'Mankind' has existed as a mass for long before it was conceived of and watered down into an idea. It foams, a huge, wild, full-blooded, warm animal in all of us, very deep, far deeper than the maternal.[5]

Canetti's warm animal that was embedded even more deeply in the psyche than the maternal bond could be expressed by a voice that was not intimate, singular or erotic, but rather feral and collective.

As I will argue in the following, Schoenberg theorized both the erotic solo voice and the noisy, collective voice as musical limit conditions. If the realization of a rarefied music of pure sensation produced by the individual voice briefly seemed like an artistic *raison d'etre* for

Schoenberg, the noisy sounds of an ungoverned mob eventually came to drown it out. The voice of the mob came to warrant a more sober artistic response.

I. Where is Moses?

In the scream of the Volk in *Moses und Aron*, the expression of the 'mass-soul' undermines music. Like the chosen people who have followed their leader into a desert, sound has lost its way. It has wandered into a wilderness where it explodes in a place beyond the established boundaries of musical expression. This sonic eruption is singularly indeterminate, the only musical event in an opera score that can be named but not notated, identified only in an overheated stage direction: 'Noise, wailing, and howling, ever louder, comes suddenly nearer; in enraged excitement, a shrieking crowd crashes onto the stage from all sides.'[6] This is the final event of Act II, Scene I. The shrieking crowd has waited forty days and nights for its leader to return.

To understand this uniquely unhinged sound, I will focus on a passage in which Schoenberg models the sounds of a coalescing mob. This is the *Zwischenspiel* between the two completed acts of *Moses und Aron*: it's an etude in whispered invertible counterpoint that occurs 112 measures before the scream. It compulsively recycles variations on an anxious question ('Wo ist Moses?') while probing the edge between singing and speaking.[7] The *Zwischenspiel* is a rendering of music straying into a phonic desert, a dry place where pitches erode into noise, vowels and consonants collide and structures break down. In this place, a chorus turns into a mob and singing turns into screaming. Seven hundred measures later there will be a human sacrifice.

Here, as always, it is easy to be mesmerized by the efficacy of Schoenberg's technique. I will focus on the ambivalent interplay of constructive and deconstructive elements involved. In this brief passage, Schoenberg weaves twelve-tone polyphony into a scheme of calls and responses that mimics the orderliness of imitative counterpoint, but here renders the murmurs of an anxious crowd in which discursive communication is falling apart. The pitches that articulate structure evaporate into static. Spoken and sung text turn into noise.

In the first sung music of the *entr'acte*, the source twelve-tone set of the opera appears in the guise of a fugal subject and countersubject. The two lines, sung by mezzo-sopranos and tenors, each contain six pitch classes. This balanced disposition is a norm of Schoenberg's musical universe; abnormally, however, the two hexachords are formed by partitioning the set asymmetrically to project non-identical pitch class collections. Here, the musical techniques of imitative counterpoint, which so often exemplify communicative intimacy in polyphonic structures, begin to signal a breakdown of communicative norms.

Below, Example 1 shows the row, the partitioning and arrangement of pitch classes in the passage, and the superimposition of texts and pitch classes.

Example 13.1

Row:
    A G# D E Eb F Db B C Bb G F#
    Partitioning of row into two lines (boldface/italic):
    A *G#* **D E** **Eb** *F* **Db** *B C* **Bb** **G F#**
    Order of Pitch Class and Words, Two-Part Texture:

Part 1:	A		E	Eb	Eb Db		G	G F#
	Nie		*Nie*	*Nie*	*kehrt*		*er*	*wieder*
Part 2:	G#	D D	D		F	G# G# D	F B C	C Bb Bb
	Verlassen	*sind*	*wir?*		*Wo*	*ist sein Gott,*	*wo ist der E-wi-*	*ge?*

The composite sequence of pitch classes in the two parts shown in Example 13.1 outlines the opera's governing structure: an ordered set (the prime form of the opera's row under inversion), but the contrapuntal arrangement of the two parts obfuscates at least as much as it clarifies. The shape, character and interval content of the subject and countersubject offer a study in contrasts. The leaping diminished seventh chord in the countersubject (with its telling repetition of the word 'Wo' on a high F) diverges vividly with the two equivalent trichords and alternation of leaps and steps in the subject.

The subject and countersubject fly by quickly, but the intensifying conflict between normative structural relationships and the expressive eccentricities that they initiate continues to unfold inexorably. A third line of counterpoint, while unexceptional in the formal design, continues to disturb the expression of balance and complementation between the parts. This second countersubject, presented in mumbling *Sprechstimme*, causes further challenges to communication, not only between the chorus and its audience but between the members of the chorus themselves. It is as if the tribe, lost in the desert, was barely holding on to the norms of mutuality.

There is a lot of structure here, but no single governing principle. On the one hand, the chorus sings a twelve-tone set in two-part counterpoint. On the other, they effectively rip the structure apart. No external authority stops them. There is no chord of nature, no inviolable principles, nor even a *sensus communis* to restore communicative norms. *Where is Moses?* The chorus continues to wander further into a desert of noise as the musical texture they speak and sing continues to thicken. Paradoxically the form comes into focus as the increasingly unintelligible texture unfolds. The orderly imitative relationships of the parts superimpose speech and singing in a way that increasingly garbles the text as well as jumbles the pitch structure's order. Sound and meaning are engaged in a war fought over the phonemes, which function neither as effective instruments for shaping the vocal tract as a rich resonant environment nor as a medium for articulating intelligible information.[8]

As the *Zwischenspiel* continues, the number of vocal parts expands and the war between sound and sense escalates. After the first statement, the configuration of subject and two countersubjects returns in invertible counterpoint at the pitch level of the original statement's combinatorial complement. This time around, the basses and altos have the sung bits, while the tenors mumble the *Sprechstimme* and the mezzo-sopranos sing something new (a *stretto* statement of the first hexachord of the row in its 'correct' order). Over the course of the next twenty seconds, a fifth and sixth voice enter as whispered *Sprechstimme* echoes. The polyphony of the six-voice texture intensifies again at the beginning of the second section of the passage (at m. 20). Here, the subject/countersubject and its echo in invertible counterpoint are superimposed in a canon. Meanwhile, the *Sprechstimme,* now whispered by altos and basses, snaps into its own strict canonic pattern.[9]

The whispered consonants in the *Zwischenspiel* threaten to bring down the firm edifice of neo-baroque, twelve-tone counterpoint. They also provide the raw material to build a new structure, a profane temple of noise. From the outset of the *entr'acte*, the mouths of the chorus become an efficient apparatus for producing a palette of unpitched sounds: labiodental and palatal fricatives (v, f), digraphs (sh, ch), bilabial nasals (m), uvular (kh) and velar stopped consonants (g). In the first four measures alone, there are a dozen different consonants. After introducing an array of consonants *ad seriatim,* Schoenberg constructs a mini-taxonomy of noisy chords: noise molecules, so to speak, constructed from the chorus' atomic consonants. At the nodal point of the passage (m. 18) pitched sounds momentarily clear out altogether to lay bare a three-voice *Sprechstimme* canon. The subject of the canon is a spoken sentence comprised of nine syllables, all but one of which begins with a different consonant. (Only the ninth (*ihn*) begins with a vowel.) The staggered speech canon produces a sequence of chords or intervals on seven consecutive half beats, each of which is comprised of a different combination of consonants. For a narrow couple of seconds, Schoenberg displays a contrapuntal dystopia of noise.[10]

Throughout the *Zwischenspiel*, noise becomes more and more structurally articulate: vowels dissolve into consonants and pitches into noise. Harmony, counterpoint and intelligible speech are collateral damage. In producing this destructive miracle in the desert, the density of consonants, the speed of attacks and the passage's brisk tempo (a function of the crowd's panic) are primary factors. Only the first three notes of the repeated fugal subject, sung on the cry, 'Nie, nie, nie' have the open vowel sounds and ample durations for full-bodied choral singing. Sharpening the focus of the first three pitches of the subject, of course, props up the *Zwischenspiel's* otherwise sagging polyphonic structure. There is, however, no question that the temple will collapse.

Throughout this passage, consonant noises fly by quickly and articulately, but the vowels are choked out. There are, for example, twenty-five consonants articulated in the first eight beats of the opening of the *entr'acte* – at quarter = eighty-eight, roughly five ensemble consonant sounds are pronounced per second. In the ensuing choral music, the chorus sings sixteenth notes at a pace of roughly a sixth of a second each. At that speed, the syllabic peaks, the portion of the vocal sounds where vowels and pitches come into focus, are attenuated almost to the vanishing point. Rather, the noisy, sonic onset attacks prevail. The setting of the consonant rich, melodically intricate and rhythmically compressed sentence, 'Lange schon hat ihn keiner gesehn!', (m. 11–12), for example, is too fast and too varied for the mezzos to squeak out much in the way of vowels or pitches, let alone syllables or words. There are ten syllables, ten pitches and pitch classes (the first ten pitch classes of the set) and thirteen consonants in two seconds. Then, in another two seconds of music, the sentence is repeated, sung to a scrambled version of the previous musical setting (in other words, the last two notes of the set, followed by a retrograde of its second hexachord). The force of this sonic compression all but annihilates the 'normal' mechanics of singing. Both singing and *Sprechstimme* head into a phonically liminal space where noise prevails.

One other factor needs to be mentioned in describing the tilt from pitch to noise and phoneme to consonant in this passage: the quiet, frantically rearticulated solo instrument doublings of the vocal parts. Here, instrumental doubling, normally to aid intonation and support polyphonic choral singing, produces contradictory effects. Instrumental doublings focus and reinforce the pitch, but they also shred the sound. Each instrumentally doubled note is rearticulated five times in consecutive thirty-second note attacks, tongued or with a thrown bow, at a speed close to the threshold of a physical limit. Each of these rearticulations introduces more onset noise into the sonority. The rearticulated instrumental doublings thus produce an aural paradox, simultaneously reinforcing and granulating the pitches being sung. The effect intensifies as the texture becomes denser; the more intricate the contrapuntal structure, the noisier the texture. In the canon in invertible counterpoint that I already mentioned (m. 20), the noise of rearticulation nearly overwhelms the orderly pitch/rhythm structures in play. Structure and sound, as well as meaning and sound, seemed to be locked in a war of mutually assured destruction.

II. 'The illusory stuff of our dreams'

The dissolving of pitch into noise in *Moses und Aron* models the ascendency of the mob. It also pessimistically mimics a couple of theoretical possibilities for the future of music that Schoenberg had presented more than ten years before the opera was written. In the closing arguments of his 1910 *Harmonielehre*, he proposed that the transmutation of pitch into tone colour was a way to bring us 'closer to the illusory stuff of our dreams'. This would occur when composers threw off the shackles of 'consonance' to investigate the full range of sensations of tone; in other words, the gamut of partial vibrations of the standing wave.

Here is Schoenberg's argument, in brief: (1) Musical experience involves attending to the full range of overtones in complex sounds. '[In] the acoustical emanations of the tone nothing is lost ... [T]he world of feeling somehow takes into account the entire complex [of overtones]'. (2) Pitch and colour are on a continuum. 'Tone colour is ... the main topic, pitch a subdivision. Pitch is nothing else but tone colour measured in one direction'. (3) If harmony and melody are derived from exploring the gamut of partial vibrations of the standing wave, that is, by translating colour into pitch, a reciprocal process was also possible – a kind of additive synthesis whereby shifts of colour would be triggered by rearranging combinations of pitches.

> [I]f it is possible to create patterns out of tone colours that are differentiated according to pitch, patterns we call 'melodies', then it

> must also be possible to make such progressions out of [what] we call simply 'tone colour', progressions whose relations with one another work with a kind of logic entirely equivalent to that logic which satisfies us in the melody of pitches.[11]

Harmony would be governed by a new phenomenology of sound and a yet undiscovered melodic logic of tone colours rather than fixed conditions of consonance and dissonance and tonal hierarchy.

In an essay written in 1908 for the *Blaue Reiter*, Schoenberg suggested that the human voice was the ideal instrument of liberated sound, especially when singing was liberated from the burden of expressing the meanings of words. By lingering on pitched vowels and so combining tones and phonemes to reshape the infinitely malleable vocal tract, the voice could be the medium of an even more radical tone colour music than the *Klangfarbenmelodie* produced by chords made out of pitches.

> [T]he outward correspondence between music and text, as exhibited in declamation, tempo and dynamics, has but little to do with the inward correspondence, and belongs to the same stage of primitive imitation of nature as the copying of a model. Apparent superficial divergences can be necessary because of parallelism on a higher level. Therefore, the judgment on the basis of the text is just as reliable as the judgment of albumen according to the characteristics of carbon.[12]

The living material, the sonorous albumen of music, gestates in the mouth. Mimesis, by comparison, was a primitive effect. In imagining the music of the future, the emancipation of sound from meaning through singing might lead to a decisive liberation of tone colour, not only from language, but even the distinction of consonance and dissonance – and from pitch itself as a primary structural element.

Schoenberg's radical speculation about sound led to a choice between two epistemological limits: on the one hand, vocal music freed from mimesis and meaning and decoupled from structure, able to express 'pure' sensations. On the other, a new kind of melodic order, made of tone colours rather than pitches, but made possible by acknowledging what he called an 'extended truce' (*Waffenstillstand*) between equal-tempered pitches and the frequency ratios of overtones. The music theorist Benjamin Steege has noted that Schoenberg swung from 'petulant irrationalism' to 'cool pragmatism' as he struggled with the enigma of pure sensation and contingent structures during the period when he composed his theory of harmony and wrote his first atonal pieces.[13] In a letter to Busoni written in 1908, Schoenberg made the case for a musical unlogic of unmediated sensation, contrary to the hope for a 'kind of logic entirely equivalent to that logic which satisfies us in the melody of pitches' that he imagined just months later in the *Harmonielehre*:

> This variegation, this multifariousness, this *unlogic* our sensations display, this unlogic, which the associations exhibit, which reveal some rising surge of blood, some sensory or nervous reaction – I would like to have this in my music. It should be the expression of sensation, as sensation really is, which brings us into connection with our *Unconscious,* and not a changeling of sensations and 'conscious logic'.[14]

There are a number of reasons that Schoenberg might have backed away from this radical polemic. In this discussion, the one that I want to emphasize is this: 'the lesson that has been forced upon me during this year [1920]', as Schoenberg famously wrote to Kandinsky, 'It is that I am not a German, not a European, indeed perhaps scarcely even a human being (at least, the Europeans prefer the worst of their race to me), but I am a Jew'. For Schoenberg, Kandinsky's anti-Semitism was above all a capitulation to conformity. 'I have seen that someone with whom I thought myself to be on a level preferred to seek the community of the lump', as he starkly put it.[15] The breakdown of intersubjective communication and the rule of the mob were two sides of the same coin. This lesson that Kandinsky's anti-Semitism conveyed to Schoenberg seemed an especially bitter pill to swallow, given the two artists' previous solidarity and their shared mission to reach beyond conscious logic and sensations to reach the unlogic of the unconscious. 'At this point', Schoenberg confessed, 'I give up the hope of reaching any understanding. It was a dream.' Disenchantment was the order of the day: 'Perhaps someday a later generation will be in a position to indulge in dreams. I wish it neither for them nor for myself. On the contrary, indeed, I would give much to bring about an awakening.'[16]

When Schoenberg revisited the question of sensation and structure in a lecture on twelve-tone music delivered at Princeton in 1934, two years after completing Act II of *Moses und Aron* and just months after reconverting to Judaism and immigrating to the United States, he had successfully brought about a kind of musical awakening and begun to explore the musical techniques to manifest it. The petulant irrationality and cool pragmatism of 1910 gave way to an altogether Mosaic project: to emulate the oneness of God by making order out of chaos using contingent structures and forms. 'The concept of creator and creation should be formed in harmony with the Divine Model', he flatly proposed in the Princeton lecture, adding that 'inspiration and perfection, wish and fulfilment, will and accomplishment [would thus] coincide spontaneously and simultaneously'.[17] Schoenberg recycled his argument about the sensations of the tone from his 1910 harmony book not to conjure the stuff of our dreams or the unlogic of the unconscious, but rather to make the case for sovereign consciousness and cognition. 'In my *Harmonielehre*', he wrote, 'I presented the theory that dissonant tones appear later among the overtones, for which reason the ear is less intimately acquainted with them'. Now, however, to become intimate with the higher partials was to overcome fear of dissonant pitch combinations – the 'fear of [the] "sense-interrupting" effect' of so-called dissonance – rather than to court ephemeral sensations.[18] The two-way traffic between pitch and tone colour must arrive in the same place – the elaboration of new pitch structures.

Over and over in the essay on twelve-tone composition, Schoenberg described the triumph of cognition and comprehension over difficulty and fear in terms of pitch structures: 'Closer acquaintance with the more remote consonances – the dissonances, that is – gradually eliminated the difficulty of comprehension ... The term *emancipation of the dissonance* refers to its comprehensibility, which is considered equivalent to the consonance's comprehensibility.'[19] The inspired genius emulated God by wresting intelligible pitch structures from the distant overtones.

Once the choice was made to pursue meaning and intelligibility over unstructured sensations, dissonant harmony could be liberated, but the singing voice would be suspect. Moreover, if the solo voice's unbound, multifarious qualities had become a threat to intelligibility, the mouth of a mob was even more destabilizing. The former would produce seductive but unintelligible sound colours; the latter, an unalloyed disturbance that would never resolve. All told, *Moses und Aron* is a parable of failed vocalization and the difficulty of creating a viable marriage of sound, sense and musical structure. Moses, the Supreme Commander's proxy, cannot sing. Aron, the *bel canto* singer, is a shallow thinker who inspires a blood sacrifice. The crowd turns to noise. The composer cannot complete the opera. Schoenberg's anxieties about the breakdown of communication in an era of emancipated dissonance are muted in his self-assured prose writing, but they break through the surface of his opera in an orgy of consonants which are, in turn, a prelude to a scream.[20] For the mob, there are two possibilities: the uncritical solidarity of noise or the atavistic solidarity of reified consonance. There is no escape hatch to *jouissance*. *Moses und Aron*, as Adorno succinctly summarized, 'does the Absolute the honour of not pretending it is present', even as it strives, meta-musically, to represent the problem of representation.[21]

Coda: 'Wie wunderbarlich ist doch diese Strafe!'

If Schoenberg's noisy crowd insinuates a crisis of subjectivity and faith, Bach's chorus in the *St Matthew Passion* enacts a profane eruption of choral turbulence but then retreats from the possibility of collective noise. Arguably, the shout is the most over-excited diminished seventh chord in the Western canon. Produced by a chorus impersonating a crowd of Jews, the shout injects a spike of unprepared and, in a sense, unresolved, dissonance into the heart of a long story about a Roman prefect, a petty thief and the Christian saviour. It disrupts a tonal cadence, truncates the end of a recitative and endangers a well-established agreement between verbal syntax, harmonic progression and narrative conventions.

In blowing up the cadence, the shout momentarily arrests the narrator's command of the surrogate voices he summoned to illustrate his story – the hallmark of his sermonizing powers. Nonetheless, the preacher barely registers the uproar. He maintains his composure as if almost nothing, certainly nothing untoward, has happened. That is, he treats the shocking choral outburst and harmonic substitution (and the corresponding substitution of Barabbas for Jesus in the story) as if they were a regular part of the narrative apparatus – the result of a conventional tonal elision that nudges the music into the next sung sentence of the story.[22] The shout might be understood as the preacher's most drastic trick, a shock effect to convey the irrepressible savagery of a mob. I prefer to think that it intrudes, unbidden by the storyteller, not as an intended narrative contrivance, but rather as a latent memory. The shout breaks through the sonic surface at a moment when the burden of narration becomes unbearable. Its aberrant harmony, which produces stinging cross-relations and a startling tritone leap in the bass, seems to come out of nowhere, or at least from another time and place. And it does: the chord would have been intense but unexceptional if it had occurred as a pre-tonic harmony in E minor, the key of the oratorio's opening, which renders the Saviour's ascent to the site of the crucifixion. Although it emanates from a naturalistic source in the fictive world of the oratorio, a chorus impersonating a mob, the shout is uniquely incongruous. It defies the conventions of storytelling and enactment. It does not seem altogether realistic or preternatural. It models a psychic rather than a narrative turn – a pre-modern return of the repressed. It is a simulacrum of the sound that Schoenberg had once sought – the sound of the unconscious. Here, a psychic experience that the preacher cannot repress not only breaks through into his consciousness but becomes audible to his congregation. For two beats, the audience vicariously feels the shock of a witness to traumatic events, rather than enjoying his virtuosity as a storyteller.

In the spatial and contrapuntal dynamics of its ensemble singing, the double chorus of the *Passion* is a strong precedent for Schoenberg's *Moses und Aron*. The comparison extends to the scheme of solo singing as well: Schoenberg's Moses expresses himself only through *Sprechstimme*, Bach's Evangelist exclusively through recitative. Both Moses and the Evangelist employ surrogates to sing arias to the people. In *Moses und Aron*, it is Aron who intensifies the communication with the Volk, and in the *St Matthew Passion*, various solo singers step forward to illustrate the story for a congregation that itself participates in the performance of the piece's chorales.

Bach stages a complicated exercise in empathy to reveal the durability of the structures in play. If the Jewish mob's ferocity momentarily threatens to break apart the musical and verbal orders of the *Passion*, its dissonance swiftly resolves into a capacious tonal structure. A transcendent movement from dissonance to consonance regulates the relationship between resonance and harmony. As a matter of faith, tonality also cradles the chorus' subjective motility throughout the work, so that the collective voice can assume a range of identities: as a Jewish mob, a Messiah's disciples and even the congregation itself, which may sing along in the chorales, reflecting on the sacrifice of a martyr, the possibility of redemption and, above all, the universality of sin. Following quickly after the chorus' ejaculation of the name, Barabbas, the Chorale, 'Wie wunderbarlich ist doch diese Strafe!' (number 46), enfranchises both chorus and congregation in a self-reflexive meditation on the dynamics of sin, punishment and atonement.

By contrast, the accomplishment of Schoenberg's grand opera can be measured in terms of the decisiveness of its failed ambitions. The scream of the Volk is irrevocable; the mob has flouted the ontological conditions of musical intelligibility and shows no signs of relenting. The third act of the opera, in which it might have regained, or perhaps better to say fully gained, its composure, remained unwritten – at least in part, I believe, because of the implausibility of restoring the musical covenant between this crowd and its maker once they have broken away from him and screamed. In Act III, the relenting Volk would have had to learn a new idiom and find a new way of singing together. It is impossible for me to envision this, that is, to imagine the Volk transformed into the lyrical congregation that Schoenberg imagined in his last choral pieces, especially *Dreimal Tausend Jahre* (op. 50a) or the unfinished *Modern Psalm* (op. 53c). After the scream, this possibility has been foreclosed.

It is just this irrevocability, however, especially set in relief against Schoenberg's relentless reflections on meaning and structure throughout the opera, that makes the scream startling. The scream still summons us to an *awakening*, as Schoenberg put it to Kandinsky. Now, in an era of lethal mobs and viral crowd noise, this wakeup call may strike us with renewed force. As a heuristic for critical thinking about vocality, the scream of the Volk portends an alternative to Aristotelian speech, Barthes' *jouissance*, Pythagoras' consonant anvils, or Cavarero's plurality of voices.[23] What would the topography of a sonic space modelled on vocal turbulence look like? Not a hierarchy of sound structures, natural or metaphysical, tonal or otherwise; not Schoenberg's linear spectrum of colour and pitch; not a sudden leap into a noisy void; not an apotheosis of collective solidarity or a nervous fear of anarchy; neither a cloistered discharge of pleasure nor a global affirmation of the voice's individuality. I hope it will not seem facile to leave the question unanswered. I will conclude, rather, with a gloomy revision of Barthes' final sentence in the *locus classicus*, 'The grain of the voice': were we to succeed in refining a certain aesthetics of vocal turbulence, then doubtless we would attach even more importance to the formidable break in tonality accomplished by modernity.[24]

Notes

1. Arnold Schoenberg, *Moses und Aron*, Act II, Scene I conclusion: https://www.youtube.com/watch?v=NKm_cdlodLQ (51:05-51:16); Johann Sebastian Bach, *St Matthew Passion*, 45a https://www.youtube.com/watch?v=HXoXPspTKyg. Accessed 31 December 2021. Throughout this chapter, I will provide links and timing indications for audio samples of the examples under discussion. In the Schoenberg examples that follow, I also note a few measure numbers to orient the reader. I hope that the argument that I am making will be clear, however, through aural experience, whether or not the reader consults the musical scores of the examples.
2. See HaCohen, 'A theological midrash in search of operatic action', for a discussion of the translation of the biblical text into an operatic libretto.
3. Prologue, *Boris Gudonov*, Modest Mussorgsky https://www.youtube.com/watch?v=pA-LLi7YZZE, Generic/folk: 5:41–6:15; Raw Cry: 6:16–6:55. Accessed 31 December 2021.

4. Giacomo Puccini, *Turandot* (opening) https://www.youtube.com/watch?v=iZn_FGQmlVQ, 0:00–2:25. Accessed 31 December 2021.
5. Canetti, *Auto-da-Fé*, 461.
6. Schoenberg, *Moses und Aron*, 157.
7. The effects of spoken and sung musical events in the *Zwischenspiel* that I will discuss here depend on a brisk (and accurate) tempo. Two successful renderings on record are Boulez/Concertgebouw *Deutsche Grammophon*, 1996 and Solti/Chicago Symphony, Decca, 1984. For reference in this chapter, I will include links to the latter recording: https://www.youtube.com/watch?v=UchqcV-4wLE. Accessed 31 December 2021.
8. *Zwischenspiel*, 0:10–0:18.
9. *Zwischenspiel*, 0:24–0:48.
10. *Zwischenspiel*, 0:48–0:50.
11. Schoenberg, *Theory of Harmony*, 421.
12. Schoenberg, 'The relationship to the text', 6.
13. Steege, *Helmholtz and the Modern Listener*, 239.
14. Schoenberg, 'Letter to Busoni', August 1909 in Theurich, *Briefwechsel*, 171. Quoted in Steege, 239.
15. Schoenberg, 'Letter to Kandinsky', *Arnold Schoenberg Letters*, 89–90.
16. Schoenberg, 'Letter to Kandinsky', *Arnold Schoenberg Letters*, 89–90.
17. 'Composition with twelve tones' in Schoenberg, 'The relationship to the text', 102.
18. 'Composition with twelve tones' in Schoenberg, 'The relationship to the text', 102.
19. 'Composition with twelve tones' in Schoenberg, 'The relationship to the text', 105.
20. This comment about the communication between Moses, Around the 'Volk' (unlike my comments on choral noise) play off of David Lewin's formulation of a 'multiple proportion-God: Moses: Aron: Volk equals 'the idea' (row): composer (Schoenberg): performer: audience … Moses, like Schoenberg, perceives directly and intuitively a sense of divine ('pre-compositional') order. He cannot communicate this sense directly, however. As he suggests in Act I, Scene 1, he would much prefer to spend his life in simple contemplation of this order. But God commands him to communicate it ('Verkuende!') and he is powerless to resist'. See Lewin, *Moses und Aron*', 1.
21. Adorno, 'Sacred fragment', 87
22. The passage under discussion is the end of Number 45a of the *St Matthew Passion*, which begins at 144:07 in this performance. https://www.youtube.com/watch?v=Tq4lxMcwYwU. Accessed 31 December 2021.
23. See, for example, Barthes, 'The grain of the voice', Cavarero, *For More than One Voice*, Heller-Roazen, *Revolution in Poetic Language*.
24. Barthes' version: 'Were we to succeed in refining a certain "aesthetics" of musical pleasure, then doubtless we would attach less importance to the formidable break in tonality accomplished by modernity'. (Barthes, 'The grain of the voice', 189.)

Bibliography

Adorno, T.W. 'Sacred fragment: Schoenberg's *Moses and Aaron*'. *Quasi una Fantasia: Essays on Modern Music*, translated by Rodney Livingstone. Verso, 1992, pp. 84–97.
Barthes, Roland. 'The grain of the voice'. *Image, Music Text*, translated by Stephen Heath. Hill & Wang, 1977, pp. 179–89.
Canetti, Elias. *Auto-da-Fé*, translated by C.V. Wedgwood. Farrar, Straus, and Giroux, 2021.
Cavarero, Adriana. *For More than One Voice: toward a philosophy of vocal expression*, translated by Paul Kottman. Stanford University Press, 2005.
HaCohen, Ruth. 'A theological midrash in search of operatic action: *Moses und Aron* by Arnold Schoenberg'. *Music's Obedient Daughter: The opera libretto from source to score*, edited by Sabine Lichtenstein. Rodopi, 2014, pp. 405–31.
Kristeva, Julia. *Revolution in Poetic Language*, translated by Margaret Waller. Columbia University Press, 1984.
Lewin, David. '*Moses und Aron*: some general remarks and analytic notes for act 1, scene I'. *Perspectives of New Music*, vol. 6, no. 1, 1967, pp. 1–17.

Puccini, Giacomo. *Turandot*. London Philharmonic Orchestra, 1973. https://www.youtube.com/watch?v=iZn_FGQmlVQ. Accessed 31 December 2021.

Schoenberg, Arnold. 'The relationship to the text'. *Style and Idea*, edited by Dika Newlin. Philosophical Library, 1950, pp. 1–6.

Schoenberg, Arnold. *Arnold Schoenberg Letters,* selected and edited by Erwin Stein, translated by Eithne Wilkins and Ernest Kaiser. St Martin's, 1965.

Schoenberg, Arnold. *Theory of Harmony*, translated by Roy E. Porter. University of California Press, 1983.

Schoenberg, Arnold. *Moses und Aron,* edited by Christian Martin Schmidt. Eulenburg Edition, 2008.

Steege, Benjamin. *Helmholtz and the Modern Listener*. Cambridge University Press, 2012.

14
Creative Translation in Emerson's Idealism
Kenneth P. Winkler

In *Emerson and the Art of the Diary*, Lawrence Rosenwald describes the literary form of Emerson's journals as a 'creative translation' of earlier traditions of diary-writing or journal-keeping:[1]

> Two of Emerson's diaristic traditions, the Lockean commonplace book and the Moodyan diary, we have already considered in describing the process by which Emerson found his form; and in that description, as in most descriptions of the relation between and innovative artist and his or her tradition, we proceeded as if the traditions were originals and Emerson's response to them a creative translation.

The Lockean commonplace book, about which I will say no more, is an indexed record of one's readings and observations. The Moodyan diary, or what I will call the Puritan diary, which is more intensely personal, is best represented by Mary Moody Emerson, Ralph Waldo Emerson's aunt, who was the most potent personal influence on Waldo's early intellectual development. In the remark I have quoted, Rosenwald uses the word 'translation' very broadly, and in this chapter I will follow him. I will apply the word not only to Emerson's creative appropriation of a literary form, but to his creative appropriation of a philosophical doctrine – one that helps to make sense of an attitude towards life, its gifts and its burdens, that Puritan diaries often express. The doctrine, now known as the Doctrine of Continuous Creation, holds that, in conserving the world, God re-creates it at every moment, making the same creative effort at each ever-advancing now that he made at the very beginning. Continuous creation was explicitly endorsed by at least one Puritan diarist, Jonathan Edwards. It was an important ingredient in his idealism and, once translated, it became an important ingredient in the idealism of Emerson. My aim in this chapter is to describe Emerson's creative translation of the doctrine as Edwards understood it. I will close by suggesting that for us, the doctrine can perhaps be a source of optimism and an incentive to action, as I believe it was for Emerson. I will also briefly consider Emerson's bearing on the themes of this volume.

I will begin in section one with Edwards' statement of the doctrine. In section two, I will document Emerson's esteem for the diaries of his Puritan forebears, Mary Moody Emerson among them. I will suggest that continuous creation makes her valiant response to life more comprehensible. I will then turn, in the third and final section, to Emerson's creative translation of the doctrine and its contribution to his idealism.

There is one preliminary: I must explain how I will understand idealism. The founding text of the idealist tradition is a passage from Plato's *Sophist*, where a 'stranger' or visitor to Athens speaks of a 'quarrel about reality' that he compares to a 'battle of gods and giants'.[2] 'How so?', young Theaetetus asks. F.M. Cornford, whose translation of the Stranger's answer I now quote, calls it a battle between 'idealists' (the party of the gods) and 'materialists' (the party of the giants):

STRANGER: One party is trying to drag everything down to earth out of heaven and the unseen, literally grasping rocks and trees in their hands, for they lay hold upon every stock and stone and strenuously affirm that real existence belongs only to that which can be handled and offers resistance to the touch. They define reality as the same thing as body, and as soon as one of the opposite party asserts that anything without a body is real, they are utterly contemptuous and will not listen to another word.

THEAETETUS: The people you describe are certainly a formidable crew. I have met quite a number of them before now.

STRANGER: Yes, and accordingly their adversaries are very wary in defending their position somewhere in the heights of the unseen, maintaining with all their force that true reality consists in certain intelligible and bodiless forms. In the clash of argument they shatter and pulverize those bodies which their opponents wield, and what those others alleged to be true reality they call, not real being, but a sort of moving process of becoming. On this issue an interminable battle is always going on between the two camps.

The Stranger's sympathies – and Plato's – are with the gods. As the entry on idealism in James Mark Baldwin's *Dictionary of Philosophy and*

Psychology reports, 'the first historical system to which the name of idealism is applied by common consent is that of Plato'.[3] The idealist thesis most emphasized by Plato in the passage quoted is metaphysical: bodies possess a diminished reality, a reality less 'true' – less real – than that of the impalpable unseen. In this chapter, I will take idealism to be the view that the mind is more truly real or more fundamental than body. To affirm the diminished reality of body is not to say that bodies are altogether unreal, or that they do not exist. This more extreme idealist thesis is a limiting case of idealism as I will understand it. The extreme thesis holds that the reality of body is so radically diminished that, in the end, it amounts to nothing at all.

I. Edwards on continuous creation

As a student at Yale College, Jonathan Edwards would have encountered the doctrine of continuous creation in the *Medulla Theologica*, a handbook of Puritan theology by William Ames.[4] God's conservation of the world, Ames writes 'is nothing else than as it were a continued *Creation*' – 'as it were' because conservation and creation do differ 'in reason' (but not 'in very deed'), since '*Creation* includes a certaine newnes which conservation excludes, & *Creation* excludes a precedent existence which conservation includes'.[5] Present-day students of philosophy first encounter the doctrine in the *Meditations* of Descartes. In the Third Meditation, Descartes explains:

> A lifespan can be divided into countless parts, each completely independent of the others, so that it does not follow from the fact that I existed a little while ago that I must exist now, unless there is some cause which as it were creates me afresh at this moment – that is, which preserves me. Hence the distinction between conservation and creation is only a conceptual one [a distinction of reason, as Ames had called it] and this is one of the things that are evident by the natural light.[6]

In the following passage, Jonathan Edwards states the Doctrine of Continuous Creation and argues for it. His argument begins with a disjunction: the present existence of any created thing, he says, can be caused in only one of two ways, either by the past existence of the thing itself or by God:[7]

> That God does, continually, by his immediate power, *uphold* every created substance in being, will be manifest, if we consider, that

> their present existence is a *dependent* existence, and therefore is an *effect*, and must have some *cause*: and the cause must be one of these two: either the *antecedent existence* of the same substance, or else the *power of the Creator*.

Edwards then denies the first disjunct: 'But it can't be the antecedent existence of the same substance. For instance, the existence of the body of the moon at this present moment, can't be the effect of its existence at the last foregoing moment.' Why not? Because a thing cannot operate where and when it does not exist:

> 'Tis plain, nothing can exert itself, or operate, when and where it is not existing. But the moon's past existence was neither *where* nor *when* its present existence *is*. In point of time, what is *past* entirely ceases, when *present* existence begins; otherwise it would not be *past*. The past moment is ceased and gone, when the present moment takes place; and does no more coexist with it, than does any other moment that had ceased twenty years ago. Nor could the past existence of the particles of this moving body produce effects in any other place, than where it then was. But its existence at the present moment, in every point of it, is in a different place, from where its existence was at the last preceding moment. From these things, I suppose, it will certainly follow, that the present existence, either of this, or any other created substance, cannot be an effect of its past existence.

The same reasoning rules out the possibility that the present existence of one creature is caused by the past existence of another (a relevant possibility that Edwards' initial disjunction had ignored):

> The existences (so to speak) of an effect, or thing dependent, in different parts of space or duration, though every so *near* one to another, don't at all coexist one with the other; and therefore are as truly different effects, as if those parts of space and duration were every so far asunder: and the prior existence can no more be the proper cause of the new existence, in the next moment, or next part of space, than if it had been in an age before, or at a thousand miles distance, without any existence to fill up the intermediate time or space.

So the present existence of a thing can be caused neither by the thing itself nor by any other thing. It must therefore be brought about by God, who causes it by creating it at every instant it occupies: 'Therefore the existence of created substances, in each successive moment, must be the effect of the *immediate* agency, will, and power of God'.

What Edwards calls 'the body of the moon' stands in for any body whatsoever. If we concentrate on the moon, and on the other bodies it represents, the idealist consequences of Edwards' argumentation seem clear. Bodies have no causal power. Every effect that we might impute to a body is the immediate effect of God's will. Consider a billiard ball that collides with a second ball at rest. Does it cause the motion of the second ball? No, because the motion of the second ball is nothing but its successive reappearance in adjacent parts of space, and each reappearance is the work of God and God alone. Nor do bodies have an inherent self-identity – or so Edwards contends in passages elsewhere in *Original Sin* and whose argument I will summarize. Consider the moon. We take it to be identical over time. But its continued existence over time is nothing but the successive creation of remarkably similar – yet distinct – *phases* or *stages* in what we think of as a single lunar career. What is it that unites those stages into the enduringly self-identical thing we call the moon? What makes them all stages in a single career or lifetime, as opposed to fleeting and disconnected bursts of being? It is surely nothing in the stages themselves. Taken by themselves, any two stages, however similar or closely packed in time, are two things rather than one. According to Edwards, only the arbitrary will of God can meet the need. Only the power of God can unite intrinsically distinct things into a whole that is genuinely one. The reality of bodies is thereby diminished: they have been drained of causal power, now wholly invested in God, and even their self-identity has been rendered dependent on Mind.

As we will soon see, though, things are not quite so tidy as they seem.

II. Emerson and the Puritan diary

Riding one September day near his home in Northampton, Massachusetts in 1748, Jonathan Edwards ran into a young minister, Joseph Emerson, from the eastern part of the state. Emerson, who was twenty-four, was returning home from the commencement of Yale College.[8] Jonathan invited Joseph to spend the night at his home. There Joseph fell deeply in love with Esther, Jonathan's sixteen-year-old daughter. He returned to Northampton two months later to court her, but he was disappointed. 'I could not obtain from the young Lady the least Encouragement to come again. ... I hope the disappointment will be sanctified to me, and that the

Lord will by his Providence order it so that this shall be my companion for Life', he wrote in his diary.[9] I tell this touching story – touching in part because of young Joseph's determination that his rejection should teach a lasting religious lesson – to indicate how close, in one way, the New England transcendentalists of the nineteenth century were to the New England Puritans of the eighteenth. The Joseph of my story was Ralph Waldo Emerson's great uncle.

More important than such external marks of closeness were the internal ones. Colm Tóibín, in his novel of the life of Henry James, brings out what these inward marks were like for some. Henry's Aunt Kate is describing the struggles of her brother, Henry's father. Henry Sr was the idealist author of *Substance and Shadow* and a member, with his friend Emerson, of Boston's Saturday Club.

> There was a battle going on, Aunt Kate used the same words each time, between his own sweetness and the heavy Puritan hand which his father, old William James of Albany, had placed on his shoulder. Everywhere he went, she said, Henry James Senior saw love and the beauty of God's plan, but the old Puritan teaching would not let him believe his eyes. Daily, within him, the battle went on. He was restless and impossible, but he was also, in his searching, innocent and easily enraptured.[10]

Jonathan Edwards, as Robert Richardson notes, was 'one of the few religious writers' of whom Henry Sr specifically approved.[11]

Standing over Ralph Waldo Emerson's own shoulder was his aunt Mary Moody Emerson. The following passage is from an entry, composed three years after her death, in Emerson's journal for 1866:[12]

> Read M.M.E'.s mss yesterday – many pages. They keep for me the old attraction ... They make the best example I have known of the power of the religion of the Puritans in full energy, until fifty years ago in New England. The central theme of these endless diaries, is, her relation to the Divine Being; the absolute submission of her will, with the sole proviso, that she may know it is the direct agency of God, (& not of cold laws of contingency &c) which bereaves and humiliates her. But the religion of the diary, as of the class it represented, is biographical: it is the culture, the poetry, the mythology, in which they personally believed themselves dignified, inspired, judged, & dealt with, in the present & in the future. And certainly

> gives to life an earnestness, & to nature a sentiment, which lacking, our later generation appears frivolous.

Among the many resolutions made by the young Jonathan Edwards, there is an all-encompassing one that I find especially stirring: 'Resolved, to live with all my might, while I do live.'[13] Emerson's great uncle Joseph also lived by resolution, as we have seen, and even if he never put Edwards' particular resolution into words, he certainly seemed to live by it. Here is the conclusion of his diary for 1748, in which he urges himself to live even more intensely than he had in the year then closing:[14]

> read some & studied some. the year is now concluded and I may well finish my Journal as *Ames* does his Almanack [.] Another year now is gone, but ah! how little have we done. alas! how little have I done for God, for my own soul, for the souls of my people. committed I find a great deal Amiss, I would fly to the grace of Christ to pardon my defects and to his strength to enable me to do more for him this year if he should please to spare my Life.

Emerson would have found the same commitment to courageous self-inspection and self-improvement in the literary remains of his maternal ancestors. The following resolution, committed to paper a year before her marriage, is from the diary of Emerson's mother, Ruth Haskins:[15]

> I desire now in a better strength than my own to resolve that from this date – April 20, 1795, – I will, as God shall enable me, from time to time carefully notice all his providences towards my friends or myself, whether prosperous or adverse, – and conscientiously note down whatever appears to be for the glory of God, or the good of my own soul.

I think it is fair to assume that between the glory of God and her own good (or the good of others), nothing could defensibly fall beneath her notice.

In lectures he gave in Boston in 1839–40, Emerson asked his audience, 'Who can read the pious diaries of the Englishmen in the time of the Commonwealth and later without a sigh that we write no diaries today?' 'How richly this old stream of antique faith descended into New England', Emerson says later in the lecture, 'the remembrances of the elder portion of my audience I am sure will bear witness'.[16] He continued:

> The depth of the religious sentiment as it may still be remembered in individuals imbuing all their genius and derived to them from hoarded family traditions, from so many godly lives and godly deaths of sainted kindred, was itself an Education. It raised every trivial incident to a celestial and religious dignity.[17]

I cannot of course say that these diarists had continuous creation explicitly in mind when they dignified every incident. But the doctrine makes very good sense of their thinking, lending it a force and urgency it may not otherwise have. The doctrine assures us that we are, at every moment, in immediate contact with God. At any instant, we are on the receiving end of a creative effort as mighty and miraculous as the effort chronicled in Genesis. Each of us is as much an Eve or Adam as Eve and Adam were.

Emerson brings out these implications of continuous creation in a letter to his aunt.[18]

> It is one of the *feelings* of modern philosophy, that it is wrong to regard ourselves so much in a *historical* light as we do, putting Time between God & us; and that it were fitter to account every moment of the existence of the Universe as a new Creation, and *all* as a revelation proceeding each moment from the Divinity to the mind of the observer.

He makes fuller remarks along the same lines in an early sermon.[19]

> Men are ever disposed to view God from afar, to look back to a distant period, put back his agency at the Creation 6000 years ago, a notion which all sound philosophy combats. It is imagined that at that time God established the laws of Nature and left it to itself as an Artist winds up a machine and leaves it to perform its work. But this is very unsound analogy. If God leaves his work it will fall asunder. For consider the difference of the two cases. The artist who constructs a watch avails himself of powers perpetually afforded him by nature, that is, by God – as the force of gravity or the elasticity of steel. If these powers should be withdrawn his machine would stop. But God has no such powers out of himself.

> The same power is needed this moment as was needed the first moment to produce the same effect. To him it is the same to uphold as to establish. It is a creation of each instant. I look then at my present being as now received, as now sustained by the Omnipresent

Father. Therefore, when I look abroad I receive directly from him these impressions of earth and sea and sun and stars and man and beast. All that we behold is not an ancient primeval work, covered with the moss of many an age but fresh with life, God's immediate act upon each of our minds, at this instant of time. And thus in a most emphatic sense, 'In him we live and move and have our being'.

If every instant is a revelation, as Emerson says in his letter to his aunt, then we are, at every moment, being addressed. Our experience is not a brute effect of the cold laws of contingency, but a carefully considered message from a cause that is warm with life. Hence in dignifying the present moment, continuous creation seems to dignify *us*. But there is a difficulty – one we can make apparent by returning to the passage from Edwards. Edwards illustrates continuous creation with a body: 'the body of the moon'. And with that illustration in mind, we are primed to appreciate the doctrine's potential to diminish the reality of body. Yet as the passage begins, Edwards speaks not of body, but of 'every created substance'. So his reader – my own self, for example – would be as fit an illustration of the doctrine as the moon. The same reasoning that diminished the reality of body would then apply no less relentlessly to me. It would deprive me of any remnant of causal power and rob me of inherent self-identity. How, then, could I in fact be addressed? Address, so far as we are able to understand it, always involves two parties, and the party doing the receiving, no less than the party doing the transmitting, pre-exists the advice or information that is being imparted. If our own existence is as fugitive as that of body, we seem to lose our privileged place as addressee.

William Ellery Channing was perhaps the most influential Unitarian minister of the first quarter of the nineteenth century. Emerson called him 'our Bishop'. Channing was an avowed opponent of the Calvinism that Edwards represented. I do not know whether Channing was aware of the selfhood-undermining reasoning I have just reviewed, but he saw the same general tendency in what he called Calvinism, and he lamented it. Channing was an idealist. He acknowledged the diminished reality of body. It was, he told his friend Elizabeth Peabody, Richard Price's *Dissertations on Matter and Spirit* that had 'saved [him] from Locke's philosophy':[20]

> He gave me the Platonic doctrine of ideas, and like him I always write the words Right, Love, Idea, etc. with a capital letter. His book, probably, moulded my philosophy into the form it has always retained, and opened my mind into the *transcendental depth*. And

> I have always found in the accounts I have read of the German philosophy in Madame de Stael, and in these later times, that it was cognate to my own.

Channing was repelled by what he saw as Calvinism's diminishment of human beings – more particularly, by its denial that human beings share in causal power. This denial, Channing argued, draws one inevitably to pantheism:[21]

> Calvinism will complain of being spoken of as an approach to Pantheism. It will say that it recognizes distinct minds from the Divine. But what avails this, if it robs these minds of self-determining force, of original activity; if it makes them passive recipients of the Universal Force; if it sees in human action only the necessary issues of a foreign impulse. The doctrine that God is the only Substance, which is Pantheism, differs little from the doctrine that God is the only active power of the universe. For what is substance without power? It is a striking fact that the philosophy which teaches that matter is an inert substance, and that God is the force which pervades it, has led me to question whether any such thing as matter exists: whether the powers of attraction and repulsion which are regarded as the indwelling Deity, be not its whole essence. Take away force, and substance is a shadow, and might as well vanish from the universe. Without a free power in man, he is nothing. The divine agent within him is every thing. Man acts only in show. He is a phenomenal existence, under which the One Infinite Power is manifested: and is this much better than Pantheism?
>
> One of the greatest of all errors is the attempt to exalt God, by making him the sole cause, the sole agent in the universe, by denying to the creature freedom of the will and moral power, by making man a mere recipient and transmitter of foreign impulse.

This is a verdict that Emerson shared. But Emerson was unwilling to abandon continuous creation. It is invoked, or so I think, in the opening paragraph of *Nature*, Emerson's first book and the fullest statement of his idealism. Here Emerson is doing what he often went on to do: joyfully anticipating new worlds and the people who would occupy them. I do not agree with Barbara L. Packer, for whom the paragraph brims with 'satire and scorn'.[22] To my ear, the paragraph's tone, though reproving, is earnest and hopeful.[23]

> Our age is retrospective. It builds the sepulchres of the fathers. It writes biographies, histories, and criticism. The foregoing generations beheld God and nature face to face; we, through their eyes. Why should not we also enjoy an original relation to the universe? Why should not we have a poetry and philosophy of insight and not of tradition, and a religion by revelation to us, and not the history of theirs? Embosomed for a season in nature, whose floods of life stream around and through us, and invite us by the powers they supply, to actions proportioned to nature, why should we grope among the dry bones of the past, or put the living generation into masquerade out of its faded wardrobe? The sun shines to-day also. There is more wool and flax in the fields. There are new lands, new men, new thoughts. Let us demand our own works and laws and worship. (Introduction 1)

I turn now to Emerson's creative translation, in *Nature*, of the Doctrine of Continuous Creation that Edwards and other modern philosophers had handed down to him.

III. Continuous creation in Emerson's idealism

The first edition of *Nature* begins with a motto attributed to Plotinus but actually borrowed from Plotinus' seventeenth-century heir, Ralph Cudworth. The motto adumbrates the idealism to come: 'Nature is but an image or imitation of wisdom, the last thing of the soul; nature being a thing which doth only do, but not know.' *Nature's* later statement of idealism, more official and less cryptic, is adapted to continuous creation:

> Idealism sees the world in God. It beholds the whole circle of persons and things, of actions and events, of country and religion, not as painfully accumulated, atom after atom, act after act, in an aged creeping Past, but as one vast picture, which God paints on the instant eternity for the contemplation of the soul. (VI 19)

But idealism so defined is not *Nature's* stopping point: 'Let [the ideal theory] stand ..., in the present state of our knowledge, merely as a useful introductory hypothesis, serving to apprize us of the eternal distinction between the soul and the world' (VII 6). Idealism is only introductory because there are urgent questions it does not settle:

> Three problems are put by nature to the mind; What is matter? Whence is it? and Whereto? The first of these questions only, the ideal theory answers. Idealism saith: matter is a phenomenon, not a substance. Idealism acquaints us with the total disparity between the evidence of our own being, and the evidence of the world's being. The one is perfect; the other, incapable of any assurance; the mind is a part of the nature of things; the world is a divine dream, from which we may presently awake to the glories and certainties of day. Idealism is a hypothesis to account for nature by other principles than those of carpentry and chemistry. Yet, if it only deny the existence of matter, it does not satisfy the demands of the spirit. It leaves God out of me. It leaves me in the splendid labyrinth of my perceptions, to wander without end. Then the heart resists it, because it balks the affections in denying substantive being to men and women. Nature is so pervaded with human life, that there is something of humanity in all, and in every particular. But this theory makes nature foreign to me, and does not account for that consanguinity which we acknowledge to it. (VII 5)

That 'matter is phenomenon, not a substance' was precisely Channing's view of matter or nature. And that idealism so defined denies 'substantive being to men and women' was Channing's complaint against Calvinism. But Emerson's complaint against idealism taken as a final view, as opposed to a hypothesis meant for eventual incorporation into a larger whole, is more specific than Channing's – and more daring. 'It leaves God out of me', Emerson objects. A mature idealism, by implication, puts God into me. And when continuous creation is translated into this new setting, the finite self becomes the creator. ('In all my lectures, I have taught one doctrine, namely the infinitude of the private man.'[24]) The truths of a mature idealism – an idealism that answers the questions that a merely introductory idealism fails to address – are offered as self-evident insights, rather than as conclusions reached by the kind of taut, linear argument we saw in Edwards:

> But when, following the invisible steps of thought, we come to inquire, Whence is matter? and Whereto? many truths arise in us out of the recesses of consciousness. We learn that the highest is present to the soul of man, that the dread universal essence, which is not wisdom, or love, or beauty, or power, but all in one, and each entirely, is that for which all things exist, and that by which they are; that spirit creates; that behind nature, throughout nature, spirit is

present; that spirit is one and not compound; that spirit does not act on us from without, that is, in space and time, but spiritually, or through ourselves. Therefore, that spirit, that is the Supreme Being, does not build up nature around us, but puts it forth through us, as the life of the tree puts forth new branches and leaves through the pores of the old. As a plant upon the earth, so a man rests on the bosom of God; he is nourished by unfailing fountains, and draws, at his need, inexhaustible power. Who can set bounds to the possibilities of man? Once inhale the upper air, being admitted to behold the absolute natures of justice and truth, and we learn that man has access to the entire mind of the Creator, is himself the creator in the finite. This view, which admonishes me where the sources of wisdom and power lie, and points to virtue as to

'The golden key

Which opens the palace of eternity',

carries upon its face the highest certificate of truth, because it animates me to create my own world through the purification of my soul. (VI 7)

What can we make of these confident promises, and of the idealism that underlies them? To mention just one difficulty, how can nature be put forth through us when we are late arrivals in the world? *Nature* was written almost twenty-five years before Darwin's *Origin of Species* (1859), but Emerson did not need Darwin to convince him that ages had to pass before the world would be prepared for us. He had learned that much from his study of geology, and he emphasized the point repeatedly in his natural history lectures of the 1830s. 'Man', Emerson explains in one lecture, was 'prophesized in nature for a thousand ages before he appeared; … from times incalculably remote there has been a progressive preparation for him; an effort, … to produce him'. 'He was not made sooner', Emerson says in summary, 'because his house was not ready'.[25] Yet the furnishing of the house, and the larger effort to *produce* humankind, could not in any straightforward way be the *work* of humankind. In what way, then, can we be the creator in the finite?

I can offer only a sketch in Emerson's defence. For Emerson, God or spirit is primary. But God exists at first, or before our arrival, only as impersonal law. That law is moral as well as physical (V 13). This means, in part, that a common verbal formula serves for both. 'Every action has an equal and opposite reaction' formulates a law of nature, a law that allows for no exceptions. Every portion of matter must conform to it. Were it not for law, every body would be a dead, inactive lump. Hence law is more real than the bodies it animates. But the sentence also formulates a moral law, a law of compensation, from which we, as conscious, willing beings, can depart. We are alone in being able to depart from it, but we are also alone in being able deliberately to follow it. Law, then, is rendered personal only in us. And when 'personalized', it assumes its most fully realized form: first when we come to understand it and, second, and finally, when we come to act in thorough accordance with it.

We thereby gain the substantive being that Edwards' reasoning had denied us. But continuous creation has not been left behind. Here I cannot even try to make sense of Emerson's suggestion that all of nature is put forth through us. But with respect to our own acts, continuous creation now presents itself as a perpetual task – a task assigned not to a God who stands outside of us, but to our own selves. We are now called upon either to renew our acts at every moment – all the wise agree, Emerson later writes, 'that as much life is needed for conservation, as for creation'[26] – or to change them. In one way this is daunting. Inertia cannot carry us forward from one moment to the next. But, in another way, it is encouraging. At any moment our slate is clean. Anything is possible. In the limited domain of acts indisputably our own, continuous creation can perhaps be a source of the optimism needed to endure the strains of commitment to 'actions proportioned to nature'. In our own perilous time, this may serve us as well as I believe it served Emerson in his.

I conclude with some remarks about the themes of this volume. My topic has been the translation of an idea from one thought environment to another, rather than the translation of text to text. Emerson never thought of texts as authoritative – at least not if their authority was supposed to derive from the person of their author, the might of their culture of origin, the persistence of a tradition or the sheer passage of time. What authority they had, he thought, came from the insights they translated into words. Emerson read text-to-text translations gratefully. He preferred reading English translations even when the original was written in a language he knew:[27]

> I thank the translators & it is never my practice to read any Latin, Greek, German, Italian, scarcely any French book, in the original which I can procure in an English translation. I like to be beholden to the great metropolitan English speech, the sea which receives tributaries from every region under heaven, the Rome of nations, and I should think it in me as much folly to read all my books in

originals when I have them rendered for me in my mother's speech by men who have given years to that labor, as I should to swim across Charles River when ever I wished to go to Charlestown.

Emerson read widely, and in diverse traditions, as his recommended readings among the 'class of books' he deemed 'the best' – namely 'the Bibles of the world, or the sacred books of each nation' – attest:[28]

> After the Hebrew and Greek Scriptures, which constitute the sacred books of Christendom, these are, the Desatir of the Persians, and the Zoroastrian Oracles; the Vedas and Laws of Manu; the Upanishads, the Vishnu Purana, the Bhagvat Geeta, of the Hindoos; the books of the Buddhists; the 'Chinese Classic', of four books, containing the wisdom of Confucius and Mencius.

Emerson listened carefully to all these sacred texts, and what he heard in them was not dissent but agreement. These texts agreed in teaching him 'the immensity of every moment, the indifference of magnitude, the present is all, the soul is God'.[29] These thoughts are corollaries of Emerson's version of continuous creation, or thoughts that continuous creation can explain. The past is dead and gone and the future is yet to come. Hence the present moment is immense; so immense that it contains all that is real, or, at least, all that is actual.

Notes

1. Rosenwald, *Emerson and the Art of the Diary,* 83.
2. Cornford, *Plato's Theory of Knowledge,* 230 in Cornford, *Plato's Theory of Knowledge.*
3. For more on Plato as the standard-bearer of idealism see Holmes, *Ralph Waldo Emerson,* 391: 'Emerson was an idealist in the Platonic sense of the word, a spiritualist as opposed to a materialist.'
4. A copy of *Medulla Theologica* now in Yale's Beinecke Library, is signed by Edwards and dated 1721.
5. I quote from an English translation of the *Medulla, The Marrow of Sacred Divinity,* 42.
6. Cottingham, Stoothoff and Murdoch, *The Philosophical Writings of Descartes,* vol. 2, 33.
7. Holbrook, *The Works of Jonathan Edwards,* vol. 3, 400–1.
8. 'Joseph Emerson's Diary, 1748–1749', 266 in *Proceedings of the Massachusetts Historical Society,* 262–82.
9. 'Joseph Emerson's Diary', 271. Phyllis Cole also tells this story, in *Mary Moody Emerson and the Origins of Transcendentalism,* 18.
10. Tóibín, *The Master,* 133.
11. Richardson, *William James,* 52.
12. Rosenwald, *Ralph Waldo Emerson, Selected Journals 1841–1877,* 846.
13. Claghorn, *Works of Jonathan Edwards,* vol. 16, 753. There are many echoes of this resolution in later American writing. They are probably clearest in Thoreau, but they can also be heard in William James: 'Live energetically; and whatever you have to do, do it with your might' (quoted in Richardson, *William James,* 327). James' resolution more directly echoes Ecclesiastes

ix:10: 'Whatsoever thy findeth to do, do it with thy might'. A 1829 sermon by Emerson is on this text; see von Frank, *Complete Sermons of Ralph Waldo Emerson*, vol. 1, 250–4.
14. 'Joseph Emerson's Diary, 1748–1749', 275. Joseph quotes from Nathanael Ames, *An Astronomical Diary, or, an Almanack for the Year of our Lord Christ, 1748*, fourteenth unnumbered page. On the importance of an end-of-year audit, in which the soul 'summon[s] her faculties before them', to 'ask them rigorously what they have done', and to determine 'how performance tallies with the promise', see Emerson's 1829 sermon 'The night is far spent ...', in *Complete Sermons*, vol. 2, 112.
15. Haskins, *Ralph Waldo Emerson: his maternal ancestors*, 44–5.
16. Spiller and Williams, *The Early Lectures of Ralph Waldo Emerson*, vol. 3, 193.
17. Spiller and Williams, *The Early Lectures of Ralph Waldo Emerson*, vol. 3, 194.
18. *The Letters of Ralph Waldo Emerson*, vol. 1, 174. His aunt does not take up these points in her reply; see Simmons, *Selected Letters of Mary Moody Emerson*, 222–3.
19. Toulouse and Delbanco, *The Complete Sermons of Ralph Waldo Emerson*, vol. 2, 21–2.
20. Peabody, *Reminiscences of Rev. Wm. Ellery Channing*, 368.
21. Channing, *The Works of William E. Channing*, vol. 1, xii–xiii.
22. Packer, *The Transcendentalists*, 47.
23. Porte, *Emerson. Essays and Lectures*. References to *Nature* will be by chapter and paragraph number and will follow the quoted passages.
24. Rosenwald, *Emerson, Selected Journals 1820–1842*, 735.
25. Spiller and Williams, *The Early Lectures of Ralph Waldo Emerson*, vol. 3, 29.
26. Porte, *Emerson. Essays and Lectures*, 734.
27. Rosenwald, *Emerson, Selected Journals 1841–1877*, 159. A revised version of this 1843 journal entry appears in *Society and Solitude*, 182.
28. Emerson, *Society and Solitude*, 194–5.
29. Here I quote Emerson's statement of the 'great and greatest' lessons of 'the religious sentiment' in his preface to *Parnassus*, edited by Ralph Waldo Emerson, v.

Bibliography

Ames, Nathanael. *An Astronomical Diary, or, an Almanack for the Year of our Lord Christ, 1748*. J. Draper, 1747.
Ames, William. *Medulla Theologica*. Johannes Janssonius, 1634.
Ames, William. *Medulla, The Marrow of Sacred Divinity*. Edward Griffin for Henry Overton, 1642.
Baldwin, James Mark. 'Idealism'. *Dictionary of Philosophy and Psychology*, vol. 1. Oxford University Press, 1901.
Channing, George E. *The Works of William E. Channing*, vol. 1. Crosby, Nichols and Company, 1849.
Claghorn, George S, editor. *Works of Jonathan Edwards*, vol. 16. Yale University Press, 1998.
Cole, Phyllis. *Mary Moody Emerson and the Origins of Transcendentalism*. Oxford University Press, 1998.
Cornford, Francis MacDonald. *Plato's Theory of Knowledge*. Routledge & Kegan Paul, 1935.
Cottingham, John, Robert Stoothoff, and Dugald Murdoch, editors. *The Philosophical Writings of Descartes*, vol. 2. Cambridge University Press, 1985.
Emerson, Joseph. *Joseph Emerson's Diary, 1748–1749*. Proceedings of the Massachusetts Historical Society 44. 1911.
Emerson, Ralph Waldo. *Society and Solitude*. Fields, Osgood and Company, 1870.
Emerson, Ralph Waldo, editor. *Parnassus*. James R. Osgood and Company, 1875.
Haskins, David Greene. *Ralph Waldo Emerson: his maternal ancestors [,] with some reminiscences of him*. Cupples, Upham and Company, 1887.
Holbrook, Clyde, editor. *The Works of Jonathan Edwards*, vol. 3, *Original Sin*. Yale University Press, 1970.
Holmes, Oliver Wendell, Sr. *Ralph Waldo Emerson*. Houghton Mifflin, 1912.
Packer, Barbara L. *The Transcendentalists*. University of Georgia Press, 2007.
Peabody, Elizabeth. *Reminiscences of Rev. Wm. Ellery Channing*. Roberts, 1880.
Porte, Joel, editor. *Ralph Waldo Emerson, Essays and Lectures*. Library of America, 1983.

Richardson, Robert D. *William James: In the maelstrom of American modernism*. Houghton Mifflin, 2006.

Rosenwald, Lawrence A. *Emerson and the Art of the Diary*. Oxford University Press, 1988.

Rosenwald, Lawrence A., editor. *Ralph Waldo Emerson, Selected Journals 1820–1842*. Library of America, 2010.

Rosenwald, Lawrence A., editor. *Ralph Waldo Emerson, Selected Journals 1841–1877*. Library of America, 2010.

Simmons, Nancy Craig (ed.). *The Selected letters of Mary Moody Emerson*. University of Georgia Press, 1993.

Spiller, Robert E. and Wallace E. Williams, editors. *The Early Lectures of Ralph Waldo Emerson*, vol. 3. Harvard University Press, 1972.

Tóibín, Colm. *The Master: a novel*. Scribner, 2004.

Toulouse, Teresa and Andrew Delbanco, editors. *The Complete Sermons of Ralph Waldo Emerson*, vol. 2. University of Missouri Press, 1990.

Von Frank, Albert J., editor. *The Complete Sermons of Ralph Waldo Emerson*, vol. 1. University of Missouri Press, 1989.

Index

Acevedo, Elizabeth 12
acrostics 20–1
Actor-Network Theory 154–5
Adam 244
Adler, Cyrus 43
Adorno, Theodor W. 232
aims of the present book 7–8
Almodóvar, Pedro 14, 214, 217
Alter, Alexandra 148
Alter, Robert 34
This American Wife 201–4
American Film Institute 198
American market for science fiction 149
Ames, William 239
The Ancestral Temple in a Box 156
Anderson, Benedict 6
Anger, Suzy 97
Anglophone readership 146, 152–6
anti-Semitism 41–2, 53, 68
appropriateness, cultural 6
art-house films 208–9
Ashton, Rosemary 108
Atta Troll 57
audiences 38, 196–9, 204, 208–9, 218, 233
Augustine, St 3–6, 13, 188–9
Auslander, Philip 200
authenticity 156
authoritative texts 5, 250

Bach, J.S. 221–2, 232–3
Badiou, Alain 194–6, 203
Baldwin, James Mark 238–9
Barthes, Roland 234
Bassnett, Susan 98
Bausch, Pina 202
Bay-Cheng, Sarah vi, vii, 13–14
Beauvais, Clémentine 12
Beijing 142
Beltrán, Lola 215–16
ben Halevi, Jehuda 36, 45–6, 57–8
Benjamin, Walter 14, 125, 195–6, 199, 203
Berliner Ensemble 120
Bhabha, Homi K. 5
Bialik, Hayyim Nachman 60–1
bias 9
the Bible 54, 81
    King James Version 34, 183, 188
biblical texts 6–10, 20
biblical translation 33–4, 38

Bicha, Fado 213–14, 217
Biden, Joseph 6
Bielski, Andrew 195
Biemann, Asher D. 43
Bin Laden, Osama 180
Black directors 218
Blanchot, Maurice 5
Bloch, Jan 65
Bodenheimer, Rosemarie 102, 105
Boris Godunov 222
Börne, Ludwig 184
Brabant, Rufa 100–3, 106
Bray, Cara 101, 104
Brecht, Bertolt (and Brechtian theatre) 11–26, 195, 202–3
Breslin, Michael 203
Britell, Nicholas 207
Brody, Martin vi–vii, 14, 222
Bruegel the Elder 119
Buber, Martin 8, 33–4, 39

Calvinism 245–8
Cambridge Companion to George Eliot 97
Canetti, Elias 222–3
Cannes Film Festival 216
cannibalism 137–42
Cao Xuenan 148
capitalism 120–5
Carlyle, Thomas 103–4
Casanova, Pascale 151–2
Cavarero, Adriana 235
Channing, William Ellery 245–8
Chen, Isabelle vi–vii, 12
Chen Qiufan 153–7
children's literature 12
China
    culture and tradition 150, 153–4
    literary history 11, 130–1, 140
    modern consciousness 139–40
    national literature 150
    'new wave' in 131–2, 140, 142
Chinese language 156–7
'Chineseness' 12, 145–54, 157
Chion, Michel 210
choral music 221–7, 232–4
Christianity 4, 51, 55, 58, 101, 183, 232
Church Fathers 3–4, 39
Cicero 4
Circle Jerk 201, 204

Clarke, Neil 152
code-switching 86
Colbron, Grace Isabel 120
Coleridge, Samuel Taylor 103–4
commonplace books 237
community-building 218
Confucianism 132
Congo 10–11
contents of the present book 15–16
continuous creation, doctrine of 237, 245–51
Cornford, F.M. 238
Covid-19 pandemic 157, 193–4, 200–5
creation of one's own world 249
Cross, John Walter 97
'Cucurrucucú Paloma' 207, 212–18
Cudworth, Ralph 247
curation of text 7

The Dangerous Age 124
Dao, Fei 141–2
Darwin, Charles 249
Darwinism 136
decolonising the future 151–7
Delitzsch, Franz 53
Denmark 123
Derrida, Jacques 5
Descartes, René 239
diaries 237, 243–4
Dick, Philip K. 148
Diggs, Daveed 198
digital representation 14
Dinezon, Yankev 66–8
Disney Corporation 198–200
dissent 10
dissonance 231–3
Dixon, Steve 200
Do the Right Thing (film) 199
Draper, Hal 47–9
Dryden, John 2–3
Dürer, Albrecht 13, 184

Eddy, Beverly Driver 121–3
Edwards, Jonathan 15, 237–42, 245–50
ekphrasis 179
Eliot, George 10, 53, 55, 95–108
Embach, Michael 184
Emerson, Esther 240–1
Emerson, Joseph 240–4
Emerson, Mary Moody 237, 242–4
Emerson, Ralph Waldo 15, 47, 242, 245–51
    idealism of 238
    journals of 237
Emmy awards 198
empowerment 146, 151
engagement, digital 200
English language 146–7, 151, 155–7, 181, 204, 250
Enlightenment thinking 138–9
ethnocentrism 149–52
evangelisation 3
Evans, Marian 10, 96–7, 109
    see George Eliot
Eve 244
exotification 152–3

Facebook 200
faith in a Supreme Being 101
faithfulness, *literal* and *literary* 153
Fake Friends (company) 201, 204
falsetto 216–17
fear of seeing 130–1
Felski, Rita 154
feminism 6, 11, 124
Feuerbach, Ludwig Andreas 10, 96–9, 108
film 13–14, 198–9
film music 208, 215
Fischer-Lichte, Erika 196–9
Foley, Patrick 201, 203
foreignization 152–4
Foreman, Richard 195
forewords 5
Fox, Everett v, vii–viii, 8
Franklin, Aretha 207–14, 218
French language 151
Freud, Anna 122
Freud, Sigmund 73
Frost, Robert 6
future prospects for music 228–9

Gaffric, Gwennaël 148
Gal-Ed, Efrat v, viii, 9
'Gehaus' engraving 185–9
Geiger, Abraham 44
Gelber, Mark 44
Gello, Joshua William 203
gender
    female gender 23
    gender issues 22–3
geography 79–80
George III, King 198–9
Germany, a Winter's Tale 57
Gernsback, Hugo 137
Gibson, William 148
Gillman, Abigail v, viii, 9
global audience 147
God 237–40, 244–9
    contact with 244
    as creator 237–40
    existence of 249
    power of 240, 246
    seen through foregoing generations 247
    as sole agent in the universe 246
Gogol, Nikolai Vasilovich 74
Golden Globe awards 198
Goldschmitt, K.E. vi, viii, 14, 214
Gorman, Amanda 6
gospels translation of 6
Gottheil, Gustav 44, 53
Greece, ancient 4, 6
Greenstein, Edward L. v, viii, 8, 34
Gregory the Great, Pope 179
Grimmelshausen, Jakob 118
Groff, Jonathan 198–9
Gross, Alex 195
Grossman, Jeffrey 44

Halevi, Judah *see* ben Halevi
Hall, Stuart 6
Hamilton (musical) 197–200
Han Song 130, 141–2
Harmonielehre 231

Harris, Jeremy O. 201
Hašek, Jaroslav 119
Haskins, Ruth 243
Hebraism 57
Hebrew Bible 34, 38, 222
Hebrew faith and literature 9, 23, 45–6, 51–5, 60–1, 68, 70, 75–83, 86, 182–4, 188–9
Heine, Heinrich 9, 41–61, 184
Hennell, Charles 100–4, 107
Hennell, Sara 100–8
Herodotus 4
Herzl, Theodor 53
Hollander, John 42, 53
Hollander, Katherine vi, viii–ix, 11
Homer 179
Horace 4–5
huapango style 215
Hudes, Quiara 198
Hugo Awards 152

idealism 238–9, 246–9
    introductory or *mature* 248
imagined communities 6
imprisonment 123, 125
In the Heights (musical) 198
Infante, Pedro 215
intercultural dynamics 10
intersectionality 10
intertextuality 10, 16, 136–7
invisibility 130–1
Isaiah 34–5, 38–9
    book of 33
iterative processes 7, 208

Jacobs, Carol 196
Jahoda, Marie 122
James, Henry (father and son) 242
Japan 133, 135
Jenkins, Barry 14, 207–14, 217–18
Jerome, St 13, 183–9
Jerusalem 8, 19–21, 24–5, 28, 35
Jewish culture 7–9, 42–5, 53–7, 61, 68, 71, 74, 78–80, 184, 230
Jewishness 43–4, 51–4, 58–9
Jiang, Jing 136
Jin, Emily Xueni vi, ix, 12, 157
Job 21–4, 28, 34
    book of 23
Johnson, Ben 3
Johnson, Samuel 65–6
Jonah's shrub 187–9

Kandinsky, Wassily 234
Kant, Immanuel 99
Kar-Wai, Wong 14
Kassabian, Anahid 208
Kattenbelt, Chiel 200
Katzenelson, Yitzchak 45
Keeling, Kara 211
Klein, Melanie 122
Kollontai, Alexandra 121
Korngold, Wolfgang 75
Kramer, Aaron 42, 55–6
Kuder, Ulrich 189

Lai Yiu-Fai 216
Lamentations, book of 19–25, 28
Larrick, Nancy 160
Latour, Bruno 154–5
law, need for 250
Lazarus, Emma 9, 41–61
Lazarus, Josephine 59
Lee, Kaifu 155–6
Lee, Spike 199
Lenin, V.I. 121
Leopardi, Giacomo 151
Levin, Gershon 76
Lewes, George Henry 95–6
Lewis, Maria 101
LGBTQ identity 213–14
Liang Qichao 132–3
Lichtenstein, Diane 42
Liu, Ken 145–6
Liu Cixin 12, 141–2, 145, 148, 150
live performances 193–6, 200–1, 204
lived experience 12
lockdown 193
Locke, John 245–6
Loreley myth 41
Lu Xun 11, 129–42
Luther, Martin 6

'A madman's diary' 130–2, 138–42
Magnus, Lady Katie 52
man
    preparation for 249
    as a type rather than a gender 22
Manheim, Ralph 195
Marengo, Enrico *see* Meyring, Heinrich
Marks, Peter 196–7
Marxism 119–23
May Fourth literary revolution 131
Medenica, Ivan 196
Mendelssohn, Moses 59
Mendez, Tomás 215
Mexico 215–16
Meyring, Heinrich 181–3
Mezzocchi, Peter 193, 204
Michaëlis, Karin 11, 112–13, 117–25
Michelangelo 183
mimesis 229
the mind 239
    problems in 248
Minnesang 57
Miranda, Lin-Manuel 198–200
Mitchell, Stephen 34
Mitchell, W.J.T. 2
Møller, Poul Martin 123
Moonlight (film) 14, 207–11, 214, 217–19
moral law 250
Moreno, Gaby 218
Morris, Leslie 61
Moses 182–4, 189, 224, 226, 231
Moses und Aaron 14–15, 221, 224, 226, 232–3
Mother Courage 114–25
mother tongues 151
multilingualism 147, 154–7
musical scores 2, 14
Mussorgsky, Modest 14, 222–3

nature 248–9
New York Times 148
Ngũgĩ Wa Thiong'o 11
Nietzsche, Friedrich Wilhelm 195
Niranjana, Tejaswini 5
Nolden, Thomas (editor) i, v, ix
North Sea Poems 57
Nottage, Lynn 11, 112–18, 122–5

Odyssey 4
'One Step Ahead' 207, 209, 212, 214, 218
online communication 200–1, 204
online performance 200
opera 14–15, 221–8, 231–3
Oppenheim, Moritz Daniel 183–4, 189
orientalism and orientalization 12, 146–55
original-language versions 250
the Other 9
Ovid 5
Oxford English Dictionary 194
Ozaki, Yukio 133

pacifism and pacifist fiction 11, 125
Packer, Barbara L. 246
Parker, Joseph 100
Parshall, Peter W. 187–8
Peabody, Elizabeth 245
Penguin Random House 155
Peretz, Yitskhok-Leybush 9, 65–82, 85–6
perseverance 7–8, 15
Pesaro, Nicoletta 150
Phelan, Peggy 200
philosophy 244, 246
Pinney, Thomas 98
Pitchfork (magazine) 213
Planck, Max 141
Plato 4, 238–9
Pliny 188
Plotinus 247
Poch, Silvina 12
poetry 6, 9, 19–24, 33, 43–6, 53–8
    biblical 20
    Jewish 44, 61
Poland 9
pop music 208, 218
possibilities for man 249
postcolonialism 6
Powell, Jakeem Dante 203
Price, Richard 245
The Producers 198
prophetic tropes 8
prose translations 56
psalms 54
public institutions 8
Puccini, Giacomo 14, 233
Pythagoras 234

Qualls, Barry 97–8
queerness 13, 208–19
quoted material 55

racial justice 10
rape as a weapon 115–18
Real Housewives series 202–3
reality television 202–4

reception of work 1
Redinger, Ruby 101
Reimer, Gail Twersky v, ix–x, 10
Reinhard, Richard 53
religion, critiques of 10
religious institutions 3
remediation 12–13, 204, 222
reputation 5
Ribot, Théodule 73
Richardson, Robert 242
Rilke, Rainer Maria 195
risk-taking 16
Rodenbach, Georges 75
Rokem, Na'ama 46, 57
Roman authors 4
Rosenwald, Lawrence i, 1, 15–16, 33, 112, 116–17, 122, 125, 187, 197–8, 237
Rosenzweig, Franz 8, 33
Rothschild family 184
Ruined 113–18, 122–5

Sachs, Michael 44
sacred texts 251
St Matthew Passion 221, 232–3
Sakai, Naoki 149
Sammons, Jeffrey L. 44
Sawyer, John F.A. 39
Schiller, Friedrich 119
Schnipper, Matthew 213
Schoenberg, Arnold 14–15, 221–34
Schor, Esther 42, 57
Schwarwald, Eugenie 121
science 140
    attitudes to and views on 11, 140
science fiction (SF) 10, 12, 130–41, 145–52, 155–7
    influences on 149
scientism 139
screen performances 197–9
scripture 8, 13
self-translation 9, 76–7, 86
Sephardic parentage 43
sexual assault 114–17
sexuality 117
Shakespeare, William 99
Shih Shu-mei 150
Shmeruk, Khone 75
'silent' translators 5
simpatico 155
social justice 10
social media 198–204
soft power 150
Soh, Yoojin 136
Sokolow, Nachum 68, 76
Sollors, Werner vi, x, 13
Song, Mingwei vi, x, 11
Song of Songs 22
Sontag, Susan 196
soundtrack choices 209–10, 215, 218
sources 4
Spinoza, Baruch 96, 98, 103–4
spirit 248–9
Spivak, Gayatri Chakravorty 5–6
Sprechstimme 226–7
Stael, Madame de 246

stage performances *see* live performances
standards 3
Star Trek 148
Steege, Benjamin 229–30
Steffin, Margarete 114, 117–25
Stephenson, Neal 148
Strauss, David Friedrich 10, 96–109
Strong, Louise Jackson 11, 134–9
'supreme' texts 7
Szold, Henrietta 43

Taylor, Diana 199
theatre 13–14
  death of 204
  digital 14, 193–7, 200–5
  role and function of 194
  as translation 195, 197, 204
  underlying economic concerns 193
theatricality 193–4
Thiel, Peter 201
Thirty Years War 118, 120
The Three-Body Problem 140–1, 147–50, 157
Tóibín, Colin 242
Tomaszów region 65–6
translation 1–3, 96–100, 103–9, 146, 151–7, 194–8, 204
  broad and *narrow* uses of the word 237
  definition of 194
  degradation in translation 204–5
  discussions about 10
  domesticated translation 152–3, 156
  focus of 81, 86
  history of 2–3, 7–8
  importance of 15–16, 100
  invisible translation 152, 156
  limitations of 179
  linked with geopolitics and power 2
  literalist translations 6
  as a medium of empathy and cultivation 155
  moral relevance of 1
  necessary components of 99–100
  no longer a linear process 155
  obscuring of text 7
  politics of 10
  principles of 3
  problems of 4–5
  process of 75–7, 155
  reading of 197
  responsibilities of 1
  status of 98
  subjects for 6
  and theatre 195, 197, 204
  theory of 2–6, 12–14
translatability 151–3; *see also* untranslatability
translation studies 7, 153, 156
translational strategy 78
Tremignon, Alessandro 182
Turandot 222–3
twelve-tone music 224–6, 230–1
Twitter 193, 196, 201, 203

United States 202
universalism 150–1
unrhymed translations 57
Untermeyer, Louis 47–50
untranslatability 12

Veloso, Caetano 207, 214–17
Venture's End 112–14, 117–25
Venuti, Lawrence 151–5
vernacular style 133, 194, 204
Verne, Jules 129, 133–4
Verso, Francesco 147–9
video cameras, use of 199
virtual performances 13
virtual reality (VR) 193, 201
virtual technology 154
visual experience 2
voice
  communal 24
  human 229, 231

Wall, Joshua Logan 57
Wall Street Journal 147–8
Ward Island 53
Washington Post 196
Weigel, Helene 113, 117
Weigel, Sigrid 179
Weis, Adolf 187–8
Wells, H.G. 137–8
Werses, Shmuel 75
Whorisky, Kate 114, 118, 122
Wicksteed, Charles 107–8
Willey, Basil 103
Winkler, Kenneth P. vi, x, 15
women
  dangers faced by 112
  lives of 123–4
  role and status of 11
Wong Kar-Wai 216–17
Woolf, Virginia 120
world-building 148
Wu Shuang 152–4
Wundt, Wilhelm 73

xenophobia 148

Yiannopoulos, Milo 201
Yiddish language 9, 75–85
Young, Bette Roth 52, 55
Young, Robert 149
younger generation 147
YouTube 200

Zenzile, Mawande Ka 13, 179–81, 189
Zhou Shuren *see* Lu Xun
Zionism and Zionist literature 53, 57
Zophar 24
Zwischenspiel 226

CPSIA information can be obtained
at www.ICGtesting.com
Printed in the USA
BVHW050526190523
664462BV00010B/119